THE OXFORD HISTORY
OF ENGLISH ART

Edited by T. S. R. BOASE

THE OXFORD HISTORY OF ENGLISH ART

Edited by T. S. R. Boase
President of Magdalen College, Oxford

Plan of Volumes

I. ENGLISH ART TO 871 A.D.

II. ENGLISH ART   871–1100

III. ENGLISH ART   1100–1216

IV. ENGLISH ART   1216–1307

V. ENGLISH ART   1307–1461

VI. ENGLISH ART   1461–1553

VII. ENGLISH ART   1553–1625

VIII. ENGLISH ART   1625–1714

IX. ENGLISH ART   1714–1800

X. ENGLISH ART   1800–1870

XI. ENGLISH ART   FROM 1870

EDWARD PIERCE: SIR CHRISTOPHER WREN, 1673. Ashmolean Museum, Oxford

ENGLISH ART
1625–1714

MARGARET WHINNEY

AND

OLIVER MILLAR

OXFORD
AT THE CLARENDON PRESS
1957

Oxford University Press, Amen House, London E.C.4

GLASGOW NEW YORK TORONTO MELBOURNE WELLINGTON
BOMBAY CALCUTTA MADRAS KARACHI
CAPE TOWN IBADAN NAIROBI ACCRA SINGAPORE

PRINTED IN GREAT BRITAIN
AT THE UNIVERSITY PRESS, OXFORD
BY CHARLES BATEY, PRINTER TO THE UNIVERSITY

PREFACE

IN his General Introduction to the *Oxford History of English Art*, which appeared in Volume V, the Editor defined the character of the seventeenth-century contribution in the following words: 'Three great artists, Inigo Jones, Van Dyck, and Christopher Wren, brought England once more to the level of European achievement though each in his own way adapted continental baroque to the more rigid and restrained tastes of seventeenth century English patrons.' This brief statement is an indication both of the major theme of this book, and also of special problems, so far without precedent in the series, with which the authors have been faced. For the story of the acceptance, assimilation, or rejection of ideas derived from the main stream of continental art is bound up, to a much greater degree than in the medieval periods so far considered, with the talents and temperament of the individual artist, with his training and his contacts with foreign art. A considerable amount of biographical material must therefore be included, as well as some discussion of the development of an artist's personal style, and the relation of his work to that of other men, working perhaps in other mediums. Indeed the claims of the individual artist, the continuity of various themes in any one art, or the pattern of art as a whole at any given date are hard to reconcile completely, especially in a book which is limited in length and must therefore be selective in character.

Our task has been made easier by the recent appearance of books which treat English art in its European context. A great impetus towards a wider outlook was given by F. Saxl and R. Wittkower's *English Art and the Mediterranean* (1948). Professor Ellis Waterhouse's *Painting in Britain, 1530–1790* and Mr. John Summerson's *Architecture in Britain, 1530–1830*, both of which appeared in 1953, contain a mass of new and well ordered material and inevitably alter the picture of the period given in such earlier books as Mr. C. H. Collins Baker's monumental *Lely and the Stuart Portrait Painters* (1912).

But the revolution wrought in English art in the seventeenth century was due not only to the work of individual artists, but also to the stimulus given by royal, aristocratic, civic or private patronage, and by English reactions to practice and theory in the arts of the Continent. This important theme has been treated, though briefly, in our introductory chapter. In architecture native artists achieved the greatest heights and its development, though perhaps more familiar, has made the first demand on our space. An attempt has been made to review the different types and styles of building of each generation and to see the architects in relation to each other. The long career of Wren does not lend itself readily to this approach, but since admirable short biographies are available it is hoped that the attempt to integrate his work with that of other architects is worth while.

The amount of sculpture produced in the period is immense, and since the larger part of it is tomb-sculpture it conveys a vivid impression of the cross-currents of taste and fashion. Much of it is of mediocre quality, but since no general chronological survey of English sculpture could be quoted, for the pioneer work of the late Mrs. Esdaile was never completed, some space has been given to an indication, at least, of the more important trends. Painting, on the other hand, demanded a fuller treatment and to the story of the birth of the 'Van Dyck tradition' some account has been added of English landscape painting in its formative stage and of the school of decorative painting which has been undeservedly neglected in earlier general histories. Little room therefore remained for consideration of the minor arts, though the furniture, tapestries, and plate, as well as the books produced within the period, are a constant source of interest in their reflection of changes of style in the greater arts, and are frequently in themselves things of great beauty. Here, however, the literature is larger and the modern methods of display in museums (above all in the Victoria and Albert Museum) make it possible for the reader to obtain a lively impression of those objects of daily use which form the background to the lives of the patrons and artists who appear in our pages.

This book owes more than we can adequately express to the owners who have helped us to see and reproduce their possessions or the works of art in their charge. Her Majesty the Queen, Her Majesty Queen Elizabeth the Queen Mother, and His Majesty the King of Sweden have graciously permitted us to reproduce works of art in their collections. We should like to thank particularly: the Dukes of Portland and Buccleuch, the Marquesses of Exeter and Northampton, the Earl of Shaftesbury, Earl Stanhope, Earl Spencer, Lord Herbert, Sir Gyles Isham, Mr. T. Cottrell-Dormer, Mr. George Howard, Col. Nigel Stopford Sackville, and Mr. John Wyndham; Sir Owen Morshead, Mr. Francis Thompson, and the Trustees of the Chatsworth Settlement; the Dean and Chapter of St. Paul's Cathedral; the Presidents and Fellows of Magdalen and St. John's Colleges, the Wardens and Fellows of Merton and All Souls Colleges, and the Provost and Fellows of Worcester College, Oxford; the Master and Fellows of Trinity College, Cambridge; the Worshipful Companies of Goldsmiths and Painter-Stainers; Mr. C. K. Adams, Mr. Noel Blakiston, and the staffs of the National Portrait Gallery and the Public Record Office; the Mobilier National, Paris, the National Trust, the British Museum, and the Victoria and Albert, Soane, and Ashmolean Museums.

We are especially grateful to: Mr. G. H. Chettle, Mr. Howard Colvin, Mr. Rupert Gunnis, Mr. Graham Hughes, Mr. Robin Hutchison, Mr. Michael Robinson, Mr. John Summerson, Professor Ellis Waterhouse, Mr. Francis Watson, Professor Johannes Wilde, and Mr. John Woodward for the patience with which they have answered endless questions; and to Professor Anthony Blunt, Mr. Edward Croft-Murray, Mr. David Piper, Mr. Graham Reynolds, Professor Geoffrey Webb and Miss Rhoda Welsford, all of whom have read part of our text in manuscript. We should like finally to record our gratitude to the staffs of the libraries of the Courtauld Institute and the Society of Antiquaries; Dr. George Zarnecki and the Photographic Staff of the Courtauld Institute, Miss V. M. Dallas of the Royal Commission on Historical Monuments, the Warburg Institute, the National Buildings Record, and A. C. Cooper Ltd., for their help with photographs; to many students and members of the staff of the Courtauld Institute for the help they gave so generously to one of the authors during a long illness; to Miss Elizabeth Clarke for the checking of references and

Miss Margaret Brown for her patience in coping with a particularly difficult manuscript; to Mr. Peter Murray for his skilled advice on the proofs; and to Mrs. Oliver Millar for the enthusiasm to which the later stages of the volume owe so much.

Finally we should like to thank our Editor for his kindness and help at all stages in the making of this book.

M. D. W.
O. N. M.

August 1955

CONTENTS

LIST OF PLATES

Frontispiece: EDWARD PIERCE: SIR CHRISTOPHER WREN. 1673. [26 in. high.]
Oxford, Ashmolean Museum.

AT END

1. SIR ANTHONY VAN DYCK: CHARLES I. 1633. Buckingham Palace.
   [Canvas: 145 × 106 in.]
   Reproduced by gracious permission of Her Majesty the Queen.

2 *a*. INIGO JONES: THE QUEEN'S HOUSE, GREENWICH. 1616–35.
   Photograph by Royal Commission on Historical Monuments. Crown copyright.

   b. INIGO JONES: THE BANQUETING HOUSE, WHITEHALL. 1619–22.
   Photograph by Royal Commission on Historical Monuments. Crown copyright.

3. INIGO JONES: THE QUEEN'S CHAPEL, MARLBOROUGH GATE. *c.* 1627.
   Photograph by The Topical Press Agency Ltd.

4 *a*. INIGO JONES: ST. PAUL'S CATHEDRAL: WEST FRONT. BEGUN 1633. From
   the etching by W. Hollar in Sir William Dugdale's 'History of St.
   Paul's Cathedral' 1658.

   b. INIGO JONES: COVENT GARDEN PIAZZA. 1630–8.
   Etching by W. Hollar.

5 *a*. INIGO JONES: DESIGN FOR WHITEHALL PALACE. *c.* 1638. Worcester
   College, Oxford. *Photograph by courtesy of the Courtauld Institute of
   Art.*

   b. INIGO JONES: MASQUE DESIGN: THE ISLE OF DELOS FOR FLORIMENE. 1635.
   *Photograph by courtesy of the Courtauld Institute of Art. Reproduced by
   permission of the Trustees of the Chatsworth Settlement.*

6 *a*. CHEVENING, KENT. *c.* 1630.
   Water-colour, 1679.
   *Photograph by 'Country Life'. Reproduced by permission of Earl Stanhope,
   K.G.*

   b. HAM HOUSE, SURREY: THE NORTH DRAWING ROOM. 1637.
   Photograph by National Buildings Record.

7 *a*. SWAKELEYS, MIDDLESEX. 1638.
   Photograph by Royal Commission on Historical Monuments. Crown copyright.

   b. SIR ROGER PRATT: COLESHILL, BERKSHIRE. 1649–62. BURNT 1952.
   Photograph by 'Country Life'.

LIST OF FIGURES

ABBREVIATIONS

Arch. Journ.	*Archaeological Journal.*
B.M.	British Museum.
Burl. Mag.	*Burlington Magazine.*
Cal. S.P. Dom.	Calendar of State Papers, Domestic.
Cal. S.P. Ven.	Calendar of State Papers, Venetian.
Cal. Tr. Bks.	Calendar of Treasury Books.
Collins Baker	C. H. Collins Baker, *Lely and the Stuart Portrait Painters* (1912).
Colvin, *Dictionary*	H. Colvin, *A Biographical Dictionary of English Architects, 1660–1840* (1954).
Evelyn	*Diary of John Evelyn . . .*, ed. W. Bray and H. B. Wheatley (1906).
Gunnis, *Dictionary*	R. Gunnis, *Dictionary of British Sculptors, 1660–1851* (1953).
H.M.C.	Historical Manuscripts Commission.
Knoop & Jones, *London Mason*	D. Knoop and G. P. Jones, *The London Mason in the 17th century* (1935).
N.G.	National Gallery.
N.P.G.	National Portrait Gallery.
R.C.H.M.	*Royal Commission on Historical Monuments.*
R.I.B.A. Journ.	*Journal of the Royal Institute of British Architects.*
Summerson	John Summerson, *Architecture in Britain, 1530–1830* (1953).
Vertue	Notebooks of George Vertue, i, *Walpole Society*, xviii (1930); ii, ibid. xx (1932); iii, ibid. xxii (1934); iv, ibid. xxiv (1936); v, ibid. xxvi (1938) ; Index, ibid. xxix (1947).
V. & A.	Victoria and Albert Museum.
Waterhouse	Ellis Waterhouse, *Painting in Britain, 1530–1790* (1953).
Willis & Clark, *Cambridge*	R. Willis and J. W. Clark, *Architectural History of the University of Cambridge* (1896).

(s.) indicates that a painting is signed; a date is inserted if the picture is signed and dated by the artist; and a date by itself in a bracket indicates that the canvas or panel bears a contemporary date or, in a few instances, can be dated from other sources without qualification.

In this book dates are given according to the New Style.

I

ASPECTS OF TASTE

THE Stuart period is one of the richest and most absorbing in the history of the arts in England. The sheer quantity of works of art that were produced between the reigns of James I and George I was far greater than in the age of the Tudors and, though much of it would be deservedly neglected by a historian of European or even of English art, it contained some of the most vigorous and beautiful expressions of the English genius. The flowering of that genius in the Hanoverian age grew partly out of a fusion in the earlier period of native and continental influences, and the English reaction to the full baroque style of the Continent is the central problem: a problem affected by growing consciousness of the arts, by rapidly increasing first-hand acquaintance with renaissance and modern art on the Continent and by varied trends in patronage, from the highly developed cosmopolitan tastes of some of the Stuart sovereigns and the aristocracy to the reactionary, or actively hostile, views of less sophisticated patrons. And it is this problem that links the artistic activity of the seventeenth century so closely with many aspects of social, political, and religious history.

Charles I was the most enthusiastic and discerning patron of the arts to grace the English throne and he assembled a collection of pictures and works of art unequalled in the history of English taste. His accession in 1625 was an event of cardinal importance for the arts in England; and the activities of the 'Whitehall group' (the small circle of collectors, patrons, and amateurs of which the King was the heart) were a new and integral part of the life of the court; that life was set against, and inevitably coloured by, the magnificent possessions with which Charles filled his palaces. 'King Charles', wrote Lucy Hutchinson, 'was temperate, chaste, and serious. . . . Men of learning and ingenuity in all arts were in esteem, and received encouragement from the king, who was a most excellent judge and a great lover of paintings, carvings, gravings, and many other ingenuities, less offensive than the bawdy and profane abusive wit which was the only exercise of the other court.'[1]

The development of the King's tastes can be traced back to the example of his elder brother Henry, prince of Wales, whose enthusiasms had been stimulated by the experience and knowledge of Inigo Jones and of Thomas Howard, earl of Arundel: the true 'father of vertu in England', the friend of Rubens and the young Van Dyck, and the first Englishman of his class to combine a passion for the arts with first-hand experience of European and antique civilization. His many months of study and excavations in Italy during the reign of James I bred in Arundel a consciously Italianate quality in his way of life, of which his contemporaries were well aware, a high standard of taste, and an insatiable and ruthless desire for works of art to swell the collections at Arundel House. His tastes were learned and eclectic, with a particular feeling for Flemish and German painting of the sixteenth century and for the Mannerists and a 'foolish curiosity [which he amply gratified] in enquiringe for the peeces of Holbien'.[2] His most serious rival, the duke of Buckingham, could afford to be more lavish as a patron and collector, but had nothing of the older man's refinement or antiquarian sense. The duke's rebuilding and redecoration of York House, and the amassing of pictures and sculpture for its gardens and galleries, were carried out with great speed and prodigal expenditure: 'out of all the amateurs, and Princes and Kings, there is not one who has collected in forty years as many pictures as your Excellency has in five'.[3] A superb collection of Venetian paintings included Titian's great *Ecce Homo* (Vienna); the duke sat

---

[1] *Memoirs . . . of Colonel Hutchinson*, ed. C. Firth (1885), i. 119–20.

[2] Mary F. S. Hervey, *The Life . . . of Thomas Howard Earl of Arundel* (1921); Sir L. Cust, 'Notes on the Collections formed by . . . Arundel . . .', *Burl. Mag.* xx (1911), 97–100, 233–6, 341–3; xxi (1912), 256–8; Mary Cox in *Burl. Mag.* xix (1911), 282–6, 323–5; H.M.C. Fourth Report (1874), *Denbigh MSS.* 258, and *Denbigh MSS.* v (1911), 67, 75–76; D. Sutton in *Burl. Mag.*, lxxxix (1947), 3–9, 32–37, 75–77; J. Hess, 'Lord Arundel in Rom . . .', *English Miscellany*, i (Rome, 1950), 197–220.

[3] Sir Balthazar Gerbier to Buckingham, 8 Feb. 1625 (G. Goodman, *The Court of King James I* (1839), ii. 369–70); Gerbier was an amateur artist (see below, pp. 52–53) and the duke's factotum and principal agent.

to Rubens for the magnificent equestrian portrait (formerly at Osterley and the most fully baroque portrait of an English sitter); his other pictures by Rubens included his own *Apotheosis*; and he had a special liking for the Caravaggisti and the school of Utrecht.[1]

From an early age the young Prince Charles had shown marked personal tastes. During his journey to Spain with Buckingham in 1623 he bought pictures, attended auctions and sat to Velazquez. Above all he saw for the first time, in the Spanish royal collection, some of the greatest masterpieces of renaissance painting. The experience strengthened his nascent love of the Venetian school and a personal devotion to the work of Titian: a devotion so great that Philip IV presented to the prince Titian's *Venus of the Pardo* (Louvre), with which Charles had been particularly smitten. In the same year he acquired the Raphael cartoons which survive in the Victoria and Albert Museum as one of the most impressive monuments to the collecting spirit of the age.[2] Before his accession the prince had built up a private collection of considerable range and quality[3] and a position at court as an *arbiter artium* to whom artistic questions should be referred.[4]

After he came to the throne works of art poured into the royal houses. Collections *en bloc* and individual objects were bought by the King's agents at home and abroad. Their greatest success was the purchase, made possible by the moral decadence and financial

[1] J. von Sandrart, *Academie* . . . ed. A. R. Peltzer (Munich, 1925), 22. Bathoe printed (1758) the list of pictures which had survived the depredations of the Parliamentarians and were preserved at York House for the young 2nd duke; for the inventory of York House in 1635 see R. Davies in *Burl. Mag.* x (1907), 376–82; see also C. R. Cammell, *The Great Duke of Buckingham* (1939), ch. xxvii, and J. Pope-Hennessy, *Samson and a Philistine by Giovanni Bologna* (V. & A., 1954).

[2] J. Pope-Hennessy, *The Raphael Cartoons* (V. & A., 1950).

[3] *e.g.* Van der Goes's *Trinity Altarpiece* (Holyrood), Rubens's *Self-portrait* (Windsor), Holbein's *Erasmus* (Louvre), Titian's *Charles V with a Dog* (Prado) and portraits by Tintoretto, Mor, Blyenberch, Bunel, Mytens, and Van Somer (W. N. Sainsbury, *Original Unpublished Papers* . . . (1859), 355).

[4] Rubens realized as early as 1621 that Charles, as much as his father, would be concerned in any scheme for the decoration of the Banqueting House (Sainsbury, op. cit. 61); and in 1622 James put in the hands of the prince a scheme for founding an academy for improving education and encouraging the patronage of the arts (P.R.O., *S. P. Dom.* cxxxi (70)).

collapse of the last members of the Gonzaga dynasty, of the greater part of the collection of the dukes of Mantua.¹ This acquisition brought into Charles's possession such renaissance and contemporary masterpieces as Titian's *Emperors*, Raphael's *La Perla*, and Andrea del Sarto's *Holy Family* (both in the Prado), Correggio's two *Allegories* in the Louvre, Mantegna's *Triumph of Caesar* (Hampton Court) and Caravaggio's *Death of the Virgin* in the Louvre. Works of art were sent as presents to the King by foreign governments,² by his foreign relatives, and by his diplomatic representatives.³ Sir Henry Wotton and Sir Dudley Carleton, for instance, were able to place at the disposal of the King and his fellow collectors their specialized knowledge of the state of the arts in Venice and Holland. And within the Whitehall group itself there were constant exchanges of works of art between the different collectors: when, for example, the 4th earl of Pembroke gave to the King Raphael's *St. George*, which is now in Washington, Charles gave to him in return the celebrated book of Holbein's portrait-drawings, but, with a kindly understanding of a fellow collector's passion, Pembroke straightway gave them to Arundel.⁴

As a patron of living artists and a lover of modern painting Charles I's achievement was to set England for a tragically short period within the orbit of most of the contemporary artistic movements on the Continent. A number of lesser foreign artists and craftsmen were at work in England during his reign.⁵ Honthorst was continuously in touch with the English court and in 1628 visited

¹ A. Luzio, *La Galleria dei Gonzaga venduta all'Inghilterra nel 1627–28* (Milan, 1913); Sainsbury (op. cit.) also printed some of the relevant documents. See also B. Reade, 'William Frizell and the Royal Collection', *Burl. Mag.* lxxxix (1947), 70–75, for the purchase of Frizell's collection by the King in 1638.

² *e.g.* the States-General of the United Provinces sent to the King in 1635 the two panels by Geertgen tot Sint Jans which are now in Vienna.

³ The earl of Ancrum brought back, before June 1633, Rembrandt's *Portrait of his Mother* (Windsor) and a *Self-portrait*, which were probably the first Rembrandts to come to this country; in 1636 Arundel was given by the city of Nuremberg Dürer's *Self-portrait* (Prado) and *Portrait of his Father* (N.G.) as presents from the city to the King.

⁴ K. T. Parker, *The Drawings of Hans Holbein . . . at Windsor Castle* (1945), 7–34.

⁵ *e.g.* Wouters, Keirincx, Stalbempt, Poelenburgh, Hendrik Gerritsz Pot, and Christiaen van Vianen.

London, where he painted the vast piece of courtly allegory which hangs on the Queen's Staircase at Hampton Court;[1] and, probably in 1626, Orazio Gentileschi had come to England, where his highly personal form of Caravaggism and angular sense of narrative were admired by the King and the duke of Buckingham. But it was the visit in May 1629 of Rubens, an artist for whom he had a deep and long-standing admiration, that must have given the King special pleasure. Rubens was on a diplomatic mission, but he was so enchanted with the peaceful country to which he had come, from a Continent which was being slowly drawn into the horrors of the Thirty Years War, that he found time to pay tributes to the prosperity of Charles's realm in the great *Peace and War* (National Gallery), and to the charms of the English scene in that splendid, magic idyll, *The Landscape with St. George* at Buckingham Palace.[2]

Rubens also presumably took back with him to Antwerp the final commission for a scheme of decoration for the ceiling of the new Banqueting House,[3] which was inspired by a great renaissance ceiling in Venice. A few years later Van Dyck began his series of portraits of the King and his court which showed, in so many cases, a like dependence on the painters in whom the King took such delight. The impact on Van Dyck of the collection of pictures by Titian which he found at Whitehall, and especially in the quiet of Charles's Privy Lodging Rooms,[4] went to form the distinctive qualities of his English style. This conscious fusion between Charles's personal tastes as a collector and his choice of artists for his service was perhaps his most significant contribution to the development of the arts in England. The Civil Wars prevented it from bearing, in his own time, more than half-ripened, tantalizing fruit in the work of William Dobson.

[1] O. Millar, 'Charles I, Honthorst and Van Dyck', *Burl. Mag.* xcvi (1954), 36–42.

[2] E. Croft-Murray, 'The Landscape Background in Rubens's *St. George and the Dragon*', *Burl. Mag.* lxxxix (1947), 89–93.

[3] See below, pp. 25–26, 287–8.

[4] In the first of these rooms hung, for example, *The Pope presenting Jacopo Pesaro to St. Peter* (Antwerp), *St. Margaret* and *The Speech of the Marchese del Vasto* (Prado), the *Entombment*, *D'Avalos Allegory* and the *Supper at Emmaus* (Louvre), and *The Woman in a Fur Cloak* (Vienna).

The feeling for works of art which brought the spectacular Caroline collections into being was restricted, even within the court, to a very limited circle: the knowledge and interest which lay behind Caroline connoisseurship were luxuries which few Englishmen of that time could afford or acquire. And in the life of the court it was those aspects which particularly fostered a love of the arts that aroused such dangerous hostility in the country at large beyond the walls of the King's palaces. The Catholic element at court, of which the Queen was the heart, stirred up the deepest mistrust and hatred among the King's opponents; it deliberately strengthened its position by giving works of art to the King, engaging him in civilized discussion of his possessions and arranging for Bernini to create, in the bust which was formally presented to the King and Queen at Oatlands on 17 July 1637, a sumptuously idealized baroque portrait of Charles on the basis of a portrait specially painted by Van Dyck. In the professional field the King's active encouragement of illustrious foreign artists, and their presence in the capital, were bitterly resented by the reactionary nationalist Company of Painter-Stainers in the City.[1]

The brittle fabric of the culture of the Caroline court, where the arts had played so great a part in fostering an illusive sense of security and isolation, was shattered by the Civil War; Van Dyck's death late in 1641 was symbolic of the passing of a society which he had recorded with such incisive brilliance. There was much artistic activity in England during the wars and the Interregnum; the usurping government was not indifferent to the arts and the influence of the Whitehall group can be felt in such undertakings as the considerable redecoration of Wilton by a renegade member of the King's circle;[2] but the effect on the development of the arts in England of the great collections made by Charles and his courtiers, and of their interest in current continental art, becomes a matter of idle speculation. During the wars and the disturbances that preceded them the worst and most embittered prejudices found an outlet in sustained and organized iconoclasm. The dispersal, under economic or political pressure, of the Caroline collections and, above all, of the King's own great collection by

[1] See below, pp. 81–82.   [2] See below, pp. 39–41, 290–1.

deliberate action, though for not wholly unworthy motives, on the part of the Council of State after the King's execution, involved a loss to the artistic heritage of this country which can hardly be over-estimated. It was only indirectly, by stimulating the enthusiasms and training the critical faculties of young royalists like John Evelyn and Richard Symonds, who made protracted visits to France and Italy during the troubles in England, that the Civil War and Interregnum contributed to the growth of English connoisseurship.

The court never entirely regained the central position which it had occupied under Charles I in the structure of patronage in England. At the Restoration a special Committee of the House of Lords succeeded in recovering for the new King some of his father's treasures and thus formed the basis of a newly constituted royal collection, to which all the later Stuart sovereigns made numerous and important additions. Charles II took great pleasure in works of art, but neither he nor his brother James II inherited their father's passion for them. Charles's delight in the practical application of the artist's or craftsman's skill was typical of the inquiring spirit which pervaded court circles from the atmosphere of the new Royal Society; but his initiation of the great baroque scheme of rebuilding and redecoration at Windsor Castle[1] showed him to be worthy of his father's memory and his cousin's example. There was the same cosmopolitan quality in the arts at the court of Charles II and James II as in their father's time. The Catholic element was even more strongly stressed in the employment by the two brothers and their consorts of such artists as Huysmans, Gascars, Gennari, Vignon, and Largillierre, and in the creation of chapels at Windsor, St. James's, and Whitehall which would not have been out of place in Rome or Versailles. The flight of James II again brought about the collapse of this ultramontane nexus of patronage and unleashed as savage a wave of iconoclasm as had vented its wrath on his mother's idolatrous equipment at Somerset House. The close association between the arts of the court and those elements in Stuart policy which precipitated the constitutional upheavals of the seventeenth century provides an illuminating

[1] See below, pp. 207–10, 296–300.

commentary on this phase of English history and on the English reaction to the full baroque style of France, Italy, or Flanders.

It is, however, misleading to attempt to link motives of taste too closely with the political views of a patron. The influence of France was very strong at the court of Charles II and Versailles was the core of the French hegemony which it was William III's life work to destroy. After the Revolution the style of painters like Rigaud and Largillierre came to be particularly associated with St. Germains; but the Peace of Ryswick in 1697 made possible a revival of interest, among William's principal supporters, in French painting and architecture, served by the dispatch of French pictures and architectural prints to England by Matthew Prior, who played the same part in Paris on behalf of collectors at home as Carleton and Wotton had done earlier in Venice and The Hague. On the other hand there was no more sustained or pervasive influence on the arts in Stuart England than the Dutch. The widespread love of pictures in Holland had impressed travellers like Evelyn and Peter Mundy, and the subject-matter and technical virtuosity of certain forms of Dutch painting ensured for them a popularity in this country which they have never lost. The inspiration for the Dutch William's great building projects came paradoxically from France, but his tastes, and those of his queen, in garden layout and interior decoration were predominantly Dutch. They evolved at Hampton Court a synthesis of the Dutch and French influences: Mary's Water Gallery was decorated with her Dutch boulle cabinets and a large collection of china and blue and white Delft ware; her little dairy, on the other hand, and her husband's project for a small palace as a retreat from Hampton Court, anticipate Marie Antoinette's *Hameau* and recall the *Grand Trianon*.[1]

But Italy, in the minds of travellers, *virtuosi* and artists, reigned supreme as '*Nature's Darling*, and the *Eldest Sister* of all other *Countries*', and, among the increasing number of Englishmen whose careers took them to Italy or who made the conventional Grand

[1] H.M.C., *Bath MSS*. iii (1908); R. W. Goulding, *Catalogue of the Pictures . . . at Welbeck Abbey . . .* (1936), 58–60; Defoe, *A Tour . . .*, ed. G. D. H. Cole (1928), i. 175; Celia Fiennes, *Journeys*, ed. C. Morris (1947), 59–60.

Tour, were some whose minds were deeply coloured by their experiences, who sat to Carlo Maratti as their descendants were to sit to Batoni, and whose position enabled them, as patrons, to infuse Italian influences into the development of the arts at home. The part played by diplomats in Venice, from the days of Sir Henry Wotton to Consul Smith, in forging artistic links between Italy and England is illustrated by the 1st duke of Manchester's initiation of a very attractive rococo period in English music and decorative painting.[1] In Florence Sir John Finch was on friendly terms with Carlo Dolci, and in Rome the duke of Shrewsbury was the complete example of the English grandee abroad, with tastes as strictly classical as those of Richard Symonds before him; with better health or a more aggressive character, he might well have had as powerful an effect on the arts in England as Arundel or Lord Burlington. British artists had been drawn to Rome throughout the Stuart period. Not until the last years of the seventeenth century did their work show more than an occasional flickering reminiscence of Italy, but in the early years of the next century William Kent and the younger Talman were forming their tastes more critically and were meeting in Italy their future patrons, who later created with them, out of their experiences, a new phase in the history of English art.[2]

Collectors at home were not only concerned with the prints and drawings or the pictures by (or copies after) Salvator Rosa, Albano, Guido, the Poussins, Maratti, and Claude, which they acquired through the friendly connoisseurship of Shrewsbury and his like or the more professional offices of the young English artists in Rome. Throughout the Stuart period collections were made for personal, and not for purely aesthetic, motives. Even Charles I's collections had had a strong iconographical basis and in the majority of English private collections family portraits and portraits of friends and political associates predominated. More specialized

[1] See below, p. 307.
[2] R. Lassels, *The Voyage of Italy* (1685–6), pt. i. 1; F. Baldinucci, *Notizie de' Professori* . . . (Florence) iv (1728), 503; H.M.C., *Finch MSS.* ii (1922), 167, 501; *Buccleuch MSS.* ii, pt. ii (1903), 746–99; M. Jourdain, *The Work of William Kent* (1948); H. Honour, 'John Talman and William Kent in Italy', *Connoisseur*, cxxxiv (1954), 3–7.

collections of portraits were being formed, as in the sixteenth century, in private or public libraries, by City companies, learned or medical institutions, and by university colleges: above all at Oxford, where during the seventeenth century the Bodleian Library was assembling groups of portraits of successive librarians, founders of colleges and chancellors of the University, and of those connected with special subjects. The greatest and most personal of such collections was that formed by the earl of Clarendon in Clarendon House, where portraits of his contemporaries hung as an inspiring commentary on the *History* on which he was engaged. The manufacture of 'historical' portraits became, particularly at Oxford, a specialized genre; and artists as varied as Kent, Rysbrack, and William Blake were to work in this tradition.[1]

The titles of the nobility are thickly spread in the pages of this book, and the influence of the Crown and aristocracy was very great throughout the later Stuart and earlier Hanoverian periods. But it is significant of the gradual spread, through a wider society, of interest in the fine arts, that Kneller and Dahl, the two leading portrait painters at the end of our period, owed their establishment in this country to the good offices of merchants, who were playing the parts which had been acted under the early Stuarts by Arundel and the duke of Buckingham. The far greater demand for portraits in the age of Kneller than in the age of Mytens indicates that many patrons were to be found among the newly enriched money-making families whose houses were as well suited for the display of pictures as those of the aristocracy. Rubens's great portrait of Buckingham, in all his baroque magnificence, now belonged to Sir Francis Child, the son of a Wiltshire clothier, who rose to be Lord Mayor of London, father of English banking, and the epitome of the financial interests in the City in which the Whig party found their staunchest support. The flow of pictures and works of art into England increased steadily, despite the protests of the Painter-Stainers, and the demand for pictures inevitably put busi-

[1] Mrs. Lane Poole, *Catalogue of Portraits in . . . the University, Colleges, City and County of Oxford* (1912–25), i. x–xx; Evelyn, ii. 234–5 n., iii. 435–56; Lady T. Lewis, *Lives of the Friends . . . of Lord Chancellor Clarendon . . .* (1852).

ness into the hands of the 'expert', the cleaner, the dealer, and the
auctioneer. By the end of the Stuart period the structure of the art
market in London as we know it today already existed in embryo.

But pictures were still a luxury. It was the engraver who brought
a knowledge of the arts to a wider public and the Stuart age saw
a great increase in the number of prints published in England.
The writings and discussions of Pepys and Evelyn throw much
light on the interests which the engraver and his publisher served
and stimulated. Evelyn's love of engravings had been aroused by
his acquaintance in France with Nanteuil, Bosse, Stefano della
Bella and Pérelle. In 1662 he published his important and largely
unreadable *Sculptura*. In it he stressed the use of engravings in the
spread of knowledge and in helping those who could not afford
to buy original works of art to cultivate an understanding of the
arts, and he published to the world the revolution that had been
wrought in the engraver's art by the discovery of a new process:
the mezzotint. Prince Rupert, who had earlier practised etching,
learnt the new method during the Interregnum, produced a number of plates, demonstrated the technique to Evelyn early in 1661
and gave him leave to publish it to a limited circle. On 5 November 1665 Evelyn showed Pepys 'the whole secret of mezzotinto'.

The details of the responsibility for the invention and perfecting
of the mezzotint are less significant than that the technique was
brought to this country by a Royal amateur artist and scientist,
discussed by him with Evelyn and published under the auspices
of the Royal Society. On 10 June 1662 *Sculptura* was presented to
the Royal Society with a dedication to Boyle. The conception of
the book, and of the abortive undertakings of which it was to some
extent the fruit, is of profound interest for the close connexion it
illustrates between science and the arts, in an age which saw a great
wave of activity in the realms of science, in the minds of a group
of men who shared an insatiable passion for collecting facts and
a conviction that painting and the graphic arts were only one
manifestation of a whole range of technical activity. The Royal
Society accepted *Sculptura* as a serious contribution to scientific
knowledge, and not only because one of its author's aims was 'that
such as are addicted to the more Noble Mathematical Sciences,

may draw, and engrave their Schemes with delight and assurance.'[1]

The new process flourished in England more than in any other country and developed so fast that by the middle of the eighteenth century practically all reproductive engraved work was done in mezzotint. It was used almost exclusively for the reproduction of pictures and is thus closely linked with the development of the English portrait: engravers like John Smith, John Simon, and the younger John Faber worked in close collaboration with such painters as Kneller, whose reputation must have been enhanced by their plates. And, in contrast to their predecessors who had worked in line, the engravers in mezzotint could provide collectors with prints which gave them a reproduction of an oil-painting the accuracy, but not the beauty, of which has only been surpassed by the photograph. The development that separates William Marshall's engraving of Bower's *3rd Lord Fairfax* from Smith's mezzotint of Kneller's *1st Duke of Schomberg* (Pl. 83 *b*) is not only in the pattern for an equestrian portrait. The *Fairfax* is wholly Elizabethan in manner, but Smith's plate gives a faithful impression of the composition and tone of the canvas from which he was working. An increasing output of political satires and crude woodcuts on broadsheets brought to an even wider public, in the shape of trenchant comments on current personalities and events, some form of visual experience.[2]

This interest in the arts, which the engraver was encouraging so greatly, was also fostered by the appearance of English writings on the fine arts. No important English contribution was made in the seventeenth century to the development of European artistic theory and most English writers on the subject were unblushing plagiarists. The works of Henry Peacham, Sir Henry Wotton, and Sir William Sanderson expanded the sixteenth-century conception of the part that the arts should play in the life of an educated gentleman and gave some practical hints on connoisseurship. These

---

[1] A. M. Hind, *A History of Engraving* . . . (1923), 257–71, and 'Studies in English Engraving', vi, *Connoisseur*, xcii (1933), 382–91; Royal Soc., *Philosophical Transactions*, iii (1668), nos. 39, 785.

[2] F. G. Stephens, B.M. *Catalogue of . . . Political and Personal Satires*, i (1870), ii (1873).

themes were taken up at the end of the Stuart period by two writers of much greater importance: Jonathan Richardson, the portrait painter, and the 3rd earl of Shaftesbury, a distinguished philosopher in the tradition of the Cambridge Platonists. Both were classicists: Shaftesbury's was the more serious mind of the two and it had been formed by many years of travel and study; Richardson, who had never been to Italy but was a practising artist with a celebrated collection of drawings and a considerable reputation as an expert, tempered his opinions with wider sympathies and with practical considerations and advice. Both men had a high ideal of the part that might be played, in a prosperous and victorious country rich in 'engravings, drawings, copyings and . . . original paintings of the chief Italian schools', by enlightened patronage of the noblest forms of artistic expression; and in Shaftesbury's desire to reform contemporary manners and taste artistic and moral issues were closely interwoven. He intensely disliked virtuosity, superficiality, and exoticism in painting and detested such painters as Adriaen Brouwer and Van der Werff; Richardson shared without reserve his admiration for Raphael and lavished all his powers of praise and analysis on the Cartoons. Of the limitations of the English school Shaftesbury was more critical than Richardson, but at the turn of the century Richard Graham and Bainbrigg Buckeridge[1] had attempted a vindication of the native school with biographies of painters who had worked in this country. In a different spirit George Vertue had begun, by the end of our period, to assemble with the passion and humility of the true scholar the great corpus of notes which remains a primary source for the history of the arts in England.

'As for . . . academies', wrote Shaftesbury, 'for painting, sculpture, or architecture, we have not so much as heard of the proposal.' He was not quite accurate, as at least two abortive schemes for an academy for painting seem to have been brought forward in the seventeenth century, but the lack of a strict Academic discipline in England such as controlled the work of artists in France gave

---

[1] Graham's *Short Account* appeared in 1695 with the English translation of Du Fresnoy's *De Arte Graphica*; Buckeridge's fuller work came out with the English edition (1706 et seq.) of De Piles's *Abrégé de la Vie des Peintres*.

to English art under the Stuarts a brilliant freshness and directness in its highest achievements and an engaging provincialism in
much that would otherwise be merely incompetent. It was not
until 1711 that the first Academy was set up in London under the
governorship of Sir Godfrey Kneller, and later of Thornhill, and
a body of Directors.[1] Artists in London were fast becoming conscious of the importance of their place in society and of the need to
organize their activities: 'painters', wrote Richardson, 'are upon the
level with writers, as being poets, historians, philosophers and
divines, they entertain and instruct equally with them'.[2] The
friendship between such painters as Richardson and Charles Jervas
and writers like Addison, Swift, or Pope, 'smit with the love of
sister-arts', is perhaps more eloquent than all the worldly success
of Thornhill or Kneller or the insistence of Richardson and Shaftesbury on the dignity of the arts.

There is no more elusive theme than the development of taste,
but the later Stuart period is the turning point in its history in this
country. The 'state of the arts' that we associate with the age of
Hogarth was already formed in the age of Kneller and Wren and
the ideals of the eighteenth century are largely implicit in the
influences which were being woven, often slowly and incoherently,
by artists, patrons, writers, and travellers under the Stuarts. Above
all there was an increasing and unmistakable awareness of the part
that the arts could play in Great Britain, and of the glory that they
might shed on her, in the wonderful era of expansion which the
triumphs of the reign of Queen Anne had made possible. The
eighteenth century was to see many of their dreams realized.[3]

[1] Vertue, ii. 125; iii. 7, 21, 74, 92; W. T. Whitley, *Artists and their Friends in England
1700–1799* (1928), i. 7–19.

[2] *An Essay on the whole Art of Criticism* (1719; *Works*, ed. 1773, 177–8).

[3] This introductory chapter is, of necessity, a very brief treatment of certain aspects
of a theme which is vital for an understanding of the Stuart period in the arts. I hope
to be able to expand some of them in the future and to indicate more fully the richness
and variety of the sources.

II

INIGO JONES

INIGO JONES was by far the most important English artist of the seventeenth century. His eminence rests not solely on his achievements as an architect. If it were so, his position might be challenged, for Wren had a far greater range, and the dome of St. Paul's can rank with any of Jones's work. Jones was, however, much more than an architect. He was probably the first Englishman to have any profound knowledge of continental art, both antique and contemporary; and he had sufficient distinction of person to be able to influence, in a remarkable degree, the taste of his employers and their associates. He was, indeed, an entirely new phenomenon in England, both as a professional architect (the controlling mind directing the whole body of craftsmen) and as a connoisseur. Further, he appears to have been the first man in England who had an interest both in the theory of his art, and in the proper prestige due to an architect as an artist rather than as a craftsman.[1]

He was born in London in 1573, the son of a clothworker who died in 1596 or 1597.[2] According to Sir Christopher Wren[3] he was apprenticed to a joiner in St. Paul's Churchyard, but nothing is really known of his early life, nor is it possible to guess precisely what drew him to Italy.[4] He was apparently in Venice in 1601, for the fly-leaf of his copy of Palladio's *I Quattro Libri dell'Architettura*,

[1] See D. J. Gordon, 'Poet and Architect: the Intellectual Setting of the Quarrel between Ben Jonson and Inigo Jones', *Journ. of Warburg and Courtauld Institutes*, xii (1949), 152.

[2] The fullest account of Jones is J. A. Gotch, *Inigo Jones* (1928), though additional evidence has since appeared.

[3] Vertue, i. 105.

[4] It is likely he went with a patron, since it is hard to believe he would have had money to go on his own account. Lord Roos, afterwards 6th earl of Rutland, the brother of the 5th earl who was Jones's first known patron (in 1603), visited France, Germany, and Italy between 1598 and 1601. There appears to be no evidence for Vertue's suggestion (v. 25) that he was sent by the earl of Pembroke.

now in the Library of Worcester College, Oxford, is inscribed
with that date and the name of the city—probably a record of its
purchase. It would therefore seem that he was already studying
architecture, using the best and most up-to-date textbook. Many
years later his pupil, John Webb, was to state in the *Vindication of
Stone-heng Restored*[1] that Jones had resided many years in Italy and
especially in Venice 'designing many works and discovering many
antiquities before unknown, until Christianus the Fourth, King of
Denmark, first engrossed him to himself'. There is possible cor-
roboration of the fact that Jones indeed worked in Denmark,
though perhaps not as an architect, for in 1603 the household
accounts of the earl of Rutland, then ambassador in Denmark
(though in England at the time), include an entry for a New Year
gift to 'Henygo Jones, a picture maker'. No certain painting by
Jones has survived,[2] but some of his drawings for masques show
great freedom and felicity in their handling of washes and their
use of light and shade, and the whole character of his draughtsmanship is that of a man whose interests were by no means confined to
architecture.[3] Whatever his work in Denmark may have been, his
first recorded employment in England was neither as an architect
nor as a picture-maker but as a designer of scenery and costumes
for the court masques. In 1605 he designed the *Masque of Blacknesse*
which was presented in Oxford and in 1606 the more famous
Masque of Queens. From then till 1640 he was to be almost continuously employed on such work.

The rise of the court masque and its place in English art belong
to the reign of James rather than to that of Charles. The great part
it played in Jones's professional career must, however, be emphasized here. It offered scope for a splendour of colour and general
effect which was to be paralleled in some of his interior decoration
(of which, alas, very little now remains), while at the same time
its personification of the Gods of Olympus satisfied his passion for

---

[1] Published in 1662. See below, p. 26.
[2] A small landscape attributed to Jones is at Chatsworth. Eighteenth-century
tradition held that he had painted views of ruins in Rome (Vertue, i. 137).
[3] For the importance to English art of Jones as a draughtsman, see Summerson,
68.

Antiquity. Moreover, it gave him an opportunity of introducing to the English court the fashions of the Continent (for, as is well known, his masque designs are derived from those of Italy)[1] and therefore of presenting himself, quite early in his career, as a man of wide knowledge and taste. For it is abundantly clear that, though the learned allegories of the masques must have been above the heads of many in the court audience, the novelty and brilliance of the settings could have been enjoyed by all (Pl. 5 *b*).[2] The masque designs, indeed, lie at the very heart of Jones's work as an artist, and the fact that the greater number of the drawings for them are from his own hand, while most of the later architectural drawings are by his assistant, suggests how deeply he loved them. But their very essence demanded that they should 'vanish like a dream'. They can hardly be re-created, though something of their fantastic and flickering charm can be sensed from the stage directions, or from the drawings which remain. Even so, our understanding of Jones can never be complete, for we now have only his architecture on which we can truly judge him.

Jones's knowledge of continental art was perhaps reinforced by a second visit to Italy about 1605, while in 1609 he was certainly in France. He visited Paris, and, either now or on a return journey from Italy, the Loire and Provence, for he knew Chambord and drew the Pont du Gard. So far there are no records of his work as an architect, but in 1611 he was made Surveyor to Prince Henry, the promising heir to the throne, for whom he created a 'cabinet room' at Whitehall, and at about the same time he was employed on minor surveying work for the Crown.[3]

After the premature death of Prince Henry in 1612 Jones was granted a reversion of the Office of Surveyor to the Crown, then held by Simon Basil.[4] Since, however, there was no immediate prospect of his succession, he left England in the company of the

[1] Allardyce Nicoll, *The Stuart Masque and the Renaissance Stage* (1937); E. Welsford, *The Court Masque* (1927); C. F. Bell and P. Simpson, 'The Masque Designs of Inigo Jones', *Walpole Soc.* xii (1924). And see below, pp. 293–4.

[2] D. J. Gordon, articles on the iconography of the masques in *Journ. of Warburg and Courtauld Institutes*, vi (1943), 122; viii (1945), 107.

[3] *Cal. S.P. Dom.* (1603–10), 570, and ibid. (1611–18), 32.

[4] On 27 April 1613. Ibid. (1611–18), 181.

earl of Arundel.[1] The notes made by Jones during his months in Italy in his copy of Palladio are revealing.[2] They rarely record his impressions of a building as a whole,[3] but consist chiefly of careful, scholarly records of the comparative use of details by Palladio and the Ancients. He is interested also in practical matters such as the arrangement and lighting of staircases, and the inadvisability of having domestic offices in cellars; and he is often emphatic in his approval of the use, or omission, of some particular moulding. He refers slightingly to the use of what he calls 'composed ornaments' which were brought in by Michelangelo and his followers, and which in his opinion 'do not well in solid architecture, but in gardens, loggias, etc. . . .' Beyond that, his very occasional references to modern Italian architects are concerned only with their use and abuse of classical detail, and there are more comparisons with books—those of Serlio, Antonio Labacco, and even Philibert de l'Orme—than with actual buildings. This scholarly preoccupation with detail, with the constant reference to the major manuals of architecture, suggests a mind deeply interested in rules and theories, eager to seize and sift the knowledge of the previous century, but unlikely to create a new and original style. This side of Jones's character was to find expression, much later in his life, in the book which he began to prepare, but never completed,[4] and which can be reconstructed from the drawings only.

Further light is thrown on his interests at the time of this Italian journey by a sketch-book, now in the collection of the duke of Devonshire at Chatsworth. It contains a few drawings of ancient buildings, a number of studies from the works of sixteenth-century Italian artists (including four drawings of the Sistine ceiling), and many figure sketches, mainly copied from Italian engravings.[5] The

[1] See above, p. 2.

[2] The greater part of these notes was printed in Leoni's English translation of Palladio, 3rd ed., 1742.

[3] The major exception to this is Palladio's Teatro Olympico. See W. Grant Keith, 'A Theatre Project by Inigo Jones', *Burl. Mag.* xxxi (1917), 61, 105.

[4] Colin Rowe, *The Theoretical Drawings of Inigo Jones, their sources and scope*; unpub. Ph.D. thesis, University of London (1947). And see below, p. 34.

[5] J. Sumner-Smith, 'The Italian Sources of Inigo Jones's Style', *Burl. Mag.* xciv (1952), 200.

draughtsmanship is free and lively, and has affinities with that of the painter Guercino (of whom there is a portrait drawing). There are also a number of written pages in the book, filled with quotations from theoretical writers, especially Lomazzo. It was perhaps also at this time that he bought the large number of original drawings by Palladio (now in the Burlington-Devonshire collection at the Royal Institute of British Architects) which both in his own lifetime and in the early eighteenth century were to play so vital a part in determining the course of English architecture.[1]

In 1615, soon after Jones's return to England, Simon Basil died, and Jones assumed the Surveyorship. He was to retain that office till 1642, all his most important work being done for the Crown. His worth was recognized by an increase in salary. Basil's annual fees (exclusive of allowances for travelling and a clerk) had been £36. 10s.; Jones was allowed £80. At first he seems to have worked mainly for the Queen, Anne of Denmark. His alterations for her palace at Oatlands were probably finished by 1617, since a view of the older house, with Jones's classical gateway before it, may be seen in the signed and dated portrait of her by Paul van Somer at Windsor. Far more important, however, was the villa he began for her at Greenwich, which has always been known as the Queen's House and is now the National Maritime Museum (Pl. 2 a).[2]

The royal palace at Greenwich had been given to Anne in 1613 (following a reconciliation with James after she had shot his favourite hound by mistake). It consisted of Tudor buildings on the river front, with a garden behind them, and beyond the latter a park, separated from the garden by the road from Deptford to Woolwich. In October 1616, Anne, who had already made some alterations to the Tudor building, began her new house farther up the hill: in the next year Chamberlain in a letter to Sir Dudley Carleton writes 'yt is said to be some curious device of Inigo Jones, and will cost above 4000l'. In 1618 work was stopped, presumably owing to the Queen's illness, and on her death in 1619 was abandoned till 1630, when Greenwich had been granted to Henrietta

---

[1] W. Grant Keith, 'Inigo Jones as a Collector', *R.I.B.A. Journ.* xxiii (1925), 95.

[2] The best modern account of the Queen's House is G. H. Chettle, London County Council, *Survey of London* (14th monograph), n.d.

Maria as part of her jointure. Only the lower part of the walls seem to have been built before 1618, but the plan must have been fixed. Alterations may have been made in the elevations before Henrietta Maria's name and the date 1635 were placed on the upper storey of the north front, but if so they were probably of detail only, and the design and plan alike heralded a revolution in English architecture, a complete break with tradition, and a direct and successful attempt to introduce a pure and very sophisticated Italian style.

It may have been rumours of the novelty of the design which caused Carleton's correspondent to refer to the building as 'a curious device', or it may have been the idiosyncrasy of the plan (Fig. 1). Some strange fancy induced the Queen to build her villa astride the Woolwich–Deptford road—it is said so that she could step into the park or into the palace gardens (and so down to the landing-stage on the river) in privacy and without muddying her feet. Such a fantastic house would have been a 'conceit' which would have been found highly intriguing in Jacobean (or even in Elizabethan) England, and is not too far removed in idea from John Thorpe's scheme for a house planned on his own initials, or the great triangular castle at Longford with its reference to the Trinity—though at Greenwich the fantasy was practical in origin, and not linked with any emblematic content.

There is, however, little that is fantastic in Jones's execution of the Queen's wishes. For him fantasy belonged to the theatre rather than to architecture, and it is not until quite late in his career, in some of the schemes for the rebuilding of Whitehall, that we can see any intrusion of it in his building designs. At Greenwich he arranged two simple rectangular blocks on either side of the road, and joined them, at first floor level, by a bridge.[1] The simple block form with no projections was in itself a complete novelty. No less new was the interior disposition of the rooms. Following the precepts laid down by Palladio that the size of adjacent rooms would be found most agreeable when they bore a mathematical ratio to each other, i.e. 1 to 2 or 1 to 3, Jones has

[1] Owing to alterations made in 1664 (see below, p. 133) the building now appears as an unbroken rectangular block. The position of the original road is marked by the two nineteenth-century Doric colonnades.

planned his house with the greatest care. The entrance hall on the
river front is a cube, running up through both storeys but surrounded by a gallery at first floor level, making it possible to pass
from the east to the west suites of rooms. The space on either side

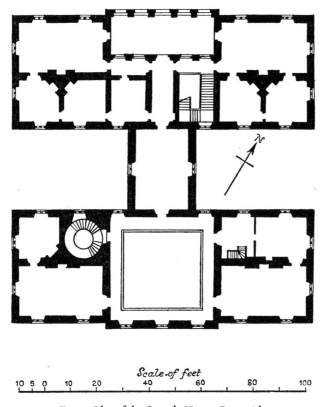

Scale of feet

FIG. I. *Plan of the Queen's House, Greenwich*

of the hall is divided into three rooms, one large and two small.
all carefully proportioned to each other. The traditional English
arrangement of the Great Hall[1] is completely abandoned. The hall
is still the one great room in the house, as it is in Palladio's Italian
villas, but it serves mainly as a vestibule to the private rooms,
though it would no doubt have been used as a reception room,
a *salone* when necessary. There can be little doubt that Jones took
his main inspiration from the villas of Palladio and Scamozzi

[1] See below, p. 43.

(without precise imitation of any one of them); though the arrangement of rooms in small suites is close to the French idea of an *appartement*.[1]

In his elevation, however, he modified considerably the normal villa scheme. Palladio's villas are usually raised on a basement, with one storey of very high rooms, and perhaps a mezzanine above. The windows are comparatively small, for the main purpose of these summer residences in Italy was to provide a refuge from the sun in the heat of the day. In England the question of heat hardly arose, and large windows were needed to let in light. Moreover, the view from the house was a consideration, and since a finer prospect of the river could be gained from the first floor, the rooms of the Queen were placed at that level. Jones therefore designed a house in two storeys, the ground storey being of rusticated stone (echoing the Italian tradition which had originated with Bramante in Rome) while the upper, slightly taller storey was of brick whitewashed over, with stone quoins and stone dressings to the windows. The simple, well-proportioned windows were originally rather taller in this floor than in the lower, thus giving emphasis to the upper floor. The balance of the design was destroyed in the early eighteenth century, when the ground floor windows were lengthened. Further damage was done to the value of the mouldings when the upper storey was stuccoed over. The fine quality of Jones's classical detail can perhaps now best be appreciated in the open loggia with which he adorned the Park front.

For all its apparent Italianism the Queen's House is not a purely Italian villa. Its long, low lines are very different from Palladio's block-like houses, which are much higher in comparison with their length. The mouldings of string course, cornice, and window casings can never have told as more than lines drawn delicately on the surface; they have none of the strong, sculptural quality of Italian detail. The long house was traditional in England, and the low-relief string courses of Perpendicular architecture had persisted, even if they were given debased classical profiles, throughout the sixteenth century. Nevertheless, the Queen's House must have

[1] For sources see F. Saxl and R. Wittkower, *English Art and the Mediterranean* (1948), 44, where the Villa Medici at Poggio a Caiano is proposed as a source for the plan.

seemed a very startling object in the English landscape, even in the 1630's when it was completed, by which time the court had had some opportunity of knowing what to expect from Jones. The impact of his first completed building, the Banqueting House in Whitehall (Pl. 2 b) (now the United Services Museum), must have been far greater.

On 12 December 1619 the Banqueting House, a brick and stone building erected in 1607 by Simon Basil, was totally destroyed when scaffolding set up for the Twelfth Night masque caught fire. The rebuilding was taken in hand immediately, and, in spite of the fact that Jones reported in 1620 that many of the masons had run away,[1] the work was pushed on so that the St. George's Feast on 23 April 1621 was 'held in the new Banquetting Room, which is too handsome for the rest of the building'.[2] Special arrangements had in fact been made for carrying out the work. William Cure, the royal Master Mason, was evidently an incompetent and negligent character, and a new post of Master Mason to the Banqueting House had been created and given to Nicholas Stone the sculptor.[3] The whole character of the building, with its mature handling of Italian forms, must, however, be due to Jones's immediate supervision of every part. An entirely new standard of precision and elegance must have been demanded of the masons and it is not unlikely that they found the Surveyor an exacting taskmaster. In two preliminary elevations at Chatsworth, as well as in the final design, Jones draws freely on Palladio for his inspiration.[4] The proportions, a double cube (fifty-five feet wide, one hundred and ten feet long, and fifty-five feet high), are those advocated by the Italian and much of the detail, especially the festoons in their

[1] *Cal. S.P. Dom.* (1619–23), 172.   [2] Ibid. 249.

[3] Perhaps partly because, having an interest in the Portland stone quarries, he was able to furnish part of the materials (W. L. Spiers, 'Note Books of N. Stone', *Walpole Soc.* vii (1919), 137). The basement was of Oxfordshire stone (recased in Portland in 1773), the main fabric in Northamptonshire, and the orders and crowning balustrade alone in Portland. The whole, including the original Portland, was renewed in Portland stone by Sir John Soane in 1833. One original capital is in the Soane Museum (London County Council, *Survey of London*, xiii (1930), 121, 124). The original would have provided colour contrasts, now lost, analogous to some Roman palaces. For Nicholas Stone see below, pp. 106 f.

[4] For an analysis of the evolution of the design see Summerson, 65, 78.

unusual position, linking the capitals of the columns,[1] suggests that he was using Palladio's book as a dictionary of measurements and motifs. But the final design is no mere pastiche. It is a new and individual statement of a given theme, a theme attempted by all the great sixteenth-century architects of Italy—the application of the orders to a palace façade. In his clear and coherent exposition Jones uses pilasters on both storeys in his two outer bays, and for the three central bays, which project slightly, he employs half-columns. The entablatures above have a marked break forward over the columns, thus emphasizing the centre (for a pediment which gave this emphasis in the earlier designs has disappeared); the break over the pilasters is slighter. The use of half-columns in the centre, with the strong break above, provides a valuable vertical accent which helps to balance the strong horizontals. As in the Queen's House, the whole structure is longer in comparison with its height than would be normal in Italy and so the vertical accents are of great importance. It is clear, however, from the abandonment of the pediment, and the fact that the design of the windows is unvaried along the whole length of the front, that Jones wished the accent on the centre to be discreet rather than emphatic, to be a delicate change of rhythm rather than the climax of his design. Had the entrance been in the centre, it would have necessarily been a focal point; but the entrance was from the end, the main façade was in fact the side of the building, and so the architectural problem was more difficult and more delicate. Its triumphant solution and the manner of handling the details, in particular the proportions and patterning of the lightly rusticated walls behind the order, show a discipline and a sensitivity of mind which is astonishing in a man who was self-taught, without apparently any previous practical experience. It is simple, clear-cut, logical architecture, the work of a man who has thought deeply and read widely, inherently academic, but academic art at its best. Like his slightly older contemporaries, the Carracci in Italy, he looks back to the simple clarity

[1] These appear in Palladio's plate of the Palazzo Thiene at Vicenza, though not in the executed building. The first of the preliminary drawings is an adaptation from Palladio's 'Designs for a Venetian House', and the second borrows the window treatment of the Palazzo Porto-Colleoni, but rearranges it.

of the High Renaissance. His view is strongly coloured by the influence of Palladio, but he deliberately ignores all that is un-academic in the Vicentine's work, all the complex, unexpected double rhythms which give a Mannerist twist to much of his executed architecture. But unlike the Carracci, much of whose work reflects the propagandist aims of the Counter-Reformation, his style is personal. It does not grow out of an older national tradition, nor is it linked with a strong contemporary expression of thought. In other countries seventeenth-century artists who sought inspiration in classical art were able to create a new 'classical-baroque' style. Domenichino and Poussin, adding to the eclecticism of the Carracci a new research into the antique, were to find a fresh impetus in Roman intellectual or religious thought. Bernini himself was to find in classical art the foundations of a new expressive style. In France François Mansart was to make of French sixteenth-century classicism a new, completely national architec-ture. It is with these men that Jones must be compared. He is linked with them in his deep respect for Antiquity and for the age of Bramante and Raphael, in his determination to ignore the dis-tortions of late sixteenth-century Mannerism. It was no small miracle that an Englishman of his day should select with such certainty from the wide vocabulary of Italian architecture. Unlike his foreign contemporaries, however, he adds too little of his own to create a new, living seventeenth-century style. He refines, he adjusts, and in the Banqueting House, by which one must most fairly judge him, since it is his least altered building, he produces an architecture which in its accomplishment is unmatched in northern Europe, and which was to be a permanent inspiration in England for nearly three hundred years. But it is the swan-song of the High Renaissance, a lyric with a dying fall; it has a nostalgia for the past and for the south, that was to be a recurring element in English romanticism.

It is difficult today to appreciate the original splendour and spaciousness of the interior of the Banqueting House, filled as it is with the glass cases containing the exhibits of the United Service Museum. It is a single great room running the full height of the building. The two-storeyed exterior does not truly express the interior pattern, but there was as yet no precedent in Italy for a single-unit domestic building in which the interior arrangement was conveyed in the exterior design.[1] The final glory of the room was not, of course, due to the architect, but to Rubens, whose ceiling paintings glorifying the rule of the Stuarts were placed in position in 1635.[2]

No other major architectural work was undertaken by Jones in the 1620's, but his activities were extremely varied. In 1620 he was commanded by the King to investigate the history of Stonehenge. His conclusions, published in 1655 after his death by John Webb,[3] show that he regarded the remains as those of a Roman temple, for he thought he had found a mathematical basis, similar to that advocated by Vitruvius for temples, in the plan of Stonehenge.[4] It is, however, revealing that in spite of this scientific approach Jones, in his enthusiastic desire to ascribe all noteworthy antiquities to the Romans, who were certainly to him the greatest and most heroic of nations, and to establish links with them in his own country, was willing to ignore the complete dissimilarity between the great monoliths on Salisbury Plain and the remains of those classical buildings he had seen in Italy. It is, in fact, another example of his romantic antiquarianism, and is in striking contrast to the careful historical approach of English medieval scholars from Sir William Dugdale onwards.[5]

In the same year, 1620, Jones was for a time member of Parliament for Shoreham,[6] and by the end of the decade he was serving as a magistrate in the City of Westminster. Much of his time, both

---

[1] Summerson, 77, is probably right in suggesting that the Roman basilica, as described by Vitruvius, served as Jones's inspiration.

[2] See below, pp. 287–8.

[3] *The most notable Antiquity of Great Britain, vulgarly called Stone-Heng, on Salisbury Plain, restored, by Inigo Jones Esq., Architect General to the King.* Jones's conclusions were challenged by Dr. Walter Charleton, Physician-in-Ordinary to Charles II, who in *Chorea Gigantum* ascribed Stonehenge to the Danes. Webb answered this in his *Vindication of Stone-Heng Restored* (1662) in which his references to Jones's life are an important primary source.

[4] See R. Wittkower, 'Inigo Jones, Architect and Man of Letters', *R.I.B.A. Journ.* lx, series 3 (1953), 83.

[5] See D. C. Douglas, *English Scholars* (1939).

[6] E. S. de Beer, *Notes and Queries*, 27 Apr. 1940, note 4.

now and in the following decade, must have been taken up with minor business connected with the Surveyor's office: dealing with nuisances of one kind or another, preparing lodgings for distinguished guests, designing a catafalque for James I, sitting on Commissions dealing with London buildings and the spread of the town. A good deal of abortive work was connected with Prince Charles's proposed match with the Infanta. Plans were made for the fitting up for her of St. James's and Denmark House (formerly Somerset House and empty since the death of the Queen in 1619) and of Durham House for the Grandees in her train,[1] and orders were given to 'Jones and Allen the old player[2] with noblemen to arrange pageants and repair the highways for her reception'.[3] Most important of all, a new chapel was begun for her use and later finished for Henrietta Maria. This building, the importance of which has only recently been recognized, is now known as the Queen's Chapel, Marlborough Gate (Pl. 3).[4] It was the first ecclesiastical building in England in a truly classical style, and is the only interior now remaining by Jones from which we can gain any idea of the impact of Rome on his imagination. The splendid coffered barrel vault of wood, which gives so great an air of monumentality to this little building, is clearly derived from his studies of the buildings of the Ancients, either in the original, or in the reconstructions in Palladio's book.[5] His design may also be tinged with a recollection of the use of such grave antique motives by Bramante and Raphael; it is clear from other drawings for work not carried out[6] that the grandeur of coffered vaults had made a strong impression on him. Jones's new opportunity, and the passion for

---

[1] *Cal. S.P. Dom.* (1619–23), 536, 560–1, 576.

[2] i.e. Edward Alleyn (1566–1626), the famous Elizabethan actor and founder of Dulwich College, where his collection of pictures still remains.

[3] *Cal. S.P. Dom.* (1619–23), 608.

[4] The Spanish Ambassador laid the first stone on 30 May 1623 (ibid. 593). See also G. H. Chettle, 'Marlborough House Chapel', *Country Life*, lxxxiv (1938), 450, where the payments for the roof are published. The present fittings date from the reign of Charles II.

[5] The pattern used in the coffering is taken from Palladio's illustration of the Temple of the Sun and Moon.

[6] e.g. for Whitehall Palace, and some of the church designs in the Worcester College collection, probably for the proposed treatise.

Venetian painting aroused in Charles by the sight of the Spanish royal collection, are the two major results of the Spanish marriage venture.

The new reign did not at once bring important new commissions, though from 1627 onwards the Surveyor was fairly continuously engaged on alterations and additions to the Queen's residence, Denmark House, which now seems to have reverted to its older title of Somerset House. But his influence was becoming evident outside immediate court circles. Although both the first Stuart kings had continued Elizabeth's policy of attempting to restrict building outside the confines of the City, the development of the land between Ludgate and Westminster continued.[1] As early as 1618 Jones was concerned with an abortive scheme for Lincoln's Inn Fields.[2] In 1625 he was made a member of a Commission appointed to inquire into buildings set up since the thirteenth year of King James, and to see that they complied with the regulations for building in brick, and in the early 1630's he was working for the earl of Bedford in Covent Garden (Pl. 4 b). Its layout of a piazza surrounded on two sides by houses which were uniform in design, the end being closed by a church and the south side by the wall of the earl's garden, was a complete novelty in England, and a vitally important step in town-planning.[3] There had been no planning, either of streets or houses, in Elizabethan London; each individual owner built his house as he chose, with no reference to those of his neighbours. The result was picturesque enough, but completely at variance with the basic classical principles of regularity and balance. Both Alberti and Palladio had discussed the planning of piazzas, the inspiration in both cases being the piazzas of the Ancients, though Alberti had combined this with a surprisingly modern sociological approach. Jones must, of course, have known both these authorities, but it seems likely that his immediate source was the work of Henri IV in Paris,

---

[1] N. Brett James, *Growth of Stuart London* (1935), 151 f.

[2] He appears to have had no hand in the buildings, including Lindsey House, set up between 1638 and 1641. See Summerson, 83, 101.

[3] Colen Campbell's plate in *Vitruvius Britannicus* (1717), iii. 20–22, which shows the piazza completely surrounded by houses, is typical of that tendency to correct irregularities which sometimes makes him dangerous as a source.

especially in the Place des Vosges, which would have been just completed when he visited Paris in 1609. The use of brick and stone in the surrounding houses is far more French than Italian, and the treatment of the church as a centre-piece with two dependent blocks has also a French flavour.[1]

The church in Covent Garden, consecrated in 1638[2] and completely rebuilt by Hardwick in the eighteenth century, more or less on the original design, has nothing French about it. Bedford, who had Puritan leanings, is said by Horace Walpole to have stated that he wanted nothing elaborate, in fact, something like a barn, whereupon the architect promised him 'the handsomest barn in England'. He chose the Tuscan, the simplest and most austere of the orders, and designed a temple with a deep portico and wide low pediment with strongly projecting eaves. It is a highly original, indeed probably a unique, conception. It has gravity and force, but with its heavy mouldings and complete lack of surface ornament it demands brilliant sunshine to make an effect, and is inappropriate to the grey skies and softer light of Northern Europe.

Jones's work as a town planner made a lasting impression on English architecture; his work at St. Paul's Cathedral made a far greater impression on his contemporaries.[3] The fabric had become increasingly insecure since the fall of the spire in 1561; the Commission (of which Jones had been a member) set up in 1620 to inquire into the decay had done little. But in 1627 Laud became bishop of London and was therefore in a position to promote much more actively his policy of increasing the dignity and decorum of church services. It must have been abhorrent to him that his cathedral church was notorious for its lack of repair, and for the desecration of the nave by a labour market and an exchange for

[1] The houses were in fact built by Isaac de Caux, which may partly account for their French character (Summerson, 83). It should perhaps be noted that John Evelyn states that the scheme was derived from that of the piazza at Leghorn (Evelyn, *Diary*, 21 October 1644). For the houses in Great Queen Street of about 1636 possibly by John Webb, but more probably by Peter Mills, Bricklayer to the City, see Summerson, 101, and the same author's *Georgian London* (1945), 13–19.

[2] Letter from the Rev. G. Garrard to Strafford, 10 May 1638, *Letters and Dispatches of Thos. Wentworth, Viscount Strafford* (1739), ii. 167.

[3] For the best record of Jones's work see Sir William Dugdale, *History of St. Paul's* (1658), plates by W. Hollar.

merchants. A new Commission was appointed in April 1631,[1] and it is clear that Laud's energetic personality, coupled with the King's sincere interest in the question, compelled action, for difficulties connected with the pulling down of houses abutting on the cathedral were swept aside. In February 1633 Jones was appointed Surveyor, with Edward Carter as his subordinate, and in May of that year Jones reported that work was ready to proceed.[2] The only remaining difficulty was money. The project was extremely unpopular, since the cost was partly defrayed from fines imposed by the hated Prerogative Courts. The King, distressed to hear of the complaints, resolved as a gesture to enlarge his personal bounty and to be responsible for the building of the west end; but though the artistic results were to be great, Clarendon's account does not suggest that public opinion was much moved by it.[3] In fact, it leaves no doubt that the work on St. Paul's contributed materially to public discontent, and so ultimately to rebellion.

The greater part of Jones's executed work at St. Paul's was of repair only; the Norman nave and transepts were to be recased, not rebuilt; and their proportions and bay design had therefore to be retained. The Gothic choir, which was in relatively good condition, was left untouched. Jones, however, did his best to transform the exterior in conformity with Italian taste by replacing the old buttresses by wide pilasters carrying an entablature, with balls on pedestals instead of finials. The round-headed aisle windows were surrounded with an architrave, with a table carried on brackets above, and the buttresses and entablature again appear at clearstorey level. The transept fronts and the west front (Pl. 4 a) presented far greater difficulties. They were too high and narrow to fall into any classical scheme, and their large windows were presumably necessary to light the interior. Beyond masking the junction of nave and aisles with great scrolls imitated from the

---

[1] *Cal. S.P. Dom.* (1631–33), 6.

[2] Ibid. 528; ibid. (1633–34), 65.

[3] Clarendon, *History of the Rebellion* (ed. W. D. Macray, 1888, i. 125). Up to 1635, however, large sums were contributed by the country as a whole and by private individuals. After that year public contributions dropped owing to the growing unpopularity of the Government. (H. R. Trevor-Roper, *Archbishop Laud* (1940), 123, 346, 350.)

Gesù in Rome, adding a classical doorway to the transepts, and using small obelisks instead of finials, Jones seems to have abandoned any attempt to grapple seriously with the problem. A drawing in the collection of the Royal Institute of British Architects[1] shows a rather unsuccessful attempt to design a Roman façade topped by a pediment for the west front, but in the executed design the medieval gable is left, though the string course below it is replaced by a Doric entablature, with lions' heads in the metopes.[2]

The lower part of the façade was ultimately masked by the great projecting portico which was the gift of the King. Its immediate purpose was, no doubt, to provide accommodation outside the church for the chaffering which had desecrated the nave. Jones evidently felt that it offered an opportunity for a grand classical effect: this is extremely difficult to gauge from Hollar's engravings, for they are drawn from a high viewpoint, and so the impact on the visitor climbing Ludgate Hill of the great row of Corinthian columns fifty feet high, and spreading one hundred feet in width, is entirely lost. Moreover, the portico projected forty feet in front of the façade and therefore, as one approached the building, the lower part at least of the windows above would have been masked, and the lack of cohesion between the portico and the upper part of the front (which is so obtrusive in Hollar's plate) would have been much less apparent.

As a piece of classical architecture the portico is interesting, for it is finished with a straight balustrade instead of the usual pediment. The latter would have been unhappy with the high-pitched gable above, and might also have taken too much light from the west windows of the nave. Fortunately, Jones could find good authority for its omission. Palladio's plate of the portico of the Temple of the Sun and Moon shows just such a portico, and Jones noted that this was 'of the architect's own invention, and was intended for the Temple of Peace'. Such an association with the

---

[1] Illustrated in J. A. Gotch, *Inigo Jones* (1928), Pl. xix.

[2] The work as a whole may well have bored Jones, and much may have been left to Edward Carter. It was certainly badly done, for Sancroft, dean of St. Paul's, writing to Wren in 1668, reported that Jones's casing of the upper part of the walls was not set squarely above the piers, but over the groins of the vaulting and that the new work was not adequately tied to the old fabric (*Wren Soc.* xiii. 46).

grandest of all antique buildings (i.e. the Basilica of Constantine) was irresistible.

To Jones's contemporaries the portico of St. Paul's was one of his two major achievements. It was shown with the Banqueting House in relief on his tombstone in St. Benet's Church, Paul's Wharf;[1] John Webb[2] states that it 'hath contracted the Envy of all Christendom upon our Nation, for a Piece of Architecture, not to be parallell'd in these last Ages of the World'. Webb might perhaps be thought prejudiced; but both Sir Roger Pratt[3] and John Evelyn,[4] who had seen and appreciated the best modern architecture of France and Italy, were unstinted in their praise. It had indeed a quality of antique grandeur without parallel in Northern Europe.[5]

The 1630's were perhaps the fullest years of Jones's life. The work at St. Paul's entailed much beyond the actual designing, for there was trouble about the shipping of stone from the Portland quarries, both men and ships having been pressed for service with the Navy;[6] there were certificates to be issued when the stone was shipped;[7] transport had to be arranged for timber from Hampshire.[8] The Surveyor was further occupied with various Royal Commissions; for instance in April 1638 one was set up to inquire into frauds in deal boards and fir-timber;[9] there are constant references

[1] Bodleian MS. *Aubrey* 8. f. 19 has a sketch of Jones's tomb (destroyed in the Great Fire), showing a bust standing on a plain sarcophagus, with the Banqueting House recognizable at the left end. At this side is a pencil note: 'The Banquetting House at Whitehall in Bas-relieve', and at the other: 'West end of St. Paules in Bas-relieve'. Vertue, i. 99, says that the west end of St. Paul's and the porch of Covent Garden church appeared on the monument, but Aubrey's drawing seems conclusive.

[2] *Stone-heng Vindicated*, 27.

[3] *The Architecture of Sir Roger Pratt*, ed. R. T. Gunther (1928), 23.

[4] John Evelyn, *Diary*, 7 Sept. 1666.

[5] The work was interrupted by the Civil War. Jones had intended to rebuild the central tower, and add a steeple 'suitable thereto'. No drawings remain, but some of John Webb's church designs give some indication of the probable style (see M. D. Whinney, 'Some Church designs by John Webb, *Journ. of Warburg and Courtauld Institutes*, vi (1943), 142).

[6] Jones reported this to Laud on 11 Apr. 1637 (*Cal. S.P. Dom.* (1636–7), 563).

[7] Nine such certificates were issued between April and June 1637. (Ibid. (1637), 4, 5, 6, 76, 78, 156, 201, 205, &c.)

[8] Ibid. (1639), 405.   [9] Ibid. (1637–8), 363.

to inquiries into possible infringements of the regulations concerning the manufacture of bricks; in 1639 he was reporting on the pollution and possible improvement of the water supply to the King's houses. This rather tedious routine business must have taken much time, and yet more was spent on his duties as a Westminster magistrate.

The increased work on masques in this decade must have been more agreeable to him. In 1631 he and Ben Jonson, who had hitherto written most of the masques, had their final quarrel; thereafter it seems probable that Jones supplied ideas as well as settings, though his ideas were turned into suitable verse by Sir William Davenant.[1] These later masque designs, especially those for *Coelum Britannicum* (1634), the *Temple of Love* and *Florimene* (1635), (Pl. 5 *b*), and above all *Britannia Triumphans* and *Luminalia* (1638), have remarkable pictorial quality and great ease and fluency of draughtsmanship. The style of figure drawing changes somewhat, the Mannerist elegance of the earlier costume studies giving place to a stronger, rather heavier proportion and handling.[2] It is, however, not only in the masque designs that the character of Jones's mature draughtsmanship can be seen. Some of the drawings, which are practically all that has survived of the sumptuous decoration (including a new type of fireplace with a picture frame as the overmantel) which he was contriving for the Queen's House, have the same ease of handling, the same fertility of invention.

From about 1635 onwards the Surveyor seems to have confined himself mainly to these rapid almost free-hand sketches. Strictly architectural drawings from his own hand in the later part of his life are rare. It is possible that he had never cared greatly for this side of his work and that he had trained his assistant, John Webb, largely for this purpose. Webb, who was born in 1611, had gone into the Surveyor's office when he was seventeen, and had subsequently married Jones's niece. At the Restoration, when Webb petitioned Charles II for the Surveyorship, he stated that 'he had been brought up by his uncle, Mr. Inigo Jones upon His late

---

[1] In 1625 Jones had already provided a text in his translation of the *French Pastoral*.
[2] For an analysis of the scenic devices used in the later masques, see R. Southern, *Changeable Scenery* (1952), 17–106.

Majesty's command in the study of Architecture, as well that
which relates to building as for Masques, Triumphes and the like'.[1]
The precise character of Charles I's interest in the young man is
obscure, but it may well be that the King knew of Jones's desire
to produce an English treatise on architecture, and was anxious
that he should train an assistant (since no English draughtsman
would have had the necessary knowledge of Italian architecture)
who could help him to see the project through.[2] Unfortunately,
so far as is known, the treatise was never written. Enough drawings, however, remain (chiefly at Worcester College, Oxford) for
it to be almost beyond doubt that a book on the lines of the great
Italian treatises was planned, containing chapters on the orders,
domestic, ecclesiastical, and probably urban building, with additional sections on gates, grottoes, fountains, &c. The great majority
of the drawings are adaptations from known sources, generally
from the books of Serlio or Palladio, but in many cases they are
developments of a theme, rather than an exact imitation.[3] It may
be that, following the example of Palladio, Jones intended to
include some of his own works also.[4] Had the book materialized
it would have clarified and rendered permanent much that is now
fragmentary and conjectural, for it would have been clear proof
of the aspirations of the little circle of connoisseurs at the Caroline
court, and would have made it far easier to estimate the balance
between aesthetic, theoretical, and historical interests in the mind
of Inigo Jones. As it is, we must deduce this from his few written
notes, his drawings, his remaining work, and the opinions of his
contemporaries. The picture is incomplete; the personality remains
a little shadowy, and sometimes, indeed, a trifle contradictory.

In addition to preparing the drawings for the treatise, Webb
acted as chief draughtsman in the office, his position being pre-

---

[1] *Cal. S.P. Dom.* (1660–61), 76.

[2] For a full discussion see Colin Rowe, *The Theoretical Drawings of Inigo Jones, their
sources and scope*, unpub. Ph.D. thesis, University of London (1947). I am grateful to
the author for permission to use his material.

[3] This is particularly marked in the domestic and ecclesiastical buildings.

[4] This might account for the careful drawings made by Webb of the proposed new
Star Chamber, the plan of which drawn by Jones is dated 1617, i.e. eleven years
before Webb entered the office.

sumably that of a personal assistant to the Surveyor.[1] All the draw-ings for the major architectural project of King Charles's reign, namely the entire rebuilding of Whitehall Palace, are from his hand, though there is good reason to believe that many, but by no means all of them, show the ideas of Jones.[2]

It is not surprising that Charles I found the rambling Tudor palace inconvenient. It had grown in a haphazard fashion, strag-gling along the water front (which was, of course, much closer to St. James's Park than it has been since the Embankment was built) and stretching back in blocks dividing the site into a series of awkwardly shaped courts.[3] The great collection of pictures was housed for the most part in the Long Gallery or the Matted Gallery, neither of them in any way worthy of their contents. It is impos-sible to say how long the idea of rebuilding had been in Charles's mind (there is no evidence for supposing that it had been con-sidered by James I when he rebuilt the Banqueting House), but it is certain that projects were being considered about 1638, for the fines imposed in connexion with the Londonderry Charter incident were to take the form of a contribution towards the erection of a new palace.[4] Sir William Sanderson, recording this, refers to a

[1] A good deal of work no longer extant was carried out about this time: Bagshot Lodge (1630-1); the New Lodge in Hyde Park (1634-5); the temporary Masking Room at Whitehall (1636; set up so that the new Rubens ceiling in the Banqueting House should not be damaged by the smoke from the torches); and much decoration at Somerset House, as well as a water gate and a costly new chapel. A large new wing was projected here (a drawing for it in Webb's hand dated 1638 is at Worcester College) but it was not built till after the Restoration; see below, p. 137. Further work was carried out for the Queen at Oatlands (W. Grant Keith, *Burl. Mag.* xxii (1912), 225). A classical screen, with figures by Hubert le Sueur, was built in Win-chester cathedral by 1638; the design for Temple Bar (R.I.B.A. collection) of 1638, based on a Roman triumphal arch, was not carried out. For country houses for private owners, possibly designed by Jones or Webb, see below, pp. 45 f.

[2] For a full analysis, see M. D. Whinney, 'John Webb's drawings for Whitehall Palace', *Walpole Soc.* xxxi (1943), 45–107.

[3] The plan of Whitehall made about 1669, and subsequently engraved by George Vertue in 1747, shows the palace substantially as it was in Charles I's time. (London County Council, *Survey of London*, xiii (1930), Pl. i and *Wren Soc.* vii, Pl. vi.)

[4] See E. S. de Beer, 'Whitehall Palace: Inigo Jones and Wren', *Notes and Queries*, 30 Dec. 1939, quoting a letter from Richard Daye dated 1638, and Sir William Sanderson's account in his *Compleat History of the Life and Raigne of King Charles* (1658).

'Model drawn by Inigo Jones'. Drawings by Jones may perhaps
have existed, but the seventy-odd drawings that survive are by
John Webb. It is unthinkable that at a time when the Surveyor was
at the height of his powers, the major commission of the day should
have been given to his assistant, and it is therefore reasonable to
consider these drawings as vital evidence of Jones's quality as an
architect. The most complete scheme[1] (Fig. 2) is for a very large
palace arranged in orderly blocks round a series of rectangular
courts—a great court in the centre running north and south (i.e.
roughly in the position of Whitehall today) with ranges of three
courts to east and west of it. The westernmost courts would therefore have spread over what is now the Horse Guards and far into
St. James's Park. This palace would, for size and splendour of plan,
have been unparalleled in the Europe of its day.[2]

It is important to note that the plan is almost symmetrical, and
consists of a series of closed rectangles. The whole is a single unit,
but made up of a number of smaller units. There is nothing that
can be called a Grand Front, no major accent, either in plan or
elevation, on a special block of buildings. The interest is diffused
equally over the whole; it has, indeed, a High Renaissance harmony
rather than a baroque sense of drama. This is even more marked in
the elevations than in the plan. All four fronts are treated in a
similar manner, (Pl. 5 a) with a central section three storeys high,
joined by two long wings of two storeys to end-pavilions which
echo the three-storey scheme of the centre. The central entrance
is in every case flanked by two towers, crowned by small cupolas.
This disposition of a façade is completely un-Italian. The use of

---

[1] This is the well-known scheme published by William Kent in his *Designs of Inigo Jones* (1727).

[2] The Escorial, designed by Herrera for Philip II and seen by Charles in 1623, contained many courts. The Louvre, of which the Great Court was unfinished in 1640,
hardly provides a parallel, though Jones may have known the triple-court project for
the Tuileries engraved by J. A. du Cerceau, or possibly Serlio's unpublished plan
(probably in France in the seventeenth century) for a royal palace (see W. Bell Dins-
moor, 'The Literary Remains of Sebastiano Serlio', *Art Bulletin*, xxiv (1942), 55, 115).
Another possible source for a building round many courts was the reconstruction of
the Temple at Jerusalem, published by the Jesuit Villalpandus in *De Postrema Ezechielis
Prophetae Visione*, 1605. This influential book would certainly have been known to
Arundel and so probably also to Jones.

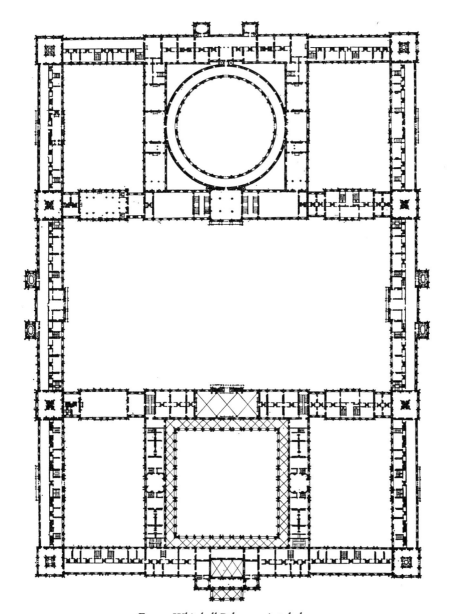

FIG. 2. *Whitehall Palace, projected plan*

taller end-pavilions may owe something to France, but the whole design is far closer to a Tudor frontage (e.g. the base court at Hampton Court) with its turreted centre block reminiscent of a great gate house, and its angle towers joined by lower walls. In fact, it is a development of an English medieval type.[1]

Though the general arrangement of the front may be English, the architecture itself is purely Italian. Each storey is treated with an order; cornices and windows are, in finished drawings, profusely decorated with festoons, reclining figures or purely classical ornaments. Many of the motives can be traced to precise sources, the plates in Palladio's book, or the back elevation of the Palazzo Farnese; others are perhaps derived from antique fragments Jones had seen in Rome. The design of the Banqueting House makes one of the principal themes, especially in the court elevations.[2] The exterior façades show, in some drawings, a much heavier rustication for the ground storey, and attempts to break up the wall surface above with a motive of a relieving arch over the windows. On one occasion rugged caryatid figures are used in front of a rusticated loggia, perhaps drawn from Serlio's loggia at Fontainebleau. The most puzzling feature is the fantastic circular court (the central of the three at the park end) which is surrounded by two superimposed caryatid loggias. No exact parallel can be found for this feature, nor can any certain use be suggested for it. Very few drawings remain which show the proposed treatment of interior decoration, but it is possible to see that some of the great vaulted halls (in themselves directly derived from Roman remains) were to be adorned by figures in niches and busts *all'antica* set on pedestals. For rather less formal rooms one can only deduce the effect from the drawings for the Queen's House, or the existing decoration, dating from the last years of Jones's life, at Wilton House.

How far the erection of the palace would have added to the

[1] For an Elizabethan building showing the same scheme, cf. Burghley House, c. 1580.

[2] In the scheme under discussion the Banqueting House would have been incorporated in the range of buildings on the east side of the great court. In other less complete schemes it appears that its destruction or its removal to another site was contemplated.

permanent prestige of Jones as an architect is hard to say. Its mere size would have been impressive, and judging from Wilton, the interiors might well have been superb. But the scale of the elevations and particularly of their orders seems a little small for their great extent, and in their lack of accent they might well have been a trifle monotonous. The general conception of so great a palace, however, reflects clearly enough the absolutist ideals of the King. That Charles himself cared greatly for the project is shown by his interest in it to the very end of his life. In 1647 and 1648, when he was held captive at Hampton Court and Carisbrooke castle, John Webb visited him with further schemes for it. These drawings, which seem to be identifiable, were probably presented again to Charles II at the Restoration. Their architecture is completely different from any certain work by Jones, and is almost certainly the independent work of Webb. It will therefore best be considered in a later chapter.[1]

The remainder of Jones's life can be reviewed very briefly. The outbreak of the Civil War swept away the foundations on which he stood, and for about eight years he seems to have done little work. He followed the King to the north (there is a receipt for a loan of £500 signed by the King at Beverley in July 1642), leaving John Webb in charge of the Office as his deputy. In 1643 Webb was ousted by Edward Carter, now a Parliament man, though he had been in charge of the hated work at St. Paul's. In 1645 Jones, apparently a sick man, was taken prisoner at the fall of Basing House. His estate was sequestrated and he was pardoned in the following year. In 1650 he made his Will 'in perfect health of mind but weake in body', and in June 1652 he died at Somerset House.

His last important work was in the south wing at Wilton House for the 4th earl of Pembroke. The old house, which was largely Tudor, was built round a quadrangle,[2] but new gardens were laid out on the south by Isaac de Caux in the 1630's, and a new and very long south front was then planned with the advice of Jones.[3]

[1] See below, p. 135.
[2] The entrance was then on the east front. It was moved to its present position on the north front by Wyatt in 1812.
[3] H. M. Colvin, 'The South Front of Wilton House', *Arch. Journ.* cxi (1954), 181.

The existing building would have been the east half only, for the design consisted of two long wings, joined by a central portico. In its fantastic length of some four hundred feet it echoes the magnificence of the Whitehall Palace projects of the same decade, but the detail is clumsy and has always been difficult to reconcile with the learning of Jones or Webb, though it has only recently become clear that it is not theirs, but by de Caux. Presumably the outbreak of the Civil War, if not shortage of money, prevented the whole project from being attempted, and the half front was provided with two towers to make it a complete design.[1] A fire occurred in 1647, and Pembroke turned to Jones for the redecoration of the interior that became necessary.[2]

He and Webb designed one of the most splendid suites of rooms in England, the great Double Cube (Pl. 8) and Single Cube Rooms. The proportions of the Double Cube Room are in fact the same as those of the Banqueting House (though the actual dimensions are considerably less), but the effect is very different, for the ceiling is coved instead of flat, and so the height is less oppressive and the space composition much more interesting.

This magnificent room, designed for the series of portraits by Van Dyck and his school which it still contains, is the only example by which we can judge the quality of Jones's interior decoration. In it (and in the Single Cube as well) he has completely abandoned the English tradition of the panelled room. Jacobean panelling, with the spacing of styles and rails conditioned by the width of the oak plank, would have made an uncomfortable setting for the large portraits. He therefore treats the room with wains-

[1] The general lines of the compromise design appear to be derived from the two-towered façade illustrated by Scamozzi (pt. i, bk. iii, cap. xv). The Venetian window with seated figures is close to that in his Villa Trissini (ibid. cap. x).

[2] There are drawings by both Jones and Webb at Wilton; others apparently not carried out are at Worcester College, Oxford, in the Gibbs collection in the Ashmolean Museum, Oxford, and at the R.I.B.A. The most interesting, inscribed by Jones: *the ceiling of the cabinett room, 1649*, shows a cupola raised on free-standing columns, a treatment adopted for the staircase of Ashburnham House, Westminster, probably built after Jones's death by an unknown architect. The new rooms at Wilton were finished when Lodewyck Huyghens saw it in 1652 (MS. *Journal of his stay in England, 1652*, Kon. Ned. Acad. van Wetensch., on loan to Roy. Lib. The Hague No. 58). I am indebted to Miss K. Fremantle for this reference.

coted walls, painted a deep cream, on which panels are outlined (but do not project) by a decorated moulding.[1] He thus obtains the maximum of plain wall surface as a foil to the richly coloured paintings. But between and above the paintings are ornaments carved in high relief and gilt; crossed palms, masks between festoons of fruit and great pendants of fruit and flowers tied by ribbons. The fine dignified doorway is treated architecturally, with flanking columns and a broken pediment above; the fireplace is also conceived architecturally, though it includes figure-sculpture. The details of the decoration are French rather than Italian, for like the designs for fireplaces in the Queen's House, they are derived from Jean Barbet's *Livre d'Architecture* and from the interiors shown in Pierre le Muet's *Traicté des cinq ordres d'Architecture*.[2] Clearly late in his life, and possibly through association with the Queen, Jones became more aware of contemporary French taste. Here, indeed, one can speak of interior architecture rather than of interior decoration, for in addition to the use of features such as the column and the pediment, the disposition of raised pendants and flat portraits articulates the wall surface like column and window in an exterior design.[3]

Wilton House, with its restrained exterior[4] and its splendid rich interior, well illustrates the dual character of Jones as an artist. In his copy of Palladio he noted, early in his life,

'Friday, ye 20 January 1614. In all inventions of capricious ornaments, one must first design the ground, and the thing plain, as it is for use, and on that vary it, adorn it . . . For as outwardly every wise man carryeth a gravity in public places, where there is nothing else looked for, yet inwardly hath his immaginacy set on fire, and sometimes licentiously flying out, as nature herself doeth oftentimes stravagently, to

---

[1] The boards of the wainscoting which are thinly cut, and must have been well seasoned, are set both vertically and horizontally. The joints are masked by the decorated beading or hidden by the pictures. I am indebted to Mr. G. H. Chettle of the Ministry of Works for this information.

[2] I have to thank Mr. John Shearman for the reference to Le Muet. Three drawings, possibly by Barbet, are among the Jones drawings in the Burlington–Devonshire collection at the R.I.B.A., and one was copied by Jones for a chimney-piece for the Queen's House, dated 1637.

[3] For the painted decoration, see below, p. 290.

[4] The general character, even if executed by de Caux, is inspired by Jones.

delight, amaze us, sometimes move us to laughter, sometimes to con-templation and horror, so in architecture, the outward ornaments ought to be solid, proportionable according to the rules, masculine and unaffected. Where within the cimeras (? chimeras) used by the ancients the varied and composed ornaments both of the house itself and the movables within it are most commendable.'

The Double Cube Room, the drawings for the decoration of the Queen's House and many of the masque designs surely show Jones with his 'immaginacy set on fire' which 'within' the house would have been 'commendable'. His exterior designs have been dis-cussed in sufficient detail for it to be clear how far they are 'solid, proportionable according to the rules, masculine, and unaffected.' Jones's peculiar position in English architecture is indeed due to the fact that he was the first Englishman with any real knowledge and understanding of 'the rules', not only as set out by Vitruvius, but also as applied by the great Italians of the sixteenth century. That his work is often derivative, and in many ways conservative, does not detract from his vital importance as an innovator, and his position as the most learned of the men about Charles I can hardly be overrated.[1]

[1] The very interesting list of Jones's library (now mainly at Worcester College, Oxford) quoted by Gotch, shows that he studied history and philosophy as well as mathematics and architecture.

ADDENDUM

While this chapter was in proof two references have come to light concerning earlier connexions of Jones with English architecture than any so far known. Mr. Mark Girouard has informed me that John Aubrey in his *Chronologia Architectoria*, f. 169 (Bodl. Lib., MS. Top. Gen. C. 25) states: 'The next step of Roman architecture was the New Exchange in the Strand, which was surveyed by Mr. Inigo Jones.' This building, named by James I 'Britain's Burse', was erected by Robert Cecil, earl of Salisbury in 1608 (A. W. Clapham and W. H. Godfrey, *Some Famous Buildings and their Story* (n.d.), 153 ff.: London County Council, *Survey of London*, xviii (1937), 94–96 and pl. 58). Though it was designed by Simon Basil it is just possible that Jones was consulted. His documented association with the same patron and his possible contri-bution to the south front and clock tower of Hatfield House in 1609–10 will be dis-cussed by Mr. Lawrence Stone in his forthcoming article, 'The Building of Hatfield House', *Arch. Journ.* cxii (1955). I am very grateful to Mr. Stone for allowing me to refer to it here.

III

DOMESTIC AND ECCLESIASTICAL ARCHITECTURE TO 1660

THE country house plays as important a part in English architecture in the seventeenth as it does in the sixteenth century, though for slightly different reasons. Elizabeth's passion for economy had meant an almost complete lack of court patronage. She was content to live in her father's palaces, but expected her subjects to provide great houses in which she could be entertained. In the seventeenth century, both in the reigns of the two first Stuarts, and again after the Restoration, the Crown embarked on palace building, and the great importance of this to architecture in the early part of the century has already been discussed. Most, though not quite all, of the greater aristocracy had built or rebuilt their houses by about 1620, though important additions or replacements, such as those at Castle Ashby or Wilton, were to be made by the middle of the century. The lesser aristocracy and the squirearchy (including merchants who bought land), who were now to play a much greater part in national affairs, built many houses, nearly always of charm, and sometimes of great interest. These men took their local responsibilities seriously, and employed their own local craftsmen to build for them. In some cases a London architect might be consulted; in very many more the patron and the estate mason and carpenter evolved the new house.

The influence of Inigo Jones on English country house design during his own lifetime was comparatively small. The majority of country houses built before the Civil War follow a line of development which originates in the Jacobean architecture of the first decade of the century. By the end of the reign of Elizabeth experiments were being made in planning, largely though not entirely linked with the decline in importance of the great hall, which with living-rooms at one end behind the high table and service rooms reached through a screen at the other, had been the core of the whole house. This disposition was used at Hatfield (1607–11) and persists as the basis of collegiate architecture throughout the century. Other houses of the same date, more modest in scale, show the break away from the domination of the medieval hall.[1] Swakeleys, Middlesex (Pl. 7 a), is a late example, reflecting the conservative taste of a City merchant.[2] It was not begun until 1638, nearly twenty years after Jones had designed the Banqueting House, but it shows no real feeling for classical architecture. There is no ordered balance between horizontals and verticals; the wall face is carried up into the area of the roof by gables, which break across the cornice; windows are still composed of many lights and their size is varied according to the size and importance of the room behind them. It is true that the mouldings have classical profiles and that considerable use is made of triangular and segmental pediments. By now, English masons were accustomed to the use of such forms (they had first appeared in the middle of the sixteenth century), and since Serlio's book had been translated (from the Dutch) by Robert Peake in 1611, Italian as well as Flemish or German models were easily available. Many other buildings of the same type can be found; Kew Palace and Broome Hall near Canterbury, both built about 1630, are good examples, and are moreover interesting for their treatment of brick. Before this date all English brickwork had been laid with fairly thick joints and in English bond, i.e. alternate rows of headers and stretchers (bricks with the 'head' or short end showing, or 'stretched' along the row, with the long side showing). Kew Palace and Broome Hall both use Flemish bond—i.e. alternate headers and stretchers in the same row, and this was to become usual in future. Joints become finer, and the use of moulded and 'rubbed' brick (i.e. bricks rubbed down to produce chamfered or moulded edges) was also imported from Flanders.[3] The finest examples of rubbed brickwork, how-

---

[1] e.g. Charlton House, Blackheath, and Nottingham House, Kensington (for the latter see P. Faulkner, *Arch. Journ.* cvii (1950), 66; see also Summerson, 52).

[2] London County Council, *Survey of London*, 13th monograph (1933). Built by Alderman Sir Edmund Wright.

[3] N. Lloyd, *History of English Brickwork* (1934), 48.

ever, such as the gate piers at Hampton Court, date from much later in the century.

Some contemporary buildings show a greater understanding of Italian models, and have therefore, without certain evidence, been attributed to Jones. Among them are the entrance front of Castle Ashby and the house at Stoke Bruerne, both in Northampton-shire. The former, built about 1630,[1] is strongly Italianate, and the central feature with the voussoirs of the entrance arch breaking up into the frieze of the order, is close to certain details of the abortive Whitehall designs of the end of the same decade. Though by a mature hand, it is less orthodox than any of Jones's remaining executed work, and it is not safe to accept it as his without reserva-tions.[2] Stoke Bruerne, built for a court official, Sir Francis Crane, the manager of the Mortlake tapestry factory, was apparently finished by 1635, when the King visited it. It no longer exists, but the engraving in *Vitruvius Britannicus*[3] shows that though the plan was perhaps the first English example of the Palladian disposition of a central block with pavilions joined to it by quadrants, the elevation was uncomfortably proportioned, with a giant applied order. It may well be that the tradition that Crane brought the design from Italy is true, and that Jones merely assisted in its execution.[4]

One important new type of house, however, appears to have been created by Jones, though no unaltered example by him remains. It may be seen in a drawing made for Lord Maltravers, dated 1638,[5] which shows a compact block, with a simple design

[1] The coat of arms over the door is that of the 1st earl of Northampton, who died in 1630.

[2] Nicholas Stone's gate of the Botanic Garden at Oxford, though less refined in handling, is not too far distant in style. York Water Gate may also be compared with it.

[3] iii, Pl. 9.

[4] J. Bridges, *History & Antiquities of Northamptonshire* (1791), i. 328, the material for which was collected before the author's death in 1724. The one pavilion that remains has a design of giant and small orders borrowed from Michelangelo's Capitoline palaces, an unlikely source for Jones. Other examples of work attributed to Jones though probably not by him are Raynham Hall, Norfolk, and the north front of Kirby Hall, Northants.

[5] Worcester College, i. 55. Lord Maltravers was Arundel's eldest son. The design was probably for a town house, since it is inscribed 'Lothbury', i.e. presumably in the

of repeated tall windows, finished at the top by a straight cornice. Above this rises a sloping roof, broken by dormers, which are set above the cornice, and so do not interfere with its horizontal emphasis. In its clear-cut lines and its repetition of the window unit, it offers the greatest possible contrast to a house like Swake-leys, built in the same year. Chevening in Kent, as shown in a draw-ing before the eighteenth-century alterations (Pl. 6 a)[1], had much the same character and was perhaps by Jones himself.[2]

By far the most important and most accomplished building of the group was Coleshill House, Berkshire (Pl. 7 b), which before its destruction by fire in 1952 was one of the most beautiful country houses in England.[3] It was begun in 1649 by Sir George Pratt and finished in 1662. Shortly after Sir George had begun his new house, his cousin Roger returned from France and Italy, where he had studied the buildings he had seen with great intelligence,[4] and forced his relative to abandon his plans, and start again on a fresh site. Jones is said to have been consulted (it will be remem-bered that though he was still working at Wilton he was now an old man, and was to die in 1652), and there is a drawing for a capital at 'Colesell' in the little Webb sketch-book at Chatsworth. Roger Pratt certainly played a major part in the execution of the house, and it is now impossible to decide on Jones's share.

Coleshill was a lower, longer house than Chevening, but the main motives were much the same. Again there were the repeated tall rectangular windows, the straight unbroken cornice, the slop-

City of London. For a discussion of the type, and its possible dependence on Rubens's *Palazzi di Genova* (1622) see G. Webb, 'The Architectural Antecedents of Sir Christo-pher Wren', *R.I.B.A. Journ.* xl (1933), 573.

[1] Chevening, according to well-informed family tradition in the eighteenth cen-tury, was built by Jones about 1630 for the thirteenth Lord Dacre. That John Webb had some hand in it is proved by two drawings for decoration 'for ye Lo. Dacres at Chevening in Kent' in the small sketch book at Chatsworth. Drawings in the book connected with other houses date from the 1650's.

[2] The type reappeared after the Restoration, e.g. Ashdown House, Berks., some-times attributed to John Webb, but more recently to William Winde (Summerson, 159), and was widely used throughout the rest of the century.

[3] H. A. Tipping, *Eng. Homes*, iv. i. 1–22, has a good description of the house and fine plates. For the accounts see *The Architecture of Sir Roger Pratt*, ed. R. T. Gunther (1928).

[4] For further discussion of Sir Roger Pratt, see below, p. 137.

ing roof with dormers. In order, however, that the long front should not be monotonous, the window and wall rhythm was very skilfully varied, the three central windows being slightly wider apart than the three at either end. The height and slope of the roof were carefully adjusted to the mass of the house below, and the chimneys instead of being scattered haphazard were used as an integral part of the design. Behind them was a flat terrace, surrounded by a balustrade with a cupola in the centre, a feature of other mid-seventeenth-century houses, from which a fine view of the countryside could be obtained.[1] The details of the stonework, simple as they may seem, were handled with supreme skill. Cornice, door, and window dressings were finely proportioned and finely cut; the rusticated quoins at the angles not only gave a change of surface texture, but bound the façade firmly at the ends. The same care was given to the egg and dart ornament which surrounded the panels on the monumental chimneys, and to the pairs of fine gateposts in the park.

The interior of the house was worthy of the exterior and in both plan (Fig. 3) and decoration represents the most advanced ideas of the time. The main door opened into a large hall (Pl. 9), which was no longer, as in the early-seventeenth-century house, a living-room. Instead, it contained a grand stone staircase, or rather two staircases, for the stairs rose on either side of the door, and ran up clinging to the wall, to a landing, which crossed the hall at first floor level.[2] Again the detail was very fine. Doorcases and balusters were boldly designed, and the carving of festoons, lions' heads, and masks which decorated the stairs must surely have been executed by a craftsman who had been trained by Jones. No local man working from a drawing could have produced work of such distinction. An outstanding feature of the decoration of the hall was the use of busts of Roman Emperors in roundels wreathed with laurel. Nothing of the kind now remains in any work by Jones,

[1] Such a roof, with a balustraded platform, appears in one of the Jones 'treatise' drawings.
[2] Derived from Baldassare Longhena's staircase in the Convent of S. Giorgio Maggiore, Venice, finished about 1643, i.e. during Pratt's visit to Italy. I am indebted to Mr. John Shearman for calling my attention to this.

though some of the few drawings for interiors among the White-hall Palace schemes show that he intended a comparable scheme for some of his great vestibules.

Behind the hall was the great parlour (almost as large as the hall itself) with the dining room above it on the first floor. The service rooms were relegated to the basement and the rooms on the two

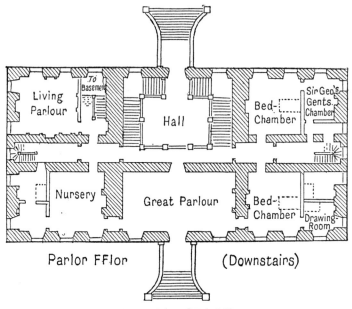

FIG. 3. *Plan of Coleshill*

main floors (some of the bedrooms were on the ground floor) enjoyed a surprising amount of privacy, for instead of opening from each other they were reached by a short corridor running off on either side of the hall.

The ceilings were admirable examples of the new type of plasterwork which certainly originated with Jones. Instead of the lightly moulded ribs and trailing vines or leaves of the Elizabethans, or the flat strap-work of Jacobean ceilings, the field is now divided, in the Italian manner, by heavily moulded flat beams. In the hall the soffit of the beams was decorated with a guilloche pattern, similar to that in Jones's Banqueting House—indeed the whole design of this ceiling is very close to the earlier example. Beneath the landing was a lovely design of wreaths of olive, oak, laurel, and bay in very low relief. The ceiling of the great dining room, later the Saloon, was richer and freer than that in the hall. It had a great oval wreath of fruit and flowers in very high relief in the centre, scrolling acanthus with boys playing in it on the soffits of the beams, and festoons and shields along the cornice. Other houses have plasterwork which is almost as fine, but none is so complete in its scheme of decoration as was Coleshill, and none has so beautiful a staircase.

In woodwork the mid-seventeenth century shows interesting developments, both in decoration and in staircases. At Hatfield (1607–11) and Aston Hall, Birmingham (1618–38), there are already fine open staircases with pierced panels of strap-work in place of balusters. A similar stair of about 1630 exists at Castle Ashby. But at Ham House, Surrey, in 1637 the strap-work has been replaced by trophies, and the ceiling is near to the Coleshill type. By the fifties, even in comparatively remote districts, scrolling acanthus forms the pierced panels, and the Jones manner influences ceiling design. At Forde Abbey, Dorset,[1] where additions were made in 1658 (this date is on the staircase) (Pl. 11 b), the plasterwork is in lower relief than at Coleshill, and the coved ceiling of the Saloon has still some reminiscences of Jacobean work in its pendants, and coarsely executed panels with Old Testament scenes. The fireplace however, with its picture frame above, is entirely in the new manner. The work at Forde Abbey, as at so many other houses, has been ascribed to Jones or Webb, but the detail suggests another hand, familiar with their work and with the new fashions in decoration. At Ham House, where the woodwork of 1637 is advanced for a house of its size, the North Drawing Room has an unusually interesting fireplace flanked by rather clumsy twisted columns wreathed with vines (Pl. 6 b). These are beyond question imitated from the Raphael cartoon of SS. John and Peter in the Temple, then being used at the Mortlake factory, where it was copied for the weavers by Francis Cleyn, the painter of the overmantel.[2]

[1] R.C.H.M. *West Dorset* (1952), 240–6, Pls. 185–92.

[2] For the Mortlake factory, see below, p. 126, and for the painted decoration, p. 289. See also the official *Guide to Ham House*, pub. by H. M. Stationery Office, 2nd ed. (1951), 39 and 42, and H. A. Tipping, *Eng. Homes*, IV. i. 111.

In a number of rather scattered houses,[1] dating from just after the turn of the century, both the interior woodwork with its lavish use of broken entablature and lugged architraves and the general design combining old and new ideas, are typical of the gradual penetration of forms originating in London, and sometimes in the circle of Inigo Jones, into the provinces. Thorpe Hall has an old-fashioned plan, with an echo of the medieval hall and screens arrangement. Its exterior, however, conforms broadly speaking to the Chevening–Coleshill type (substantial alterations were made to the windows in the nineteenth century); the handling of such details as gateposts is mature and able and one of the ceilings borrows freely from a drawing for Wilton. In spite of its plan, it has been persistently attributed to John Webb. Recently, however, it has been proved to be beyond question the work of Peter Mills, Bricklayer to the City of London[2] and like his patron, Oliver St. John, a Parliamentarian.[3] Wisbech castle, also for a Roundhead patron, may well be by the same designer, but Thorney Abbey was almost certainly designed by the local contractor.[4] All are indeed craftsman's rather than architect's houses, often relying for their details on French and Flemish engravings, and are therefore interesting as proof (if proof were needed) that the sixteenth-century tradition of the employment of a master craftsman rather than the new-fangled 'architect' was by no means dead.[5] It was indeed to persist for very much longer.

Lamport Hall, Northamptonshire, was without question de-

[1] Thorpe Hall, Northants., 1651; Thorney Abbey House, Cambs., 1660; Wisbech Castle, Cambs., 1654–8; Tyttenhanger, Herts., 1654; Wimborne St. Giles, Dorset, 1650. Woodwork with similar characteristics appears also at Cromwell House, Highgate, 1637, and Ham House, Surrey, 1637. For these houses, see G. Webb, 'The Architectural Antecedents of Sir Christopher Wren', R.I.B.A. Journ. xl (1933), 577 ff.

[2] H. M. Colvin, 'The Architect of Thorpe Hall', Country Life, cxii (1952), 1732, where the contract found in the British Museum is printed, and a summary of the career of Peter Mills is given.

[3] According to Evelyn (Diary, 30 Aug. 1654) Thorpe Hall was 'built out of the ruins of the Bishop's palace and cloister'.

[4] The contract between the earl of Bedford and John Lovin, contractor of Peterborough, is published in G. Scott Thomson, Family Background (1949), 180.

[5] For further discussion of craftsmen's buildings in London and elsewhere see Summerson, Ch. 10 'Artisan Mannerism', 97–105.

signed by Webb for Sir Justinian Isham in 1654, though it has been much altered. The special interest of the house lies, however, in the drawings and correspondence which are still preserved there.[1] They reveal clearly the relationship between patron, designer, and contractor. Webb sent his drawings (which included full-size details) to his client, and not to the contractor, John Sargerson, with accompanying notes which make it clear that a country gentleman was expected to have a good general knowledge of architecture. Sargerson then turned to the client for instructions. Other letters show that Webb was employed not only as an architect, but also as a picture expert. Isham asked him to look at pictures in London which he was thinking of buying, and in return was advised that originals were a better investment than copies. Most of the pictures mentioned are still in the house, and the over-mantel in the Music Hall, with its swan supporters (the Isham crest) to the picture frame, conforms almost exactly to Webb's drawing for it.[2]

A brief mention must be made of two other figures who con-tributed to the history of English architecture. Sir Henry Wotton, Ambassador in Venice, later became Provost of Eton. In 1624 he published 'The Elements of Architecture', an essay without illus-strations which defines the qualities of good building as 'Com-moditie, Firmness and Delight'. This still has links with Bacon's 'Essay on Building' which starts, 'Houses are built to live in, not to look at, therefore let use be preferred before uniformity, except where both may be had'. Wotton, however, as he enlarges his theme, makes it abundantly clear that he had not only read but understood the Italian theoretical treatises from Alberti onwards. Indeed, much of his book, since he draws on many of the same

[1] Some, but not all, of the papers were published by J. A. Gotch, *R.I.B.A. Journ.* xxviii (1921), 19. See also Sir Gyles Isham, 'Historical and Literary Associations of Lamport', *Northamptonshire Past and Present*, i (1948).

[2] The only other houses with which Webb was certainly concerned were Gunners-bury House, near Brentford (1661) (now destroyed), a Palladian villa with a loggia in the same position as that of the Queen's House (*Vitruvius Britannicus*, i, Pls. 17, 18); some work at Belvoir (1654) for which there are schemes among the Burlington-Devonshire drawings at the R.I.B.A., and possibly the portico of The Vyne, near Basingstoke (1654). For his continuation of his master's work as a stage designer, see below, p. 294.

sources, reads like a commentary on the work of Inigo Jones. Like Jones, he was fascinated by Palladio's theory of musical proportions. He speaks of the two principal consonances in music that 'most ravish the ear', the fifth and the octave, which arise from the proportion between two and three or two and four. These, if properly used in architecture, and especially in the design of windows and doors, 'reduce Symmetrie to Symphonie and the harmonie of Sounde to a kinde of harmonie in Sight'. Since a knowledge of music was widespread in seventeenth-century England, it can be supposed that these parallels were more easily understood than they are today, and that Wotton's book helped many a gentleman towards an understanding of the new architecture.

The part played by Sir Balthazar Gerbier (1591–1667) is less clear.[1] He was born in Middelburg of a French Huguenot family, and by 1616 was in England in the service of Buckingham.[2] While Keeper of the duke's collections at York House he altered the apartments and advised on their decoration, and may have designed York Water Gate, which has always been regarded as by Inigo Jones.[3] On Buckingham's death he entered the King's service and was knighted. Rubens stayed at his house during the winter of 1629–30, and at the same time Gerbier was arranging with Le Sueur for the equestrian statue of Charles I for Lord Treasurer Weston.[4] He was evidently regarded as a general agent on all artistic matters. His treacherous nature, which had already revealed itself during his diplomatic career, became more evident under the Commonwealth when to ingratiate himself with the new rulers he produced one of his many pamphlets, 'The None-such Charles', in which he referred to 'great sums squandered away on braveries

[1] For a short life, see H. Ross Williamson, *Four Stuart Portraits* (1949), 26–60. His rather shady political career cannot be discussed here, though it was through it (in France in 1625) that he first came into contact with Rubens.

[2] See above, p. 2.

[3] Summerson, 92. Nicholas Stone's great-nephew, Charles Stoakes, states, however, that it was designed and built by Stone (*Walpole Soc.* vii (1919), 137). Though it does not resemble the architecture of Stone's monuments of the 1620's, the statement cannot be lightly ignored, and Gerbier himself never claims it.

[4] See below, p. 118.

and vanities; on old rotten pictures and broken-nosed marbles'. It is perhaps not surprising that Charles II did not at the Restoration grant him the Surveyorship, the reversion of which he said had been promised him.[1] He was, however, concerned with architecture in his last years,[2] for in 1661 he designed for Lord Craven the house at Hampstead Marshall[3] which was to be presented to Elizabeth of Bohemia. Though she died soon after it was begun, the work continued and in 1663 Gerbier himself died there before it was finished, and is buried in the village church. So far as can be judged from engravings the design was strongly dependent on Rubens's *Palazzi di Genova*,[4] while the drawing for a gateway is far more florid in character than York Water Gate.[5]

It was while he was working at Hampstead Marshall that Gerbier published his two architectural pamphlets, *A Brief Discourse concerning the three chief principles of Magnificent Building, viz. solidarity, convenience and ornament* (1662), and *Counsel and Advise to all Builders* (1663). The former is a very small work (in which Wotton's basic qualities are taken over and rearranged); the latter, though almost half of it is taken up with fulsome dedicatory epistles, is more interesting, because it is practical. It lays down the duties of the surveyor, the clerk of the works, and the workmen, and provides much advice about materials and prices. Gerbier has his importance as a go-between in the collector's world; it seems that he was also something of an architect.

Ecclesiastical architecture in the first half of the seventeenth century was, except for the few buildings of Jones himself, far less touched by Italianism than domestic building. The unswerving

---

[1] He makes this claim in his pamphlet *A brief Discourse concerning the three chief principles of Magnificent Building* (1662). John Webb made the same claim, probably with more justification.

[2] Three drawings in the Burlington–Devonshire coll. at the R.I.B.A. for triumphal arches for the coronation of Charles II are attributed to him.

[3] The house was destroyed by fire in 1718; only gateposts remain. After Gerbier's death the work was carried on by Captain Winde, see below, p. 219.

[4] For other buildings showing this influence, particularly Furnival's Inn, see A. E. Richardson, '17th century buildings in search of an architect', *R.I.B.A. Journ.* lx (1933), 625, in which he follows up suggestions made by G. Webb, ibid. 577.

[5] Bodleian, *MS. Gough Drawings* a2, ff. 24–25, and see Bodleian Picture Books, no. 7, *Architectural Drawings* (1952), no. 2 (illus.).

support given by Charles I to the Anglican Church owed much to the stimulus of Archbishop Laud. This bustling, active man, whose personality commands respect but never affection, was the dominant figure in the English Church from the time of his advancement from the see of Bath and Wells to that of London in 1628, to his fall in 1641. Inevitably he left his mark on English church architecture.[1] Since, however, his whole policy was directed towards conservatism, towards an uncompromising restatement of those disciplines and doctrines which episcopacy had preserved, it is not surprising that he fostered no novelty in architecture. Except when compelled to do so (i.e. at St. Paul's), he did not employ Inigo Jones, and it is fairly clear that he had no sympathy with the artistic sensibilities of the King. His ceaseless efforts were directed to the enforcement of order and decency of worship and to the arrest of neglect of fabric or fittings. He had no quarrel with older styles of building or craftsmanship on aesthetic grounds, and indeed his whole outlook and policy encouraged a survival of what was established rather than an introduction of what was new.

As President of St. John's College (1611–21) and Chancellor (1630–41) he had long and close connexions with the University of Oxford. The hybrid style of his major collegiate building, the Canterbury quadrangle of St. John's College (Pl. 10 b),[2] erected between 1631 and 1636, at a time when he was certainly in touch with Inigo Jones over the renovation of St. Paul's, suggests something of his architectural taste. Both ends of the quadrangle have an open loggia, which is admittedly Italian in feeling, but the façades above are extremely medieval, with their two-light windows, their string courses broken by grotesque beasts, and their battlemented parapets. The centrepieces continue the Oxford

[1] This section owes much to Sir Alfred Clapham's posthumous paper 'The Survival of Gothic in 17th century England', *Arch. Journ.* cvi, Supplement (1952), 44.

[2] R.C.H.M. *City of Oxford* (1939), 103, 106, and Pls. 181, 184; H. R. Trevor-Roper, *Archbishop Laud* (1940), 284. It has constantly been suggested that Jones played some part in the design (see H. R. Trevor-Roper, loc. cit.) but it bears no relation to any of his known buildings or drawings. Nicholas Stone (see below, pp. 106 f.) is a possibility since the carvers Anthony Gore and Harry Acres are known elsewhere as his assistants. John Jackson, who later worked at Brasenose College, was put in charge in 1632, after the work had begun (*V.C.H., Oxfordshire*, iii (1954), 262).

tradition of coupled superimposed columns,[1] though the relative purity of the orders and the lavish use of cartouches as decoration suggests a good knowledge of pattern books. The iconography of the sculpture is characteristic of Laud's love of the ordered formulae of the Schoolmen, for the spandrils of the loggia are filled by busts of the Theological and Cardinal Virtues on the west and the Liberal Arts on the east,[2] while half-length figures of angels appear above the central arch. Such a programme was common in ecclesiastical art of the middle ages, but it is probably unique in secular art of the seventeenth century. The only concessions to contemporary taste are the bronze figures of Charles I and Henrietta Maria by the King's sculptor Le Sueur, in niches above the entrances.

There was considerable building activity at Oxford, where much of the damage done in the Reformation was still imperfectly repaired. In Magdalen College chapel a new black and white marble floor was laid, and the stalls partially remade. Classical pediments and swags of fruit were curiously intermixed with Gothic tracery and finials. In 1631, the President, Accepted Frewen, afterwards as archbishop of York a noted builder at his palace of Bishopthorpe, 'changed the Communion-table into an altar, which was the first set up in the University after the Reformation': a crucifix was placed upon it, which afterwards was to figure in charges against Archbishop Laud, and painted hangings by Richard Greenbury with scenes of the life of Christ were hung behind the altar, where the broken carving of the reredos had been plastered over. A corona of lights was suspended from the roof: a fine brass eagle lectern, which still survives, was introduced: and one of the Christmas brothers provided eight statues. Laud noted in his diary in 1635 that the work at Magdalen 'was completely finished'.

The compromise at Magdalen between up-to-date Renaissance

---

[1] Cf. the gatehouses of the Fellows' quadrangle at Merton (1608–10) and of Wadham (1610–13), though these have four instead of two storeys. The motive is ultimately derived from France, e.g. the centrepiece from Anet by Philibert de l'Orme, now in the courtyard of the École des Beaux-Arts, Paris, though a form of it had appeared in England about 1550 at Somerset House.

[2] To both the groups, which normally include seven figures, one has been added, i.e. Piety to the Virtues and Learning to the Arts. (R.C.H.M., loc. cit. 107.)

detail and a general Gothic setting is characteristic of building in Oxford as a whole. Lincoln College Chapel[1] (Pl. 10 *a*) (consecrated in 1631), the gift of Bishop Williams, Laud's life-long opponent, is predominantly Gothic with its traceried windows and its wooden canted roof divided into panels by small ribs, though the fittings are far less medieval. Perhaps the most splendid part of the decoration of the chapel is the glass, the east window being filled with a series of Old and New Testament types and anti-types (a medieval form of iconography but with a contemporary allusion, for the figures of Adam and of Christ are given the features and characteristic beard of Charles I) and the side windows with figures of prophets and apostles, almost certainly the work of Bernard van Linge.

There was indeed much fine glass painting associated with this movement, though nearly all of it is the work of foreigners. Bernard van Linge, a native of Emden, made the east window in Wadham Chapel, and the windows in Lincoln's Inn chapel, London (1623–4).[2] He was also associated with the cathedral at Oxford, which was refitted under Dean Brian Duppa between 1629 and 1638.[3] The figure of Bishop King in the south aisle of the presbytery is probably his work, while the splendid pictorial window in the north aisle of the nave, showing Jonah under the gourd, with the city of Nineveh in the background, is signed by his brother or son Abraham.[4] The impression made by all this activity was recorded in 1636 by George Garrard, chaplain to the earl of Northumberland, who wrote:

'the Churches or Chapels of all the colleges are much beautified, extraordinary cost bestowed on them; scarce any cathedral churches, nor Windsor nor Canterbury, nay nor Paul's Choir exceeds them, most

---

[1] R.C.H.M., loc. cit. 64, 67, and Pls. 121–6.

[2] C. Woodforde, *English Stained and Painted Glass* (1954), 42.

[3] R.C.H.M., loc. cit. 37, 42, and Pl. 98. The fittings were removed in 1856, and the whole building restored by Sir Gilbert Scott in 1876. Some of the seventeenth-century glass has been replaced (often in fragments) during the present century. It is possible that the pulpit (ibid., Pl. 42) may be part of Duppa's fittings, though it seems rather archaic in style.

[4] C. Woodforde, loc. cit., Pl. 50. The latter also carried out windows at the Queen's College (1635), Balliol (1637), and at University College in 1641.

of them new-glazed; richer glass for figures and painting I have not seen, which they had most from beyond the seas.'[1]

Despite some controversy as to their seemliness most of these windows survived the Commonwealth and are still extant.

Other Gothic buildings during Laud's chancellorship include the Convocation House with its fan-vault (1634–7)[2] and panelling related in style to that of Lincoln College chapel, the gate-house of University College, also with a fan-vault (1635–7),[3] and most spectacular of all, the staircase of Christ Church (c. 1640)[4] designed by 'Smith, an artificer of London'. This excited the interest of John Evelyn,[5] and is indeed very remarkable, for (to quote Sir Alfred Clapham) 'its proportions and details are alike admirable and might well be mistaken for medieval work'. The style persisted long after Laud's death. The chapel of Brasenose College[6] was begun in 1666. It has a plaster ceiling imitating a fan-vault, designed by John Jackson, but the exterior shows an attempt to combine Gothic and classical motives, for traceried windows are set between Corinthian pilasters, and the large window above the ante-chapel door is rectangular (though still traceried) with a broken pediment above it. Fan-vaults were to continue in Oxford right down to the end of the century, that under Tom Tower dating from 1682–3,[7] while the Radcliffe Gateway of University College[8] is as late as 1716–19. Up to that time Gothic was still a living tradition in Oxford: Hawksmoor's Gothic at All Souls[9] is different in character, for it is a more self-conscious attempt to design in an alien style.

In Cambridge one building had an immediate connexion with the Laudian movement, namely, the chapel of Peterhouse[10] built between 1628 and 1632, during the Mastership of Dr. Matthew Wren, though the exterior facings at the east and west were done

---

[1] *Cal. S.P. Dom.* (1636–7), 113; cited more fully in Preface, xxiii.

[2] R.C.H.M., loc. cit. 9 and Pl. 56.   [3] Ibid. 116 and Pl. 5.

[4] Ibid. 29, 33, and Pl. 84.   [5] *Diary*, 12 July 1654.

[6] R.C.H.M., loc. cit. 23, 27, and Pls. 77, 78. The ceiling masks a hammer-beam roof, brought from St. Mary's College.

[7] Ibid. 29, 30, and Pls. 5, 198.   [8] Ibid. 114, 118, and Pl. 5.

[9] See below, p. 350.

[10] R. Willis and J. W. Clark, *Cambridge* (1896), i. 40.

at the expense of Dr. John Cosin, who succeeded as Master in 1634.[1] The exterior, which has been a good deal mutilated, originally combined a Jacobean frieze (probably of strap-work) with perpendicular tracery in the window above, but judging from Loggan's print the two styles were not so happily combined as in contemporary Oxford buildings. The inside was adorned with statues of the Evangelists and St. Peter, as well as with figures of angels and cherubim, the destruction of them being recorded with glee by William Dowsing, the iconoclast.[2] Cosin's love of ritual had even before this been challenged by puritanical elements within the Church. In 1630, when he was Prebendary of Durham, a long indictment against him had been drawn up by Canon Peter Smart.[3] In this he was accused, in the most violent language, of having introduced in Durham Cathedral 'popish baits and allurements of glorious pictures and Babalonish vesturs', of setting up many images about the choir, 'some of the angells, in long scarlett gownes, greene petticotes, golden winges and gilded heads'. The altar was not of wood, as was prescribed, but 'a double table very sumptuous, of stone . . . upon 6 stone pillars, curiously polished, and fastened to the ground, having upon every black pillar 3 cherubim-faces, as white as snow'. The font had not only been moved four times in seven years but had been renewed: 'they have taken out . . . the old holy Font, which was comely like to that in St. Paul's at London and in other cathedrals, and instead thereof they erected a Mausoleum, tow'ring up to the roph stone, which cost about 140^l, a fantastical and caprecious piece of work. . . .' Cosin's font cover (Pl. 11 a) has miraculously survived, and is one of the most remarkable pieces of early-seventeenth-century woodwork in the country. It, and Smart's naïve vindictiveness, give some faint picture of the visual results of Laud's church policy.

Cosin's taste for the medieval was to last till the end of his life.

[1] Cosin left money in his will for the finishing of the north and south sides of the chapel.

[2] W. Dowsing, *Diary*, quoted Willis and Clark, 46. Cosin's altar is described in W. Prynne, *Canterbury's Doom* (1646), 73, 74.

[3] 'Articles to be exhibited by His Majesties Commissioners against Dr. John Cosin etc.', Bodleian, *Rawlinson MSS.*, A. 441, f. 28, quoted at length in *Correspondence of John Cosin, D.D.*, Surtees Soc. lii (1869), i. 161.

At the Restoration he became bishop of Durham, and in 1668 rebuilt the chapel at the episcopal palace at Bishop Auckland with octagonal buttresses and traceried windows. Elsewhere the Gothic style was used for a number of churches, though not all of them (on grounds of date) can be ascribed to the immediate influence of Laud. In London, the church of St. Catherine Kree[1] was reconstructed in 1628 in the hybrid manner with classical arcades, ribbed plaster vaults, and a rose window at its east end. Lincoln's Inn Chapel[2] (1620–23) has perpendicular windows and a vaulted undercroft; St. Luke's, Charlton,[3] largely rebuilt under the will of Sir Adam Newton (who had once been tutor to Prince Henry), has a fine Gothic tower of brick.[4] One of the most important and least altered churches of the time is St. John's, Leeds, consecrated by Laud's friend Archbishop Neile in 1634. It is a completely Gothic structure, and still retains its screens and pews which are markedly Jacobean in style. At Leighton Bromswold, Huntingdonshire, the nave and tower are linked with the Anglican community established by Nicholas Ferrar at Little Gidding, for they were built under the supervision of John Ferrar.[5] A gallant example of loyalty to the Church during the Commonwealth period can be found at Staunton Harold, Leicestershire. Here in 1653 a perpendicular church with an east window in the fourteenth-century style was erected. A clumsy classical frontispiece was set at the west door, with an inscription above it:

'When all things sacred throughout the nation were either demolished or prophaned Sir Robert Shirley Bart. founded this church whose singular praise it is, to have done the best things in the worst time.'[6]

---

[1] See Summerson, 107, for possible designer.

[2] Formerly wrongly ascribed to Inigo Jones. See ibid. 87, and *Black Books of Lincoln's Inn* (ed. 1898), ii. 199, 209.

[3] R.C.H.M. *East London* (1930), 17, and Pls. 52, 173.

[4] Another tower of the same period, built of flint, remains at Hillingdon, Middlesex (R.C.H.M. *Middlesex* (1937), 75, and Pl. 2). The church of Great Stanmore was built by Nicholas Stone for Sir John Wolstenholme, and consecrated by Laud in 1632. Only the tower now remains. A chapel at Groombridge, Kent, with perpendicular windows and a Renaissance porch, was built by John Parker in 1623 'in gratitude for the safe return of Charles, Prince of Wales from Spain'.

[5] M. Whiffen, *Stuart and Georgian Churches outside London* (1947), 11, and Pls. 2, 3.

[6] Ibid. 13.

IV

VAN DYCK IN ENGLAND

THE name of Anthony van Dyck is indissolubly associated with the age of Charles I. With his characteristic sensitiveness to the environment in which he was working, Van Dyck evolved in England a style entirely distinct from the resonant Mediterranean splendour of his Italian portraits or the strong simplicity of his second Flemish period, and particularly suited to the ephemeral civilization of the English court. It is through this style, with its subtle romanticism, that we see the dramatis personae of the years between the death of Buckingham and the summoning of the Short Parliament. Van Dyck's portraits of Charles, his family and courtiers are, with their withdrawn grandeur, frigid magnificence, and brittle elegance, a penetrating commentary on the Caroline court.

Van Dyck's English period is the most important single factor in the development of portrait painting in this country, infinitely more profound and far reaching in effect than Holbein's second visit to England nearly a hundred years earlier. Nevertheless, before Van Dyck came to this country early in 1632, a competent and modern school of portrait painting had grown up in London and had shown a marked advance on the more formal style of later Elizabethan and early Jacobean portraiture. This new style was simple, realistic and worldly. Its inspiration came directly from Holland (and particularly from The Hague and Delft) and its principal exponents were Daniel Mytens and Cornelius Johnson.

Mytens was actually trained in The Hague, probably in the studio of Miereveld; Johnson, born in London of Netherlandish stock, was affected more by English, or Anglo-Netherlandish, painting 'in large' and in miniature. Though both artists were closely bound to the leading school of Dutch portrait painters and though their feeling for texture and surface remain fundamentally Dutch, they each made personal and distinctive contributions to this common stock. Mytens was a more ambitious painter than Miereveld and developed a distinguished style in the full-length, a form rarely essayed by Miereveld; Johnson infused into fundamentally Dutch forms of composition a restraint and delicacy of feeling which are essentially English. Both men, moreover, were far more competent than their immediate predecessors in England. Their works show a quality of draughtsmanship and paint which surpasses Gheeraerts's impersonal technique and Van Somer's coarse and lifeless brush, though both Gheeraerts and Van Somer (who was related to Mytens by marriage) were in their later work affected by this new Anglo-Dutch style.

Daniel Mytens was born about 1590, almost certainly in The Hague; in 1610 he entered the Guild of St. Luke in that city and two years later he was married there. He came to England in or before 1618 and certainly had English connexions some years earlier. In the summer of 1618 he was working for Arundel. He was also hoping for the patronage of Prince Charles[1] and, perhaps at Arundel's instigation, the Prince seems to have taken Mytens under his protection. Charles realized, no doubt, that he was the best painter in London. On 19 July 1624 Mytens was bound to the royal service and granted an annual pension of fifty pounds[2] and on 4 June 1625, soon after Charles's accession, he was appointed 'one of our Picture-Drawers of our Chamber in ordinary' and granted an additional twenty pounds per annum.

From now onwards he was fully employed in the manufacture of royal portraits, many of them for dispatch overseas, and in the humbler tasks to which royal painters were so often put: painting copies of some of the King's Italian masterpieces or working up posthumous portraits of Prince Henry or of such remoter figures as James IV, Margaret Tudor, and Mary Queen of Scots.[3] On 10 August 1626 he was granted a pass to travel for six months to the Low Countries; and on 11 May 1631 his wife, her three children,

[1] W. H. Carpenter, *Pictorial Notices* . . . (1844), 176–7.
[2] W. N. Sainsbury, *Original Unpublished Papers* . . . (1859), 356–7.
[3] See C. Stopes, 'Daniel Mytens in England', *Burl. Mag.* xvii (1910), 160–3, and 'Gleanings from the Records of the Reigns of James I and Charles I', ibid. xxii (1913), 276–82.

and two maids were granted a pass to the Low Countries with their 'trunks of apparel'. The payments to him continue until 1634, but it is possible that he was contemplating a return to The Hague before Van Dyck's arrival. He was in The Hague early in February 1635,[1] and in 1637 he was looking out for works of art for Arundel in Amsterdam and Dordrecht.[2]

One portrait of an English sitter by Mytens is known from as early as 1610: the *3rd Earl of Southampton* (*s.* 1610) at Althorp. Painted on panel, it follows the conventional form of martial portrait which was evolved in Miereveld's studio; but it is hesitant and thin in handling and lacks the robustness of Miereveld or Ravesteyn.[3] Mytens's advance upon the most elaborate school of Jacobean portraiture can be seen particularly clearly at Redlynch, in a series of splendidly decorative full-length portraits of members of the earl of Suffolk's circle. The portraits (*c.* 1617) of the Earl of Banbury and of Elizabeth, Countess of Banbury (Pl. 12) can be ascribed with some certainty to Mytens and are fundamentally different from the rest. In place of the brilliant colour, elaborate pattern, polished ivorine surface, and the emphasis on a spectacular piece of decoration rather than the sitter's personality, these two portraits show the painter aiming at something simpler, warmer, and more personal. The earl stands with assurance against a plain dark background; the expression of his face is shrewd and humorous and the painting of the head is much looser and more spontaneous than in the other portraits. The more timid portrait of his wife shows the same tendencies and also Mytens's favourite combination of greens, greys, and silvers. The countess's left hand rests on a chair which shows a real desire to present an illusion of depth within the canvas, in contrast to the entirely two-dimensional treatment of both figures and accessories in the other portraits. The handkerchief in her right hand amounts to Mytens's signature; it is painted in a broken and impressionist manner, very far from the entirely formal treatment of the same motive in, for

---

[1] A. Bredius and E. W. Moes, 'De Schildersfamilie Mytens', pt. ii, *Oud-Holland*, xxv (1907), 94.

[2] M. F. S. Hervey, *The Life of Thomas Howard Earl of Arundel* (1921), 404–5.

[3] R. W. Goulding, 'Wriothesley Portraits', *Walpole Soc.* viii (1920), Pls. xxii, xxiii.

example *Diana, Countess of Oxford* or *Anne, Countess of Stamford* (Pl. 13), in the same series.

The full-lengths at Arundel of the Earl of Arundel and his Countess, which were painted before August 1618, show a marked advance in the grasp of structure in the figures themselves, although the relation of the figures to the floor and to the backgrounds, with their careful pictures of the growing riches of Arundel House, is not yet fully understood. The full-length portraits from the early 1620's show more assurance; *Prince Charles* (c. 1623; Parham)[1] or the young *3rd Marquess of Hamilton* (s. 1624) in the Tate Gallery are limited in range, but have an unaffected distinction quite new in English painting. The *Ernst von Mansfeld* and *Christian, Duke of Brunswick* (both 1624 and at Windsor) are ambitious reinterpretations of the formulas of Miereveld and Ravesteyn.

His two visits to the Low Countries in 1626 and 1630 had a marked effect on Mytens's style. In the full-lengths of his later years in England the figures are set against more ambitious backgrounds and have a grander swagger. Yet at the time of the first of those two visits Van Dyck had not embarked on his second Flemish period and it is not easy to define the source from which Mytens derived this new elegance. He produced in the years immediately before Van Dyck's arrival in England some of the most powerful full-length English portraits of the century. The colour is remarkably fine and the handling sensitive and assured. The magnificent full-length *Duke of Buckingham* (s. 1626) at Euston with its striking combination of silver, cool browns, and crimsons; the *1st Lord Baltimore* (s. 1627) at Wentworth Woodhouse[2] in deep glowing black against a setting of soft grey and cold crimsons; and the *2nd Earl of Warwick* (Pl. 14: s. 1632), where Mytens's new elegance is almost pushed to mannerism, are among the finest examples of this fine phase. Mytens's masterpiece is the full-length of the 3rd Marquess of Hamilton (s. 1629),[3] the most mature portrait of its kind painted in England before the advent of

---

[1] F. M. Kelly, 'Mytens and his Portraits of Charles I', *Burl. Mag.* xxxvii (1920), 84–9.

[2] Waterhouse, Pl. 30.

[3] Ibid., Pl. 31. The background is unfinished.

Van Dyck. The figure is set with absolute assurance against a simplified repertory of some of the more elaborate trappings of court portraiture. The canvas is startling in colour: the marquess is clad entirely in pale grey, richly embroidered with silver, against a harmony of varying blues and greys which are used as a foil to the head, the one warm area in the canvas. With portraits such as this Mytens can claim a high place among his contemporaries on the Continent. Perhaps his years in London inspired a strain of courtliness in his grave sense of character and innate feeling for the solid structure of a figure. He proved himself to be more ambitious than the painters with whom he spent his early years and he can stand comparison with any but the very greatest Dutch portrait painters in the first half of the century. He surpassed the majority of contemporary court painters, Karel van Mander III, the Elles, the Beaubruns, and Bunel; and his finest portraits could hang safely beside the more formal portraits of Philippe de Champaigne.

Cornelius Johnson[1] is a less robust spirit. His parents had fled from Antwerp during the religious persecutions and their son was born in London in 1593. He was brought up within that group of closely connected families of French or Flemish origin who 'came for relygyon': the Olivers, the Gheeraerts's, the Colts, and the De Critzes, whose lives revolved round the Dutch Reformed Church in Austin Friars.[2] It is not known where the young Johnson received his training as a painter, but his early work is based on a combination of the Anglo-Netherlandish style with a strain of a purer English quality which is normally, and rather loosely, associated with the younger Gheeraerts and is reflected in the later works of Hilliard.

Although his early years are still obscure, Johnson is the only painter 'in large' working in England in the seventeenth century who signed and dated a considerable number of his pieces. We can trace his development year by year, up to and beyond his departure

---

[1] Johnson or Jonson were the only two variants of his name which he used himself; he seems to have been anxious that he should be regarded as an English armigerous gentleman. A Cornelius Johnson received a grant of denization on 13 November 1637 (*Cal. S.P. Dom.* (1637), 537).

[2] Mrs. Lane Poole, 'Marcus Gheeraerts, Father and Son, Painters', *Walpole Soc.* iii (1914); see also Waterhouse, 26–29.

for Holland in October 1643.[1] The earliest date on a portrait signed by Johnson is 1617.[2] A pair of portraits dated 1619 at Lamport Hall[3] are valuable documents for his early style. They are already set, though not very happily, within the painted oval which Johnson used so constantly and which was a popular form in Anglo-Dutch portrait painting and engraving; it also has an obvious connexion with the oval framework within which almost all miniaturists of this period, including Johnson himself, put their sitters, and with the oval or circular surrounds on sculptured monumental portraits. The panels at Lamport arc effective studies of personality; that of the woman (Pl. 16 b) is particularly sensitive. The colour is very unambitious and, though the heads and the details of the costume are carefully drawn, there is a lack of balance between the fully modelled head of the woman and the spiky, formless drawing of her ruff and cap. The portraits have none of the depth which even the earliest of Mytens's portraits reveal. They are essentially the work of a young painter who has infused something of the native English temper into the Netherlandish elements in his style.[4]

Johnson's development during the 1620's, from the meticulous and enamelled manner of his early work into something freer and more sensitive, was partly hastened by his increasing use of canvas instead of panel. There is a gain in breadth and atmosphere in the broad and vigorous *Unknown Man* (s. 1627) in the National Portrait Gallery (1344), the sensitive *Sir John Cooper* (s. 1628) at St. Giles's House or *George Sandys* (s. 1628) at Ombersley Court. Johnson usually restricted himself to heads and shoulders with an occasional hand introduced. The three-quarter-length portraits

[1] A. J. Finberg's 'Chronological List', *Walpole Soc.* x (1922), is well illustrated and is still useful, but many portraits could now be added to it (e.g. K. E. Maison, 'Portraits by Cornelius Jonson in Scotland', *Burl. Mag.* lxxiv (1939), 86–91); see also Sir L. Cust, 'Cornelius Janssen van Ceulen', *Burl. Mag.* xvi (1910), 280–1.

[2] Waterhouse, 38.

[3] The female portrait is signed and there are the remains of a signature on the pendant.

[4] Perhaps the closest parallel with Johnson in Dutch painting is provided by the work of Salomon Mesdach; e.g. in four portraits in the Rijksmuseum, dated between 1619 and 1625, in which the handling of the flesh is almost indistinguishable from Johnson in the early 1620's.

which he painted before he became aware of Van Dyck (particularly *Sir Kenelm Digby* (c. 1628) at Althorp and the splendid *Sir
Thomas Coventry* (s. 1631)[1] in the Clarendon collection) are solid
and convincing; but such full-lengths as the *Unknown Woman* (s.
1630)[2] at Boughton, or *Frances, Marchioness of Hertford* (s. 1633) at
Petworth are cumbersome pieces with nothing of the movement
of Mytens's last portraits.

Johnson had, however, a delicate sense of colour, an increasingly
light and feathery touch, and a fineness in painting such details as
the lace collars of his sitters which is never allowed to upset the
balance of a portrait. His quiet and fragile charm is seen at its best
in such portraits as *Dorothy Godfrey* (Pl. 16 a: s. 1636), where the
painted oval is used to great effect, and the *2nd Earl of Northampton*
(s. 1633) at Castle Ashby, which has an unusual richness in the
golden-brown doublet with silver lace and the scarlet ribbon of the
Bath. Although he was sworn in as 'his Majesty's servant in ye
quality of Picture Drawer' on 5 December 1632,[3] he never seems
to have attempted to build up so illustrious a clientele as that served
by Mytens or Van Dyck. And he may deeply have resented the
Laudian persecution of his church. At some period in the 1630's
he lived and worked at Bridge in Kent, probably staying with the
Dutch merchant, Sir Arnold Braems, and he painted the local
families: Campions, Oxendens, Peytons, Masters, Hammonds, and
Dormers. Van Dyck is permanently associated in our minds with
the court of Charles I and Henrietta Maria, but Johnson gives us
a no less vivid picture of the quiet country families of the 1630's.

There are subtle changes in Johnson's style during the last ten
or twelve years of his life in this country. Van Dyck was responsible
for a slight increase in elegance in his smaller portraits and for a
rather more liquid technique. In his larger compositions Johnson
was wholly under the new influence. In his later full-lengths, such
as the *Earl of Elgin* (1638) and his *Countess* at Redlynch, or *Mary
Coventry* (s. 1641) at Longleat, he uses an assortment of accessories
which are taken straight from Van Dyck. But Johnson's technique
and treatment of detail retain their individual delicacy and his

---

[1] Finberg, loc. cit. 52 (Pl. xxxvi).   [2] Ibid. 43 (Pl. xxviii).
[3] C. Stopes, *Burl. Mag.* xxii (1913), 280.

quiet, rather startled sitters do not take very readily to this new manner. The delightful group of the *Capel Family* (Pl. 17: *c.* 1640) demonstrates the extent of Van Dyck's influence on Johnson. The central group is based almost verbatim on Van Dyck's first large royal piece, the group of the King and Queen with their two eldest children,[1] which was painted in 1632, and Johnson was content to string out the surplus children along the canvas in a display or Van Dyckian motives. In the portraits produced by Johnson in Holland, after his departure from this country, his technique gains in fineness and lightness and, as if to show that he had been in contact with one of the most celebrated portrait painters of the age, his portraits are often on a bigger scale. His group of the *Dukes of Hamilton and Lauderdale* (of which there are versions, both *s.* 1649, at Ham House and in the Hamilton collection) bears witness to the popularity, which he shared with Hanneman, among Englishmen travelling in the Low Countries or attached to the exiled Stuart court.

Nothing is known of the personnel of Johnson's studio in England; in January 1625 a certain John Evoms was turned over to Johnson as an apprentice by the Painter-Stainers' Company.[2] For some years Johnson was assisted by his nephew Theodore Russell, who is loosely associated with small copies on panel of heads from Van Dyck's portraits, though there is no certain evidence that they are by his hand.[3] The only extant signed portrait by Russell[4] shows him to have worked in his uncle's manner, to have little of his quality, and to have taken on a certain elegance and affectation from Adriaen Hanneman.

The possibility that a native school might flower under the influence of the sound craftsmanship of Mytens and Johnson was eclipsed by the arrival of Van Dyck and by the dazzling sophistication

---

[1] G. Glück, *Van Dyck, Klassiker der Kunst* (Stuttgart, 1931), 371; this can now be supplemented by, e.g. C. H. Collins Baker, *Catalogue of the Petworth Collection* (1920), and catalogue R.A., *Flemish Art* (1953–4).

[2] *Booke of Orders and Constitutions* of the Company, i. f. 11; the name is obscure.

[3] The series of such panels (copies after Van Dyck and Lely) in the Royal Collection was said *temp.* Queen Anne to be by Leemput.

[4] An *Unknown Man* (*s.* 1644), wrongly identified as Henry Cromwell, Christie's, 30 March 1951 (24).

of his English style. The rising reputation of the young Flemish painter had brought him to the attention of Jacobean connoisseurs and in the winter of 1620-1 he had actually spent a few months here in King James's service. He was probably under Arundel's protection and it seems to have been Arundel who secured for him, on 28 February 1621, leave to travel for eight months.[1] He did not return for eleven years, but he was constantly in touch with English travellers and collectors: he painted Nicholas Lanier when he was abroad; a *Madonna and Child* by him was given to the King by Weston as a New Year's gift; and in 1629 he painted for Charles I the sumptuous *Rinaldo and Armida*, which is now in Baltimore. The circumstances of his return to London early in 1632 (probably in March or April) are not precisely clear, but there is no doubt of the warmth with which he was received or of the King's delight in having secured the services of such a painter. He was knighted on 5 July 1632, set up in a house at Blackfriars by the King, awarded an annual pension (which was constantly in arrears) of two hundred pounds and given the gold chain and medal which he displays so proudly in his *Self-portrait with a Sunflower*.

Van Dyck himself does not seem to have regarded his establishment in London as more permanent than his earlier sojourns in Antwerp or Italy. In 1634 he returned to Flanders for a visit of some months and the last months of his life, after Rubens's death had left him as the acknowledged head of the Flemish school, were distracted by visits to Paris and Antwerp to try and claim the position and secure the commissions that he thought were his due. Prematurely aged and worn out, he died in London on 9 December 1641, and was buried near the tomb of John of Gaunt in St. Paul's Cathedral.

That was appropriately the crowning moment in a career spent in the most illustrious circles. Van Dyck was an entirely new phenomenon in English society: a painter of international repute, wide knowledge, and considerable personal distinction. His influential acquaintances, his manners, and his deep knowledge of Italy and of the Renaissance ensured him a place in the Whitehall group to which even a painter of Mytens's ability could not hope

[1] W. Hookham Carpenter, *Pictorial Notices* . . . (1844), 10.

to aspire. It is hard to imagine such a *grand seigneur* as Newcastle writing to any other painter in the elaborately flattering style that he adopted towards Van Dyck.[1] Van Dyck stood quite outside the craftsmen's tradition in which painters in England still worked,[2] and was, in other words, the last kind of person over whom the Painter-Stainers' Company could hope to exercise any control.

One of the most significant elements in Van Dyck's English portraits is the renewed dependence that they show on the work of Titian. A profound study of Titian and the other great Venetians, of which the Chatsworth Sketch-Book is the most eloquent testimony, was the major formative influence on the evolution of Van Dyck's style. Direct borrowings from Titian are rare in his work before 1632; but in England he saw one of the finest collections of Titians that has ever been made, he was in the service of one of Titian's most passionate admirers,[3] and such borrowings can be found again and again. The portraits of Strafford, who was 'so often with Sir Anthony Vandike', provide clear examples of the effect on Van Dyck of the Titians he saw in London. The full-length at Welbeck is taken from the principal figure in Titian's *Speech of the Marchese del Vasto* and the superb full-length at Went-

---

[1] R. W. Goulding, *Catalogue of the Pictures . . . at Welbeck Abbey . . .* (1936), 485.

[2] Even Mytens and Johnson seem to have been quite ready to use each other's patterns; see O. Millar, 'An Attribution to Cornelius Johnson reinstated', *Burl. Mag.* xc (1948), 322.

One small episode shows how far Van Dyck stood from this milieu. A type of portrait which was popular at court was that in which an elaborate perspective scene was painted as a setting for the figure. The most obvious example of this is the full-length of *Charles I* by Mytens in Turin (s. 1627; reproduced on p. 112 of the 1899 catalogue of the Pinacoteca at Turin), where the architectural background is independently signed and dated (1626) by Steenwyck. Charles I owned five little cartoons of perspectives by Steenwyck which were to serve as patterns for these backgrounds and a large canvas on which Steenwyck had painted one of these elaborate backgrounds against which Van Dyck was to paint a double portrait of the King and Queen: 'but Sir Anthony Vandyck had no mind thereunto.'

[3] Charles seems to have realized fully Van Dyck's knowledge of Titian; when it was found that the *Vitellius* in the set of Titian's *Emperors* was irreparably damaged, Van Dyck was ordered to paint a *Vitellius* to make up the set. He also repaired the *Galba*.

In an obituary notice of Van Dyck Dr. Hamey described Van Dyck as *autem Titiani imprimis aemulus* (MS. in Royal Coll. of Physicians, kindly communicated to me by Mr. David Piper).

worth Woodhouse echoes *Charles V with a Dog*, which the King had brought back from Spain. The design of the powerful *Strafford with his Secretary*, also at Wentworth Woodhouse, is probably taken from a Titianesque or North Italian variant on the theme of a statesman with his secretary rather than from Sebastiano del Piombo's *Cardinal Carondelet and his Secretary* (Thyssen collection) which was then in Arundel's collection as a Raphael.

Van Dyck's most vital contribution to the development of English portrait painting was to introduce into this country a completely new range of idioms and conventions. His own style was strongly eclectic and he presented his contemporaries and his successors down to the twentieth century with an incomparable pattern-book, which has been the major influence in the history of the English portrait. A fascinating game can be played by following the variations on a theme, introduced by Van Dyck, by successive generations of painters. The equestrian *Charles I* in the National Gallery derives (as Van Dyck's contemporaries already realized) from Titian's *Charles V at the Battle of Mühlberg* (and also probably from a conventional type of English engraving of equestrian martial portraits) and directly inspired Gainsborough's *General Honeywood*; the full-length *Strafford* at Wentworth Woodhouse is the first example of a favourite English motive; the design of a statesman with his secretary was very popular in the eighteenth century and Van Dyck's use of it for the earl of Strafford inspired Reynolds's portrait of Rockingham (who owned the prototype) with Edmund Burke. Even the celebrated *Blue Boy* is taken from one of the figures in Van Dyck's *Villiers Boys* at Windsor, which was particularly admired in the eighteenth century.

To patrons who had been accustomed to seeing themselves on Mytens's canvases Van Dyck's portraits must have been a revelation. Even in Mytens's grandest pieces the relation of the figure to the picture-plane hardly ever varies and the head is set at the same angle to this plane as the shoulders and torso; and the backgrounds even in his later portraits are rigid and conventional. In Van Dyck's courtly baroque style the figures have an elegant poise, made up of a subtle play of twists and thrusts, and are set against backgrounds of which they are fully aware. The portrait of the 2nd Earl of Warwick (Pl. 15) with its ease and grace, glance away from the spectator, picturesque pile of armour and rocky shore is already nearer to Reynolds's *Captain Keppel* of 1753 than to Mytens's portrait of Warwick at Greenwich, with its solid frontal stance and formal seascape framed by a balustrade and a wall. Nor was Mytens capable of the *bravura* of the fine full-length *1st Earl of Denbigh* (National Gallery) or of its allusion to the earl's travels in the East. In the portraits of his royal patron he transformed the inarticulate little King of Mytens's portraits into the cavalier with his air of languid romance and with a prescient aura of martyrdom which has surrounded the popular image of King Charles ever since. We forget the rather comic figure in Garter robes in Mytens's portrait of 1633 in front of the graceful full-length in robes of state at Windsor (*s.* 1636),[1] or the pedestrian portrait of the type used by Mytens and Johnson before the idealised visions of the King dismounted in the hunting-field (Louvre)[2] or riding out of a wood with bared head in a Venetian landscape (National Gallery).

His more grandiose compositions were completely new to Caroline England. The formal 'greate peece of oʳ royall selfe, Consort and children' (1632) at Buckingham Palace and the superb double portraits of the gilded youths of the Caroline age[3] lead up to the sumptuous family group of the Herberts at Wilton (*c.* 1634),[4] the crowning glory of the Double Cube Room (Pl. 8). With its echoes of Rubens and the great Venetians in the rhythmical mounting line of figures, it is a brilliant piece of decoration. The sweep and drama of its prototypes have been transformed into a two-dimensional surface-pattern. This is even more marked in the *modello* (Belvoir Castle) for one of the four scenes from the history

[1] Waterhouse, Pls. 32, 33.

[2] There is an echo of the artist's early days in the motive of the equerry (in this case the duke of Hamilton) and the horse pawing the ground. It occurs in Rubens's sketch of *Pax Romana* in the Mauritshuis and in the *Consecration* scene in the *Decius Mus* cycle. The motive perhaps derives from Titian's *Adoration of the Magi* (Escorial).

[3] e.g. the *Earls of Bristol and Bedford* (Althorp) and *Lords John and Bernard Stuart* (Broadlands).

[4] It had great effect on the English group-portrait. It inspired Closterman's and Hudson's groups of the Marlborough families at Blenheim, it was studied by Gainsborough and was a formative influence in the development of Reynolds.

and ceremonial of the Order of the Garter with which it was proposed to decorate (possibly with tapestries based on Van Dyck's designs) a room in Whitehall.[1] All movement into the scene has been flattened into a flowing, linear pattern. Within the group of knights who parade in front of an architectural back-cloth, which is taken straight from Veronese, there is the same subtle interplay of elegant movements and gestures that make up the canvas at Wilton; but the movement is entirely within this narrow stage and along this one plane. Something of Van Dyck's thwarted ability as a designer of great baroque compositions can be gauged from the equestrian portrait of the King with M. St. Antoine (Pl. 1: 1633); its effect at the end of the Gallery at St. James's must have been most spectacular, as if Charles were riding out through the arch to join the Roman Emperors of Titian and Giulio Romano.

For all their apparent ease there is a withdrawn quality about Van Dyck's English portraits. It is very clear in the contemptuous glance of the magnificent *10th Earl of Northumberland* (Pl. 26), but it is present in portraits on a smaller scale, such as two of his most delicate portraits of the Queen at Windsor, the three-quarter-length and the profile (Pl. 18 *b*). The sense of false security which was nurtured by the Caroline poets lurks beneath the mannered ease of the double portrait at Windsor of Thomas Killigrew and Thomas Carew (*s.* 1638).[2]

With a sitter whom he knew well Van Dyck could achieve the burning intensity and deep sympathy of the wonderful *Strafford* (Pl. 18 *a*); by contrast a composition like *Dorothy, Viscountess Andover and Lady Elizabeth Thimbleby* at Althorp, with its playful allusion to the matrimonial achievements of the two ladies and its harmony of silvers and golds, has a refinement which trembles on the brink of decadence and which no pupil or imitator could hope to achieve. Many of the portraits which poured from his studio in the last years of his career in England, even some of those for which Van Dyck was himself responsible, reveal the slackness and lassitude of a tiring painter. His finest portraits, however, continue

[1] O. Millar, 'Charles I, Honthorst and Van Dyck', *Burl. Mag.* xcvi (1954), 36–42.
[2] Carew's poem, 'In Answer of an Elegiacal Letter upon the Death of the King of Sweden', exactly reproduces the mood of this canvas.

to show a brilliance of technique, a keen grasp of character, and a spontaneity combined with infinite remoteness.

The handling of Van Dyck's portraits varies considerably and within the Van Dyck Room at Windsor the change of surface can be seen clearly. The *Three Heads of Charles I*[1] is painted in a thin, fluent manner through which the canvas shows clearly. In *Killigrew and Carew*, which is slightly later, the head of Killigrew is opaque and carefully worked, in contrast to that of Carew (if it really be he), which is painted with a dashing *bravura* in a glowing, Venetian style. In the enchanting *Three Children of Charles I* (s. 1635) the golden costume of the little Prince of Wales is rich and juicy, but the dogs are painted with a fluency and precision which were not to be surpassed by Gainsborough. And the portraits of their mother are painted in a cold silver key which Velazquez was to achieve some twenty years later.

The subject-pictures which Van Dyck painted in England catch no less surely the Caroline mood. Between the portraits and the subject-pictures lie the portraits of sitters in some allegorical context. The elaborate and highly misleading *Venetia, Lady Digby*[2] as Prudence (Windsor) or such portraits of 'Noble Persons . . . in pastoral habit' as the nostalgic Arcadian *Lord Wharton* (Washington) must have been peculiarly pleasing to patrons who spent so much of their lives in an atmosphere of masque.

Even more significant for the Caroline court is Bellori's account of the religious pictures which Van Dyck painted: a *Crucifixion*, a *Deposition, St. John the Baptist in the Desert, The Magdalen listening to the Harmony of Angels*, and *Judith and Holofernes*, all for Sir Kenelm Digby; a *Crucifixion*, with the angels catching the Blood of Christ in golden vessels, for, most strangely, the earl of Northumberland; and for the Queen *The Rest on the Flight* with dancing putti.[3] This may be the picture in Leningrad; but all the

---

[1] The pattern was presumably taken directly from Lotto's *Three Heads of a Jeweller* (Vienna) which was in Charles I's collection as a Titian. See above, p. 6.

[2] It may be a posthumous portrait and is not of autograph quality; the theme was most carefully worked out for Van Dyck by Sir Kenelm Digby (see Glück, 563).

[3] Bellori's account of Van Dyck's years in England (*Le Vite* . . . (Rome, 1672), 259–64) is of great value; it was largely based on information given to him by Sir Kenelm Digby when the latter was Henrietta Maria's resident in Rome in 1645.

other canvases have disappeared. So have the mythologies which were painted for the King: a *Dance of the Muses on Parnassus, Apollo and Marsyas*, some *Bacchanals* and a *Venus and Adonis*.

The only extant subject-picture painted by Van Dyck for the English court is the enchanting *Cupid and Psyche* (Pl. 23 *b*).[1] With its cool colour, exquisite draughtsmanship and delicate forms, it is nearer to Boucher than to Rubens. There is an echo of Titian and a premonition of Gainsborough and this supremely poetic and idyllic wood-note was not heard in England again until Gainsborough painted his *Diana and Actaeon*.

Although his influence on painting in England was immediate and profound, little is known about the organization of Van Dyck's studio in London from which this influence spread.[2] A large studio was established to cope with a fashionable practice and to enable the master to live in the state to which he aspired. The borderline between some of Van Dyck's portraits, especially those of his later years, and the canvases carried out under his surveillance by his pupils is extremely vague. The 1640's and, to a lesser extent, the 1650's produced a very large number of Van Dyckian portraits which attempt, with varying incompetence, to exploit his patterns or to imitate different aspects of his technique.

The two styles which have been discussed so far are the loadstones within whose field almost all the portraiture of the period was drawn. There were minor painters who worked in the Anglo-Dutch manner; others who began within this tradition and later

---

[1] See A. P. Oppé, 'Sir Anthony van Dyck in England', *Burl. Mag.* lxxix (1941), 186–90. For Van Dyck's landscape drawings, see below, p. 261.

[2] Among his assistants was probably Remigius or Remy van Leemput, a Frenchman who was established in London by 1635, flourished as a copyist until after the Restoration, and specialized in Van Dyck. The Dutchman, Jan van Belcamp, was employed in the royal collection as 'an under copyr to another Dutchman that did formly keepe the King's pictures' (Richard Symonds, B.M. Egerton MS. 1636, f. 100*v*.) He was sent to France by the King to paint portraits of Louis XIII and Anne of Austria (*Cal. S.P. Dom.* (1635–6), 159) and also painted for Charles the fantastic full-lengths *Edward III, The Black Prince* and *Edward IV* which are still in the royal collection. The Stone family is very confused: Symon Stone was certainly a copyist and was associated with the Northumberland collection both before and after 1660; Henry Stone, who is so often loosely associated with copies after Van Dyck, was also an independent portrait painter.

succumbed to the new influence; and their later contemporaries who are only known as straightforward imitators of Van Dyck. The works of Mytens and Johnson are only the most distinguished examples of a style of portraiture in which many less competent, less familiar, or more migratory painters worked. Abraham Blyenberch, perhaps a native of Antwerp, is recorded in England in the latter half of the second decade of the century. He painted the full-length *Prince Charles* and the *Ben Jonson* (both in the National Portrait Gallery); his *3rd Earl of Pembroke* (s. 1617) at Powis Castle is painted in the manner of Pourbus and is livelier in character and handling than Mytens at that date. The painter confusingly named John Eycke was apparently English and his full-lengths at Milton of the 1st Lord Fitzwilliam (s. 1630) and his wife are coarser and flatter than Mytens or Johnson, but follow them closely in design.[1] A group of portraits at Woburn of the children of the 4th earl of Bedford, painted in 1627 by the obscure Hungarian Johann Priwitzer, includes an ambitious full-length *Lord William Russell with a Dwarf*,[2] which shows a certain dependence on Mytens, and portraits of the remaining children on a smaller scale in the familiar painted ovals; they are fresh and very much alive, but are technically less accomplished than Johnson at that date. Finally (though these are only a few instances of an extremely prevalent style) there is the impressive *Sir John Backhouse* (National Portrait Gallery) proudly displaying a little landscape of London with the view of the new river-head, which bears the monogram *V.M.* and the date 1637 and is close in arrangement and handling to Johnson's three-quarter-length portraits of a slightly earlier period.

The career of the ubiquitous George Geldorp would probably show the successive influences at work in England and their effect on a portrait painter of very limited ability, but much of it is

[1] J. W. Goodison, 'John Eycke—A Seventeenth-Century English Portrait Painter', *Burl. Mag.* lxxiii (1938), 125.

[2] Collins Baker, i. 62; if Priwitzer is to be identified with 'pintor hungaro Juan Privisier', who is recorded in Valladolid in 1647 (see J. Martí y Monśo, *Estudios histartíst, &c.* (1898/1901), 6), he can probably be identified with 'John Previsour' who was recorded among foreign artists in London in March 1627, and again in July 1635, when he was stated to have been born in Italy (*Booke of Orders . . . of the Painter-Stainers' Company*, i, f. 28; *Cal. S.P. Dom.* (1635), 283–4).

obscure. He was a native of Cologne; in 1610 he was a member of the Guild at Antwerp; and he seems to have come to England in 1623.[1] The pair of full-lengths at Hatfield of the 2nd Earl of Salisbury and his Countess, for which (with other portraits of the family) he was paid in December 1626,[2] are his most important extant works. The male portrait is a gawky rendering of one of Mytens's stock patterns, set in a landscape with a hunting scene outside Hatfield House; the pallid portrait of the countess is scarcely distinguishable in arrangement from the full-lengths of Johnson in his pre-Van Dyckian phase. Geldorp was later an intermediary with Rubens and a friend of Van Dyck, and he seems to have specialized in copies after Van Dyck.[3]

The career of Adriaen Hanneman is a more interesting object-lesson in the early stages of the Van Dyck tradition. Born, and presumably trained, in The Hague, he came to London in 1626. He may have worked for a time under Mytens and he was on friendly terms with the Johnson and Russell families. His earliest works, such as the *Peter Oliver* (Hampton Court) or the *Unknown Man* (Pl. 19 *b*: *s.* 1632?), combine a texture which is akin to that of Mytens or Johnson with a poetry that owes as much to Titian as to Van Dyck. Hanneman was back in his native town in 1637 and thus was the first to introduce the Van Dyck manner into Holland. Thereafter his style became exaggeratedly Van Dyckian and it is significant that his bloodless extension of Van Dyck's style was especially popular in the upper ranks of Dutch society; he was employed mainly by the Dutch nobility, by the house of Orange, and by Charles II and his exiled courtiers.[4]

The most slavish dependence on Van Dyck by an English painter is to be seen in the work of Robert Walker. He was perhaps 'Walker A picture maker' who was mentioned at the court of the Painter-Stainers' Company on 28 February 1641. On 4 March 1650 Mr. Robert Walker was made free of the Company with

[1] *Cal. S.P. Dom.* (1635), 592.

[2] Collins Baker, ii. 112; i. 66–68.

[3] Symonds (B.M. Egerton MS. 1636, f. 93*v*.) saw 'Abundance of Coppyes of Ritrattos of Vandyke' in Geldorp's house in June 1653.

[4] M. Toynbee, 'Adriaen Hanneman and the English Court in Exile', *Burl. Mag.* xcii (1950), 73–80.

Edmond Marmion and Francis Barlow and on 18 October 1652 he was chosen to be one of the two Stewards of the Company for the following year.[1] Symonds records his copies of some of the Titians from Charles I's collection,[2] but Walker was the favourite portrait painter of the parliamentarian party. His association with Cromwell seems to have lasted at least until 1655,[3] but the obvious superiority of Lely's and Cooper's images of the Lord Protector may well have been a blow to Walker's prestige.

In Walker's portraits of the parliamentarians their heads are attached to bodies lifted straight from Van Dyck. The incongruity of *Henry Ireton* (National Portrait Gallery) set in the pattern used by Van Dyck in one of his noblest portraits of King Charles, and the highly inappropriate reminiscences of Lord Goring and the earl of Strafford in the *Cromwell* (National Portrait Gallery) and *Colonel Hutchinson* (Milton), detract to a large extent from the austere sincerity of some of Walker's heads. He was actually taxed for this plagiarism and 'was asked why he did [not] make some of his own Postures, says he if I co^d get better I wo^d not do Vandikes, He [Walker] wo^d not bend his mind to make any Postures of his own.'[4] His dry and impersonal use of paint and his lack of any feeling for colour were perhaps well suited to his sitters, and the portraits of Cromwell and of Colonel Hutchinson and his wife[5] are convincing studies of the Puritan temperament (the portrait of the colonel is so bad as to verge on caricature), but are equally typical of Walker's limp lay-figures against pedestrian backgrounds. No works are known from later than 1656 and, although there is a tradition that he died just before the Restoration, he seems to have survived to comment on Lely's style after 1660.[6] Perhaps his most personal achievements are his *Self-portrait*[7] and the portrait of John Evelyn, leaning on a skull with

[1] *Booke of Orders . . .*, i. f. 155; ii. ff. 8, 21.

[2] B.M. Egerton MS. 1636, ff. 98*v*., 101.

[3] A receipt, dated 25 June 1655 and signed by Walker for twenty-four pounds 'for the draught of his highnesse picture', is at Hinchingbrooke.

[4] B.M. Add. MSS. 22950, anon., f. 41*v*.   [5] Waterhouse, Pl. 49.

[6] See below, p. 174.

[7] Several versions exist (e.g. in the Ashmolean Museum); that at Belvoir is rep. in the cat., *Exhibition of Paintings*, Worcester (1951), Pl. v.

an air of conscientious melancholy (Pl. 20 a). This is of great iconographical interest and painted in a pleasant range of cool browns, greys, and blacks. It hardly justified the praise with which Evelyn recorded his sitting on 1 July 1648 to 'Mr. *Walker* that excellent Painter', but it is largely independent of Van Dyck and is more purely English in feeling than much that we have discussed hitherto.

In a period so dominated by foreign influences we can catch little more than occasional flickers of an English spirit. Certain native painters, though they were affected by foreign influences, retained the essential qualities of English painting at this date: a fresh approach to character; an ingenuously direct attempt to apply the results of that approach to canvas or panel; restricted technical means and a very mediocre sense of composition. They naturally worked for a less illustrious clientele than their foreign rivals, and much of their work was on the more or less impersonal level of the journeyman. Richard Greenbury, for example, was a straighforward portrait painter and worked in the royal collection as a glass painter, copyist, frame-maker, and picture-restorer. In the 1630's at Magdalen College, Oxford, in connexion with Frewen's redecorations, he painted a portrait of the Founder and designed and painted the glass in the ante-chapel. And he painted a picture of the Massacre of Amboyna and the Persian Ambassador's portrait for the East India Company, restored the Barber-Surgeons' forty-one portraits of philosophers and in 1636 took out a patent for painting hangings.[1]

Other native painters, such as Gilbert Jackson and Edward Bower, were probably based in London, but had local connexions in the provinces. Jackson's signed and dated works range between 1622 and 1640. His most ambitious portrait is the full-length *John Williams* at St. John's College, Cambridge (s. 1625), which is much closer in design, feeling and quality, as well as in its limitations, to

---

[1] Mrs. Lane Poole, *Catalogue of Portraits . . .*, ii. xv–xxiii; and T. S. R. Boase, 'An English Copy of a Carracci Altarpiece', *Journ. of the Warburg and Courtauld Institutes*, xv (1952), 253–4, for Greenbury's copy of Annibale Carracci's *Canaanite Woman before Christ*. The latter provides an interesting sidelight on the slightness of the demand for religious paintings in England at this date. See also above, pp. 55–57.

Gheeraerts's *Sir Henry Savile* in the Bodleian than to Mytens's more robust portraits.[1] His small extant *œuvre* includes a number of portraits at Oxford and a group of portraits of the Thornhaugh, Hickman, and Bacon families, formerly at Thonock. *Samuel Radcliffe* and *Robert Burton* (*s.* 1635) at Brasenose and the *John Tolson* at Oriel (1637) are adequate examples[2] of his style: completely frontal and flat, dry in quality, with no ability to convey the third dimension and far more provincial than Johnson's portraits, whose main convention Jackson sometimes exploits. The set from Thonock is more ambitious: *Bridget, Lady Hickman* (*s.* 1634)[3] shows a slight influence of Van Dyck, and the little full-length of *Master William Hickman* (Pl. 21 *a*: *s.* 1634) has a naïve provincial gaiety.[4]

Edward Bower or Bowers perhaps came from the south-west.[5] Complaints were lodged by the Painter-Stainers against an 'Edward Bowers' on 27 March 1629, and again on 31 July 1634, and in 1644 and 1646 he was in trouble for non-payment of fines and for contempt of the Company's orders, perhaps at the period when he was working in the west country. Thereafter 'the famous painter at Temple Barr' was a loyal member of the Company and on 24 October 1661 was sworn in as Master for the ensuing year.[6] The earliest extant piece by Bower is a full-length *Unknown Man* at Dunster (*s.* 1638). It is the work of a very provincial painter in an exotic style which he cannot assimilate. The *2nd Lord Fairfax*[7] (*s.*) at Acomb House has been associated with the sitter's letter of 30 June 1646 to his son from Bath in which he refers to the 'ability of the workman who was servant to Anthony Vandike, [which] made me and some others patient under his hand a few hours'.

[1] Mrs. Lane Poole, 'Gilbert Jackson, Portrait Painter', *Burl. Mag.* xx (1911), 38–43; see *Catalogue of Portraits . . .*, ii (1925), xxiv–xxvi.

[2] *Loan Collection of Portraits*, Oxford (1905), Pl. iii.   [3] Collins Baker, i. 52.

[4] C. H. Collins Baker, 'More Notes on Gilbert Jackson', *Burl. Mag.* xxi (1912), 169–71.

[5] E. K. Waterhouse, 'Edward Bower, Painter of King Charles I at his Trial', *Burl. Mag.* xci (1949), 18–21.   [6] *Booke of Orders . . .*, i. ff. 43, 96, 187, 207; ii. ff. 42, 69.

[7] Collins Baker, i. 115–16; the signature is in an unsatisfactory state. A portrait at Beningbrough Hall of John, 1st Viscount Scudamore is confusingly signed and dated *Bowar. fecit. / 1642*; it is practically indistinguishable from Johnson's latest English portraits.

There is little of Van Dyck in Bower's portraits of King Charles at his trial (Pl. 21 *b*). Three versions are signed as painted at Temple Bar and dated 1648 (O.S.). It was a very popular piece and many inferior unsigned versions are in existence, but the variations in the signed originals indicate that Bower made drawings in Westminster Hall on that tragic occasion; the portraits are historical documents of great value and their *gaucherie* enhances their pathos.

There was a great deal of local work done in the provinces, generally of a humble nature, in the period between the payments by the earl of Rutland in 1592 to John Matthews of Nottingham for 'newe paintinge of diverse pictures and hanginge of the same in the long gallerye' and for 'inricheinge' the family tombs,[1] and the Vicar of Wakefield's 'limner, who travelled the country, and took likenesses for fifteen shillings a head'. Among this limner's prototypes may perhaps be included men like Edward Bellin,[2] Thomas Leigh, who was responsible for a small group of portraits of which the best is probably the light and timid little *Robert Davies* (Major P. R. Davies-Cooke);[3] or the shadowy figures of the monogrammists *I.W.* (or *I.W.F.*), who seems to have worked in Leicestershire in 1648, and *J.H.*, who apparently enjoyed a practice in the north-west between 1647 and 1662 and specialized in portraits of children.[4] The detailed record, by John Souch of Chester, of the bereavement of Sir Thomas Aston in 1635; Des Granges's slightly later scene of the *accouchement* in the Saltonstall family;[5] or a remarkable group (*c.* 1643) at Deene Park of the Salusbury family,

---

[1] H.M.C., *Rutland MSS.* iv (1905), 404.

[2] E. K. Waterhouse, 'Portraits from Welsh Houses', *Burl. Mag.* xc (1948), 204; Bellin's canvas is said to be signed and dated 1636, but the inscription gives the date 1630 which fits the costume better.

[3] Ibid. 207; a Thomas Leigh was paid by the Middle Temple in 1656 for the posthumous full-length of Robert Ashley, and 'Mr. Leigh' was accused by the Painter-Stainers on 30 July 1652, with Lely and Flesshiers, of neglecting the Company's ordinances.

[4] A. C. Sewter, 'The Master I.W.F.', *Burl. Mag.* lxxvii (1940), 20–24 and M. Toynbee, 'A Mystery Portrait-Painter , *Country Life*, cviii (1950), 840–2, and 'New Light on a Mystery Portrait-Painter', ibid. cxv (1954), 1503.

[5] The Souch is now in the City Art Gallery, Manchester, and the Des Granges belongs to Sir Kenneth Clark; see C. H. Collins Baker, *Connoisseur*, lxxx (1928), 131–3, and Waterhouse, 40, Pls. 36, 37.

are primitive attempts on a large scale to record events in the lives of ordinary English families.

We have come a long way from Whitehall, but Greenbury, Bower, Jackson and their like stood for the native tradition in painting; there is evidence in their support of the Painter-Stainers' Company, an essentially medieval and reactionary body, that they felt it their duty to join in protests against the success of their foreign rivals who were practising in the metropolis. The foreigners had constituted a threat to the Painters and Stainers when they had been amalgamated as far back as 1502, but the danger was greatly increased by the flow of refugees from the Low Countries later in the century and by Charles I's encouragement of continental artists. On 28 February 1627 it was agreed by the Company that they would support measures against 'Strangers and Englishmen' who neglected to obey the Company's ordinances. On 7 March 1627 Greenbury, and others who were to act in alliance with the Company, presented a list of those whom they wished to prosecute: Gentileschi and Mytens head the list, which includes Geldorp, Belcamp, Vroom, Steenwyck, De Neve, and Van der Doort. It was a quixotic gesture of defiance against the Whitehall group, which was doomed from the start and to some extent frustrated by the Company's inactivity. The Company's last serious effort to assert its claims came in December 1640. Meetings had been held with Greenbury and 'other pfesso^{rs} of that p^t of o^r Art wch they call to the Life, not free as yet of o^r Society' to discuss measures against the hated foreign painters. It was decided that six established English painters (among them Jackson, Greenbury, and Eycke) should be sworn in as freemen of the Company and should discuss with the Company measures for their common good. Again the allies seem to have achieved nothing, and the Civil War came unexpectedly to their aid, but the whole episode is of deep significance and it stirred the conscience of many English painters at the time. In the early months of 1641 a number of native painters offered their allegiance to the Company; among them were 'Mr. Ager', the obscure Peter Trovell and 'John Gybbes Picture maker dewelling At Canterburye', Sheppard, Walker, and Robert Streeter.[1]

[1] See the *Booke of Orders* . . ., i, ff. 28, 61, 91, 110, 153–6 for the main references

In their ordinances of 1582 the Company had excepted from those from whom they expected obedience 'gentlemen exercising the art for recreation or private pleasure'.[1] 'Cunning in drawing, and the knowledge in the verie art of painting' had been rated among the complete gentleman's accomplishments by writers of conduct books since the time of Castiglione, and the purpose of writers such as Peacham and Norgate was partly to help their readers to indulge in 'a Recreation soe inoffensive and ingenious.'[2] In his *Compleat Gentleman*, first published in 1622, Peacham, a keen amateur draughtsman himself, describes painting as one of the 'generous Practices of youth' and recommends amateur draughtsmanship as a suitable employment for leisure hours and as a useful talent for travellers. His *Gentleman's Exercise* of 1612 contains a fuller initiation into technical methods.

Of all the noble amateurs of England, none surpassed in Peacham's eyes 'Master *Nathaniel Bacon* of *Broome* in Suffolk ... not inferiour in my judgment to our skilfullest Masters.'[3] Sir Nathaniel Bacon, who died in 1627, is the most interesting English amateur of the century; his smaller *Self-portraits*, such as those in the National Portrait Gallery (Pl. 19 *a*) and at Raveningham,[4] seem to have been painted late in his life. They are so full of character, so clear and individual in colour, and painted with such assurance that they do much to justify Peacham's claim for his friend. They are set in painted ovals, but in technique Bacon is quite distinct from Mytens and Johnson. The arresting full-length *Self-portrait*[5] at

to this: after the war the Company seems to have accepted defeat, though Lely was a thorn in their flesh in the fifties. The Company's records are now deposited at the Guildhall Library; I am grateful to the Painter-Stainers' Company for allowing me to consult this very rich source. W. A. D. Englefield, *The History of the Painter-Stainers Company* (1923) barely indicates the wealth of material it contains.

The histories of Guilds in other countries in Europe would provide parallel episodes, e.g. the attempts by the Painters' Guild at Paris to thwart the foreign painters and the artists working under special Crown protection.

[1] W. A. D. Englefield, op. cit. 68.

[2] Edward Norgate, *Miniatura or the Art of Limning*, ed. M. Hardie (1919), 3 (dedication to Arundel).

[3] *Compleat Gentleman*, ed. G. S. Gordon (1906), 126.

[4] *17th Century Art in Europe* (R.A. 1938), illustrated souvenir, Pl. 87.

[5] Waterhouse, Pl. 28. See below, p. 261, n. 1.

Gorhambury might serve as an illustration to several chapters of the *Compleat Gentleman*.

Attempts to define too clearly the trends in portrait painting, or to classify too rigidly achievements of individual artists in England from the accession of Charles I to the Restoration, are bound to be misleading. The picture which the period as a whole presents at the moment is still too hazy. Our ignorance is under-lined by the numerous portraits, or groups of portraits, by un-identified painters and conversely by the disturbing number of names of painters whom we know to have been at work, but to whom no single piece can be attributed with certainty.[1] A typical problem is presented by the portraits of the Tradescant family, which are with one exception (Pl. 20 *b*) in the Ashmolean Museum, and their tentative association with the De Critz family.[2] The family had fled from Antwerp to England to avoid the religious persecutions of the sixteenth century and John De Critz I had held the office of Sergeant-Painter for many years before his death in 1642.[3] The only portrait painter in the family of whom we know anything was his son Emanuel, but, although he seems to have enjoyed some reputation during the Commonwealth, his full-length *Sir John Maynard* (s. 1657) at Helmingham Hall is a feeble Van Dyckian piece, far below the level of the Tradescant portraits.

The portraits themselves are some of the most unusual painted in England in the seventeenth century. The two canvases in which Hester Tradescant appears (one is dated 1645) are thinly painted in a harmony of browns and greys with areas of cool, clean colour. The flesh is crisply drawn and details like the ungainly placing of the daughter's head in the other portrait are reminiscent of Cuyp.

---

[1] In a volume of this kind little is to be gained by listing these names, but three sources show the extent of our ignorance: the records of the Painter-Stainers' Com-pany, which are crowded with names; the returns of aliens living in London, which include many 'limners' or 'picture-makers' (see *Cal. S.P. Dom.* (1635), 283–4, 456–7, 592–3); and Symonds's notebooks. See also Waterhouse, 39–40.

[2] For this problem, see especially Mrs. Lane Poole, 'An Outline of the History of the De Critz Family of Painters', *Walpole Soc.* ii (1913), and *Catalogue of Portraits . . .*, i (1912), xx–xxvi, and nos. 414, 426–8, 439, 440, 443.

[3] See below, pp. 286–7.

The air of melancholy in both portraits is also felt in the portrait of her husband gazing up at the face of his extraordinary bottle-nosed friend, though the eye is distracted by the remarkable display of still-life painting, and is more intense in the searching portrait of Tradescant with his hand on a spade against a brooding sky with pallid orange clouds. A tentative attribution to Dobson was once suggested; and the warm, fused quality of the paint, the soft, warm reds and greys in the flesh and the light, unimpasted texture are faintly suggestive of Soest. There is also in the Ashmolean a portrait, perhaps by the same hand and with the air of a self-portrait, which is inscribed *Sr Oliver de Crats A famous Painter*. Oliver was another son of John II, but is entirely obscure.

The Civil War shattered the civilization which Van Dyck recorded and affected the careers of many painters in England. It was the cause of Johnson's return to Holland and perhaps of the journeys to Italy of such younger native painters as Michael Wright and William Sheppard,[1] but it also provided the setting for the most accomplished native portrait painter before the advent of Hogarth: the short-lived William Dobson.[2]

He was baptized at St. Andrew's, Holborn, on 24 February 1611;[3] his father, William Dobson, was a gentleman and was said to have been at some period Master of the Alienation Office. He was a protégé of Francis Bacon and was employed in the additions and redecorations at Gorhambury and in the building of Verulam House which occupied Bacon's later years. Aubrey, who provides some of the very few contemporary references to Dobson,[4] describes the father as 'a St. Albans man'; the work which was carried out under his father's surveillance may have impressed young Dobson at a very early age and Aubrey's account of the ornate and ingenious scheme of decoration is curiously suggestive of

---

[1] Sheppard's feeble portrait of Thomas Killigrew, painted in Venice in 1650, is a melancholy reminiscence of Van Dyck's brilliant portrait painted twelve years earlier. The signed version formerly at Woburn is now in the N.P.G. For Wright, see below, pp. 184–7.

[2] The fullest account of his life and work is to be found in the catalogue of the exhibition of his work at the Tate Gallery, 1951.

[3] Registers of St. Andrew's, Holborn, Guildhall Lib. MS. 6667/1.

[4] *Brief Lives*, ed. A. Clark (1898), i. 38, 78; ii. 318.

certain elements in Dobson's later vocabulary: pictures of gods and goddesses, painted busts of classical heroes and emperors, and an elaborate picture of the kings of England, France, and Spain in the gallery 'donne only with umbre and shell gold'. Dobson *père*, again according to Aubrey, was a 'very ingeniose person', but wasted his estate on women, and it was thus necessity which 'forced his son to be the most excellent painter that England hath yet bred'. He was perhaps apprenticed at an early age to Peake, a stationer and picture dealer, but at some period he was working with Francis Cleyn; Symonds stated categorically that he 'was Dobsons Master & taught him his art'.[1] It is therefore possible that Dobson assisted Cleyn in such decorative schemes as the work done at Ham in the 1630's.[2] The forms and types of the symbolical figures, and the small monochrome medallions in Cleyn's designs for the borders of Mortlake tapestries,[3] probably suggested the reliefs and statuary which Dobson later used to fill out his portraits and to illustrate his sitter's tastes and occupation. The wealth of heavy symbolism in the elaborate monochrome framework to Dobson's *Civil Wars of France* is reminiscent of Cleyn's ponderous Jacobean style.

In Cleyn's house near Covent Garden Symonds saw 'He & his family by Candle light' and it may have been through Cleyn, as well as through a knowledge of the great Caroline collections, that Dobson acquired a passing interest in the school of Utrecht: his Caravaggesque *Executioner with the Baptist's Head* is a very close copy of a picture, almost certainly by Matthias Stomer, in Mr. Denis Mahon's collection.[4] It was clearly impossible for any young English painter to remain unaware of Van Dyck, but there is curiously little indication in his extant *œuvre* of Van Dyck's direct personal influence on his style. Dobson's technique is fundamentally un-Van Dyckian. His feeling for character is entirely English and the colour and texture of his canvases are strongly Venetian;

[1] B.M. Egerton MS. 1636, f. 89*v*.
[2] See below, pp. 289–90.
[3] See Pls. 30 *b*, 31 *b*.
[4] The Dobson is now in the Walker Art Gallery, Liverpool; see also the catalogue of the Dobson exhibition (26).

a study of the royal collection seems to have been a potent ingredient in the formation of his style.

The Civil War gave Dobson his great opportunity and he is as closely associated with the war as Van Dyck had been with the years before it. We know nothing of his early years or of the circumstances in which Dobson entered the King's service. Nothing can be attributed to him with certainty before 1642 and we only know him as the painter of the war-time court at Oxford. When Princes Rupert and Maurice and many of the royalist officers and gentlemen rode out of Oxford after the surrender of the city in June 1646 Dobson's uncertain little world collapsed. He probably returned to London in the spring or early summer of 1646 and on 5 August he was among those elected by the Painter-Stainers' Company to stand for nomination as Steward.[1] Significantly he was not elected; his life was probably as precarious as it was irregular and he was thrown into prison for debt. He was released in time to die in great poverty at his house in St. Martin's Lane and he was buried at St. Martin's on 28 October 1646.

His career as a painter is therefore almost completely confined to the period when he was painting portraits of the King's officers in intervals snatched from campaigning or in the winter months. There is a look of anguish in many of his sitters and a sense of uncertainty even in those who parade most bravely against the stone reliefs and stormy skies. Dobson also mixed in learned circles in Oxford and designed, with the help of Sir Charles Cotterell, the frontispiece,[2] which seems never to have been used, for Sir Thomas Aylesbury's translation of Davila's *Istoria delle guerre civili di Francia*.

The *Unknown Officer with a Page* (1642)[3] at Knole is the earliest extant portrait by Dobson and is already very mature. It has a simplicity and solidity quite foreign to Van Dyck, a blunt and homely feeling for character, a loving attention to military accoutrements (faintly reminiscent of Miereveld and Ravesteyn) and

---

[1] *Booke of Orders . . .*, i. f. 209.

[2] O. Millar, 'A Subject Picture by William Dobson', *Burl. Mag.* xc (1948), 97–99.

[3] Collins Baker, i. 92; see catalogue, *Flemish Art*, R.A. 1953–4 (136) for a possible Van Dyckian source for this type of design. The Dobson does not represent Lord Essex.

Venetian elements in the stormy landscape and the page, who is uncomfortably cramped in the corner of the canvas. It is rich in colour and full and meaty in texture; the flesh is warm and very thickly painted. *Endymion Porter* (Tate Gallery), presumably slightly later, is drier and rougher with strong, sticky impasto over a uniform reddish surface. The composition is more elaborate and the crowded accessories, the full-blown, uncompromisingly English, sitter and the thrusting forward of the figure into the foreground recall Eworth's portrait of *Thomas Wyndham* (s. 1550) at Longford Castle.

Dobson's most elaborate portraits, the *1st Lord Byron* (Pl. 22) and *Charles, Prince of Wales* (Scottish National Portrait Gallery), can probably be dated *c.* 1643. They are most unusual compositions: long three-quarters, cut off just above or below the knees, coming out of the canvas at the spectator and set off in a welter of ponderous accessories. They are not comparable to anything painted in England or elsewhere and represent a highly personal form of English baroque. The mixture of heavy learning and unequivocal portraiture in *Lord Byron* is completely individual. The same cumbersome inelegance marks Dobson's two groups with their strange, introspective heads: the unexplained *Self-portrait with Sir Charles Cotterell and Sir Balthazar Gerbier* (?) (Albury) and *Prince Rupert with Colonels Russell and Murray* (Pl. 25), which are worlds apart from Van Dyck's *Killigrew and Carew*. The last stage in Dobson's development as we know it is marked by two portraits dated 1645, *Sir Charles Lucas* (Woodyates Manor) and an *Unknown Girl* (City of Birmingham Art Gallery), the only canvas which certainly bears Dobson's signature. They are very unsubstantial in contrast with the earlier portraits and the grain of the canvas is seen throughout; they seem to be the work of a painter of ability and imagination, who had been forced to work in unsettled circumstances and had been starved of the influences which would have nourished his style. It is understandable that it was Dobson's final manner which influenced painters working in Oxford slightly later: John Taylor's *John Nixon* (1658), *Joan Nixon*, *John Wall* (1664) and *Richard Hawkins*,[1] all in the Town Hall at

[1] *Loan Collection of Portraits*, Oxford (1905), Pls. viii, x, xvii.

Oxford, show a combination of the English tradition with elements of the later Dobson; and the draperies in Robert Fisher's portrait of John Wilson (s. 1655)[1] in the Music Schools at Oxford are a flashy imitation of Dobson.

Dobson's repertory was inevitably very limited and a genuine feeling for paint tended to degenerate into a rather inadequate impressionism; but he occupies an isolated position among English portrait painters and he was the most ambitious native portrait painter of the century. The extraordinary full-length *2nd Earl of Peterborough* at Drayton,[2] with a snub-nosed putto awkwardly, and with understandable trepidation, handing a helmet to the earl, has a compelling ungainliness. The splendid piece at Castle Ashby of Sir William Compton or his brother the 3rd Earl of Northampton (Pl. 27) is his masterpiece. A comparison with the frigid grandeur of Van Dyck's *10th Earl of Northumberland* (Pl. 26) emphasizes the simplicity and the forceful sincerity of the Dobson, with its fine colour scheme of red, scarlet, buff, silver, and sombre black, vigorous handling and stormy background. It is the most successful portrait of its kind evolved by an Englishman before Hogarth and was not surpassed until Reynolds painted his *Captain Keppel* more than a hundred years later.

[1] *Loan Collection of Portraits*, Oxford (1905), Pl. xi.

[2] Dobson catalogue, Pl. vi; the inscription giving the artist's name, the sitter's titles and age and the date (1644) seems to be a strengthened contemporary inscription rather than a signature and date.

V

THE MINIATURE

THERE is no form of artistic expression in which English painters have more excelled than in the portrait miniature.[1] Its ancestry can be traced back to a fusion of the delicacy and technical methods of medieval illumination and the concentrated psychological interest of the portrait medal. This synthesis was evolved at the court of the early Tudors and consummated in the handful of miniatures painted by Holbein during his second visit to this country. The Stuart and early Hanoverian periods saw the introduction of more complicated and artificial techniques, but the miniature in its purest form was painted in water-colour and opaque body-colour on vellum mounted on card. The majority of miniatures were of oval form and normally were only concerned with the heads and shoulders of the sitters. In the exquisite jewelled or enamelled cases in which so many of them were set, these little works of art were gifts of special value and significance. They could be worn as tokens of love: 'Cavaliers . . .', wrote Sir Kenelm Digby in 1641, 'are ever more earnest to have their Mistresses picture in limning than in a large draught wth oyle colors'.[2] On the other hand they could be put to more official uses and the Stuart sovereigns presented their portraits in miniature, in particularly splendid settings, to foreign rulers and ambassadors. The Council of State continued this practice during the Commonwealth, when they presented portraits of Cromwell by Samuel Cooper to the Swedish Ambassador in 1656 and to Admiral Blake in the following year.

[1] I am very grateful to Mr. Graham Reynolds for reading the manuscript of this chapter. The miniatures themselves can be well studied in the V. & A. and Fitzwilliam Museums and the royal collection is particularly rich in certain Stuart miniaturists. The greatest private collections belong to the dukes of Portland and Buccleuch.

[2] Letter to Sir Tobie Mathew, 15 September 1641 (B.M., Add. MSS. 41846, f. 56v.). Miniatures can frequently be seen worn in contemporary portraits.

In the seventeenth century the art of the miniaturist flourished ('Noe painting in the world soe well paid for as Lymning') and it attained, in the achievement of Samuel Cooper, a height which rivals the eminence of Nicholas Hilliard and overshadows the shallower brilliance of Cosway and Engleheart. Cooper was probably, in continental minds, the most celebrated English artist of the day; nor could any other country in Europe at that time approach the quality or the quantity of the work of the English miniaturists. A number of painters worked in miniature as well as 'in large' and an understanding of the development of portrait painting on these two widely different scales is enhanced if they are seen in relation to each other.

At the time of the accession of Charles I in 1625 the leading miniaturist at court was Peter Oliver. His father, Isaac, had been brought as a child to England in 1568, when his Huguenot parents fled from Rouen at the time of the religious persecutions. In London the Olivers were closely linked by marriage and friendship with the colony of exiled artists and craftsmen in the neighbourhood of Austin Friars which is of such importance for the artistic life of the capital.[1] The strong, confident style of Isaac Oliver had nothing of the lyrical beauty or exquisite linear sense of his English rival, Nicholas Hilliard, whom he predeceased in 1617. The Mannerist elements in Hilliard's style had come from France; Oliver's full modelling, polished surface, brilliant decoration and direct characterization were essentially Flemish and well suited to the florid magnificence of the Jacobean court. His style at its most splendid is epitomized in the full-length of the 3rd Earl of Dorset (s. 1616)[2] in the Victoria and Albert Museum which comes very close to the more robustly ornate type of Jacobean portraits in oil.[3]

---

[1] See above, p. 64.

[2] Other good examples are the large *Henry, Prince of Wales*, and *Anne of Denmark* (both at Windsor, reproduced in catalogue *Nicholas Hilliard*, V. & A. (1947), Pls. xxxviii, xli).

[3] Waterhouse, Pls. 24–25 for a comparison between the Isaac Oliver and a portrait 'in large' from the set at Redlynch (see above, p. 62) of the same sitter. Oliver's miniatures of *Prince Henry* (s., Fitzwilliam Museum) and the *Duke of Buckingham* (Windsor), both in profile and in elaborate Roman costume (*Nicholas Hilliard* (1947), Pls. xli, xliii), come close in mood, and even in texture, to such life-size portraits in

Peter Oliver was a contemporary, and probably a close friend, of Cornelius Johnson and was painted by Adriaen Hanneman.[1] His earliest works are almost indistinguishable from his father's; but although his portrait of Prince Charles (s.: c. 1618; Windsor)[2] is wholly in the manner of the stereotyped royal images which had occupied so much of his father's and Hilliard's time, it is a little freer and softer in modelling and there is already a strain of English feeling grafted on to his father's idiom. In the portraits of Sir Francis Nethersole (s. 1619) and the so-called *3rd Earl of Pembroke* (s.), which are both in the Victoria and Albert Museum, *Sir Robert Harley* (s.)[3] at Welbeck, or in the two miniatures of Prince Charles (both s. 1621)[4] at Windsor, the mood and quality are very close to Cornelius Johnson or to some of the more restrained Jacobean full-lengths, such as *Sir John Kennedy* (1614)[5] at Woburn. *Sir Kenelm Digby* (Pl. 57 a: s. 1627), with its unusually fine, soft finish, is strikingly akin to Johnson's contemporary portrait of the same sitter at Althorp.

Isaac Oliver had painted a number of 'history pieces' in miniature, which would probably have revealed, as clearly as his surviving drawings, the Italianate (and especially the Parmesan) elements in his style. His drawings are in the same heavy Jacobean form of international court Mannerism as the earlier drawings of Inigo Jones. Peter Oliver finished for Charles I the 'greate lim'd peece' of the *Entombment*, which had been begun by his father and was apparently dated 1616,[6] but his contributions to the superb

oil as *Lord Herbert of Cherbury* and *Sir Thomas Lucy* at Charlecote. These were traditionally ascribed to Oliver, but may be by Larkin, one of whose portraits of Herbert was certainly copied in miniature by Oliver at the request of one of his female admirers, who wore it 'set in gold and enamelled . . . about her neck' (J. Lees-Milne, 'Two Portraits at Charlecote Park . . .', *Burl. Mag.* xciv (1952), 352–6).

[1] See above, p. 76.

[2] R.A., *Kings and Queens* (1953), illustrated souvenir, Pl. 34; a convenient parallel in Isaac's work is also at Windsor (*Nicholas Hilliard* (1947), Pl. xxxix).

[3] R. W. Goulding, 'Welbeck Abbey Miniatures', *Walpole Soc.* iv (1916), Pl. vi.

[4] R.A., *Kings and Queens*, Pl. 34.

[5] Collins Baker, i. 20. Lawrence Hilliard, who succeeded his father as limner to the King, never quite fulfilled his father's hopes of him: his miniatures are close to Gilbert Jackson in spirit, but archaic in conception.

[6] It measured, according to Van der Doort's catalogue, $11\frac{1}{2} \times 15\frac{1}{2}$ in.; the design is now only known from the preparatory drawing in the B.M.

collection of contemporary and sixteenth-century miniatures in the Cabinet Room at Whitehall[1] consisted largely of copies in miniature of some of the more celebrated Italian paintings in the King's collections.[2]

The career of John Hoskins is of particular interest for the inter-acting influences between painting in miniature and in oil. He was probably born in the last years of the sixteenth century and he died in 1665. The large number of miniatures which bear the signature of John Hoskins makes it possible, though by no means certain, that his son of the same name worked as a miniaturist. An early miniature, such as the *Unknown Woman* (s.: c. 1620) in the Victoria and Albert Museum,[3] is close in design, in its silvery tone and hesitant touch, to Cornelius Johnson's earliest portraits.[4] In one of his most impressive miniatures, the *Unknown Woman* (Pl. 57 b: s., c. 1640) at Windsor, the plain bright blue background marks a return to an earlier convention; and the sensitive understanding of the sitter's character and the adaptation of the design, with its simple pattern of black and grey, effect a concentration which sounds an echo of Holbein's *Mrs. Pemberton*.

The logical development of Hoskins's style was jeopardized by the impact of Van Dyck. He became a specialist in copies of Van Dyck's portraits, on a larger scale than his own miniatures *ad vivum*: 'I pray', wrote Strafford to his agent in 1636, 'get Hauskins to take my picture in little from my original that is at length, . . . and desire Sir Anthony from me to help him with his direction.'[5]

[1] Oliver was granted an annuity of £220 in March 1637 in consideration of his work on his father's limning and of all future work to be done by him (P.R.O., Index 6748, P.S.O.), and in 1635 had been paid £200 'for pictures made for his Matie' (B.M., MS. 18764, f. 30v.)

[2] A. P. Oppé, *English Drawings . . . at Windsor Castle* (1950), 79–80. They are more useful as a secondary source for a study of Charles's collection than impressive as works of art in their own right. The copy (s. 1634) of Correggio's *Venus, Mercury and Cupid* (N.G.) shows it as it was before it was cut down.

[3] G. Reynolds, *English Portrait Miniatures* (1952), Pl. vii.

[4] A close parallel is provided by a miniature in oil at Windsor which is almost certainly by Johnson. Johnson's miniatures are always in oil and are very close in mood to his portraits in large ; see R. Edwards, 'Oil Miniatures by Cornelius Johnson', *Burl. Mag.* lxi (1932), 131–2, to which could be added examples at Audley End, Chatsworth, Ombersley Court, and St. Giles's House.

[5] Earl of Birkenhead, *Strafford* (1938), 181.

This is a classic instance of the demand for miniature copies of an existing portrait in oil which is heard throughout the seventeenth century, though such a close co-operation between two painters, in enabling a patron to distribute copies of his portraits, was unusual. Hoskins's copies, such as the two of Henrietta Maria in the Rijksmuseum (s. 1632)[1] and at Chatsworth, are of the highest quality and have considerable charm in their own right. The latter has a pretty little view of London in the background, which was Hoskins's independent contribution to the design; it is a link between the art of the miniaturist, which Norgate thought particularly suitable for landscapes, and the development of English landscape painting in oil and water-colour. His association with Van Dyck inspired Hoskins to increase the scale and scope of his portraits, but great technical skill and elaboration cannot conceal an inevitable dullness in such miniatures as *Lady Catherine Howard* and the *4th Earl of Dorset* (both s.) in the Victoria and Albert Museum or the very large *Countess of Dysart* (s. 1638) at Ham House. In his later years Hoskins returned to a more normal scale and to a simpler and more direct style. The breadth, restraint, and understanding in such miniatures as *Charles I* (Pl. 57 c: s., c. 1642) or the so-called *Algernon Sidney* (Pl. 57 d: s. 1659) show without doubt the influence of Hoskins's great pupil and nephew, Samuel Cooper.

Cooper was born in 1609 and, with his elder brother Alexander, was probably in his uncle's establishment by about 1625. Of his very early work little is known, but he seems already to have

---

[1] Catalogue of *William and Mary* exh., V. & A. (1950), Pl. iii. Hoskins was granted an annuity of £200 on 20 April 1640 on condition that he worked for no other patron than the King without his permission (*Cal. S.P. Dom.* (1640), 53), but this was greatly in arrears by July 1660, when he petitioned the King for over £4,000 that was due to him (*Cal. S.P. Dom.* (1660–1), 111). The annuity was renewed on 24 March 1662 (*Cal. Tr. Bks.* (1660–7), 380). Charles also owned 'a little Booke wherein . 6 . drawings [by Cleyn] upon blew Papper wch were don for patterns for the greate Seale wherein 2 more very Curiously don by Haskins aloe for patterns'; this provides a link with Hilliard, who had been ordered to design Elizabeth I's second Great Seal.

The French miniaturist Jean Petitot, who was in England in the 1630's (and living in St. Martin's Lane by 1636), was the first to produce miniatures in enamel in this country. He specialized in copies after Van Dyck, such as the elaborate enamel (s. 1643) at Chatsworth of Van Dyck's *Countess of Southampton*. The earliest miniatures by David des Granges (see also above, p. 80), such as his *Unknown Woman* (s. 1639) at Windsor, are closely dependent on Van Dyck.

evolved in the 1630's a style of startling maturity and from 1642 a steady stream of signed and dated works carries us down to his death on 5 May 1672. The remarkable *Margaret Lemon* (Pl. 24 *a*: *s*.) was probably painted before Van Dyck's death.[1] The handling is already very free; the composition is far more ambitious than anything in Hoskins's *œuvre*; and Cooper already shows the mastery with which he had absorbed the influence of Van Dyck and a baroque sense of design which marks a complete break with the tradition of the Olivers, Hilliard, and Hoskins. On a smaller scale, in the so-called *Robert Walker* (Pl. 57 *e*: *s*. 1645), the baroque pose, full, direct modelling and unerring draughtsmanship are those of an oil painter, but skilfully adapted to the miniaturist's art. The colour is wholly mature, with the lovely soft greyish tone (in this case against a deep rich brown) which is peculiar to Cooper.

Cooper was probably living in Covent Garden in 1640. By 1650 he was established in his house in Henrietta Street and in the same year he was busy with work for Cromwell and his family;[2] his portrait of the Lord General[3] is incomparably the finest portrait in the latter's iconography and was repeatedly copied in the seventeenth and eighteenth centuries. In some of his miniatures at this period Cooper comes close in feeling and design to Lely: in his *Robert Dormer* (*s*. 1650)[4] at Rousham, for example, the pattern of the black silhouette, against a grey background and relieved by a small white collar, is very near to Lely's more sombre Commonwealth portraits. There is the same austerity in the moving portrait of the Rev. Mr. Stairsmore (Pl. 57 *f*: *s*. 1657), Vicar of Edmonton; the extreme simplicity of the design enhances the wonderful sympathy with which the parson's odd, bony face is drawn and with which his character is set before us.

Cooper and Lely had both flourished in the Interregnum, but at the Restoration their position and success were, if possible, enhanced. Aubrey, on the eve of the Restoration, thought it inevitable that the King 'could not but suddenly see Mr. Cowper's

---

[1] G. Reynolds, *English Portrait Miniatures* (1952), 57–58.
[2] W. N. Sainsbury, *Original Unpublished Papers* (1859), 354.
[3] C. Holme and H. A. Kennedy, *Early English Portrait Miniatures* . . . (1917), Pl. xxx.
[4] Dormer paid £12 to Mr. Cooper on 8 September 1650 (MS. at Rousham).

curious pieces', and, indeed, a few weeks later the King sat to Cooper and was 'diverted by Mr. Hobbes's pleasant discourse' as he was being painted. The King himself, on 10 January 1662, discoursed . . . 'on several things relating to painting and graving' to John Evelyn while Cooper was drawing the profile for the coinage.[1] In May 1663 a warrant was issued for a yearly salary of two hundred pounds to Cooper who is referred to later in the year as 'His Majestys Lymner'.[2] There is an appropriate expansion in Cooper's style in the last twelve years of his life. Soest's best portraits provide the closest parallel in English painting before the eighteenth century to the power and sympathy of such male portraits as *James, Duke of York* at Upton (s.) and Ecton (s. 1661), *Prince Rupert* in the National Maritime Museum, *Noah Bridges* (s. 1666) at Ecton or the incomparable series at Welbeck.[3] Female portraits of the same calibre emphasize the shallowness of Lely's fashionable female portraits: the so-called *Duchess of Orleans* (s.) in the Victoria and Albert Museum, *Lady Nicholas* (?) in the Buccleuch collection,[4] the two enchanting miniatures, both wrongly called *Lady Carlisle*, at Ecton and in the Fitzwilliam Museum (s.), or the *Duchess of Cleveland* (s. 1661) at Windsor, with its lovely harmony of silver, grey and white, are all of the highest quality and wholly individual in character and in design.

Cooper's qualitites are seen at their most refined in the *Duchess of Richmond in male attire* (Pl. 24 b: s. 166–), but, despite the extreme softness and delicacy with which the hair and flesh are painted, the touch and colour remain wonderfully fresh and subtle and the drawing and modelling masterly. In his larger miniatures, such as the half-length *Charles II* (s. 1665) at Goodwood and the very late *1st Earl of Shaftesbury* (s.) at St. Giles's House, there is a new elaboration in the accessories. There are no such distractions in the set of five large unfinished heads at Windsor (c. 1662), which were probably painted to provide standard types for repetition. Only

[1] G. Reynolds, op. cit. 52–53. Of the drawing of Charles II there are two versions at Windsor (see A. P. Oppé, *English Drawings . . at Windsor Castle* (1950), nos.133–4, Pl.1).

[2] *Cal. S.P. Dom.* (1663–4), 152; *Cal. Tr. Bks.* (1660–7), 565.

[3] Particularly nos. 55, 57, 60, 62, 69 in Goulding's catalogue (Pls. ix–xi). The collection of miniatures at Ecton was sold at Sotheby's, 11 Oct. 1955.

[4] Holme and Kennedy, op. cit., Pl. xxxvii.

the faces are finished; the rest is indicated with broad areas of body-colour or lightly suggested with water-colour. The flesh is delicately modelled in cool Indian red and grey and the tone in the portrait of Catherine of Braganza (Pl. 58 a) is particularly silvery. Cooper's unfailing understanding of character is matched by the breadth and fluency with which he handles his medium; and the quality and romance of the celebrated *Monmouth* in this group stands between Van Dyck and Gainsborough.

It is difficult not to speak of Cooper's work in superlatives, but his contemporaries had no hesitation in doing so. Nor was it only compatriots like Pepys and Aubrey who thought so highly of his work. To them he was 'the prince of limners of this age', 'the greate, (tho' little) limner, the . . . famous Mr Cooper', of whose painting Pepys said in 1668 that he did 'never expect to see the like again', and for whom Graham claimed that 'for a Face . . . his *Talent* was so extraordinary, that . . . he was (at least) equal to the most famous *Italians*'; but Cooper's reputation stood equally high abroad and for miniature painting 'he was esteemed the best artist in Europe'. In 1669 the Grand Duke Cosimo III of Tuscany sat in London to the miniaturist of whom he had heard so much and whose work was 'in the highest degree of estimation, both in and out of the kingdom'.[1] Cooper had travelled and was a good linguist and a skilful performer on the lute; among his friends were Aubrey, Samuel Butler, Hobbes and Sir William Petty. The delight which his contemporaries took in his work epitomizes the seventeenth-century love of the 'ingeniose' and Cooper, 'one to whom espous'd are all the arts', was to perfection the liberal artist in the Renaissance tradition. As a portrait painter he hardly ever failed to present, with his magnificent virile technique, a compelling image of his patron. No other painter of the Stuart period produced portraits of such deep sympathy.[2]

[1] L. Magalotti, *Travels of Cosmo III* . . . (1821), 166, 343. Two years earlier Magalotti had met Cooper in London and said of him: 'fa ritratti in piccolo a meraviglia, se li fa pagare trenta lire l'uno [this is confirmed by Pepys] . . . è un piccinetto tutto spirito e cortesia. È ancor egli assai ricco, e in casa non sta meno honorabilmente di Lelley . . .' A. M. Crinò, 'Il Ritrovamento della Miniatura di Cosimo III . . .', *Rivista d'Arte*, xxix (Florence, 1954), 148–55.'

[2] Cooper's elder brother, Alexander, worked for many years abroad, particularly

Thomas Flatman was much influenced by Cooper and, like him, was a man of parts and education.[1] From Winchester and New College he passed to the Inner Temple and was called to the Bar in 1662; as a minor poet his songs were set to music by Blow and Purcell; he was a Fellow of the Royal Society; Faithorne, Cotton, Walton and Nahum Tate were among his friends; and he was a close member of the Beales's family circle with its strongly clerical atmosphere.[2] He thus stands, with painters like Sir Nathaniel Bacon, Sir James Palmer, Francis Place and Hugh Howard, as a classic instance of the gentleman artist.

His earlier miniatures, such as *Charles Beale* (*s.* 1664) in the Victoria and Albert Museum, have something of Cooper's quality.[3] In such slightly later pieces as the *Unknown Man* (Pl. 58 *b*: *s.*) the sense of bulk and the sweep of drapery are akin to Soest, but the colour is cooler and the modelling flatter and thinner than in the work of Cooper. To some extent Flatman can be set in the same relationship to Cooper as Greenhill to Lely and his miniatures remain essentially the work of an amateur, with the freshness of the amateur's unspoilt vision. And there are few more moving English portraits in the Stuart period than Flatman's *Self-portrait* (Pl. 58 *c*: *s.* 1673), where the simplicity and force of the pose and handling bring out to the full the melancholy and introspection with which his poetry is over-charged and which may ultimately have driven him to suicide in 1688.

in Holland and Scandinavia; his miniatures are of very high quality, but lack his brother's breadth and are outside the main development of native miniature painting.

[1] G. Reynolds, 'A Miniature Self-Portrait by Thomas Flatman . . .', *Burl. Mag.* lxxxix (1947), 63–67.

[2] See below, p. 181.

[3] The same lively English quality, but in a rather more gauche and provincial form, is seen in the small group of miniatures signed by D. Gibson (i.e. *Lady Catherine Dormer* (*c.* 1655) in the V. & A. and portraits (*s.*) at Badminton of the earl and countess of Carnarvon). He (or she) was probably related to Richard Gibson, the dwarf, miniaturist and copyist. A painstaking head of Henrietta Maria in water-colour by Richard Gibson after Van Dyck is at Windsor. In later years he was drawing-master to the daughters of James II and was in Holland in the service of Mary II before her accession. In his early days he had probably been in the service of the 4th earl of Pembroke: it is very probable that he was *Little Dick my L*[d] *Chamberleine's Page* and *dwarfe*, who was allowed by the King to make copies from Peter Oliver's miniatures after Titian.

After the age of Flatman and Cooper there is no English miniaturist of the first rank until the great men of the next century,
and even before Flatman's death a steep decline had begun in the
quality (and to some extent in the quantity) of miniature painting,
parallel to the equally steep descent to the nadir of oil painting 'in
large' in the early years of the eighteenth century. The majority
of miniatures by Nicholas Dixon, who succeeded Cooper as *mini-
culator regis* in 1673, are cold, thin, and bright, with nothing of his
predecessor's grandeur, and often reflect the same Gallicisms that
Lely and Wissing affected;[1] his large miniature of a boy and girl
with a negro page (s. 1668) at Burghley is light and gay, with the
fussiness of Michael Wright's more elaborate portraits, but his
Lady Crisp (s.) at Ecton is a very powerful piece in the tradition of
Hoskins, in which Dixon was probably trained. Like so many of
his predecessors Dixon occupied much of his time with small copies
of existing pictures and in 1700 he mortgaged seventy limnings
which, early in 1708, passed into the possession of the duke of
Newcastle; many of them survive at Welbeck and are the crowning example of the popularity of these rather monotonous little
pieces. The miniatures of Charles Beale are thoroughly competent
and recognizably close in mood and handling to his portrait drawings; the handful of portraits by P. Cross, such as an *Unknown Man*
at Burghley (s. 1677) and the so-called *Duke of Lauderdale* (s.) in
the Ashmolean Museum, are perhaps closer to Dixon than to
Cooper; and the free, painterly work of Lawrence Cross(e) provides a very close parallel in miniature to contemporary portraits
by Kneller and Dahl.[2] The general atrophy and degeneration in a
great tradition was not stemmed by the introduction of new technical methods. The work of the painters of the Lens dynasty is no
less dreary for being painted on ivory; and the success of the
Swedish enamellist, Charles Boit, who had been trained as a
jeweller, is only justified in modern eyes by the great skill with

[1] For example, the two signed miniatures (c. 1670–5) at Windsor of an *Unknown
Woman* and the *Countess of Ossory*, or an *Unknown Woman* in the V. & A., which is
particularly close to Wissing.
[2] His *Princess Anne* (s.: c. 1700) at Windsor, for example, is very close in character,
colour and mood to Dahl; *Miss Wells* (s.) in the V. & A. is wholly Knellerian.

which he exploited a fresh medium. He had first worked in England in the time of William III and he returned in the next reign after a tour of the Continent. He and his pupil, Christian Friedrich Zincke, were very successful; but there is an inevitable monotony and lack of spontaneity in the enamelled portrait.[1] In their portraits Boit and another Swede, Christian Richter, come very near to the mood and quality of their friend and compatriot, Michael Dahl.

A slight, but very charming, expression of the English seventeenth-century spirit is to be found in the finished portrait drawings, for which there was a renewed demand in the second half of the Stuart period.[2] Some of the professional portrait painters in oil, especially Lely and such members of his circle as Greenhill, Charles Beale, and Thrumpton, drew a number of heads which are not related to their painted canvases, and a handful of minor English draughtsmen specialized in portraits in coloured chalks; their ancestry can perhaps be traced back to the great French portrait drawings of the sixteenth century, and the vogue for them cannot be unconnected with the popularity of such artists as Claude Mellan and Robert Nanteuil in France. Edward Lutterell and Edmund Ashfield developed the pastel technique and applied their colours in a more painterly manner than their predecessors. Their work, for all its attractive freshness, lacks the supreme competence of the French pastellists of the seventeenth century. Ashfield was a gentleman and probably studied under Michael Wright; Buckeridge claimed for him that he had so 'multiply'd the Number and Variety of Tints' that there was 'no subject which can be express'd by Oil, but the Crayons can effect it with equal Force and Beauty'. Such portraits as the *Duke of Lauderdale* (s. 1674–5) at Ham House or the *Unknown Man* (s. 1676) in the collection of Mr. W. Plowden[3]

---

[1] Boit's work on a large scale can be seen in his *Queen Anne with Prince George of Denmark* (s. 1706) at Windsor. For the Swedish miniaturists in England see W. Nisser, *Michael Dahl . . .* (Upsala, 1927), 135–68.

[2] J. Woodward, *Tudor and Stuart Drawings* (1951), and C. F. Bell, 'English Seventeenth-Century Portrait Drawings . . .', *Walpole Soc.* v (1917), 1–18, and (with Mrs. Poole) xiv (1926), 43–80.

[3] C. H. Collins Baker, 'Notes on Edmund Ashfield', *Walpole Soc.* iii (1914), 83–87.

are very soft in colour and of a delicacy in handling and quiet, solid sincerity which come close to Riley. The portraits by Lutterell (who may have been his pupil), such as an *Unknown Man* (s. 1689) at Melbourne Hall, or the *Duke of Bedford* (s. 1698) in the National Portrait Gallery, are more lightly drawn, but sensitive and full of character. An unusual pastel by Lutterell (s.) also at Melbourne is one of the earliest instances of a direct copy of Rembrandt by an English painter.

William Faithorne is a more important artist. His drawings are slighter than Ashfield's, though his *John Aubrey* (1666) in the Ashmolean[1] is deeply sympathetic, but they are closely linked with his plates and he was the most distinguished English line-engraver of portraits in a century which saw an unprecedented output of engraved portraits. He is the only Englishman who can stand comparison with Nanteuil. Like Nanteuil he often engraved the work of other painters, but even his early plates reinterpret Van Dyck and Dobson in robust and vigorous terms.[2] His engravings after his own studies *ad vivum* earn him a place in the highest rank of native seventeenth-century portraitists. He had been with Hollar in the royalist garrison at Basing House, under the command of Sir Robert Peake, but in the later 1640's he went to Paris. There he absorbed the influence of Mellan and Nanteuil, which was so strong on the quality, technique and composition of his plates: Faithorne's *Henrietta Maria*, in her widow's weeds, was probably engraved at this time and is very close to Mellan in design, handling and character. In England many of his plates were engraved as frontispieces and some of them are traditional in form, but even in many of his smaller 'neat-wrought Pieces' Faithorne shows

[1] Woodward, op. cit., Pl. 22.

[2] e.g. his *Prince Rupert* and *Endymion Porter* after Dobson, *Fairfax* after Walker, and *William II* and *Princess Mary* after Van Dyck. Faithorne also did a number of historical portraits for book-illustrations; they show, on the whole, a conscientious study of available models. L. Fagan, *A Descriptive Catalogue of the Engraved Works of William Faithorne* (1888), is still useful; see A. M. Hind, *A History of Engraving and Etching* (1923), 152–4, and 'William Faithorne', *Connoisseur*, xcii (1933), 92–105; Vertue, i. 140–2; and C. F. Bell, *Walpole Soc.* xiv, 50–51. In 1662 Faithorne published a technical treatise, *The Art of Graveing and Etching . . allso The manner & method of that famous Callot, & Mr. Bosse . . .*, which made use of the latter's *Traicté des manières de graver* (1645).

much of the honest sympathy of Samuel Cooper.[1] Perhaps his finest prints are those of the late 1650's: *Sir Robert Henley* (Pl. 59 *a*; 1658), the companion prints of *Sir William* and *Lady Paston* (1659), or the *Sir William Sanderson* and *John Ogilby*, which are after Soest and Lely respectively, show a mastery of design in the placing of the figure within a simple framework and are most compelling portraits. In his later pieces Faithorne's technique becomes finer and more elaborate and almost achieves the fullness of the mezzo-tint, though it lacks the swelling vigour of his earlier line; but there is no lack of power in such prints as *Sir Francis Englefield* (1661) or the very late *Samuel Collins* (1685). As his friend Flatman wrote, 'A *Faithorn sculpsit* is a charm can save from dull oblivion, and a gaping grave'.

As an engraver and seller of books and prints 'at his Shop next to yᵉ Signe of yᵉ Drake, without Temple Barr',[2] Faithorne was the classic, as well as incomparably the best, example of his flourish-ing profession. David Loggan, who was of Scottish descent and came to England in the Interregnum, also worked as a dealer, occasionally painted in oil,[3] and was virtually the last distinguished engraver to work in pure line in face of the formidable challenge of the mezzotint. His drawings *ad vivum* are in plumbago (i.e. graphite on vellum), which can anticipate the fineness of the en-graver's line, and for all their modest size and unassuming patterns there are few more sensitive and appealing English portraits than Loggan's best plumbagos (e.g. Pl. 58 *d*: *s*. 1681).[4] The technique, which is very reminiscent of Nanteuil, is of extreme delicacy, but with no lack of freshness; it was carried to an even higher pitch

---

[1] e.g. his *Sarah Gilly* and *Mary Langham*, which was prefixed to her *Funeral Sermon* (1662), *Noah Bridges* (frontispiece to his *Vulgar Arithmetique*, 1653), *Edmund Elys* (for his *Miscellanea*, 1662), or *Christopher Simpson* for his *Compendium of Practical Musick* (1667).

[2] There are interesting references in Hooke's *Diary* to Faithorne in this connexion.

[3] His varied activities emerge from his letters to Sir Thomas Isham (MSS. at Lam-port); his portrait of Sir Thomas's mother is eloquent testimony of his plea that 'it is Exciding harde to make a graet pictor after a Littel one.' An important source for Loggan is Sandrart's *Academie*, ed. A. R. Peltzer (Munich, 1925), 356, 368. See also below, p. 270, n. 1, and C. F. Bell, op. cit.

[4] His so-called *Earl of Rochester* (*s*. 1671) in the B.M. and *2nd Duke of Ormonde* (*s*. 1682) in the V. & A. are wholly typical.

of refinement in the portraits by Thomas Forster, where the sense of character and the play of light and shade in the hair and draperies of his sitters link him closely to Michael Dahl.[1]

The allied arts of the miniaturist and portrait-draughtsman provided amateurs with an agreeable and civilizing diversion. In his *Miniatura or The Art of Limning* the Herald Edward Norgate wrote of his hope that 'some of the Gentry of this Kingdome (for whose sake and service it was principally intended)' would be encouraged to practise an art so 'honest, harmles and innocent.'[2] Norgate himself was the best illuminator of patents and commissions of his time, taught his craft to the sons of the earl of Arundel, and through their father was linked with the Whitehall group. The original draft of *Miniatura* was undertaken at the request of Sir Theodore Mayerne, physician at the court of James I and Charles I, and other members of that brilliant society may have profited from Norgate's instructions: the King himself is said to have had some skill as a draughtsman; Sir James Palmer, Gentleman Usher of the Privy Chamber, painted between 1614 and 1623 a small group of miniatures which are close in style to Isaac Oliver;[3] and the versatile Sir Balthazar Gerbier, who was described as the 'Duke's painter', painted life-size and miniature portraits of Buckingham and at the time of the Spanish Marriage was contemplating an allegorical picture of the return of the prince and duke with the Infanta.[4] Later in the century the miniature of John Hough by Simon Digby, bishop of Worcester, in the National Portrait Gallery, or the copies after Samuel Cooper by Mrs. Rosse (who was Richard Gibson's daughter) are amateur works of respectable quality. The amateur artist in pencil or crayons would also have found encouragement in Norgate's pages. His advice to the beginner to

---

[1] e.g. *Dr. Drake* (s. 1700) at Welbeck or an *Unknown Woman* (s. 1704) at Windsor. The two other leading draughtsmen in plumbago, John Faber and Robert White, who was Loggan's pupil, were less competent.

[2] *Miniatura*, ed. M. Hardie (1919), 64; it was probably finished shortly before Norgate's death in December 1650 and it was the most important sequel in the seventeenth century to Hilliard's *Arte of Limning*.

[3] G. Reynolds, 'A newly identified Miniaturist . . .', *Burl. Mag.* xci (1949), 196–7.

[4] G. Goodman, *The Court of James I* (1839), ii. 260–7. His equestrian miniature (s. 1618) of Buckingham at Alnwick and his pen and ink drawing of Prince Charles (s. 1616) in the V. & A. show considerable skill. See above, pp. 52–53.

copy carefully 'the best prints cut in Copper you can get' was carried out by Samuel Pepys when, on 7 November 1666, he 'called
at Faythorne's, to buy some prints for my wife to draw by this
winter.' Mrs. Pepys, sitting at her work under her husband's
absorbed and enthusiastic eye, and her more illustrious contemporaries like Lady Bathurst and the princess of Orange, were
developing a polite accomplishment which helped to fill the leisure
hours of English ladies in the Georgian and Victorian ages.

Much of the work of the later professional limners of the Stuart
period is dull and stereotyped or only remarkable for the particular form of technical virtuosity in which that age delighted:
'there is no Art wherein Curiosity can be more expressed then in
the Art of Limning'.[1] But in the work of artists like Hoskins,
Flatman, Loggan, Faithorne, and Samuel Cooper are to be found
unaffected and spontaneous portraits in which the emphasis on the
countenance of a sitter enabled them to avoid the tiresome affecta-
tions which can become so monotonous in the work of their
rivals on a larger scale. The charm and intimacy of their portraits
are intensified by the effort of concentration needed to study these
small masterpieces. It is an effort which brings a rich reward.

[1] B.M., Harl. MS. 6376; quoted in *Miniatura*, op. cit. xxi.

VI

SCULPTURE AND TAPESTRIES
BEFORE THE COMMONWEALTH

ENGLISH sculpture of the seventeenth century is far less lively and distinguished than English architecture, nor does it rise to the level of contemporary painting, for though several foreign sculptors worked here, they none of them had the brilliance of Van Dyck or the accomplishment of Lely, and were not of the stature to found a school. The reasons for this comparative failure are manifold and complex. Much sculpture, some of it notable work, had been produced for the adornment of churches in the middle ages, but the break with the Roman Church had cut off suddenly the demand for such pieces. To the Puritans all sacred representation was anathema, and even to moderate churchmen the carved image was more suspect and nearer idolatry than its painted counterpart.[1] The tradition of religious sculpture was therefore broken and the masons' yards which had maintained it were forced to seek other work. It was never really to be revived and one of the major fields for sculptors in Catholic countries was closed to the English.

Tomb-sculpture, however, continued to flourish. Like the portrait, it appealed to the English sense of personal and family prestige, whether of the greater or lesser aristocracy, or of the merchant classes; and by far the larger part of the work of English sculptors during the sixteenth and seventeenth centuries was devoted to this purpose. The same reasons that led men to build country houses caused them to be buried in country churches. The material is consequently widely scattered, difficult to survey, and often impossible to photograph. Moreover, much has been lost, for during the nineteenth-century Gothic revival a drastic removal of seventeenth- and eighteenth-century monuments occurred. There are, however, still many hundreds of tombs or wall-tablets of dignity

[1] An extreme expression of this may be found in Canon Peter Smart's indictment of Cosin's work at Durham, see above, p. 58.

or interest in village churches.[1] In secular buildings relatively little use was made of sculpture; Jones, in spite of his Italianism, made slight demands upon sculptors, and the country house before the Restoration offered little field for their activity. Moreover, in sculpture the general standard of taste had been formed on Flemish rather than on Italian or antique models. In architecture the sixteenth-century treatises could at least be used as guides by those who had seen neither Italian nor Roman buildings. But there were no such works on sculpture. Few major Italian works were to be seen in England:[2] Buckingham owned Giovanni Bologna's *Samson*,[3] but it does not seem to have been widely known; Arundel's interest in the antique was something entirely new. Links with Flanders were, however, strong. Many Protestant refugee craftsmen had settled in England in the sixteenth century, among them families of sculptors who had founded workshops (mainly in Southwark) and captured the greater part of the trade in monuments. Tombs more or less on the same pattern were turned out in great numbers and sent all over England. In these workshops apprentices were trained who when they had finished their Articles were allowed to work under a master (not necessarily their own) as journeymen, and later were usually admitted as Freemen of the Masons' Company.[4] Nicholas Stone and his sons, Edward and

[1] All writers on post-Reformation sculpture owe much to the energy of the late Mrs. K. A. Esdaile, who rescued the subject from almost complete oblivion, and spent a lifetime recording information. Her general works are: *English Monumental Sculpture since the Renaissance* (1927); *English Church Monuments, 1510–1840* (1946). Her attributions of unsigned monuments must sometimes be regarded with caution, but her small book, *Monuments in English Churches* (1937), contains a list of signed or documented works. For sculptors after the Restoration, R. Gunnis, *Dictionary of British Sculptors, 1660–1851* (1953), is invaluable, since it collects information published in scattered articles, adds new documentary evidence, and omits attributed works. Some sculptors discussed in this chapter who were active before and after 1660 are included. I am indebted to Mr. Gunnis for allowing me to read certain entries in proof while drafting this book.

[2] Torrigiano's tombs made for Henry VII at Westminster are a notable exception, but even there the effigies conform to the English Gothic tradition.

[3] John Pope-Hennessy, *Samson and a Philistine*, V. & A. Monographs 8 (1954).

[4] Much useful information is contained in: D. Knoop and G. P. Jones, *The London Mason in the 17th Century* (1935).

Joshua Marshall, Thomas Stanton and his nephew William, and great-nephew Edward, all had family shops, while other sculptors, in the second half of the century, Abraham Storey, Thomas Stayner, Thomas Cartwright, and Richard Crutcher, were Masters of the Masons' Company. It is probable that mason-sculptors established shops in other centres, especially in those where good local stone was available. Certainly much work was produced by local men, and it is often old-fashioned and very provincial in quality.[1]

Nicholas Stone (1583–1647) was the outstanding mason-sculptor of the first half of the century. We know a great deal about his activities, for he left a Note Book which summarizes his main jobs throughout his life, and an Account Book covering the years 1631–42 in detail.[2] These record the making of more than eighty tombs or monuments, and nearly the same number of other commissions—chimney-pieces or marble floors and one or two figure subjects.

Stone, the son of a Devon quarryman, was trained in an Anglo-Flemish workshop in London, that of Isaac James,[3] and in 1606 went as a journeyman to Hendrick de Keyser, architect to the City of Amsterdam, the sculptor of the tomb of William the Silent at Delft. Stone remained with him till 1613, and married his daughter.[4] In his first two big tombs (both of 1615), the earl of Northampton's,[5] now dismembered, and Thomas Sutton's in the

---

[1] Exact dates for monuments are tricky, for surviving contracts show they were often set up in a patron's lifetime, or by relatives some years after his death. The latter is sometimes, but not always, recorded in the inscription. Failing other evidence, however, a death date may be taken as an approximate date for a work.

[2] Now in the Soane Museum. Both were published in full by W. L. Spiers, *Walpole Soc.* vii (1919).

[3] James's most important certain work is the Norris tomb in Westminster Abbey (K. A. Esdaile, *Country Life*, cvii (1950), 464).

[4] He may perhaps have assisted de Keyser with the sculpture on the screen from s'Hertogenbosch, now in the V. & A. For other possible works by Stone in Holland, see Dr. Elisabeth Neurdenburg, *De Zeventiende Eeuwsche Beeldhouwkunst in de Noordelijke Nederlanden* (Amsterdam, 1948), 93.

[5] Made for the chapel of Dover castle, but now in fragments in Trinity Church, Greenwich. For a drawing showing the original form see K. A. Esdaile, 'Three Monumental Drawings from Sir Edward Dering's Collection', *Archaeologia Cantiana*, xlvii (1935), 220. The source is the sixteenth-century French royal tombs at St. Denis, probably via a Du Cerceau engraving.

Charterhouse, London,[1] he was associated with older sculptors (Isaac James and Nicholas Johnson respectively) and it is impossible to say how much was his. Both tombs are elaborate versions of types already in use, but the Bodley monument of the same year at Merton College, Oxford (Pl. 28 a), is more original in design.[2] The elegant little figures of Arts and Sciences, with their long necks and closely clinging draperies, are of a type frequently found in Stone's early work. They seem more like an echo of the Fontainebleau school of the mid-sixteenth-century than of contemporary Dutch or English sculpture, and are clear proof of the way in which artists imitated a style they had probably never seen, but which they could have known through engravings. The coarse architecture of the Bodley monument (admittedly rendered more clumsy by the 'device' of using piles of books to form pilasters) and the strap-work label below are, however, purely Flemish in origin, and the bust cut off by the oval of the medallion is a type in common use at the time.

The most beautiful of Stone's early tombs, indeed one of the most accomplished of all his works, is the Lady Carey at Stowe-Nine-Churches, Northamptonshire (1617). Here again he uses a traditional type, the recumbent effigy on a free-standing altar tomb. But he emphasizes a new colour contrast of black and white marbles, which he had seen in Holland.[3] In the effigy, too, there is a new tendency. Hitherto, the great majority of recumbent figures had been carved lying rigid on their backs with their hands joined in prayer.[4] Lady Carey, however, lies sleeping; her head raised on an embroidered pillow is slightly turned; one hand rests on her breast, the other by her side. This new and tender naturalism extends to features and dress; the interest in the latter is clearly very

---

[1] *Walpole Soc.* vii (1919), 40, and Pls. iii and iv; K. A. Esdaile, *English Church Monuments* (1946), 82.

[2] J. Woodward, 'The Monument to Sir Thomas Bodley in Merton College Chapel', *Bodleian Library Record*, v. 2 (1954), 69.

[3] The contrasting colour-scheme had already been used in the tomb of the earl of Salisbury at Hatfield (1612), made by Maximilian Colt.

[4] The effigy on the Sutton tomb was of this type. Stone was to use it again later in, e.g., the Villiers tomb in Westminster Abbey (1631), and the Spencer tomb at Great Brington, Northants. (1638), probably on the instructions of his patrons.

great, for the embroidered bodice and fur-lined mantle are rendered with care, but the mechanical emphasis of the Elizabethan tomb-makers on details of dress rather than of head has disappeared, and the figure has become a distinguished and individual piece of sculpture. In the monument to Sir Charles Morison of 1619 at St. Mary's, Watford, a big canopied tomb, made of rich variegated alabaster, there is the same life-like ease of movement in the representation of the figures.

Stone's work in the first few years after he came back from Holland shows him quickly building up a practice (mainly outside court circles), using traditional types, but giving his figures a greater individuality. Very broadly speaking, his work shows a parallel to the change from Elizabethan to Jacobean portraiture. In 1619, however, he came into immediate contact with the new Italianism of Inigo Jones, for he was made Master Mason at the Banqueting House.[1] It does not, however, seem that this caused any immediate change in Stone's style, though his range was certainly enlarged in the following decade. He executed a standing figure of Queen Elizabeth I for the Royal Exchange (now in the Guildhall, London) which did not give satisfaction, probably because she is not shown in contemporary costume, but in loose flowing draperies, standing on a phoenix.[2] And, perhaps more important, the two Holles monuments in Westminster Abbey show a clear reference to Michelangelo's Medici tombs. The seated figure of Francis Holles (d. 1622) is based on that of Giuliano de' Medici, but the *contrapposto* which gives fire and energy to Michelangelo's figure has been completely misunderstood, and the result is a clumsy, rather flabby, seated warrior. The monument to Sir George Holles (d. 1626) shows a standing armed figure with a very long neck above a tablet flanked by two female draped figures seated on scrolls, resting their heads on one hand, a pose borrowed from Michelangelo's 'Night' on the Giuliano tomb. Below is a battle relief in the Dutch tradition. The proportions of both monuments are awkward, but they are nevertheless a landmark in Eng-

[1] See above, p. 23.
[2] J. E. Price, *A Descriptive Account of the Guildhall of the City of London* (1886), 147 f.; K. A. Esdaile, *Country Life*, xcv (1944), 162.

lish art, for they are at once the first examples of the use of Roman costume and of the direct influence of Michelangelo. The channel for the latter is unknown, but was presumably a drawing made by some artist who had visited Italy. Another work of the twenties of considerable interest and charm is the wall monument to Sir Edward Pinchon at Writtle, Essex (probably c. 1625), which shows the parable of the Sower with the Angel of the Resurrection above a rocky ground with sheaves of corn at the foot, and angelic reapers (in large straw hats) resting at either side. That so complex and vivid a scene is rare in Stone's work and indeed in English sculpture of the time is probably due to the general disapproval of 'images', and it is significant that this example is based on a parable where neither sacred figures nor saints are needed.

After about 1630, a marked change appears in Stone's work. The old tomb types still remain, but they are treated in a much more sober manner. He no longer uses richly coloured alabasters, but restricts himself to black and white marbles. Out of some twenty recorded monuments after this time only two have the little long-necked figures reclining on the canopy. Architectural settings are more severe, often heavier, but with details which are Italian rather than Netherlandish. And above all, the treatment of drapery changes. The thick material with broken, dimpled folds is replaced by thinner stuff treated in small unbroken parallel folds.[1] Perhaps the most striking example of the new manner is the monument to two boys who were drowned while bathing, John and Thomas Lyttelton (1634) in the chapel of Magdalen College, Oxford (Pl. 28 b). Here the treatment of the nude as well as of the drapery makes it clear that the new source of inspiration is antique sculpture, almost certainly that described by Peacham:[2]

'King Charles also ever since his coming to the Crowne, hath amply testified a Royall liking of ancient statues, by causing a whole army of

[1] The change in architectural detail can be seen by a comparison between two monuments at Paston, Norfolk, i.e. Katherine, Lady Paston (1629), and Sir Edmund Paston (1635), (Walpole Soc. vii (1919), Pl. xvii, b and c); in both architecture and figure treatment between the first Morison tomb at Watford (1618) and the second (1630) (ibid., Pls. x and xix), though photographs cannot convey the marked difference in colour.

[2] Compleat Gentleman (2nd and enlarged ed., 1634: ed. 1661), 107.

old forraine Emperors, Captaines and Senators all at once to land on his coasts, to come and doe him homage, and attend him in his palaces of Saint James and Sommerset-House. A great part of these belonged to the late Duke of Mantua . . .'[1]

Since Stone was paid for small mason's jobs at St. James's in 1628–29,[2] he would presumably have had ample opportunity of studying this sculpture. From a series of drawings in the Royal Library at Windsor,[3] it is possible to guess at the wide range of material—nudes, full-length figures and busts—available to him. He was in even closer touch with the court, and presumably especially with Inigo Jones, from 1632 onwards, for in that year he succeeded William Cure as Master Mason to the Crown. He was never, however, to become Master Sculptor, for that post had in 1608 been granted for life to Maximilian Colt, a refugee from Arras,[4] who survived until after 1645, but whose work does not seem to have pleased the court circle. Stone, however, who was able to modify his style to a far greater extent than Colt, was allowed in 1636 to make for Windsor a 'carved piece that stands over the Gate of Diana or chast love taking her repose having bereaved Cupid of his bow and arrow and turned him to flight'. This has unfortunately disappeared, and the only survivor of a series of statues of pagan deities made for the Pastons at Oxnead in the 1630's is a figure of Hercules so battered that nothing can be deduced from it. For his new style we are compelled therefore to rely on his tombs where he had not always a free hand, since conditions were often dictated by his patrons. In the monuments of the mid and late 1630's, such as the Lady Catherine Paston at Oxnead of 1636, or the Peyto monument at Chesterton St. Giles, Warwickshire, of 1639, a classical type of bust on a pedestal is

[1] See above, p. 4.

[2] P.R.O., A.O.I. 2425/59. 1 Oct. 1628–30 Sept. 1629. The Royal Accounts for 1629–30 include, under St. James's Palace, an item for 'mending statues damaged by sea'. (Ibid., A.O.I. 2426/60. 1 Oct. 1629–30 Sept. 1630). I am indebted to Mr. John Summerson for these and other references from *Declared Accounts*.

[3] Made for Sir John Stanley who was in the Lord Chamberlain's Office when Whitehall Palace was burnt down in 1698.

[4] His most important work falls in the reign of James I, and is therefore outside the scope of this volume.

used. This may either reflect a further influence of the antique, or the use of this form by Hubert Le Sueur, the King's Sculptor, in, for instance, the Lady Cottington (1634) in Westminster abbey.

During this decade Stone was a busy man. He was Master of the Masons' Company in 1633 and 1634; in 1632 he designed and built the gateway to the Botanic Garden at Oxford, full of reminiscences of sixteenth-century Italian garden architecture.[1] At the same time, for the same patron, the earl of Danby, he added to Cornbury House, Oxfordshire;[2] he did work at the new church of Great Stanmore for Sir John Wolstenholme in 1641,[3] and he probably built the north front of Kirby Hall about 1638.[4] He carried out innumerable small mason's jobs for the Crown, he worked for Lady Arundel at Tart Hall, St. James's (now destroyed), executed the portico of St. Paul's, designed and built Goldsmiths' Hall (which according to his great-nephew had 'a noble entrance of the Doricke Order'),[5] and probably the porch of St. Mary the Virgin, Oxford, the gift of Laud's chaplain, Dr. Morgan Owen.[6] This last, with its twisted columns, is without parallel in English architecture. Beyond all this, there were many commissions for tombs, and it is not surprising that the quality of some of these is poor when compared with the early work, for he can have done but little himself.[7] Their design is, however, often both varied and interesting, and in almost his last tomb, that of Sir Dudley Carleton, Viscount Dorchester, in Westminster abbey (1640), he sets the pattern for many later abbey tombs. The figure reclines easily on an altar tomb set under a frame of large columns with a curved broken pediment above. The motive was to run right through the century, until the frame disintegrates in the Gibbons monu-

---

[1] He had already built York Water Gate for Buckingham, see above, p. 52.

[2] His work was subsequently altered by Hugh May, see below, p. 142.

[3] R.C.H.M., Middlesex (1937), 114.

[4] See above, p. 45, note 4. The bust in the courtyard dated 1638 is probably that of Apollo 'almost twise as bigge as the life' for which Stone was paid £4 in 1640. (Walpole Soc. vii (1919), 129).

[5] Ibid. 137.

[6] V.C.H., Oxfordshire, iii (1954), 217, 262.

[7] For instance, two assistants, John Hargrave and Richard White, were paid £14 and £15 respectively for making the effigies on the Spencer tomb at Great Brington, Northants., in 1638, for which Stone received £500 (Walpole Soc. vii (1919), 75, 120).

ment to Sir Cloudesley Shovell.[1] In the suave lines of the figure of this friend of Rubens, Stone comes nearer in spirit to the court art of Van Dyck than at any other moment in his career.[2]

Stone died in 1647 and his second son, Nicholas, in the same year. John Stone, his third son, survived till 1677, following in the main patterns established by his father.[3] Of the independent work of the journeymen and assistants mentioned in Stone's Note and Account Books, little is known, though there is a signed tomb of Sir John Wentworth by Anthony Ellis at Somerleyton, Suffolk, (1651) and another by Humphrey Moyer (who had worked with Stone on the shrouded effigy of John Donne for old St. Paul's Cathedral, re-erected in the present building) at Greenford, Middlesex.[4] Neither of these has much quality, but there are a great number of monuments scattered up and down the country, some of them of considerable competence, which show the immediate influence of Stone's workshop.

Other big masons' yards were, however, beginning to appear. Of these, two which were to last for more than one generation of the same family were founded by Edward Marshall (1598-1675) and Thomas Stanton (c. 1610/11–1674). Marshall, whose yard was at the corner of Fetter Lane and Fleet Street, was apprenticed to a John Clarke (probably the mason who had built Lincoln's Inn Chapel, 1619–24), became a member of the Masons' Company in 1626/7 and was Master in 1650.[5] At the Restoration he was to become Master Mason to the Crown.[6] His tomb of George Carew,

---

[1] See below, p. 246.

[2] For Carleton see above, p. 4. A weathered copy of this monument stands at the base of the north-west tower of the abbey of Holyrood, erected by the nephews of Robert, Lord Belhaven (d. 1639), a member of the Royal Household. According to Vertue (i. 98) it was made by John Schorman, whose name appears in the Stone Account-Book as having carved the arms on the Spencer tomb at Great Brington in 1638 (*Walpole Soc.* vii (1919), 75 and 124). He also made a *Hercules and Antaeus* for Sir John Danvers at Chelsea, and the effigy of Sir Thomas Lucy at Charlecote, Warwicks. The Belhaven monument is a good example of the habit of ordering a workshop repetition of a successful work.

[3] Some of these are illustrated in *Walpole Soc.* vii (1919), Pls. xlv–xlix.

[4] Moyer (or Mayer) was admitted to the Masons' Company in 1626/7, and was Master in 1653 (D. Knoop and G. P. Jones, *London Mason* (1935), 23).

[5] Ibid. 34.

[6] See P.R.O., A.O.I. 2433/85, 1 June 1660–31 May 1661, when his 'Entertain-

earl of Totnes (d. 1629) and his wife (d. 1636), at Stratford on Avon,[1] reveals, in its arched canopy on columns, Flemish ornament, and wealth of coloured heraldry, connexions with Southwark work. His later monuments show a type much used in the middle years of the century. For instance at Tottenham, Middlesex, the tomb erected by Sir Robert Barkham to his wife Mary (d. 1644) includes, in a rather heavy architectural frame, in which much emphasis is given to floreated scrolls above and at the sides, two half-length figures shown as in life. These are forceful rather than sensitive in cutting, but the dominating character of Dame Mary is well displayed. A number of other monuments with half-length figures or long busts and some without figures, from the Marshall workshop exist; the standing shrouded figure on the Curwen monument at Amersham, Buckinghamshire (Pl. 29 *a*) emerging from a tomb, the doors of which are held open by two angels, is a fair sample of the quality of his best work.[2]

Thomas Stanton was apprenticed as a mason to Christopher Kingsfield, became a member of the Company in 1630/1, and rose to be Master in 1660.[3] Judging from his most important certain work, the tomb of Dame Jane Bacon and her two husbands at Culford, Suffolk[4] (1657–8), Stanton was a clumsier sculptor than Edward Marshall (Pl. 29 *b*). This tomb, however, serves to introduce a type not so far mentioned, that with a seated figure. Dame Jane, with a small child on her lap, sits in a stiff frontal position, while on either side stand older children, also seen from the front. Below lies her first husband, Sir William Cornwallis, rigidly propped on one elbow. Though the architectural framing and its treatment in black and white marble is close to the later

ments and Fees' amounted to £83. 3s. 2d. per annum. He held the office till his death, when he was succeeded by his son Joshua (see below, p. 256).

[1] R. Gunnis, *Dictionary*, 254.

[2] Edward Marshall also signed the brass of Sir Edward Filmer at East Sutton in Kent (a late example of this art). For a list of his monuments, see R. Gunnis, loc. cit.

[3] D. Knoop and G. P. Jones, *London Mason* (1935), 20, 21. See also K. A. Esdaile, 'The Stantons of Holborn', *Arch. Journ.* lxxxv (1928), 149 f., where it is suggested that he received his training as a sculptor under Isaac James or his partner, Bartholomew Atye.

[4] Contract printed in H.M.C. *Verulam MSS.* 1906, 54. Stanton was paid £300 and provided the stone, while the patron provided transport from Ipswich.

style of Nicholas Stone, the sculpture is much inferior to his. Stanton had previously made and signed the monument to Sir Thomas Lyttelton (1650) at Worcester cathedral. No later certain works are known though several have been attributed to him. In its conservatism his work clearly pleased old-fashioned sections of the landed gentry and is paralleled by scattered and anonymous pieces.

A somewhat similar artist, William Wright of Charing Cross, was, judging from a letter from Sir Ralph Verney, noted for his representation of shrouded figures.[1] The popular shrouded tomb seems to replace the double representation (the effigy above and the skeleton below) of the middle ages, and recalls irresistibly the theme of Death which runs through many of Donne's most famous sermons. His own figure in St. Paul's, for which he posed wrapped in his shroud, is vividly recalled by his words, 'We have a winding sheet in our mother's womb which grows with us from our conception, and we come into the world wound up in that winding sheet, for we come to seek a grave. . . . This whole world is but an universal churchyard.'[2] Donne's thunderous periods are scarcely paralleled in English sculpture; they are reduced to emblems such as skulls and bones and hour glasses; but the lovely shrouded effigies of Anne, Lady Kinloss, at Exton, Rutland, or of Rachel Gee of 1649 at Bishop's Burton, Yorkshire, (to name two only) prove how his thought had permeated English society.

Shrouded figures, but here half-lengths emerging from a coffin, with the Angel of Judgement sounding a trumpet above, may be seen in the two very similar signed monuments by John and Matthias Christmas, to Temperance Browne (1634), at Steane, Northamptonshire, and to Mary Calthorpe (d. 1640) at East Barsham, Norfolk. These two sculptors, who signed a number of

---

[1] *Memoirs of the Verney Family* (1894), iii, 124. A shrouded monument possibly by Wright is the Deane tomb at Great Maplestead, Essex (1633). He evidently had connexions with the Parliamentarians, for he made the tomb of Henry Ireton (with two effigies) for Westminster Abbey, which was destroyed at the Restoration (R. W. Ramsey, *Henry Ireton* (1949), 201). See also K. A. Esdaile, *Monuments in English Churches* (1937), 21, 26, 41.

[2] 'Death's Duell', preached at Whitehall in Lent 1630 (*Ten Sermons by . . . John Donne . . .*, Nonesuch Press (1923), 147).

monuments in the 1630's,[1] were Master Carvers to the Navy and Pageant Masters to the City of London. Their work is unequal but the best is not without some quality in the handling of drapery.

The gulf between work for the inner Whitehall circle and that produced for the majority of English patrons is, in some ways, less immediately evident in sculpture than in the other arts. The reasons are not far to seek. Although at least three foreign sculptors, Hubert Le Sueur, Francesco Fanelli, and François Dieussart (or Dusart), were employed by the court, they were none of them of the calibre of Van Dyck. Moreover, except in the case of Le Sueur, relatively few works remain in England by which they can be judged. Even so, it is clear that they make a chapter of some importance in the history of English art, for they introduced new types and new materials. Most of the seventeenth-century English sculptors followed the medieval tradition of effigies made in alabaster. Le Sueur and Fanelli were, however, both of them linked with the great Italian bronze tradition.[2]

Hubert Le Sueur,[3] a Frenchman whose birth date is unknown, is said by Henry Peacham to have been a pupil of Giovanni Bologna.[4] Though not physically impossible, if Le Sueur went to Italy before Bologna's death in 1608, it is unlikely on grounds of

[1] Rochester, St. Nicholas, Thomas Rocke (1635); Ipswich, St. Stephen's, Robert Leman and wife (1637); Ruislip, Middlesex, Ralph Hawtrey (1638); Denham, Suffolk, Sir Edward Lewknor (1638); Ampton, Suffolk, Henry Calthorpe (1638); Stratfield Saye, Hants, William Pitt (1640). They also finished the tomb of Archbishop Abbot at Guildford, begun by their father Gerard Christmas. (J. Burke, 'Archbishop Abbot's Tomb', *Journ. of Warburg and Courtauld Institutes*, xii (1949), 179). I have to thank Mr. Rupert Gunnis for several items in this list, and also for the reference to Matthias's epitaph in Chatham churchyard (now lost) given in Thorpe, *Registorum Roffensi* (1769), 731. He died in 1654.

[2] Confusion between them was begun by unsound attributions made by Horace Walpole or his nineteenth-century editor, James Dallaway, and continued by some later writers.

[3] See G. Webb, 'Notes on Hubert Le Sueur', *Burl. Mag.* lii (1928), 10, 81; K. A. Esdaile, 'New Light on Hubert Le Sueur', ibid. lxvi (1935), 177. Some tentative amendments to these articles will be suggested here.

[4] *Compleat Gentleman* (1634; ed. 1661), 108. The statement is repeated by Vertue (ii. 86), and Walpole. Peacham, however, states that Giovanni Bologna went to France, which is untrue.

style. He may perhaps have had some contact with the pupils who in 1614 set up, on the Pont Neuf, the equestrian statue of Henri IV, begun by Bologna and finished by Pietro Tacca.[1] But before this, in 1610, Le Sueur must have been a fully trained artist, since he had the title of 'Sculpteur du Roi'.[2] His work after he came to England suggests that though he was influenced by the Henri IV statue, he had also strong links with French sculptors such as Barthélemy Tremblay, active in the late sixteenth and early seventeenth centuries, and may perhaps have been trained in one of their workshops. He is mentioned as 'Officier' or 'Sculpteur du Roi' in 1618 and 1619, and in 1624 as an artist with special skill in bronze casting.

The exact date of his arrival in England is unknown,[3] but in 1626 he was paid £20 for making twelve figures for the catafalque of James I in Westminster Abbey.[4] He quickly found favour at the court, and was soon given two important commissions for the tombs of the duke of Lennox and Richmond (d. 1624)[5] and of the duke of Buckingham in Henry VII's Chapel at Westminster. The Lennox tomb, which is superior in craftsmanship and has not been damaged like that of the hated Buckingham, is in the form of a great hearse, with four bronze caryatid figures supporting a pierced metal canopy over the effigies. The whole is surmounted

---

[1] The chief of these was Pietro Francavilla (Pierre Francheville), who was in France for some years, dying there in 1615. He made the Slaves, set up in 1618 and now in the Louvre, which adorned the base of the statue, itself destroyed in the French Revolution. Le Sueur's name does not appear among the list of artists generally cited as setting up the statue. Sir L. Cust (D.N.B., and Burl. Mag. xx. (1912), 192) says Le Sueur was a pupil of Tacca, but the latter did not go to France with the statue.

[2] G. Webb, in Burl. Mag. lii (1928), 10.

[3] Mrs. Esdaile (loc. cit.) suggests that he was domiciled here by 1619, when his wife witnessed a baptism at the French church in Threadneedle Street; but this hardly seems to tally with his French appointments.

[4] P.R.O. Declared Accounts, A.O.I. 2425/57, 1 Oct. 1626–30 Sept. 1627; and see above, p. 27. It seems possible that he was encouraged to come by Buckingham, who was in Paris in 1625.

[5] The Lennox tomb was in place by 1628 (Cal. S.P. Dom. (1628–29), 329). No document records Le Sueur's authorship, but it is clearly by the same artist as the Buckingham tomb, which is attributed to Le Sueur in E. Chamberlayne, Angliae Notitia (ed. 1687), pt. ii, 303. For suggestions as to assistants working on it see Mrs. Esdaile, loc. cit.

by a bronze winged figure of Fame with a trumpet. In both cases the bronze effigies are in the traditional English pose with the hands joined in prayer, and it is rather in the supporting figures that Le Sueur reveals at once his training and his limitations. They are heavily built, with strangely cylindrical limbs, smoothly and rather clumsily modelled, giving almost the impression of being inflated from within. The Lennox caryatids are muffled in voluminous draperies and their stolidity ill accords with the large bronze tears which trickle down their cheeks. These heavy figures are far removed from the Mannerist elegance of the Fontainebleau school, but here and there details recall the work of French sculptors such as Prieur and Biard.[1] The tombs must have seemed very impressive to a people used only to mason-sculptors' work, but by contemporary continental standards they are undistinguished and certainly show no close influence from Italian masters or models.

The tendency to treat a figure as if it were blown out from within, instead of built up of bones and flesh, is characteristic of Le Sueur and appears both in his standing figures and his busts. The former include William, 3rd earl of Pembroke (c. 1629) in the Schools Quadrangle at Oxford, Charles I and Henrietta Maria (1634) (Pl. 70 b), ordered by Laud for the gates of the Canterbury Quadrangle of St. John's College, Oxford, and the figures of Charles I and James I (1639) which alone remain of Inigo Jones's screen for Winchester cathedral.[2] The Pembroke, according to family tradition, was based on a drawing by Rubens. No such drawing is known, and the whole style, with the emphasis on the dress and rank rather than on the character of the sitter, is typical of the rather dull court portraiture current in France, as exemplified for instance by the work of the Fleming Pourbus. Richly decorated armour, such as Pembroke wears, was common enough in English tombs (e.g. the kneeling figures flanking the tomb of Lord Norris by Isaac James in Westminster Abbey), but its reproduction

[1] The figures of Fame for instance are draped versions of the nude Fame by Pierre Biard of c. 1597 now in the Louvre.

[2] For the contract with Laud see Cal. S.P. Dom. (1633–4), 43; and with the King for the Winchester figures, W. N. Sainsbury, Original Unpublished Papers . . . (1859), 319. A further standing figure by Le Sueur is that of Admiral Leveson (1633) in St. Peter's, Wolverhampton (Rev. S. Shaw, History and Antiquities of Staffordshire (1801), ii. 158).

in metal gave it a far greater verisimilitude, and allowed for much finer detail. It is therefore easy to understand the popularity in court circles of this competent but rather uninspired craftsman, whose art appeared to be at once novel and linked with a continental tradition. That ungainliness of pose in his standing figures is not solely due to the restriction of armour is proved by the Henrietta Maria. Here details of dress are rendered with equal care, but the Queen stands stiffly, and the head has little character. There seems, moreover, to be no development in his style, since the Winchester figures are neither better nor worse than the Pembroke made ten years earlier.

His most important work, the equestrian statue of Charles I at Charing Cross, was begun in 1630 for Lord Treasurer Weston, for the garden of his house at Roehampton. The artist was instructed to take the advice of the 'King's riders of great horses for the shape and action of the horse and of His Majesty's figures on the same'.[1] Whatever advice may have been given him, Le Sueur in fact imitated very closely the Henri IV on the Pont Neuf. He shows ability in handling the contrast between the smooth surfaces of the horse's body and the rich decorative chasing of the armour, but detail photographs reveal all too clearly the extreme emptiness of the modelling of the face.[2] Viewed from a distance, it is not unsuccessful as an image of majesty, though it cannot compare with the equestrian portraits of Van Dyck.

The most important and by far the most influential innovation of the foreign sculptors was the portrait bust existing in its own right and not as part of a tomb. Although Pietro Torrigiano had probably made a few such busts,[3] he had not created a fashion, and portrait busts seem to have been confined to monuments, where

[1] Cal. S.P. Dom. (1629–31), 121, 165, 167. The work was to be finished in eighteen months for a fee of £600. Weston died in 1635 and the statue was not set up before the Civil War, but according to Vertue (i. 122) remained in the artist's workshop near Covent Garden till Parliament sold it to a founder to be melted down. He buried it instead, and after the Restoration it was set up at Charing Cross on a pedestal, probably designed by Wren and executed by Joshua Marshall.

[2] See H. D. Molesworth, Sculpture in England, Renaissance to Early XIXth century (1951) (pub. for the British Council by Longmans, Green), Pl. vii.

[3] e.g. the terra-cotta bust of Henry VII in the V. & A. Museum and that of Bishop Fisher in the Metropolitan Museum, New York.

they were set in roundels, Nicholas Stone's Bodley monument being, in this sense, typical of a large class. On the continent, the portrait bust on a pedestal had been fairly common since the sixteenth century.[1] The bust of Henri IV, almost certainly by Barthélemy Tremblay, the best version of which is in the Jacquemart André collection in Paris,[2] seems both in its treatment of armour and of drapery to be the basis of Le Sueur's most popular bust of Charles I, though it is far more lively in modelling. The Charles I busts present a difficult and confusing problem, since it is evident that many versions were made. Moreover, some of those now in existence are certainly not of the seventeenth century.[3] The earliest datable example is the marble in the Victoria and Albert Museum which is inscribed on the back, *Hubertus Le Sueur faciebat 1631*. The King is shown in Italian armour decorated with acanthus, wearing a scarf over his left shoulder with the George hanging below it. The condition is not now good (the moustaches seem to have been broken), but it is doubtful if the modelling was ever sensitive.[4] Linked with this are a number of bronze busts. They all, however, differ from it in the treatment of the gorget, which in the marble continues the acanthus pattern of the breastplate and pauldrons, but in the bronzes shows plain, studded armour. The one with the best pedigree is that presented to the Bodleian Library at Oxford by Archbishop Laud in 1636. Another which seems of rather better quality, but without the George, is at Windsor. Perhaps the most interesting is the bronze with the dragon helmet[5]

[1] e.g. Leoni's busts of the Spanish royal family and the Germain Pilon of Charles IX of France in the Wallace Collection.

[2] An inferior marble version is in the Louvre. Both are illustrated in P. Vitry and G. Brière, *Documents de Sculpture Française* (1911), Renaissance, ii, Pl. clxxxvi. A good bronze with slight variations is at Windsor.

[3] They may have been made (probably with busts of Cromwell and Milton) to supply the eighteenth-century taste for series of English 'Worthies', others may have been produced in the nineteenth century in pairs with a Cromwell.

[4] It was bought for the Museum about 1912 in Holland. Sir L. Cust (*Burl. Mag.* xx (1912), 192) suggested it had been made for the king of France, though there seems no evidence for this. That Le Sueur was in the royal service soon after this is indicated by a Crown debt to the money-lender Burlamacchi dated 25 Aug. 1632 for an advance for a house for Le Sueur (B.M., MS. 18764 (*Misc. Exchequer Accounts, 1620–34*), f. 19).

[5] An identical helmet is worn by the seated figure of Mars at the foot of the Buckingham tomb.

now at Stourhead (Pl. 30 *a*), which Van der Doort records in the Chair Room at Whitehall. It shows the King as a slightly older man, dressed in pseudo-classical costume.

Occasionally Le Sueur provided busts for monuments such as the Sir Thomas Richardson (signed and dated 1635) and the Lady Cottington in Westminster Abbey[1] and here he sets a fashion of some importance, quickly imitated by English sculptors.[2] An unusual work is the severely classical bust of Archbishop Laud at St. John's College, Oxford, not signed or documented, but with all the artist's characteristic smooth emptiness of treatment. Here the head and neck only appear, with no drapery or adjuncts of office. There must surely again be a direct influence from some of the classical sculpture which adorned the royal palaces by the 1630's.

Le Sueur had indeed himself added to the King's collection of 'antique' sculpture, for Peacham informs us[3] that it was he who had made the series of bronzes from famous antique models which are now in the East Terrace garden at Windsor. These include the Borghese Gladiator, the Farnese Hercules, the Belvedere Antinous, and the Diana of Versailles.[4] Two of his bills give some insight into Le Sueur's character, for they were signed 'Praxiteles, Le Sueur'. This pretentiousness, which is only matched

---

[1] *Cal. S.P. Dom.* (*1634–5*), 158, quotes the contract (witnessed by John Webb) with Lord Cottington for 'a great tomb' for which Le Sueur was to be paid £400. Sir L. Cust, *D.N.B.*, 'Le Sueur', states that the marble figure of Lord Cottington was 'executed at a later date by F. Fanelli'. I have been unable to trace the authority for this.

[2] See above, p. 111.

[3] *Compleat Gentleman* (ed. 1661), 108. Le Sueur was sent to Italy in 1631 to obtain 'moulds and patterns of certain figures and antiques there' (P.R.O. E 404/152, *Exchequer of Receipt Issue Warrants, 1630–1*).

[4] The pedestal for the 'brasse gladiator' was made for the privy garden at St. James's in 1629–30 (P.R.O. *Declared Accounts* A.O.I. 2426/60). It was later in the century moved to the end of the Long Water in St. James's Park, and appears to have been mistaken for a true antique (F. Colsoni, *Le Guide de Londres* (1693), reprinted 1951 for the London Topographical Soc., ed. W. H. Godfrey, 10 and 61, speaks of 'le beau canal, à la tête duquel il y a une excellente statue Romaine qui en fait la perspective'). The whole set of casts was moved by Queen Anne to Hampton Court, and subsequently taken by George IV to Windsor. Le Sueur also made a series, now lost, of classical figures and busts for the Queen for Somerset House, which may have been original work or copies. (*Cal. S.P. Dom.* (*1636–7*), 325, 409.)

by the shallow character of his style, is revealing. Possibly the King found his 'Praxiteles' a little tiresome, for there are annotations in State Papers, probably in the King's hand, cutting down the prices, and once stating, 'this I will not have'. By 1636 Charles may well have realized the second-rate quality of Le Sueur's work. The project for the bust to be commissioned from Bernini was already on foot, and he must have had some inkling of the brilliance of that master's work.[1] Moreover, by that date two more able sculptors, Francesco Fanelli and François Dieussart, were working in England.

The date of Fanelli's arrival is unknown. A misreading of an entry in Van der Doort's catalogue led to the supposition that he had worked for Prince Henry. This is extremely unlikely, since very little of his work survives, and nothing can be dated before the mid-1630's.[2] He had evidently been trained in a good tradition, and seems to have specialized in small bronzes.[3] Charles owned a group of two Cupids with a horse, and a St. George and the Dragon,[4] and nine similar pieces, all groups including horses, were seen by Vertue at Welbeck.[5] These were no doubt commissioned by William Cavendish, duke of Newcastle, that passionate horseman, when Charles, prince of Wales, was in his care, for Fanelli's only signed work, a bust of the boy then aged ten, is still at Welbeck, dated 1640 (Pl. 31 a). It is small ($11\frac{1}{2}$ in. high) but is far more lively and more realistic in modelling than any work by Le Sueur. The richly chased Italian armour with the prince of Wales's feathers on the breastplate, the soft crumpled collar falling over the gorget and the curling hair all have a brilliance of treatment which reveals the quality of Fanelli's art. The same skill in modelling appears in the bronze bust on the monument of Sir Robert Aiton

[1] See above, p. 6. The bust, which disappeared after the fire at Whitehall in 1698, is thought to be recorded in a copy by Francis Bird (K. A. Esdaile, *Burl. Mag.* xci (1949), 9–14). Another version of it can be seen in Vertue's self-portrait (Vertue, i, frontispiece).

[2] He received a pension from the King in 1635 (*Cal. S.P. Dom.* (1635), 63).

[3] J. Pope-Hennessy, 'Some Bronze Statuettes by Francesco Fanelli', *Burl. Mag.* xcv (1953), 157. Since this was published further small pieces have been identified at Buckingham Palace and Windsor.

[4] Van der Doort lists these in the Cabinet Room at Whitehall as made by 'Francisco Fanelli the one-eyed Italian'.   [5] Vertue, iv. 110.

(d. 1637) in the south ambulatory of Westminster Abbey,[1] though the marble flanking figures of Apollo and Athena are a trifle tame.

Fanelli's superior modelling suggests that he, and not Le Sueur, as has always hitherto been supposed, was responsible for the tomb of Lord Treasurer Weston in Winchester cathedral.[2] The head is extremely sensitive, the armour with fettered figures and trophies on the splendidly chased breast-plate, is close in handling to the Welbeck bust, and the sarcophagus has ornaments with masks that are purely Italian in style. That Fanelli was in his own day regarded as the better sculptor is suggested by the fact that the earl of Arundel, who of all men in England might be expected to show discrimination, intended Fanelli to make his tomb. His will specifies a figure '. . . (of white marble or Brasse designed by Sign[r] Francesco Fanelli) sitting and looking upwards. . . .'[3]

The only other certain work by Fanelli is the Diana Fountain now in Bushey Park. This was formerly in the Privy Garden at Hampton Court, and is described by Evelyn as including 'sirens, statues, etc'.[4] Fanelli, like many Florentine artists, was evidently interested in fountain design, for after he left England in the early 1640's he published in Paris a book of designs of fountains and architecture, in which he calls himself 'Scultore del Re della Gran Bretagna.'

The third foreign sculptor whose works can still be traced is the Fleming, François Dieussart.[5] He had been trained in Rome, perhaps in the studio of his fellow countryman, François Duquesnoy,[6]

---

[1] Not signed or securely documented but stylistically completely convincing.

[2] No documents exist. Le Sueur's authorship has always been assumed because he made the equestrian Charles I for Weston, but the work seems of a higher standard. The tomb has been mutilated, and the marble busts are certainly by an inferior hand. Mrs. Esdaile (*Burl. Mag.* lxvi (1935), 183) attributed them to John Colt, a known assistant of Le Sueur.

[3] See M. F. S. Hervey, *Thomas Howard, Earl of Arundel* (1921), Appendix ii, 460. Arundel died abroad, and the tomb was never executed.

[4] *Diary*, 9 June 1662. Moved to its present position and altered in the early eighteenth century.

[5] François Anguier, who was a leading sculptor in France shortly after the middle of the century, is said to have spent some years in England in his youth (D'Argenville, *Vie des plus fameux architectes et sculpteurs* (1787), ii. 169). Unfortunately no work can be traced, but his most likely employment was for the Queen at Somerset House.

[6] See below, p. 234.

and therefore came to England with a knowledge of the new trends of baroque art. His help was consequently enlisted by the Capuchins who served the Queen's chapel at Somerset House, and for the first Mass celebrated there in 1636 he devised 'a machine . . . to exhibit the Holy Sacrament, and to give it a more majestic appearance'.[1] In this he employed a full baroque illusionism, and combined architecture, sculpture, and painting in a single whole. The machine

represented in oval a Paradise of Glory, about forty feet in height . . . a great arch was supported on two pillars towards the high altar. . . . Over each side appeared a Prophet, with a text from his prophecy. . . . Behind the altar was seen a Paraclete, raised above seven ranges of clouds, in which were figures of archangels, of cherubim, of seraphim, to the number of two hundred, some adoring the Holy Sacrament, others singing and playing on all sorts of musical instruments, the whole painted and placed according to the rules of perspective . . .[2]

Nothing so closely linked with contemporary religious art in Rome had yet been seen in England, and indeed its only real successor was to be the chapel at Whitehall decorated for James II,[3] but it is doubtful if even there the full baroque armoury was so skilfully employed.

Not much is known of Dieussart's other work in England, but his ability as a sculptor is revealed in a signed marble bust (dated 1636) of Charles I in the collection of the duke of Norfolk. Also at Arundel castle is another bust, dated the next year, of Charles Louis, Elector Palatine.[4] Both are of good quality, sensitive in characterization and modelling. They lack the extreme penetration of the best Roman busts of, for instance, Algardi, and they have not the *panache* of Bernini's later busts of princes,[5] but the slight turn of the head and the deep undercutting of the hair

[1] 'Memoirs of the Mission in England of the Capuchin Friars of the Province of Paris from the year 1630 to 1669, by Father Cyprien de Gamache . . .', trans. in T. Birch, *The Court and Times of Charles I* (1849), ii. 310 f.

[2] The chapel was dismantled after the execution of the King, and nothing remained of its decoration.   [3] See below, p. 217.

[4] Both came from the collection of Thomas Howard, earl of Arundel. Vertue saw them at Norfolk House, St. James's Square (Vertue, ii. 66).

[5] e.g. the Francesco d'Este at Modena, or the Louis XIV at Versailles.

differ from the more conservative approach of Le Sueur and even Fanelli, and reveals the sculptor's admirable training.[1]

Portraiture of high quality was also produced by medallists, most of whom were French.[2] The greatest artists in this field were, however, English: the Simon brothers, Abraham (1617–c. 1692) and Thomas (1618–c. 1665), who carried the tradition through the Commonwealth into the Restoration, when they were supplanted by the Dutchman, John Roettiers. In addition to their beauty, many medals possess considerable iconographic interest.

Another aspect of court patronage of foreign artists and craftsmen may be seen in the fine productions of the Mortlake tapestry factory.[3] This enterprise had been founded in 1619 in imitation of Henri IV's establishment (generally known as the Pre-Gobelins factory) of 1609.[4] Though, however, James I was the official patron, the project may well have originated in the prince of Wales's circle for his secretary, Sir Francis Crane, was made controller of the factory and all the early sets of tapestries seem to have been made for the prince rather than the King. In August 1619 Crane bought houses at Mortlake to be turned into a factory, and in the next year fifty Flemish weavers and their families arrived. They were led by Philip de Maecht, who had been head weaver under Marc de Comans at the Paris factory, and whose monogram with that of F. C. (Francis Crane) and the Mortlake shield, a red cross on a white ground, appears on a number of the

[1] He left England for Holland in the early 1640's. A bust in the Rijksmuseum, Amsterdam, of Charles II as a young man, seems to be by him, and may have been made during the sitter's exile in Holland during the Commonwealth.

[2] *Guide to the Exhib. of Historical Medals*, B.M. (1924); H. Farquhar, 'Portraiture of our Stuart Monarchs on their Coins and Medals', *Brit. Numismatic Journ.* v (1909)– xi (1915).

[3] A full, though not quite up-to-date, account of the Mortlake factory is given in W. G. Thomson, *Tapestry Weaving in England* (1914), 66 ff. This was largely based on a privately printed paper by J. E. Anderson of 1894. A remarkable collection of material relating to tapestries of all kinds amassed by H. C. Marillier is deposited in the Textile Department of the V. & A. and is indispensable for any serious work on the subject. See also the Introduction by G. Wingfield Digby to the *Catalogue of the Exhibition of English Tapestries*, Birmingham Art Gallery (1951).

[4] It should be noted that the work produced here and also at Mortlake was woven on the *basse-lisse* (i.e. on horizontal looms) process, which was quicker than the *haute-lisse* process until then used in France.

best early pieces. The names of many of the weavers have been recovered from the parish registers, and from them and the accounts it is possible to get a fair idea of the organization of the factory.

It is, however, far more difficult to get a clear picture of its output. Designs were repeated many times, sometimes with additions and sometimes possibly with omissions. Moreover, at the time of the attempted revival of the factory after the Restoration, and again when the factory itself was dying at the end of the century and Mortlake workmen set up elsewhere on their own, the old designs were re-used.

The first two subjects to be woven were from sixteenth-century Flemish designs. The history of Venus and Vulcan[1] (of which at least three sets were woven before 1625) may have been copied from a series mentioned in Henry VIII's Inventory of 1547, though new borders were devised for them. The set bearing the prince of Wales's feathers and monogram already shows both the fine materials—silk and wool in strong rich colours, with metal thread in the borders—and the fine weaving which was to be characteristic of the Mortlake factory.[2] The second subject, the 'Months' which was very popular, was also woven for the prince of Wales, for he wrote from Madrid in 1623 saying he hoped the work would be finished by his return. His set is still in the English royal collection.[3] Soon, however, Charles was dissatisfied with the repetition of older Flemish patterns. An artist, Francis Cleyn (or Clein), was engaged to produce original designs, and at the same

[1] E. S. Siple, 'A Flemish Set of Venus and Vulcan Tapestries', *Burl. Mag.* lxii (1933), 212, and lxxiv (1939), 268.

[2] Pieces are in St. James's Palace, the V. & A. and two private collections in America. Remains of other early sets are the five pieces with Crane's monogram in the Mobilier National probably bought by Cardinal Mazarin at the Commonwealth sale and owned by Louis XIV in 1673, and the single piece with the arms of Buckingham given by Louis XIV to Charles X of Sweden in 1657 and still in the Swedish royal collection. The V. & A. piece has 23 warp (upright) threads and 50 weft (horizontal) threads to the square inch. Some of the finest Gobelins pieces to be made for Louis XIV were to have 8 warp threads to the centimetre, and so are coarser.

[3] See *Cat. Holbein Exhib.*, R.A. (1950), 353. Further sets belong to the earl of Ilchester at Melbury, Dorset, and the earl of Onslow at Clandon, Surrey. Some later sets with floral borders are also known.

time Charles with the factory in mind was negotiating one of the most important of all his purchases, that of the Raphael cartoons, bought in Genoa in 1623.[1] Cleyn (1582–1658) had been born at Rostock, had studied in Italy (including four years at Rome), and had then been employed by Charles's uncle, Christian IV of Denmark, on decorative paintings for his castles of Frederiksborg, Christiansborg, and Kronborg.[2] He arrived shortly before Prince Charles's return from Spain in 1623, but evidently returned to Denmark for a time, since he was paid for work there in 1625. The rest of his life, however, was to be spent in England.[3]

It is impossible to say if Cleyn's first work for the factory was the designing of an original set of tapestries, or the copying of the Raphael cartoons and the invention of new borders for them.[4] The exact date of the first weaving is not known, but the petition of a certain Dru Burton against Crane at the end of 1629 refers to 'the Apostles' as 'a greate worke' about to be undertaken.[5] The preparations at least were therefore in hand by then. Three different types of border were devised, more in keeping with seventeenth-century taste than the narrow borders of the original Vatican tapestries. The set woven for the King, now in the Mobilier National in Paris,[6] has a splendid design with putti and medallions

---

[1] See above, p. 3. The existence in Genoa of a set of the 'Months' with the same borders as the Prince of Wales's set may be connected with the purchase of the cartoons. They bear the arms of the De Franchi family, a member of which was Doge from 1623 to 1625.

[2] See F. Beckett, 'The painter Frantz Clein in Denmark', *Mémoires de l'Acad. Roy. des Sciences et des Lettres de Danemark*, 7th series, v, pt. 2 (1936); H. Walpole, *Anecdotes of Painting*, ed. Dallaway, ii. 25.

[3] For his work as a decorative painter, see below, p. 289.

[4] The cartoons of the *Death of Ananias* and the *Blinding of Elymas* were copied by Cleyn, and the border for the former designed by 1631 (P.R.O. E 404/153, *Exchequer of Receipt Issue Warrants*, 1630–1). I am indebted to Mr. William Myson for this reference. A set of small copies in pen and ink, possibly made for engraving, belongs to Wadham College, Oxford (on loan to the Ashmolean Museum) (F. J. B. Watson, 'The Raphael Cartoons in England', *Burl. Mag.* lxxxv (1944), 227). Four are dated, two 1640, and two more 1645 and 1646. Evelyn, *Sculptura* (ed. C. F. Bell, 1906), 111 f., says these copies, which were shown to him by Charles II, were made by Cleyn's sons, Francis and John, both of whom worked as engravers.

[5] Quoted in W. G. Thomson, *Tapestry Weaving in England* (1914), 80.

[6] Bought by the Spanish Ambassador at the Commonwealth sale (G.-J. de Cosnac,

showing scriptural scenes (Pl. 31*b*); in other sets the borders have winged putti climbing twisted columns[1] or terminal figures at the sides[2] and festoons of fruit at the top. It is not known how many sets from the cartoons were woven before the Commonwealth period.[3] They were used again after the Restoration, several sets being known such as that with the arms of Daniel Finch, 2nd earl of Nottingham,[4] which must be about 1700. The sets of the Acts of the Apostles were always, and indeed must always be regarded as the finest and most important products of the Mortlake enterprise.[5] The Royal set, even in its present faded condition, gives perhaps a truer impression of the magnificence which Charles I loved than any surviving works of the period except for the grandest of Van Dyck's portraits and the Rubens ceiling at Whitehall.[6]

Many other subjects were woven at the factory, one of the most popular being a series of six or seven pieces designed by Francis Cleyn showing the story of Hero and Leander. The figures in their rich costumes are a rather clumsy echo of Paolo Veronese, though Cleyn's association with the Raphael cartoons is shown in the twisted and decorated columns of the temple[7] in the scene of Leander's farewell (Pl. 30 *b*). It cannot be claimed that the compositions are very distinguished, though they tell the story clearly

Palais Mazarin (1884), 25) and later acquired by Mazarin (*Inventaire des Meubles de Mazarin en 1653*, ed. duc d'Aumale (1861), 158), who left them to Louis XIV.

[1] e.g. the set with the arms of Henry Rich, earl of Holland, in the Mobilier National, ordered in 1639 (*Cal. S.P. Dom.* (1639–40), 143).

[2] e.g. those with the arms of Pembroke in the Buccleuch collection sold by the factory in 1638 (*Cal. S.P. Dom.* (1637–8), 173).

[3] In addition to those already mentioned, sets (or parts of sets) exist at Dresden (before 1939), Belvoir, Woburn, Chatsworth, &c. Some of these, however, almost certainly date from after 1660.

[4] Sold Christie's, 12 June 1947, lot 169. Probably woven by Stephen De May, a Mortlake craftsman working at Lambeth.

[5] Sets woven at the Gobelins factory from copies specially made from the Vatican tapestries are markedly inferior to the best Mortlake examples.

[6] For the later history of the cartoons, for which a gallery still called the Cartoon Gallery was provided by Wren at Hampton Court, see John Pope-Hennessy, *The Raphael Cartoons* (V. & A., Large Picture Books, no. 5) (1950).

[7] Copied from the cartoon of the Healing of the Lame Man. The motive goes back to the late antique columns in St. Peter's, thought in the middle ages to have come from the Temple of Jerusalem. For another use of them, see above, p. 49, and Pl. 6 *b*.

enough. One fine set (now only of five pieces) woven in silk and wool with borders of putti playing among strap-work, and the monogram of Sir Francis Crane and Philip de Maecht, is in the Swedish royal collection, and is probably the set for which the King owed the factory £1,704 in 1636.[1]

At the time of Crane's death in 1636 the finances of the factory were in a poor state. He had, in 1629, been accused of profiteering, but his behaviour was probably only that normal in the seventeenth century in the case of a gentleman who had been granted what amounted to a monopoly. Moreover, it is clear that the King had not paid for the sets woven for him, and Crane had presumably had to find a good deal of ready money out of his own pocket. For a short time his brother managed the factory, but in 1637 it was taken over directly by the Crown. The workmen fared no better, since their pay was always in arrears, and they eked out a sorry existence down to 1650. A good deal of work was, however, produced. Certain designs were based on works in the King's collection of pictures. Titian's *Supper at Emmaus*, now in the Louvre, was exactly copied. Since an example belongs to St. John's College, Oxford, it is possible that the undertaking was in some way directly connected with Archbishop Laud, and was either done at his request, or as a present to him from the King.[2] A second series linked with the King's paintings was probably the 'Playing Boys'—a charming set with little naked putti climbing trees and gathering fruit, the inspiration coming from paintings by Polidoro da Caravaggio, now at Hampton Court.[3]

---

[1] It bears the English Royal Arms, and was given by Charles I to Count Johan Axelsson Oxenstierna, Swedish Legate in London in 1634, who presented the hangings to King Charles X of Sweden on his marriage in 1654. Another good set with similar borders was at Lyme Park, Cheshire. Three pieces remain there, one is in the V. & A., and one was burnt. A coarser late set is at the Lady Lever Art Gallery, Port Sunlight. Other subjects probably designed by Cleyn were a set known as 'The Horses' (see H. C. Marillier, *Burl. Mag.* l. (1927), 13) and the Five Senses, of which a set with the Royal Arms is now at Haddon Hall, Derbyshire.

[2] Another tapestry of this subject now hangs in St. George's Chapel, Windsor. A piece appears in the Mazarin Inventory of 1653 (*Inventaire des Meubles de Mazarin en 1653*, ed. duc d'Aumale (1861), 352).

[3] *Cat. Exhib. English Tapestries*, Birmingham (1951), 32. For Cleyn's use of the same theme in decorations at Ham House see below, p. 49 and Pl. 6 b. Van Dyck's

Although work continued during the Civil War, it is obvious that the court had neither time nor money to give to patronage. The weavers turned for help in 1645 to the Dutch church in London, and offered to make a set of the Acts for £357. 10s. 0d. This offer, however, was refused and the Congregation ordered instead a secular subject, 'The Hunters' Chase'.[1] Five hangings of these genre scenes, which are strongly Flemish in character, remain at Chatsworth, rather incongruously combined with borders of putti climbing vine-wreathed columns which were probably first invented for the Raphael cartoons. The quality of the work produced at Mortlake and the prestige it enjoyed (it was perhaps the best tapestry of its time in Europe) is proved by the competition by connoisseurs for the pieces belonging to the King when his goods were sold after his execution. Cardinal Mazarin was a particularly eager buyer, and acquired before his death at least eleven Mortlake sets.[2]

It will be convenient to summarize here the later history of the Mortlake factory. The number of weavers was declining fast; over forty are recorded in 1655 and only twenty-five in 1663. In 1661 Sir Sackville Crow petitioned the King[3] for the foundation of a new company, pointing out that the factory had decayed from lack of purchasers of the richer sorts, and that inferior tapestries were being imported from France and the Netherlands. In the next year he was granted control of the factory with a subsidy of £1,000 a year. Probably this was not paid, for in 1667 he resigned and three years later he was imprisoned for debt. From letters to the countess of Rutland written at this time,[4] it is clear that he had been producing sets from the old designs; he also refers to the first set woven from Mantegna's *Triumphs* as being still

Self-Portrait with Endymion Porter (Prado) is copied in tapestry at Knole, and a tapestry portrait of Sir Francis Crane, which must surely be based on a painted original, is with other pieces at Ingatestone Hall (W. G. Thomson, *Tapestry Weaving in England* (1914), 70).

[1] See A. J. B. Wace, 'The Hunters' Chase', *Burl. Mag.* lxvii (1935), 29.

[2] A short list of the best pieces was made for Mazarin in May 1650 (G.-J. de Cosnac, *Palais Mazarin* (1884), 410).

[3] *Cal. S.P. Dom.* (1661–2), 110.

[4] Quoted by W. G. Thomson, *Tapestry Weaving in England* (1914), 100.

on the looms. It was said to have been for the King, and has presumably disappeared, since the only examples now traceable are slightly later, for they bear the arms of Ralph, earl (and afterwards duke) of Montagu, who was in control of the works from 1674 to 1691. These three fine pieces now belonging to the duke of Buccleuch show that Mantegna's designs were re-arranged for the weavers.[1] Two interesting new sets were woven during the interregnum between the directorships of Crow and Montagu,[2] when the factory was held together by the master weavers, Francis and Thomas Poyntz. The hangings of Stuart portraits, signed *Fr. Poyntz* and dated 1672, now at Houghton, Norfolk, are still in the great Mortlake tradition. They are finely woven, with much gold, and with very grand borders. They show figures of James I, Anne of Denmark and her brother Christian IV of Denmark, Charles I and Henrietta Maria based on portraits by Van Mander, Van Somer, and Van Dyck. The other venture was the better known Solebay tapestries showing stages of the incon-clusive battle between the Dutch and English fleets fought off Southwold in 1672.[3] Three pieces of this series remain at Hampton Court (signed by Francis Poyntz, with the Mortlake shield), and two signed 'T. P.' belong to Lord Iveagh. It is interesting that these late designs are the only Mortlake productions in which the subject is related to English history. The purpose may have been to attract patrons away from the purchase of Gobelins tapestries by appealing to patriotic sentiment. If so, the venture failed.[4] Indeed, Mortlake as a centre was rapidly dying. Before his death in 1685 Francis Poyntz had moved to the Great Wardrobe in Hatton Garden.[5]

[1] The largest tapestry is made up from sections iv and viii of the Mantegna series; the car of Caesar is section ix, plus the trumpeters from section iv. Another set of five pieces formerly at Burley-on-the-Hill seems to have disappeared.

[2] These years are very confused; a good deal of financial jobbery seems to have gone on, in which the earl of Craven and the earl of Sunderland were involved.

[3] *Cat. Exhib. English Tapestries*, Birmingham (1951), no. 31.

[4] There is at least one instance of the copying of Gobelins designs at Mortlake, i.e. the 'Elements' designed by Charles le Brun in 1664. A set with the Mortlake mark and the arms of Montagu as duke (i.e. woven between 1689 and 1708) belongs to the duke of Buccleuch.

[5] See H. G. Marillier, *English Tapestries of the Eighteenth Century* (1930), Intro-duction, for a review of the general position in the late seventeenth century. The Great

Stephen De May, another Mortlake weaver, was at the Great Wardrobe by 1673; William Benood moved to Lambeth. The old designs were woven either at the Great Wardrobe or in small factories in London at least until the early years of the eighteenth century, but new designs were introduced in the reign of Queen Anne, some showing chinoiserie subjects in imitation of lacquered furniture.[1] Mortlake itself lingered on until 1703, when Queen Anne granted the use of the land 'for other purposes than tapestry weaving'.

Wardrobe was moved from Hatton Garden to Great Queen Street in 1685 and is then generally referred to as the Soho workshop.

[1] For Ovidian subjects woven at this time, see G. Wingfield Digby, 'Late Mortlake Tapestries', *Connoisseur*, cxxxiv (1954), 239.

VII

RESTORATION ARCHITECTURE AND THE GREAT FIRE

BETWEEN 1642 and 1660, little large-scale building had been undertaken. The Restoration, however, seemed to hold out hopes of renewed court patronage, and John Webb, the most experienced architect in England, not unjustifiably hoped that his opportunity had come at last. John Embree, the former Sergeant Plumber, who had held the Surveyorship since 1653, was tumbled out of office, and Webb was called upon to prepare Whitehall Palace for the reception of Charles II. He petitioned the King for the Surveyor's office saying that he had been trained by Inigo Jones, with the approval of Charles I, as his successor, and that he had acted as Deputy Surveyor during his uncle's lifetime.[1] His hopes, however, were to be disappointed. Charles II had contracted obligations during his years of exile, which he was prepared to fulfil even at the expense of his father's servants. He granted the Surveyorship to Sir John Denham and the Paymastership to Hugh May. Neither of these men had so far as is known had any experience in architecture. Denham was a poet of some accomplishment, who had lent the King money during his exile. He was never to produce architecture of any distinction (Burlington House, Piccadilly was perhaps his most important building), and he must have relied greatly on the technical knowledge of Webb, who worked as his assistant. Hugh May, whose cousin, Baptist May, was to become Keeper of the Privy Purse, had certainly been in touch with Royalist interests in Holland[2] and is on one occasion referred to as a servant of Sir Peter

---

[1] *Cal. S.P. Dom.* (1660–61), 76. For architecture after 1660, H. Colvin, *Dictionary of English Architects, 1660–1840* (1954) is indispensable.

[2] In 1650 or 1651 Sir Charles Cotterell, then steward to George, duke of Buckingham at Antwerp, met May in Holland, apparently in connexion with the sale of works of art from the duke's collection (T. Cottrell Dormer, 'Hugh May in Holland', *Country Life*, cviii (1950), 1198).

Lely when, in May 1656, a pass was granted for travel to Holland. Possibly he came into contact there with the exiled prince. He was later to prove himself an able architect, whose work must be discussed in some detail. It is not surprising that Webb resented these appointments. His training and experience had fitted him for the post (he was perhaps the first professionally trained architect in England) and his independent work of this decade suggests that he would have filled it well.

The building by which we can best judge the quality of John Webb's architecture is King Charles's Block at Greenwich (Pl. 32 b). The old Tudor palace had fallen into bad repair under the Commonwealth, and the Queen's House was presumably too small to house the court, but Charles liked the river. In October 1661 John Evelyn (who was very scornful of Denham's powers as an architect) discussed the placing of the new palace with the Surveyor,[1] and in March 1663/4 Pepys records that the foundations were laid.[2] The same authority tells us that it was still building in 1669.[3] Charles's palace was indeed never finished, and Webb's block was to remain a fragment until the end of the century, when it was incorporated in Wren's hospital.

Drawings, almost certainly by John Webb[4] (Fig. 4), show that the palace was to consist of two blocks on the east and west sides of an open court running down to the river, joined at the back of the court by a range of buildings with a dome in the centre which would have spoilt the view from the Queen's House. The plan may owe something to the traditional French château plan with a corps de logis at the end of a court. King Charles's Block (that on the

[1] Evelyn, *Diary*, 19 Oct. 1661.

[2] Pepys, *Diary*, 4 March 1663/4.

[3] Ibid., 16 March 1668/9. While the work was being done Webb increased the accommodation in the Queen's House by building two additional bridges over the road (each containing one good-sized room) and proposed four towers at the angles. The foundations of these were dug in 1662, but were filled in in 1669. A design for a house with four angle towers is among the drawings connected with Jones's projected architectural treatise, so Webb may have felt the towers would not be too serious a mutilation of the original.

[4] At All Souls College, Oxford. See *Wren Soc.* vi, Pl. xviii; ibid. viii, Pl. xx. There are also a number of drawings, including some for interior decoration, in the Burlington–Devonshire collection at the R.I.B.A., many of them titled and dated by Webb.

west side of the court[1] is grave and massive in design, and shows a very different style of architecture from Jones's Banqueting House. There each storey is sharply separated from the other, each has its own order, and the building owes much to its decoration. At Greenwich the storeys cannot be separated, for they are

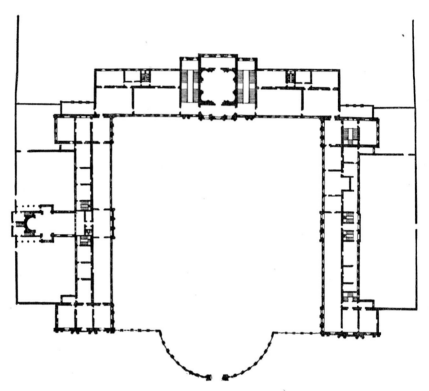

Fig. 4. *Greenwich Palace: plan by John Webb*

tied together at the centre and ends by a giant order. It is not now a case of single units added together; the unit of design has grown till it embraces the whole façade. The architect is no longer thinking in High Renaissance terms, but is producing instead a modified and very restrained form of baroque architecture. The building, except for the fine Corinthian capitals, is without

[1] Only the court side of the block remains as in Webb's time; the river front was doubled in the early eighteenth century.

decoration.[1] Its character is achieved by the fine balance between verticals and horizontals and by the carefully planned rustication of parts of the surface. As it stands today, the attics at either end appear a little heavy. Webb's elevation of the block planned across the end of the court, however, makes it clear that he introduced these attics to act as repoussoirs to the low semicircular dome which was to form an accent over the central entrance. There are still motives borrowed from Palladio; the general design of the end-pavilions with the giant order for instance bears some relation to his Palazzo Valmarana: but Palladio's flat pilasters are fattened into half-columns, and the overlapping and interlocking of orders, which gives a great feeling of tension to his façade, is omitted. The result is a solid, rather simple architecture, static in character, with no Mannerist tension, or baroque 'movement', but baroque in its feeling for size and mass. It is, however, entirely English in its long, low proportions; in Italy the height would have been greater compared with the length, and in France the end and probably the centre pavilions would have risen more sharply above the rest.

King Charles's Block is the only building from which we can judge the mature and independent style of John Webb. There is, however, ample evidence in the shape of drawings that he began to develop this manner as early as the late 1640's, when owing to ill health and adverse conditions Jones's energy was slackening. The design for Durham House,[2] dated 1649, has a giant order at the centre and ends of the long façade, though the handling of proportions and surface treatment is much less assured than in the later work at Greenwich.

This Durham House design is closely linked in style with some of the Whitehall Palace schemes. That the whole project for the latter was revived at the Restoration is certain, for the only dated drawing in the whole series (a small sketch plan showing the lay-out, with an elevation of the entrance below it[3]) is inscribed by

---

[1] Webb's drawing of the centrepiece (Burlington–Devonshire collection, R.I.B.A.) shows, however, a cartouche flanked by two reclining figures in the pediment which is surmounted by three statues breaking the sky-line.

[2] Worcester College collection, i. 21. Probably made for the earl of Pembroke, who had been granted possession of Durham House by Bishop Morton (*Corres. of John Cosin, D.D.*, ii, Surtees Soc. lv (1870), 148).   [3] At Chatsworth.

Webb '17th Oct. 1661'. It also seems likely that Webb submitted to Charles II designs which he had discussed with Charles I during his captivity, probably the two large and elaborate plans and an elevation signed by Webb and inscribed *The pallace of King Charles ye First, taken*.[1] This extravagant scheme, in which the Banqueting House is uncomfortably included in a front which has a giant order at centre and ends, was obviously too costly to interest Charles II, but one further scheme for a much smaller palace was probably produced for him.[2] This project, for which there is a plan and several alternative elevations, shows a building of the same type as Webb's plan for Greenwich—two long blocks on either side of a court open to the river. At the farther end the range of buildings was to include the Banqueting House, and a repetition of it (probably to be fitted up as a chapel) with a portico between, while behind were to be two small square enclosed courts divided by a block of buildings running back to the west range on the park front which contained the royal apartments.

The change of plan from the closed rectangle to the open court is interesting and significant. There is now one façade—that at the back of the court—on which attention is focused; the evenly diffused interest of Jones's designs is replaced by a new, more dramatic and more baroque emphasis. One of the alternative elevations,[3] indeed, is surprisingly baroque, for there the whole central feature of the main front is planned on a concave curve. Giant half-columns are ranged round it, and the two ends of the curve are marked by turrets with cupolas. The architecture is clumsy (none of the alternatives is in fact very happy) but they, with other designs under discussion, form an interesting and not unimportant chapter in seventeenth-century architecture. They show that John Webb, trained by Jones to appreciate the architecture of the Ancients, and its use by Italian sixteenth-century masters, was late in life moving towards a freer use of architectural forms. There is no evidence that he travelled, but he may well

[1] For a detailed discussion see M. D. Whinney, *Walpole Soc.*, xxxi (1943), 45 f.

[2] This may be the plan which the King showed Evelyn on 27 Oct. 1664 (*Diary*).

[3] Chatsworh, 62. For a further discussion of its significance see G. Webb, 'Baroque Art', *Proc. Brit. Acad.* xxxii (1947).

have heard accounts or even seen drawings of the baroque experiments in Rome,[1] and so been aware that his master's formulae were outdated. He had not, however, sufficient imagination, or sufficient opportunity, to create a lasting English baroque architecture, perhaps because he could never entirely rid himself of his Palladian upbringing. It needed the very different approach of Wren before a living English baroque could be evolved. Webb was not a fortunate architect, for during the years of his early maturity before the Civil War he was overshadowed by Jones. In the long troubled period from 1642 to 1660 he carried out a limited amount of domestic work, though it is difficult to get a clear picture of his style. Expediency prevented him from obtaining his rightful position at the Restoration, and when Denham died in 1668, his claims were once more disregarded, and the Surveyorship given to Wren, who had as yet hardly proved himself as an architect. Webb's reply to the reception of his last petition is pathetic but dignified: he offers to serve jointly with Wren, but not as his Assistant, and he reminds the King of his past promises. But his request was unheeded, and he retired to the country, dying in 1672.[2] His work, however, was not without influence. Half a century later Hawksmoor and Vanbrugh turned from the serenity of Wren's architecture and found the brooding mass of King Charles's Block more to their liking. St. Alphege, Greenwich, and even the south front of Blenheim are closer in spirit to Webb than they are to Wren.

The other architect still working in the 1660's who had grown up in Jones's lifetime was Sir Roger Pratt. He had held no public office, having been out of England until 1649. During the

[1] It is possible that he knew Falda's *Chiese di Roma*, which was first published in 1655.

[2] The only other important building carried out by Webb after the Restoration was the new Gallery at Somerset House for the Queen Mother (*Vitruvius Britannicus*, i (1715), 16). This has recently been dated *c.* 1635 by J. Lees-Milne (*The Age of Inigo Jones* (1954), 89), who quotes no documents. Much work was carried out at Somerset House about that time, but there are no payments for masonry, and topographical paintings by C. Bol (at Dulwich: see below, p. 263) of *c.* 1660 do not show the building. It may, however, have been based on a design by Jones, for a similar elevation appears on one of the sheets of Whitehall drawings of *c.* 1638. It was to be extremely influential in the eighteenth century.

Commonwealth period he lived as a private gentleman,[1] constantly advising his cousin, Sir George Pratt, over the building of Coleshill,[2] and he was also engaged in collecting a remarkable architectural library.[3] Pratt studied his books with care, weighing what he found there against his own shrewd comments on the buildings he had seen in his travels.[4] Some of his conclusions, which he set down in his notebooks, are dated 1660, and it seems likely that by this time at least he was putting together notes for a treatise. This was never finally formulated, but it would probably have concerned itself chiefly with domestic building of all kinds. Thus it would have been linked with such seventeenth-century books as Rubens's *Palazzi di Genova* (to which frequent reference is made) or Le Muet's publications, and would not have been, like Jones's projected treatise, based on a sixteenth-century Italian model. The change of character is revealing. Pratt's work would not have been directed towards patrons of great public buildings, but to the class to which he himself belonged, and whose way of life he understood, namely the squirearchy. These were the men who held the real power in the Restoration Parliament, and it was surely to them that Pratt offered advice when he noted in July 1660,

First resolve with yourself what house will be answerable to your purse and estate, and after you have pitched upon the number of the rooms and the dimensions of each, and desire in some measure to make use of whatsoever you have either observed, or heard to be excellent elsewhere, then if you be not able to handsomely contrive it yourself, get some ingenious gentleman who has seen much of that kind abroad and been somewhat versed in the best authors of Architecture: viz Palladio, Scamozzi, Serlio etc. to do it for you, and to give you a design of it in paper . . .[5]

[1] *The Architecture of Sir Roger Pratt*, ed. R. T. Gunther (1928), 3.

[2] See above, p. 46.

[3] *The Architecture of Sir Roger Pratt* (1928), 7, 302. The list is of interest, for in addition to the standard sixteenth-century architectural books, it includes contemporary works such as Falda's *Palazzi di Roma*, Jacob van Campen's *Stadthuys van Amsterdam*, and Le Muet's *Traicté des cinq ordres d'Architecture*. It would seem that Pratt's taste was more catholic than that of Inigo Jones, and that he was less obsessed by the Ancients.

[4] Ibid. 289–300. The arrangement of Pratt's notebooks is somewhat arbitrary and many interesting references to foreign buildings will be found elsewhere in the book.

[5] Ibid. 60.

Though one can hardly doubt which 'ingenious gentleman' the author had in mind, the reference to the amateur designer is interesting.[1] Pratt proceeds to give him many useful hints about materials, the placing of the kitchen 'so that you shall not be disturbed with the least noise or smell from thence, but yet not so far off as that your meat will be cold in bringing from it or your servants not presently at hand upon the least ringing or call . . .',[2] upon the placing of beds so that they are out of a draught, upon proper ornaments for chimneys and ceilings (here he quotes examples from the work of Jones), and upon endless other matters, combining scholarly with practical advice and great common sense.

Even though his book was never completed Pratt found clients among the men to whom it would have appealed. Coleshill was probably finished about 1662, and within two years[3] the architect was superintending the work for Sir Ralph Bankes at Kingston Lacy in Dorset. This house, which was much altered by Sir Charles Barry in 1834, is of the Coleshill type, depending for its effect mainly on the proportion of roof to wall, and on the grouping of its windows. At about the same time (1663–5) he was building Horseheath, near Cambridge, for Lord Allington, which was destroyed in 1777.[4]

Pratt's most important house, and probably his most influential, was Clarendon House, Piccadilly,[5] built between 1664 and 1667 for Edward Hyde, earl of Clarendon (Pl. 33 a). The patron was perhaps the greatest man in England, but he had sprung from the same class as Pratt himself, and preferred him to Denham or Hugh May.[6] After Clarendon's fall the house was sold, in 1675, to the

[1] Some knowledge of architecture was then part of the normal education of a gentleman (cf. above, p. 52). When Webb petitioned the King for the Surveyorship (see above, p. 132) he argued that 'though Mr. Denham may, as most gentry have some knowledge of the theory of architecture, he can have none of the practice', whereas he himself had had thirty years' experience.

[2] *The Architecture of Sir Roger Pratt* (1928), 63.   [3] Ibid. 98.

[4] *Vitruvius Britannicus*, iii. 91, 92.

[5] *The Architecture of Sir Roger Pratt* (1928), 133; C. L. Kingsford, *Early History of Piccadilly* (1925), 106.

[6] One of the carver's bills is, however, certified by Hugh May (*The Architecture of Sir Roger Pratt* (1928), 157), who seems to have been specially interested in interior decoration (see below, p. 207).

2nd duke of Albemarle, who again sold it in 1683, when it was demolished to pay his debts.[1] The engraving shows, however, that even for a town house of importance Pratt made no attempt to design an elaborate façade adorned with orders. The building was composed of three blocks round a forecourt, but the exterior is still the Coleshill type, though with a pediment, as at Horseheath, in the centre of the main block above the entrance. The top of the pitched roof is again flattened and surrounded by a balustrade, making a platform from which a 'noble prospect' could be seen.[2] The accounts[3] suggest that the interior was panelled throughout in wood, but that there were no elaborate painted decorations. It is, indeed, at first sight a little difficult to understand how a house so unpretentious by continental standards should have fostered, on the one hand, the intense hatred of the people (who believed it had been built with the money the state received from the sale of Dunkirk to the French) and on the other hand, the eulogies of Pepys[4] and also of Evelyn,[5] who once declared it to be 'without hyperbole the best contrived, most useful, graceful and magnificent house in England'. It must, however, be remembered that even in 1663, great town houses in the modern manner were practically non-existent.

In 1667 Roger Pratt succeeded to the family estates at Ryston in Norfolk, and in 1669 rebuilt his own house;[6] thereafter, until his death in 1684, he devoted most of his time to the management of his estates. But he naturally did not abandon completely his interest in architecture. He had, in the mid-1660's, been consulted about St. Paul's Cathedral,[7] and was in 1672 to put on paper his views concerning Jones's alterations to the old cathedral,[8] and his objections to Wren's first model.[9] Perhaps at the same time he

[1] For the subsequent speculative building on the site see B. Johnson, *Berkeley Square to Bond Street* (1952), and C. L. Kingsford, loc. cit. 108.

[2] Pepys, *Diary*, 4 Feb. 1666.

[3] *The Architecture of Sir Roger Pratt* (1928), 157 f.

[4] *Diary*, 31 Jan. 1666; 14 Feb. 1666; 9 May 1667.

[5] Evelyn, *Diary*, 28 Nov. 1666; 18 Sept. 1683 (see also his letter to Lord Cornbury (*Diary and Correspondence*, ed. Bray, 1852, iii. 177)).

[6] For the accounts and illustrations, see *The Architecture of Sir Roger Pratt* (1928), ch. xii.   [7] See below, p. 148.

[8] *The Architecture of Sir Roger Pratt* (1928), 198.   [9] Ibid. 213; and see below, p. 164.

added the long passages in his notebooks about the continental churches he had seen, passages which reveal, perhaps more clearly than any other of his writings, the hard and careful work of his years of study abroad and the good sense of his judgements.

Webb and Pratt, though both only middle-aged in 1660 (Webb was born in 1618 and Pratt in 1620) were nevertheless representatives of the older generation, and as is usually the case with men who have had the misfortune to live through great social and political upheavals, their lost experience in what should have been their most active years caused them to drift to one side of the main stream of development. The 1660's (and indeed most of the 1670's as well) were to be a time when the new men were to emerge, learning their art while practising it, maturing rather slowly and hampered partly by their own lack of experience and partly no doubt by the lack of skilled craftsmen. The men trained by Jones before the Civil War were dying out, and the generation that had grown up after them had had few demands made on them. There were notable exceptions, but the clumsiness of much of the work of this period, for example the exterior detail of the City churches of the seventies, suggests that the general standard was low.

The pause in the development of English architecture is not, however, due only to lack of experience in architects and craftsmen. It is partly the result of a shift of intellectual interests. In the first half of the century men had turned to Italy and to the Ancients when they endeavoured to shake off the last links with the middle ages. Milton's *L'Allegro* and *Il Penseroso* show this no less surely than Arundel's marbles or Jones's Banqueting House. But after 1660 a newer learning replaced the belated Humanism of the Caroline court. On 13 August 1662[1] the Royal Society held its first meeting under its Charter and the scientific and mathematical enterprise which had impressed Evelyn so greatly at Oxford in the mid-1650's was thus publicly acknowledged.

And further, though the prestige of Italy as the fountain-head of the arts was never completely overthrown (Vitruvius, Serlio, and Palladio were still studied as the grammar of architecture), other influences contributed to the development of a new movement.

[1] Evelyn, *Diary*.

Charles II and his court had no especial interest in Italy but they had had first-hand experience of both France and Holland. Wren visited Paris on his only journey to the Continent, and Dr. Robert Hooke (1635–1702) bought French and Dutch as well as Italian books on architecture, and was keenly interested in descriptions of Dutch buildings.[1] Hugh May had been in Holland, and his visit had a marked effect on English architecture. In Holland the 1640's had seen a transformation of Dutch architecture from the exuberant, profusely decorated style of the Dutch Renaissance[2] to a more classical manner. The Mauritshuis in The Hague, built by Pieter Post between 1639 and 1645, is the most familiar example of the new style, and it must certainly have been seen by many English refugees before the Restoration. Its combination of brick and stone— giant stone pilasters and stone dressings on a brick ground—with widely projecting eaves, reappears in England in two of May's early buildings, Eltham Lodge (1664) (Pl. 33 *b*)[3] and Cassiobury Park, Hertfordshire (probably *c.* 1675).[4] The wing which he added for Lord Clarendon at Cornbury, Oxfordshire,[5] is in stone, since it is in the heart of a good stone-producing district, but the style is, in general, the same. The projection of pilasters and mouldings from the wall face is curiously low, the whole effect of the façade being flatter than is usual in stone building.

Eltham Lodge, built for a rich vintner, Sir John Shaw, is a modest long rectangular house, showing several new features. Brick houses before the Restoration tended, generally speaking, to

[1] *Diary of Dr. Robert Hooke*, ed. H. W. Robinson and W. Adams (1935), only covers the years 1672 to 1680. It contains numberless references to the purchase of books and prints, a fact of major importance when one remembers Wren's intimacy with him. A drawing perhaps by Hooke (B.M. Add. MSS. 5238) appears to be of the Nieuwekerk at The Hague, so he may have visited Holland. See also M. I. Batten, 'The Architecture of Dr. Robert Hooke', *Walpole Soc.* xxv (1937), 83. For a discussion of Hooke's work, see below, pp. 152, 206.

[2] The Vleischmarkt at Haarlem, and the original façade of the Town Hall at Leiden (extended in the nineteenth century), both by Lieven de Key, are typical examples of the style.

[3] H. A. Tipping, *English Homes*, IV. i. 93.

[4] Cassiobury Park was pulled down early in this century. Before that it had been greatly altered by James Wyatt. W. Kip, *Britannia Illustrata* (1709), 28, shows May's house. See also Evelyn, *Diary*, 18 April 1680.

[5] *Country Life*, cviii (1950), 922.

have stone quoins at the angles, as at the original Chevening,[1] or else to imitate such quoins in brickwork.[2] In other words, the Italian emphasis on a firm angle treatment, accentuating the block of the house, is carried over from stone houses like Coleshill, into the very different material. At Eltham, May follows Dutch practice. He does not emphasize his angles by any break in the even surface of his brickwork; on the side fronts there is a slightly projecting but unbroken strip at either end, and on the side and garden fronts there are blind windows recessed, but unframed, in the brick wall.[3] Stone is reserved for the giant order on the main front, with its entablature which runs all round the house, the string course above the basement and the carved shield and festoons in the pediment. It is a new combination of the two materials, in which greater emphasis is laid on large expanses of brick. Its characteristics, with some modifications, reappear in many medium-sized houses throughout the country, houses which are popularly described as 'Wren' houses. Very few indeed of them have any connexion with Wren, who had little time for domestic work, and it seems nearly certain that the type was, in fact, created by May.

It is only within the last twenty years that the work of Webb and Pratt, May and Hooke has received any attention. Until then the seventeenth century was regarded as the age of two architects only, Jones and Wren. That is far from the truth, for both May and Hooke contributed greatly to the development of the late seventeenth-century style. Wren, however, with his surpassing ability as an engineer, and with the great range and flexibility of his mind, must always dominate the period. Born in 1632, in an age still linked with that of Shakespeare (for Ben Jonson lived till 1637), he was to survive to see the age of Sir Robert Walpole, and to die in 1723, the year in which Reynolds was born. Few other prominent men of his generation enjoyed so unbroken a career, or weathered so serenely the storms of public life. But in spite of the fact that he

[1] See above, p. 46, and Pl. 6 a.
[2] e.g. Tyttenhanger, Herts., probably of the 1650's (H. A. Tipping, *English Homes*, IV. i. 63).
[3] Such blind windows are common in Holland, e.g. the Gravensteen at Leiden.

held office under the Crown for forty-five years, and was three times for brief periods (in 1685, 1689, and 1690) a member of Parliament, he can have been in no sense a partisan. His interests lay outside politics, in science, engineering, and architecture; his intimates were his fellow members of the Royal Society, and being, if we may judge from his portraits, an urbane, humorous, and tolerant man, he was willing to adjust himself to circumstances, and serve whatever king held the throne.

His family life[1] may well have warned him against partisanship. His father, dean of Windsor, was imprisoned for his adherence to Charles I, and so was his uncle, Matthew Wren, the Laudian Bishop of Ely. From boyhood he showed a remarkable aptitude for mathematics and scientific invention, and after he went to Oxford (where he was admitted as a Gentleman Commoner of Wadham College in 1646) he enjoyed the teaching of two of the greatest mathematicians of the time, Dr. John Wilkins, then Warden of Wadham, and Dr. Seth Ward, the Savilian Professor of Astronomy. In 1653 he became a Fellow of All Souls, and in the next year John Evelyn, who visited Dr. Wilkins, speaks of 'that miracle of a youth, Mr. Christopher Wren'.[2] By 1657, that is when he was twenty-four, he was appointed to the Chair of Astronomy at Gresham College, London, and in 1661 he became Savilian Professor of Astronomy at Oxford. He was one of the original members of the Royal Society, and in 1680 was to be its President. His services to science were by no means negligible. Like most seventeenth-century scientists, he was interested in the empirical rather than the theoretical aspects of his subject. He was concerned with furthering methods of gauging atmospheric pressure (in which he was associated with the great Robert Boyle),

[1] The best source for Wren's life and work is *Parentalia*, i.e. the lives of Sir Christopher and Bishop Matthew Wren, published in 1750 (reprinted 1903) by Sir Christopher's grandson Stephen, but mainly compiled by his son Christopher (who had worked with him) partly about 1728 and partly about 1735. It also contains certain papers written by Sir Christopher. Letters, contracts, accounts, and other relevant documents have been published, with a vast quantity of drawings, in the twenty volumes of the *Wren Society*, which are indispensable for any study of his work. The best modern biographies are by G. F. Webb (1937) and J. Summerson (1953). See also H. Colvin, *Dictionary*, 699.   [2] *Diary*, 11 and 13 July 1654.

of taking observations at sea, of injections into the blood stream and with other investigations in the fields of physics and pure mathematics. At the command of Charles II (who was deeply interested in the proceedings of the Royal Society), he made a model of the moon which stood in the King's Closet—but asked to be excused the further command of 'delineating with the help of the microscope the Figures of all the Insects and small living Creatures you can light on'.[1]

This background of science, which was to be constant throughout Wren's life (though naturally as his other activities increased he could give less time to practical inventions), is vital for the understanding of his architecture. It developed his interest in experiment, in solving a given problem, often in a number of different ways. It gave him a flexibility of mind, so that, when one solution proved unsatisfactory, he could adjust himself, and start from a different angle. And above all, it encouraged his genius for applied mathematics, enabling him to grasp and control the complex questions of engineering which were to face him later in his career.

His earliest important building, the Sheldonian Theatre at Oxford (Pls. 32 *a*, 44 *b*), was to display this scientific bias. Before it was begun (the foundations were laid in 1664 and the building not finished until 1669) he had probably undertaken a commission for his uncle Matthew, who gave a new chapel to Pembroke College, Cambridge. It had offered no particular problems, since it is a comparatively small single-span building. The Sheldonian, for his own University, was a far greater challenge, since it entailed the covering of an exceptionally wide space. The plan of the building is that of a Roman theatre, probably taken from Serlio's plate of the Temple of Marcellus; but Serlio could give him no help with the roof, since Roman theatres were open to the sky, though covered by a velarium. It was essential that the floor space should not be encumbered with supports, but the span of seventy feet was wider than the length of any available timber. Wren therefore

---

[1] It was presumably his reputation as a mathematician that brought him an offer before 1663 of directing fortifications and harbour works at Tangier. For his scientific achievements see J. Summerson, *Wren* (1953), chapter 2.

applied to his ceiling an invention of his former Professor of Geometry, Dr. John Wallis, known as the 'Geometrical Flat Floor', and so achieved his purpose.[1] The Sheldonian was greatly admired by Wren's contemporaries: Evelyn, who was present at the opening ceremony, thought it 'a fabric comparable to any of this kind of former ages, and doubtless exceeding any of the present,'[2] and to the end of Wren's life it was regarded as one of his major buildings. It was certainly its scientific virtuosity which gave it its great reputation. The spacious interior has, it is true, a noble dignity, but the exterior, especially the flat south front, is extremely immature. The proportion of the storeys and the management of the windows is not very happy, and Wren had clearly turned to pattern books for most of his detail.[3] One has only to compare this building with Webb's contemporary work at Greenwich to see how little the young scientist yet knew about the handling of architecture. He was, however, quickly gaining a reputation, for by 1665, Evelyn, sending him a copy of his translation of Fréart's *Parallel*, referred to it as 'less a thing in the least assistant to you (who are yourself a master) but as a token of my respect, as the book itself is of the affection I bear to an art which you so happily cultivate'.[4]

In that same year Wren was greatly to enlarge his knowledge, for he paid his only known visit to the Continent, spending some months in Paris. His visit coincided with that of the greatest architect of the century, Bernini, who was producing designs for the east front of the Louvre. Wren, in the one highly interesting letter which has survived,[5] tells how he saw Bernini's drawings, though the 'old reserv'd Italian' would only give him a 'few minutes view'. He describes vividly the buildings he had seen: Versailles, where the 'mixtures of Brick, Stone, blue Tile and Gold make it look like a rich Livery'; the College of the Four Nations (now the Institut de France) where he criticized Le Vau for showing off his

[1] A diagram showing the method used is set out in *Parentalia*.

[2] *Diary*, 9 July 1669. For the painting of the ceiling, see below, p. 292.

[3] For the south front cf. Serlio (1619 ed.), bk. iv, 177.

[4] Letter dated 4 April 1665, Evelyn, *Diary and Correspondence*, ed. Bray (1852), iii. 154.

[5] *Parentalia* (1750), 261, and *Wren Soc.* xiii. 40.

dexterity in dealing with an awkward site. Above all, he was impressed with the organization of the building of the Louvre and with Colbert's personal care of the work, also with the richness and splendour of the 'glorious Appartement of the Queen Mother at the Louvre, which I saw many times'. These rooms of Anne of Austria (the decoration of which can still be partly seen above the classical sculpture shown there) had been decorated by Italians. To Wren their style of high relief stucco seemed infinitely preferable to the French work at Versailles, which he thought 'crowded, with little curiosities of ornament'.[1] It is indeed in his criticism of the Versailles decoration that he makes one of his rare generalizations about architecture (he was far more a practical than a theoretical architect): 'works of Filgrand and little Knacks are in great vogue, but Building certainly ought to have the Attribute of eternal, and therefore the only thing incapable of new Fashions'. This, like Jones's 'solid, proportionable according to the rules, masculine and unaffected,' has a true English ring. At no time in the history of English architecture has sheer virtuosity, as seen in the French Flamboyant style, the work of Borromini, or German rococo, dominated. The sobriety and serenity of Perpendicular, the solid weight of the architecture of Vanbrugh and Hawksmoor, even the decoration of Robert Adam with its stiffening of rococo grace, all bear witness to the continuance of this tradition. Wren's own work, baroque in its freedom of experiment, its frank adoption of devices which mask, for reasons of effect, the construction of the building, its employment of dramatic accents, has a reticence, a modesty in its treatment of surface and of line, which renders it English. It has neither the brilliance nor the richness of Roman seventeenth-century architecture and it lacks the clear logic, the intellectual discipline of the best work of seventeenth-century France. It owes its character partly to the abiding English reserve, partly to the scientific bent of its creator, but largely also to the fact that architecture was a far more isolated art in England than on the Continent. For reasons discussed elsewhere, English sculpture in the seventeenth century lacked vitality; and painting early in Wren's career was practically confined to portraiture. In both

[1] The work Wren could have seen no longer exists.

Italy and France architects either practised more than one art, or were in the closest touch with a brilliant team of collaborators. Wren lacked this support, and though by the nineties he had trained an able group of decorative craftsmen they were subordinate craftsmen only, and not fellow artists who could provide a stimulus for him. He never, throughout his career, worked with another artist who was anywhere near his intellectual equal, and until he came into contact with Vanbrugh, late in his life, he scarcely met one (except during his French journey) with any imaginative force.

From the time of Wren's return from Paris in the spring of 1666 he was, in spite of his duties at Oxford, to give more and more of his time to architecture. One of his first tasks was to present his proposals for dealing with St. Paul's. Inigo Jones had left the work of repair only partly done, and by the early 1660's the condition of the central tower had become dangerous. A Commission had been set up in 1663, of which Wren was not an original member, but with which he was soon associated.[1] The older men on the Commission, Denham, Webb, and Pratt, were in favour of patching up the old building, but Wren and Evelyn felt the only safe solution was to take down the centre part entirely. Wren's report[2] is full of interest for its estimate of the aesthetic qualities of the medieval buildings, its practical suggestions for overcoming the problems of erection of new work, and above all for the two major ideas in the new design. From his very first association with St. Paul's Wren ardently desired two things. First, a great open space at the crossing (to be achieved by the destruction of the end piers of both nave and choir arcades),[3] and the covering of that space with a feature of sufficient height to be a landmark comparable to 'Old Paul's Steeple', though a 'cupolo' would have 'incomparable more grace in the remote aspect than it is possible for the lean shaft of a steeple to afford'.

Arguments among the Commissioners went on until 27 August 1666.[4] Less than a week later they were rendered useless, for on the

---

[1] *Wren Soc.* xiii. 40.   [2] Ibid. 15.
[3] The effect would have been similar to the crossing of Ely cathedral, which must have been known to Wren, since his uncle was Bishop.   [4] Evelyn, *Diary*.

night of 2 September the Great Fire broke out, and on the 4th Evelyn reported 'the stones of Paul's flew like grenadoes, and the melting lead running down the streets in a stream'.[1]

After the Fire the cathedral was no longer the first consideration. About seven-eighths of the City had been destroyed, only a small area to the east being left. Moreover, the Fire had spread westwards beyond the City walls, reaching along Fleet Street to the Temple. The King immediately appointed a commission to deal with the problem of rebuilding. His nominees were Hugh May, the Paymaster (Sir John Denham, the Surveyor, was losing his reason), Sir Roger Pratt, and Dr. Wren. The City delegates were Peter Mills, who was the City Surveyor, Dr. Robert Hooke, Professor of Mathematics at Gresham College, and Edward Jarman, 'an experienced man in buildings'.[2] Even before the Commissioners met both Wren and Evelyn had submitted plans to the King.[3] Both have been preserved, but plans made by Hooke and Mills are lost. In spite of Evelyn's complacency there is no doubt that Wren's plan (Fig. 5) is by far the best of them. Streets of three widths were proposed (the widest being 90 feet). A civic centre was planned, with the Exchange on an island site in the middle of an oval space round which were to be placed the Mint, the Post Office, the Excise Office, 'Ensurances', and two sites for the Goldsmiths. From this streets were to radiate (linked by narrower streets), while St. Paul's formed a second focal point where two great streets converged. There were also to be other centres of less importance. The basic layout is not unique. Town-planning was a widespread interest in the seventeenth century, and the scheme of radiating streets linked by lesser streets was familiar enough from the time of Henri IV onwards. Wren, however, shows considerable ingenuity in his placing of public buildings and churches so that, while they occupy important sites, and often close a vista,

[1] Ibid.

[2] *The Architecture of Sir Roger Pratt* (1928), p. 12. His name also appears as Jerman or Germain.

[3] *Diary*, 13 Sept. 1666, and letter to Sir Samuel Tuke, *Diary and Correspondence*, ed. Bray (1852), iii. 187. Wren's and Evelyn's plans are illustrated in *Sir Christopher Wren Bi-centenary Memorial Volume* (1932), 164, 168. The article on them has some stimulating criticisms, but contains factual errors.

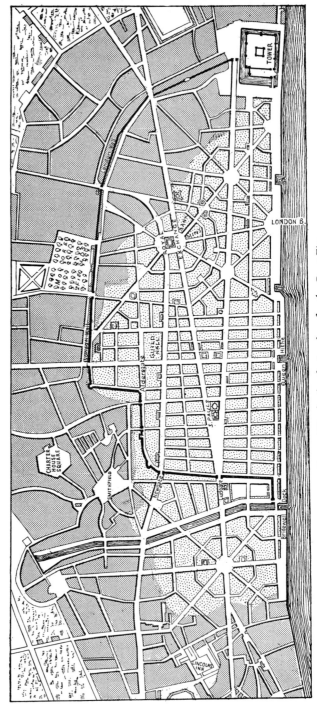

FIG. 5. *Wren's plan for London after the Great Fire*

they do not obstruct the highways. Evelyn's plan is of the same type, but much less skilful, and Hooke apparently used the 'grid-iron' type,[1] making no use of radiating streets, and showing no interest in vistas.

In spite of its great qualities, Wren's plan was, however, a somewhat Utopian scheme. The initial survey of the ruins had to be abandoned. Requisitioning of sites resulting from the new plan would have been costly, and rebuilding on schematized instead of individual designs would have been slow. The idea of a complete new layout was therefore abandoned; the citizens of London were not prevented from building up their own houses on the old sites, where foundations and cellars often remained, though steps were taken to regulate the type of building, so that the danger of fire should be lessened. By the Act for the Rebuilding of the City of London of 1667 timber houses and projecting upper storeys were forbidden, and therefore sober façades mainly of flat brick of the type introduced in the 1630's in the Covent Garden area replaced the picturesque, dangerous and insanitary medieval buildings. A standard of height was also set, four storeys for the most important streets, three for lesser streets, and two for 'by-lanes'.[2]

The cost of domestic rebuilding fell on the owners, and the speed with which it was done is a sure indication of the wealth and vitality of the trading community. Both Evelyn[3] and Sir John Reresby[4] comment on the great progress made in three or four years. This is the more remarkable in view of the almost complete cessation of building in the winter months, a practice which was general in the seventeenth century, and which can be clearly traced in, for instance, the building accounts of St. Paul's.[5]

For public buildings, however, public money was found. The Corporation and the City Companies were responsible for the

---

[1] M. I. Batten, 'The Architecture of Dr. Robert Hooke', *Walpole Soc.* xxv (1937), 86.

[2] For fuller treatment of this subject see T. F. Reddaway, *The Rebuilding of London* (1940). An excellent summary of the main points will be found in J. Summerson, *Georgian London* (1945), chapter iv.   [3] *Diary*, 17 Aug. 1669.

[4] *Memoirs of Sir John Reresby* (ed. A. Browning, 1936), 84.

[5] Hooke refers to this in a letter to Lord Conway (see M. I. Batten, loc. cit. 102) of 1680, in which he says he has three times had experience of work that had to be taken down because it was damaged by frost.

civic buildings; the churches were paid for by Parliament by means of a tax imposed on 'sea-coal', i.e. coal brought into the Port of London by sea. This division of responsibility is of some importance for its results in architecture. The City buildings, the Exchange, and the halls of the City Companies, were designed by City craftsmen. The churches, on which work began in 1670, were designed by Wren, whose profession as architect rather than scientist had been finally established by his appointment as Surveyor General in 1669.[1] Dr. Robert Hooke forms a link between the two groups. As has been said, he was one of the City's delegates on the Commission immediately after the Fire. He was to build Bedlam Hospital and the College of Physicians, both public buildings, and to undertake much surveying for the City Corporation. On the other hand, he and Wren had been friends since the inception of the Royal Society, and this friendship was to develop into a virtual partnership in the work on the City Churches.[2]

The civic buildings are very revealing, for they show how narrow had been the influence of the Italianism of Inigo Jones. The Royal Exchange (Pl. 44 a), the commercial centre of London, was designed by Edward Jarman, the City Surveyor.[3] With him was associated Peter Mills, then Clerk of the Works to the City Corporation. The new building followed the same pattern as Gresham's old Exchange, being set round an arcaded court, with further arcades forming the ground storey all round the exterior. In the court, above the slender Doric columns, was a blind wall with niches for statues of the kings and queens of England.[4] The proportions and handling of the order suggest a use of some late sixteenth-century Flemish pattern-book, such as that of Vredeman de Vries, while the open walk is covered by cross vaulting on ribs which must surely be a survival of the medieval tradition. Outside,

[1] He was knighted in 1673.

[2] *Parentalia*, 263, states that immediately after the Fire Wren 'took to his assistance his ingenious and able associate Robert Hooke'.

[3] Jarman was dead by January 1668/9 when John Oliver was sworn as Surveyor in his place (T. F. Reddaway, *The Rebuilding of London* (1940), 108, 266–9). The work on the Exchange was carried on after November 1668 by Thomas Cartwright, with advice from Wren and Hooke (*Wren Soc.* xi. 63). Jarman's Exchange was burnt in 1838.   [4] For these, see below, pp. 239, 247, 251, 254.

the main elevation, with its Ionic order and crowning balustrade, appears to owe a little to Jones's Banqueting House but the ambitious centrepiece, modelled on a triumphal arch motive, is extremely maladroit, for the two pediments create two centres of interest, and tear the composition apart.[1] The tower above it again suggests links with the Low Countries, for it is most closely paralleled by the churches of Hendrick de Keyser in Amsterdam. Indeed, the Exchange (which is, after all, only a year or two later than Webb's King Charles's Block at Greenwich) shows the great gulf between the taste and knowledge of city and court patrons and artists.

Jarman was also engaged by the richest of the City Companies—the Mercers', the Drapers', the Goldsmiths', and the Fishmongers'—to design their new Halls.[2] The Cheapside front of the Mercers' building, like the Exchange, combined a mixture of ill-assorted Italian and Flemish motives with an overloaded entrance based, probably, on a Serlio model but so confused with brackets, niches, and grotesquely large putti, as to be almost unrecognizable. He seems to have been happier in less opulent buildings, such as the Goldsmiths' and Fishmongers' Halls, where he could use the more modest combination of brick and stone. In spite of rather uneasy proportions they have an agreeable, almost vernacular quality (though there seems a faint echo of Holland) which suggests that Jarman was working in a medium he understood.

The less wealthy Companies could clearly not afford the services of the City Surveyor; some indeed could not rebuild for some years. The great majority, however, had rebuilt their Halls by the beginning of the 1670's.[3] The new buildings generally included a

[1] A similar disorganization appears in some of the City Church reredoses.

[2] Good brief accounts of these will be found in *The Builder* as follows: cx (1910), 251 (Mercers'), 353 (Drapers'), 422 (Goldsmiths'); cxix (1920), 666 (Fishmongers'). Individual histories of the Companies quoted in T. F. Reddaway, op. cit., may also be consulted. Most of them had been rebuilt or refronted before the Second World War.

[3] Some Companies employed a surveyor; i.e. John Oliver designed the Skinners' Hall, and the Brewers had a draught made by a Mr. Whiting which was carried out by Capt. Caine, who himself made a model which he executed for the Tallow Chandlers' Company. The Apothecaries used a design by Mr. Edward Cooke. In other cases a bricklayer seems to have been responsible. For further discussion of City building, see Summerson, 125–8.

Court Room and a Drawing Room as well as the Hall itself, all of them with fine woodwork and rich ceilings. The fittings in the Brewers', the Merchant Taylors'[1] and the Vintners' were among the finest, and the loss of much of this work during the Second World War is a disaster second only to the loss of Wren's churches.

The City Churches[2] are vital for the understanding of Wren's character as an architect. They are not only of great intrinsic interest; they were also of major importance in his career, for in this great flood of invention, falling mainly between 1670 and 1686, he gained practical experience of immense value.[3] The problems he faced were not inconsiderable, but they were relatively limited. The stature of their architect can, however, be seen in the many different solutions he found. The major determining factors were the requirements of the worshippers, the necessity for quick and relatively cheap building, and the restricted and often irregular sites. These churches were to be created for Protestant use (not adapted to it, like the many cruciform village churches).[4] Fortunately, we know how Wren regarded the matter, for when in 1711 further churches were needed east and west of the City, he drew up a statement for the Commissioners.[5] From this it is clear that to him 'a convenient auditory' in which 'everyone should hear the Service and both hear and see the Preacher' was the major requirement. The altar was not, as in the Counter-Reformation churches of the Continent, the chief focal point of the whole design, emphasized by plan, decoration, and lighting. It must, of

[1] Designed by Dr. Robert Hooke (M. I. Batten, 'The Architecture of Dr. Robert Hooke', *Walpole Soc.* xxv. (1937), 90 and Pl. xxxvi).

[2] Vols. ix and x of the Wren Society are devoted to the City churches and contain much documentary material (including the accounts of some printed in full), original drawings, and a fine set of measured drawings made in the early nineteenth century. R.C.H.M., *London*, ii, *The City*, is the best source for the state of those surviving in 1929. G. Cobb, *The Old Churches of London* (1942), with a brilliant introduction by G. F. Webb, contains much useful information and particulars of those destroyed in 1941.

[3] Since all the churches were being built together, no chronological analysis will be attempted. A development can, however, be traced in the larger churches, see Summerson, 129 f.

[4] The question of the adaptation of churches to Protestant ritual is fully discussed in G. W. O. Addleshaw and F. Etchells, *The Architectural Setting of Anglican Worship* (1948).   [5] *Parentalia*, 318; *Wren Soc.* ix. 15.

course, be decently placed, in the altarwise position against the east wall of the church, and not table-wise in the centre of the church as before the Laudian reforms. It must be guarded from desecration, or from a press of worshippers, by altar rails, but it should be within the church, and not in an apse or chancel, so that all could share in the Lord's Service. The pulpit was of almost greater importance, for preaching played a dominant part in services of the seventeenth century.[1] It is only necessary to read the Diaries of Evelyn or Pepys, where the name of a preacher is so constantly recorded (and his performance so often criticized) to see the contemporary view.

The need, in fact, was for not much more than a plain hall, containing an altar and a pulpit. Wren's inventive capacity, however, led him to ceaseless experiment in the interior arrangement, and especially in the roofing of his halls. And further, a certain limited richness of treatment was acceptable. The Anglicanism of Restoration England was very much less austere than Lutheranism or Calvinism (one has only to compare the interior of a Wren church with a seventeenth-century Dutch example to see proof of this), and even the sober City of London was tired of the excesses of Puritanism. Both painting and figure-sculpture were reduced to a minimum, but the merchants, who had a high standard of comfort in their own homes, had also an intense pride in their City, a pride which showed itself in the provision of fine wood fittings, generally superb in craftsmanship, which were often the gift of one of the City Companies to the church of its Ward.

More than eighty churches had been destroyed or severely damaged. It was decided to rebuild fifty-one of them: thus even though the whole population of the burnt-out areas did not return after the Fire, each rebuilt church had to hold a larger congregation than its predecessor. To provide the necessary accommodation Wren made great use of galleries, and it was in his disposition of these, together with his handling of awkward and irregular sites, that his practical ability was to be displayed. Galleries were, of

[1] In the Counter-Reformation churches of the Jesuits preaching was also taken into account in planning—hence the short broad nave of the Gesù in Rome—but the emphasis on the altar was of major importance.

course, unknown in English medieval churches. They had, however, been adopted on the Continent, by the Jesuits in northern Europe, and also by the Huguenots in France, both, it will be noted, communities in which stress was laid on preaching.[1] Further, since so early in his career and in a problem almost without precedent, Wren is likely to have sought the authority of source books, the basilica as described by Vitruvius may well have been the basis of most of his larger churches.[2] In them, however, a constant variation can be seen in the relation of interior columns to galleries, and there is further great variety in the design of the vaulted roofs. At St. Bride, Fleet Street (Pl. 34 a), which was probably the most closely dependent on the Vitruvian theme, the galleries ran awkwardly against the coupled columns of the main order, and the roof was a simple barrel vault.[3] In Christ Church, Newgate Street (Pl. 34 b), the design, and consequently the interior space composition, was quite different, for the galleries were set rather low above square piers carrying large columns. Here the roof consisted of segmental cross vaults over the nave and flat ceilings over the galleries; between these were large clerestory windows. In St. Clement Danes and St. James's, Piccadilly,[4] the galleries were raised fairly high on square piers, with columns above carrying the main barrel vault, further vaults (either cross or transverse barrels) over the aisles permitting large windows at the back of the galleries. In these last three churches and also in St. James's, Garlickhythe, Wren allowed his invention full play, and moved far from Vitruvian models. In St. Mary-le-Bow (Pl. 35 b), however, his intention was avowedly antique since, as *Parentalia* states, the design was based on the Templum Pacis (or Basilica of Constantine) with its compound piers, its wide nave arches and narrow aisles, the bays of which are sharply separated from each

[1] e.g. the Jesuit Church at Antwerp, built 1615–21 and burnt 1718, and Salomon de Brosse's Temple at Charenton (1623), which Wren would certainly have visited while in Paris.

[2] This illuminating suggestion was first made by Summerson, 129.

[3] W. Godfrey, London County Council, *Survey of London*, 15th monograph (1944).

[4] Though not strictly City churches they were contemporary, and must be considered with them. Unfortunately most of the three-aisled churches were destroyed in the Second World War, though St. James's, Piccadilly, has been restored.

other. Wren clearly followed the engraving in Serlio and here provides one of the most direct proofs of his respect for antiquity.

Interesting, however, as the larger churches are, it is in the smaller that the greatest ingenuity is displayed. Many of these were on extremely confined and often irregular sites. Some are treated as single span interiors (though always with variations in the treatment of the roof); others have one aisle; while in those where the site was approximately square Wren adopted types of centralized planning. The simplest of the last group were perhaps St. Mary Abchurch, covered by a dome carried on cantilever arches, and St. Mildred, Bread Street (Pl. 36 a),[1] where the dome was supported on pendentives (decorated with particularly fine plaster work) over an oblong space reduced to a square by the introduction of a barrel-vaulted section at the west utilized for a gallery and organ. Others, for example St. Anne and St. Agnes (Pl. 36 b), St. Martin, Ludgate, and St. Mary at Hill, have a 'cross-in-square' plan. Four free-standing columns carry four short barrel vaults (forming the arms of a cross) running inwards from the four walls; the central space is covered either by a higher cross vault (St. Anne and St. Agnes) or by a dome (St. Mary at Hill), while the four corners of the square between the arms of the cross are roofed by low flat ceilings. This is almost certainly an adaptation of a Dutch type of church; the Nieuwe Kerk at Haarlem, built by Jacob van Campen between 1645 and 1649, may well be the prototype.[2]

Wren's most accomplished interior is that of St. Stephen, Walbrook (Pl. 35 a),[3] in which he combines a large domed central space with the cross-in-square plan, though since the site is a long rectangle, the arms of the cross are not equal, and there is an additional bay to the west (see plan, Fig. 6). Twelve Corinthian columns surround the central square, joined by eight arches bringing the square to the circle required for the base of the dome. The ceilings in the corners (outside the central square) are flat, but

[1] St. Mary Abchurch was damaged and St. Mildred, Bread Street, destroyed in 1941.

[2] Summerson, 130, regards a Vitruvian origin as more probable. But, in view of Hooke's recorded interest, at a time when he was collaborating with Wren, in such Dutch buildings as the Great Synagogue at Amsterdam, the possible derivation from a Dutch model so close in type cannot be entirely ruled out.

[3] Damaged in 1941 and since restored.

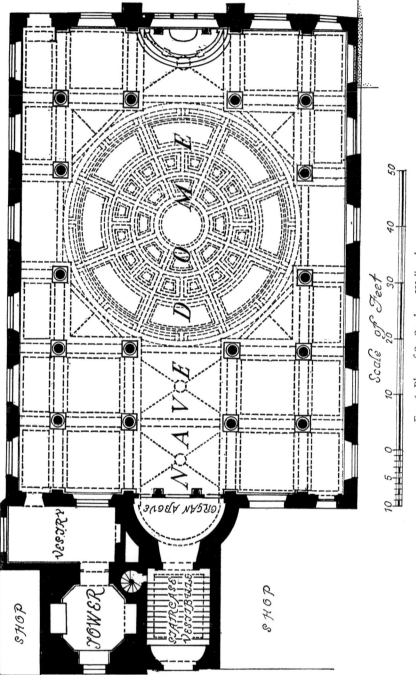

FIG. 6. *Plan of St. Stephen, Walbrook*

Scale of Feet

above them is an ingenious arrangement of windows flanking a cantilever arch, which with the great windows at the ends of the arms of the cross, make the interior unusually light. It has, however, none of the austerity of a Dutch seventeenth-century church, for the fine high relief plaster-work (executed by Grove and Doogood, who worked for Wren elsewhere) and the elaborately carved and gilt wood fittings give it a richness of texture which can be compared with the richness of the seventeenth-century prose heard within its walls.[1] To admirers of the contemporary architecture of southern Europe it is lacking in colour, and in that combination of massive supports and unexpected vistas with complex effects of space composition which characterize the baroque churches of Rome. Such critics should perhaps remember that Wren was compelled to build cheaply. Stone was the most costly material within his range, and had to be used sparingly (for columns, door frames, &c.); most of the work in the churches is of plastered brick. A Borromini, it is true, can achieve effects of immense sophistication and complexity with such materials. But such sophistication and such independence in the handling of classical forms can only be achieved in a country where they have been in long and familiar use. Only fifty years separate St. Stephen, Walbrook, from Jones's first experiments (so completely strange in England) in classical church design. It is therefore surely a remarkable achievement that Wren, relatively early in his career (St. Stephen's was built between 1672 and 1679, though the fittings were not completed till 1687), should be able to handle classical forms with assurance, fitting them to his constructional requirements, and creating a clear, lucid, and original architecture.

It would, however, be misleading to suggest that all the work on the City churches is of equally high quality. In some the detail is surprisingly poor but much was clearly left to the masons.[2] City craftsmen tended to lean on old-fashioned Flemish and German

[1] Here, as in many other seventeenth-century churches, the effect has been marred by the substitution of benches for the original high pews which would have hidden the pedestals of the columns and have formed a dark mass throwing the columns into stronger relief.

[2] See the *Parentalia* account of St. Mary at Hill, quoted in *Wren Soc.* x. 31, where the pilasters of the east window are described as 'the workman's own invention'.

pattern-books, and even in the Royal Works there can by the 1670's have been very few men left trained in the Italian manner under Jones (though admittedly some who had worked under Webb at Greenwich). There can be no doubt that early in his career Wren suffered from this dearth of experienced labour. By the time he was carrying out his great works of the late eighties and nineties he had trained men to work to his requirements, and the quality of the detail is uniformly higher.

The exteriors of Wren's churches are, generally speaking, less interesting and less skilful than the interiors. Owing to the un-controlled haphazard development of the medieval city, the plan of which was being repeated, the sites were seldom at right angles to the street (in fact many of them lay back from the street sur-rounded by other buildings, with only a short frontage to it). There was therefore no question of a façade problem, which so much concerned contemporary Italian and French architects.[1] Though, however, the exterior elevations did not make demands of the kind which produced his best architecture, the steeples which surmount them are among his most individual achievements. In his Memorandum of 1711 he makes it clear that he considers expense may be saved in the enrichment of the outward walls of churches 'in which Plainness and Duration ought principally, if not wholly, to be studied', while 'handsome Spires or Lanterns, rising in good proportion above the neighbouring Houses (of which I have given several Examples in the City of different Forms) may be of sufficient Ornament to the Town'.[2] Fortunately in them he was fascinated as much by construction as by effect. He covered the interior of the towers below with small domical vaults, and in many cases erected tall interior cones to form the core of his steeples. It was these vaults and cones which saved the steeples from destruction in the great fire-raids of 1940–41, which gutted so many of the churches,[3] and they still stand as a visible sign of Wren's creative power.

[1] For exteriors see Summerson, 134.   [2] *Parentalia*, 318 f.; *Wren Soc.* ix. 15.
[3] At St. Mary-le-Bow the tall interior cone contained a wooden circular staircase. This was destroyed by the fire, but the cone itself, though badly calcined, prevented the flames from damaging the outside of the steeple.

The steeples have been described and classified many times: they have indeed received more attention than the churches themselves, though perhaps not more than is their due. Many but not all of them are later than the buildings to which they belong, but it will be more convenient to discuss them here. In some cases, notably at St. Mary-le-Bow, the steeple was completed with the church. In others, the steeple, and often the fittings, were added later, when the accounts record that the church was 'beautified'. St. Vedast, Foster Lane, for instance, has a steeple of 1694; St. Bride, Fleet Street, of about 1700, while that of St. Magnus the Martyr, London Bridge, is as late as 1705.

The tall stone steeples of many tiers (e.g. St. Mary-le-Bow, St. Bride, St. Vedast, Christ Church, Newgate Street) are the most spectacular. Of these, St. Mary-le-Bow (Pl. 38 a) with its infinite variety of outline, its skilful change from the square of the tower to the circle of the lowest storey of the steeple, and then back to a square (now lightened by breaks on each face) and so up to the pyramid which carries the vane, is outwardly the most skilful. But though the elegant steeple of St. Bride (Pl. 38 b), with its simple repetition of pierced octagons, may appear a little tame in comparison, its interior construction is far more original.[1] St. Vedast, the most baroque of all, is built up on a Borrominesque pattern of alternate concave and convex storeys.

These tall steeples built in stages are Italianate in inspiration, and may be compared with such sixteenth-century designs as Antonio da San Gallo's scheme for St. Peter's.[2] Others again, linked with them, but more modest, since they are of one or two stages only, are probably inspired by the lanterns designed by the Italians as the climax of a dome. St. James, Garlickhithe, St. Michael, Paternoster Royal (Pl. 39 b), and St. Stephen, Walbrook all have a major tier in which columns either coupled at the angles, or standing out as buttresses all round the central core, give variety of outline and of light and shade, the first two, which are late, being distinctly baroque in character.

[1] For section, see *Wren Soc.* ix. 17.
[2] Wren probably also knew the Italianate steeples which appear in several of the Jones-Webb treatise drawings.

Some churches have a lead cupola surmounting the tower; St. Magnus the Martyr is the most elaborate of these, since it has a pierced stone octagon below it:[1] others have towers with spires, usually of lead. Of the latter, perhaps the most beautiful is St. Martin, Ludgate (Pl. 39 a), where the slender spire is set above a bell-shaped storey surmounted by a balcony, and is slightly Dutch in character. It is most frequently seen silhouetted sharply against the great brooding mass of the dome of St. Paul's. About twenty years divide the two, but one can hardly doubt that from the first Wren realized they would be seen in juxtaposition, and planned the maximum contrast.

The splendid wood fittings which adorned the churches do not, chronologically speaking, belong to this chapter, since they mainly date from the later years of the century, but they can, for convenience, be briefly mentioned here. Elaborate sculptured or painted altarpieces would, of course, have been regarded as Popish; the altar was therefore usually backed by panelling (sometimes framed by columns or pilasters) often elaborately carved with flowers and fruit (Pl. 37). The altar itself was not necessarily a plain table; that at St. Stephen, Coleman Street, was supported by four eagles and a straddling cherub. The rails were of well-proportioned twisted balusters, sometimes separated by panels of carving or occasionally of wrought-iron work. Much care was lavished on pulpits, which show an infinite variety of design and carving (Pls. 34 b, 35 b). Most have plain rectangular panels on each face, framed with bands of fruit and flowers; occasionally cherubs' heads, or heraldic beasts are introduced, but without direct religious symbolism.[2] Many of the pulpits were surmounted by

[1] Though St. Magnus was one of the last steeples to be built (1705) the design is early, since it appears in a drawing connected with St. Mary-le-Bow (identifiable by the door in the base of the tower) which must have been made before 1680. It is a simplified version of the tower of St. Charles at Antwerp, a drawing of which, by an unknown hand, is among the Wren drawings at the Soane Museum (*Wren Soc.* xii. Pl. xxxii, wrongly titled).

[2] A notable exception to this otherwise almost universal rule is the reredos in St. James's, Piccadilly (Pl. 37), carved by Gibbons and showing the pelican in her piety. This church, however, was sponsored by a private individual, Henry Jermyn, earl of St. Albans, in the new aristocratic west end, and was not supervised by the City Fathers. The only work, contrary to popular opinion, by Gibbons in the City churches

widely spreading sounding boards, which again offered further opportunity for carving. Doors, organ cases, pews, and lecterns presented further scope for fine joinery and carving, while ceilings were decorated with rich plaster work in high relief (Pls. 35 *a*, 36 *a*).

The rebuilding of St. Paul's[1] was to take nearly thirty-five years, and must, during its whole history, have been one of the major interests and responsibilities of its architect. He came to it with little experience of large-scale design or organization. Progress was perhaps fortunately slow, since the necessary money was provided out of that same tax on sea-coal which financed the City churches, and down to 1687 the larger proportion of it was given to the latter. Wren therefore had time to gain his experience, and by the end of the seventies when St. Paul's was at last taking material form, his knowledge was practical and no longer purely theoretical. And later, in the nineties, when he was faced with great undertakings at Hampton Court and Greenwich, there can be little doubt that the experience of large-scale organization which he had gained during the long history of St. Paul's was of great value to him.

The Fire left the choir in ruins, but in January, 1667, Wren, reporting on the fabric, suggested that temporary accommodation could be provided in the nave, pending the rebuilding of the east end. He does not, however, seem to have been altogether surprised when, in the next year, the fall of one of the nave piers made it clear that the remaining parts of the old cathedral were unsafe, and that the whole must be rebuilt. A Royal Warrant was issued for the demolition of the choir, and Wren was asked by the dean, William Sancroft, to design a new choir.[2] This established the dual

was the reredos of St. Mary Abchurch; see Rev. R. M. Laporte Payne, *Guide to St. Mary Abchurch* (1946).

[1] The whole of the building accounts for St. Paul's, as well as other documents, have been published by the Wren Society (vols. xiii–xvi). Drawings also appear in other volumes, e.g. i, ii, and iii, so that the index to the whole work in vol. xx must be consulted. For a short account of the history of the building, with good plates, see M. D. Whinney, *St. Paul's Cathedral*, Cathedral Books, i (1947).

[2] For the correspondence between Wren and Sancroft at this time, see *Wren Soc.* xiii. 45 f.

control over the work, that of the Government which provided the funds, and the Cathedral Chapter who commissioned the design. Both were to play a part in the evolution of the final scheme.

Wren's first design for St. Paul's was approved by the King in November 1672.[1] The battered model in the Cathedral Library was identified in 1936 from a study of the criticisms that had been levelled against it.[2] It shows a curious building, which originally consisted of two parts, a rectangular choir with a domed addition at the west end.[3] The choir was to be a comparatively narrow unaisled building, with loggias running the whole length on either side, presumably intended to fulfil the same function as Inigo Jones's portico,[4] and burial vaults beneath. The upper part of the church was wider, running out over the loggias so that the windows lighting the interior were set in a wall flush with their arcades. Galleries would have been ranged on each side within the church, with columns rising in front of them and supporting the roof. The arrangement of the upper part of the church might, indeed, have been very similar to that of St. James's, Piccadilly, a design which Wren himself regarded as satisfactory.[5]

It is not entirely surprising that the first model, in spite of its acceptance by the King, met with little favour. Some of Pratt's criticisms are clearly those of a jealous and disappointed rival, but he had, after all, seen the great churches of Italy and France, and his statement that it was unlike any cathedral in the whole world is true. This would not have mattered had it been a grand and original design, but there can be little doubt that it was unworthy of its purpose. *Parentalia*, however, defends it on the grounds that the architect had done as he was asked:—'to contrive a fabric of moderate bulk but good proportion, a convenient choir with a vestibule and porticoes and a dome conspicuous above the houses',

---

[1] *Hooke Diary*, 2 Nov. 1672.

[2] *The Architecture of Sir Roger Pratt*, ed. R. T. Gunther (1928), 213, and *Parentalia* (reprinted *Wren. Soc.* XIII. xii. 25). For this model see *Wren Soc.* xiii. 14.

[3] Both Hooke and Pratt refer to the domed section, the former calling it a 'library body': only the rectangular part remains. For discussion of a recently discovered drawing which throws new light on the design, see N. Lynton, 'A Wren drawing for St. Paul's', *Burl. Mag.* xcvii (1955), 40.   [4] See above, p. 31.

[5] He commends it in his Memorandum of 1711.

and adds that it would have been 'very fit for our way of worship, being also a convenient auditory'.[1]

The design was soon abandoned, and by September 1673 Wren was preparing a new and far finer scheme. This was embodied in the Great Model (still in St. Paul's cathedral library) which took nine months to make and cost £465. It is eighteen feet long and is undoubtedly the finest English model for a building which has survived. From it a real impression of the design may be gained. The new scheme was far more in line with continental tradition. It proposed a centralized building in the form of a Greek cross (Fig. 7), with the addition of a domed vestibule at the west, and the unusual feature of concave walls joining the four arms of the cross. The dome above the great central space was to be carried on eight piers with an unbroken ambulatory surrounding them (Pl. 41 a). The exterior was to be treated with a simple order of pilasters, while at the west was a great Corinthian portico (Pl. 40 a). It is not hard to find precedents for many of the features of the Great Model. The plan with its eight piers may owe something to François Mansart's design, made the year Wren was in Paris, for the Bourbon chapel for St. Denis;[2] the portico is certainly reminiscent of Inigo Jones. The treatment of the exterior may also be derived from Jones, since among the church designs probably connected with Jones's treatise there is one in which the wall treatment is very close.[3] For the dome he went to the best models, for it combines characteristics of both Bramante's and Michelangelo's designs for St. Peter's, taking the high drum with the continuous peristyle from the first, and the ribbed dome from the second.[4] In spite, however, of these borrowings, the Great Model cannot be dismissed as a derivative design. It has a unity, a dignity and a mastery of interior space-composition which are astonishing when one considers the architect's relative inexperience, and it is easy to believe the boast in *Parentalia* that it pleased 'persons of

[1] *Parentalia*, 281; *Wren Soc.* xiii. 26.

[2] L. Hautecœur, *Hist. de l'Architecture classique en France*, ii. i (1948), 70.

[3] Worcester College, i. 40. It shows a Greek cross church, with a dome carried on eight piers, the arms of the cross being joined by convex and not concave walls.

[4] The source for Bramante's dome would have been Serlio's plate (bk. iii, cap. iv); for Michelangelo's, Dupérac's (or other) engravings.

FIG. 7. *St. Paul's Cathedral: plan of Great Model*

distinction, skilled in antiquity and architecture'. This cathedral, unlike the previous design, would indeed have stood comparison with the great contemporary churches of the Continent.

But though some interests were now satisfied, others were not. The King and the connoisseurs might approve a design, but the commission had actually been given by the Chapter. And the clergy disliked the new design, which was 'not enough of a cathedral fashion'—in other words, it was untraditional. The Anglican Church did not, like other Reformed Churches, wish to sever all links with medieval Christianity. In fact, it had emphasized its belief in continuity by its insistence on maintaining the apostolic succession, and in the Prayer Book of 1662 English versions of many Latin prayers were retained. The Church, indeed, aimed at conserving the pure essence and discarding the errors of Roman Christianity. The medieval cathedral form, with its Latin cross plan, was the outward and visible symbol of traditional religion and its retention would be further evidence of the desired continuity. Here there is a considerable and interesting difference between the official ecclesiastical attitude to the cathedral and the parish churches. In the latter purely practical considerations prevailed, and a new type of church was accepted. In the far more important matter of the cathedral, wider questions of policy were involved. Further, there can be little doubt that Wren's new design, fine as it is, was less practical than the traditional form, especially for the metropolitan church of London, where the regular services would be attended only by a relatively small congregation (who would be lost under the great dome) but where on state occasions there would be a great crowd of worshippers, some of whom would expect to reach their seats in a processional manner. For the latter, the length of a nave was better suited.

So, though foundations had been marked out in 1674, and some preliminary work done, 'the Surveyor then turned his thoughts to a cathedral form (as they call it) but so rectified as to reconcile as near as possible the Gothick to a better manner of architecture; with a cupola and above instead of a lantern a lofty spire, and large porticoes'.[1] This third scheme was approved by Royal Warrant

[1] *Parentalia*, 282.

in May 1675, and is always known as the Warrant Design. The Warrant accepting it[1] suggests a further and probably decisive reason why the Great Model design was abandoned, for it states that there was now enough money to *begin* rebuilding, 'to put a new choir in great forwardness' and that among the designs submitted this had been chosen 'because it was so ordered that it might be built and finished by parts'. Such would not have been the case with the Great Model which had no separate choir that could be finished first and put into use.

The Warrant Design accepted the traditional Latin cross form, and consisted of a choir of three bays, a nave of five, with short transepts between (Pl. 40 *b*). But the architect compromised between his wishes and those of the clergy, by stopping his rows of piers outside the crossing and thus arranging a great central space to be covered with a dome. The eight supports of the Great Model were retained, and so was the great portico at the west. The great portico is indeed the most distinguished part of the exterior design. The elevations suggest haste, for they are very closely modelled on Inigo Jones's casing of the old nave (Pl. 4 *a*). And the whole is surmounted by a curious erection composed of a low dome (which would have been almost invisible from the ground) with above it a high dome carried on a buttressed drum, and topping all a tall, many-tiered steeple. It would almost seem that Wren, sick of delays, and finding that he could get a plan approved, had thrown together a series of undigested elevations, knowing that he would adjust them as the work proceeded. The vital step, however, was at last taken. On 1 July 1675 contracts were signed with the masons Joshua Marshall and Thomas Strong, and work was begun at the east end of the choir.[2]

---

[1] *Wren Soc.* xiii. 31.
[2] For the further history of St. Paul's, see below, p. 211.

VIII

LELY AND KNELLER

IN October 1661 an annual pension of two hundred pounds
was granted to Peter Lely;[1] it was to be paid 'as formerly to S^r
Vandyke' and marks the official recognition of his status as the
leading fashionable portrait painter in London. Thereafter until his
death in 1680 his position was threatened, but never successfully
challenged. Soest, Wright, and Huysmans, the three most important painters who stood rather outside his orbit, were either un-
fitted by temperament or lacked the technical ability to become
considerable rivals. By the time of Lely's death, however, Kneller
had nearly reached the heights from which he in his turn largely
dominated the scene until his death in 1723. The two men almost
span the period between the death of Van Dyck and the advent
of Hogarth. They ran large studios and their styles spread far beyond the confines of Covent Garden and Great Queen Street. The
organization of these portrait factories was essential to painters in
their position if they were to cope with the enormous demands
on their talent, but they have done well-nigh irreparable harm to
their reputations and their names continue to be loosely linked with
the mass of perfunctory canvases which poured from their establishments. In fact Lely and Kneller were sound, and sometimes
brilliant, painters; Kneller could, on occasion, show flashes of real
psychological insight, though he was a less consistently conscientious craftsman than his predecessor.

The success of these foreigners was at the expense of an embryonic native school of portrait painters and they overshadowed
their English contemporaries. Riley seems to have been eclipsed by
Lely and Kneller in turn at both ends of his career. But there was
no English painter of the calibre to compete with the foreigners,
and the studios of Lely and Kneller provided opportunities for
training in sound technical methods without which native

[1] P.R.O., S.P., 44/5, f. 27.

painting would have remained on an even more uniformly provincial level.

Lely's family, whose name was Van der Faes, came originally from Flanders. They owned a number of houses in The Hague and among them was one known as 'In de Lely', from which the painter took the familiar nickname. He was born at Soest in Westphalia, where his father, a captain in a Dutch regiment in the service of the elector of Brandenburg, was stationed.[1] In October–November 1637 he is recorded, apparently as a recent arrival, in the studio of Frans Pietersz. de Grebber in Haarlem. By 1647 he was in London.[2]

The earl of Northumberland was probably Lely's first important patron and secured him commissions from the earls of Leicester and Salisbury. The three noblemen were related by marriage and formed a loosely knit political group of moderate views, a milieu far from the atmosphere in which Dobson had spent his short career. After the surrender of Oxford, the young duke of York had been placed under Northumberland's care with the two youngest royal children, Princess Elizabeth and the duke of Gloucester, and in 1647 Lely painted for their guardian a series of portraits of his distinguished charges. They are now divided between Syon House and Petworth. The most ambitious are the group of the three children (Pl. 46) and the double-portrait at Syon of the duke of York handing a penknife to his father,[3] presumably painted at Hampton Court on one of the occasions when the King was visited by his children. The double-portrait is a hesitant essay

---

[1] J. A. C. Ab. Wittenaar, 'De geboorteplaats en de naam van Peter Lely . . .', *Oud-Holland*, lxvii, pt. ii (1952), 122–4. The earliest lives of Lely are by Richard Graham, in his *Short Account*, 343–4; Buckeridge, in *An Essay towards an English School*, 444–7; and Arnold Houbraken, *De Groote Schouburgh . . .* (1718–21), ii. 41–48. Certain sources give 1617 as the date of his birth, but 1618 is the generally accepted year.

[2] Graham and Buckeridge state that Lely arrived in 1641. Houbraken confuses the issue by stating that Lely came in the train of William of Orange, when he married Princess Mary, and that the portraits painted on that occasion were very successful; the marriage took place in 1641, but Houbraken places this event in 1643. There is no evidence to support this tradition and no certain portraits by Lely of the young couple are known; the design of the problematic double-portrait in the Rijksmuseum (G. Glück, *Van Dyck*, 505) must be Van Dyck's.

[3] R. B. Beckett, *Lely* (1951), Pl. 13.

in a conventional Van Dyckian formula; the larger group is a reminiscence of Van Dyck's *Three Children of Charles I* (which Lely later owned for a short period), but in very baroque and, especially in the emphasis on the landscape, Dutch terms. Both canvases show the weaknesses in construction which Lely took so long to overcome, but the fine sense of colour, forceful handling, rich pigment, and bold, confident drawing were beyond the powers of any other painter working in England at that period.

In Northumberland House, with its magnificent collection of portraits, and possibly of subject-pictures, by Van Dyck,[1] Lely had the opportunity for careful study of the work of his great predecessor, and some of the portraits painted by him for the earl recall portraits which may have surrounded him as he worked. The weaknesses in Lely's early style are largely due to an ill-digested surfeit of Van Dyck, but the ingenuousness of his early portraits, such as *Mrs. Sackville* at Knole,[2] in warm fawn-grey against a rich brown background, recaptures something of the spirit of Cornelius Johnson and is a refreshing contrast to the overweening arrogance with which Lely invests his sitters in his later and more familiar style. The same rather timid mood is felt in his portraits of children dressed as shepherds. This conceit was exceedingly prevalent in contemporary poetry and was sometimes exploited by Van Dyck,[3] but Lely's gaily dressed young Arcadians are more robust and are closer in spirit to Jan Mytens or Gonzales Coques. The sitters are drawn almost entirely from the Sidney and Percy families and they may all have sat (*c.* 1650) at Penshurst. The full-lengths of Henry Sidney (Penshurst) and the *Little Girl in Green* at Chatsworth,[4] with their fine greens, cool greys and pinks, and their slightly overawed sprightliness, are two of Lely's most charming portraits in any period of his career. Their rich pastoral settings provide a link between Lely's formal portraits and his subject-pictures.

There seems little doubt that on his arrival in England Lely 'pursu'd the natural bent of his *Genius* in *Landtschapes*, with *small Figures*, and *Historical Compositions*', but found them unprofitable

---

[1] See above, p. 73.
[2] Beckett, *Lely*, Pl. 17 (caption misplaced); *c.* 1650.
[3] See above, p. 73.
[4] Beckett, *Lely*, Pls. 48, 47.

and turned to portraiture.[1] One of his first friends in England, Richard Lovelace, had composed a fulsome eulogy on the portrait of Charles I with the duke of York, and lamented in a sympathetic *Panegyrick*[2] to 'Pow'rful Lilly' the neglect with which his subject-pieces had been treated and the obsession of English patrons with 'their own dull counterfeits'. Most of the 'Historical Compositions' were painted before about 1655, and they inspired no imitations; but, with the activities of Honthorst, Gentileschi and Poelenburgh in England, they form a minor appendix to the history of Cara-vaggism in the north.[3] Some of them are so inept that they are probably earlier than any of his extant portraits[4] and they range from such clumsy compositions as the earlier of two canvases in Lady Lee's collection to the delightful *Idyll* (formerly at Chilham Castle)[5] or the *Sleeping Nymphs* at Dulwich. Derivative though they are, they have a quite personal, nostalgic tranquillity and Lely's maturer essays in this genre are light and fluent in handling and unusually gay in colour. His few subject-pieces on a larger scale, such as the *Girl with her Music Master* (s. 1654),[6] which is perhaps the finest of them all, are close to Metsu.

By 1654 Lely was justly described as 'the best artist in England'.[7]

[1] Graham, *Short Account*, 343.

[2] *Works*, ed. C. H. Wilkinson (1930), 180–3; Lely and Lovelace were made free of the Painter-Stainers' Company on 26 October 1647 (*Booke of Orders . . .*, i, f. 221). Lely produced two illustrations for his friend's *Lucasta* (1649) and *Lucasta. Posthume Poems* (1659).

[3] There are marked affinities between Lely's subject-pictures and Jan van Bronck-horst, Netscher, Backer, and Flinck, whose drawings are often close to Lely. There is also in some of the heads in the subject-pictures a reminiscence of Gentileschi. The feeling for landscape owes much to Both. An instance of the complete Dutchness of Lely's subject-pictures is the painting hanging in the background of Vermeer's *Letter-Writer* in the Beit collection (L. Gowing, *Vermeer* (1952), Pl. 70), which, in scale, in its triangular composition, in the relation of the figures to the landscape, in the stormy sunset and in what can be seen of the handling, is indistinguishable from Lely.

[4] The signature and date on a *Diana and her Nymphs* at Nantes are obscure, but the date is said to be 1640 or 1646; it may therefore be the earliest extant piece from Lely's hand. A portrait of a girl (1640) at Hovingham Hall seems also to be by him.

[5] Beckett, *Lely*, Pls. 23, 24.

[6] Ibid., Pl. 37; in the collection of Lord Dulverton.

[7] James Waynwright to Mr. Bradshaw, 6 October 1654 (H.M.C. Sixth Report, i (1877), 437 *b*–38 *a*).

He was prosperous enough to acquire works of art at the dispersal of the royal collections. He is recorded, possibly in 1650 and certainly in 1651, in the house on the Piazza at Covent Garden in which he was to die. It was also occupied at this period by Hugh May,[1] who was Lely's lifelong friend and accompanied him in 1656 on a visit to Holland of unspecified length.[2] Lely's practice was unaffected by political prejudice. At some date before the dissolution of the Long Parliament on 20 April 1653 he submitted a proposal, with Gerbier and Geldorp, to record the achievements of the victorious party during the life of the parliament, and his reputation must have been enhanced by the powerful portrait of Cromwell which he painted soon after his installation as Protector.[3]

After the Restoration the grant of his pension and his naturalization in 1662 established him securely under the new régime. These satisfactory events coincided with complete maturity as a painter, for at the turn of the decade Lely achieved portraits in which he successfully combined the elusive elegance of Van Dyck with a Dutchman's sense of volume. Portraits like the *2nd Earl of Carnarvon* (Pl. 47 *b*: *s.*) and *Lady Jenkinson* (Pl. 47 *a*) are unsurpassed in his career: the paint is still very rich, the colour glowing and resonant, and the composition lucid and completely assured.

After the Restoration Lely was increasingly occupied with the production of the monotonous society portraits with which his name is still immediately associated. These fashionable female portraits are devoid of psychological insight and increasingly stereotyped in form, but continue to be distinguished in colour and thoroughly sound in technique. The 'Windsor Beauties' (Hampton Court), the series of Maids of Honour (e.g. Pl. 48 *b*) painted for the duchess of York and seen by Pepys on 21 August 1668, epitomize this aspect of Lely's work. The uniform heavy languor, half-closed eyes and suggestive dishevelment, which seem to coincide so closely with the most familiar aspect of life at the court of Charles II, were criticized even by his contemporaries: 'Sir Peter Lilly when

[1] MSS. at Rousham and the Rate Books in the Westminster Public Library.
[2] P.R.O., S.P., 25/77, 150; 25/112, 313. See above, pp. 132, 142.
[3] The signed original of this portrait, which is very familiar in copies, is now in the Birmingham Art Gallery. It is apparently dependent on Cooper's image (see above, p. 94).

he had painted the Dutchess of Clevelands picture, he put some-thing of Clevelands face as her Languishing Eyes into every one Picture, so that all his pictures had an Air one of another, all the Eyes were Sleepy alike. So that Mr. Walker ye. Painter swore Lilly's Pictures was all Brothers & sisters.'[1]

In one commission at this period Lely was able to escape the hot-house atmosphere of the court: the series of portraits (e.g. Pl. 48 a), for the duke of York, of the victorious flag-officers in the Battle of Lowestoft. On 18 April 1666 Pepys saw nine of the heads, 'some finished, and all begun', in Lely's studio. Nowhere does Lely reveal his Dutch origin more clearly than in the finished portraits: in mood and type they are indistinguishable from the naval portraits which were being painted across the North Sea by, for example, Van der Helst or Maes, of the men engaged in fighting the duke of York's 'Flaggmen'. There was some studio assistance in the series, especially in the draperies and hands, which have a soft, dead quality characteristic of this period and in contrast to the nervous, vibrant touch of such passages of autograph quality in works of the same type, like the *2nd Earl of Manchester* (National Portrait Gallery) or *Sir George Carteret* (St. Ouen, Jersey). Lely's painting of the heads at this date is full and direct and shows unerring precision in recording the planes of the face in a crisp, sculptural manner.[2] *Sir Jeremy Smith* in the series at Greenwich is a portrait of rare penetration and deep sympathy.

From the rich and fluent technique of the early 1660's there is a steady development in Lely's style towards a thinner texture, cooler key, restricted palette and simplified handling. The affecta-tions which become so marked in Lely's final period may be due in part to an attempt to defeat some of his rivals at their own game.

---

¹ B.M., Add. MS. (anon.) 22950, f. 41. It is needless to point out that there are many female portraits by Lely of this period which are sincere and unstereotyped; at the other end of the scale are the portraits of the more notorious ladies of the court in religious guise or in none at all.

² These qualities can also be seen in Lely's drawings, which often reveal him in an unusually sensitive and wistful vein; for them see J. Woodward, *Tudor and Stuart Drawings* (1951), 30–35, 49–52. Lely's pastels were regarded as a more important aspect of his work in his own day than they are now; in 1663 Christiaan Huygens was much interested in his technique in this medium (*Correspondance*, iv (1891), 361–2, 370–2, 393–4).

Like Hogarth after him Lely seems to have learnt to his cost that 'if a painter comes from abroad, his being an *exotic* will be much in his favour'. The success enjoyed in court circles by the Frenchman Henri Gascars and the Frenchified Simon Verelst was perhaps the most serious threat to his reputation that he had to endure; it was especially formidable because both men, though neither had a fraction of Lely's ability, were championed by the duchess of Portsmouth and the 2nd duke of Buckingham. The duke's encouragement of Verelst to turn from flower painting to portraits was probably merely one of his 'ten thousand freaks that died in thinking', but the duchess 'stuck firm to the French interest and was its chief support'. She may have been responsible for Gascars's coming to London and, though his portraits represent the nadir of decadent French court portraiture in the earlier years of Louis XIV, his 'gay Cap and Feather' manner had considerable success at Lely's expense.[1] Lely's reaction to these painters was not unlike that of Hogarth towards Vanloo and the other French portrait painters whom he affected to despise.

The two full-lengths at Arundel of the 6th Duke of Norfolk and his Duchess (Pl. 50 *b*) are excellent examples of Lely's most formal portraits in his latest phase.[2] The paint is thin, dry, and rough; the underpaint is clearly visible and suffuses the canvas with a deep red-grey tone; the draperies in the female portrait are drawn in simple, blocked-out shapes and are of two standard tones, cool blue and red-brown; and the figure is elaborately staged on a step, leaning against a ledge and set off by the standard accessories. The construction of these late portraits can be traced back to Van Dyck; the *Duchess of Norfolk*, as a type, marks a definite stage in

---

[1] Buckeridge, *An Essay*, 421–2. See above, pp. 7–8. Hooke saw 'Lady Wrens Picture at Monr. Caskades in Leicester feilds' on 27 July 1675; Gascars was still here in March 1678. He returned to France via Holland and was in Paris in 1680. His work can be studied most easily at Goodwood. The full-length of the duke of York at Greenwich is more accessible and no less typical. Philippe and Claude Vignon were sworn in as limners in ordinary on a warrant of 4 October 1669 (*Cal. S.P. Dom.* (1668–9), 516).

Verelst's remarkable portraits of Charles II (Parham) and Prince Rupert (Petworth) are redolent of the lay-figure; they are painted in a flat unimpasted style which is quite unmistakable and the necks appear to be dislocated.

[2] Both are *s.* 1677; the last digit is obscure in both cases. There are repetitions for other sitters of these particular patterns.

the Van Dyck tradition and remained the standard pattern for elaborate fashionable portraiture for some years. Riley, Wissing and Kneller exploited this formula freely and with little variation in composition or colour; and it is significant of Grinling Gibbons's association with Lely and Hugh May that he provided a pattern-book for female portraits of this type in the two reliefs on his monument (1686) to Viscount Campden at Exton.[1] From Lely's studio the convention was exported to France. Largillierre on his second visit to England was closely associated with Lely;[2] his brief return in the reign of James II brought him again into contact with fashionable studios in London and his *Prince James Francis Edward and Princess Louisa* in the National Portrait Gallery (s. 1695) displays some of the accessories with which he must have been familiar in Lely's *atelier*.

Lely was knighted on 11 January 1680, but died suddenly on 30 November of the same year. He lived in great style and to those who did not know him well he was the 'mighty proud man, and full of state' who overawed Pepys, but he appears in a more sympathetic light with his friends: to the Norths he was 'a well-bred gentleman, friendly and free' and even 'the good old gentleman' whose affairs Lord Guilford undertook to put in order in return for friendly initiation into the art of connoisseurship.[3] His position as *arbiter artium* was based, like that of the elder Richardson, not on a personal experience of Italy, which he was prevented from visiting by the pressure of work, but on the impressive collection of pictures and drawings which he built up as a substitute.[4] He gave advice on the preservation of the Wilton Diptych; in 1670 he attested

[1] K. A. Esdaile, *English Church Monuments* (1946), Figs. 103, 104. See below, p. 248.

[2] He was probably in England on this visit, 1674–8; his exact status in Lely's entourage is not clear. Lely owned a *Dead Fowl* by Largillierre and two still-lifes by him are known; one in Dr. Hannema's collection and a study of grapes belonging to Dr. Lugt (both s. 1677).

[3] Roger North, *Lives of the Norths*, ed. Jessopp (1890), i. 124, 194, 393, 408–10, 434.

[4] See 'Sir Peter Lely's Collection', *Burl. Mag.* lxxxiii (1943), 185–91, for the catalogue of his sale, 18 April 1682, which raised over £6,000; it was particularly rich in Venetian pictures of the sixteenth, and Dutch pictures of the seventeenth, centuries, and in Van Dycks. Lely also owned a very fine collection of drawings and engravings (sold later); his sculpture included Bernini's bust of Mr. Baker in the V. & A. (R. Wittkower, *Gian Lorenzo Bernini* (1955), 201).

the fitness of George Freeman as a designer of tapestry;[1] and the contract between Cibber and the countess of Dorset (12 October 1677) for the monument at Withyham makes the final payment dependent on 'ye well liking of Mr. Peter Lilly . . . or any other Artis'.[2] Grinling Gibbons owed much to his good offices[3] and the double-portrait at Audley End in which Lely appears with Hugh May, in front of the bust of Gibbons and a view of Windsor Castle, indicates that he was in some way associated with the work which May carried out for Charles II and in which Gibbons was employed.

It is unlikely that Lely's establishment was very considerable before the Restoration. Imitations of his style are rare before that date,[4] but after the Restoration repetitions of a few stock patterns came increasingly from the house on the Piazza. Obviously the assistants would be made largely responsible for the sets of portraits, such as those painted for Lord Clarendon (whose interests were iconographical rather than aesthetic) or the series at Cirencester of full-lengths of peers in robes and selected commoners which was probably produced about 1670.[5] Lely's patterns became more stereotyped as his invention flagged; he would evolve a new design, use it himself for two or three sitters and then hand it over to the assistants to be used for other clients. Finally, through the means of engravings, the patterns would become available to painters in the provinces.

Of all Lely's pupils the most precocious, and the one best qualified to inherit his fashionable clientele, was William Wissing, a native of Amsterdam who studied in The Hague under Arnoldus van Ravesteyn and Doudijns and came to London in July 1676, perhaps after a visit to France.[6] A portrait at Ham House of Mrs.

---

[1] *Cal. S.P. Dom.* (1670), 463–4.   [2] See below, p. 242.

[3] Vertue, i. 125–6. See below, p. 207.

[4] Robert Hooke was with Lely for a short period after the death of his father in October 1648; the Painter-Stainers' Company was informed on 25 November 1652 of a request from Lely 'that he might have an apprentice bound to some member of this Company and then to be turned over to him' (*Booke of Orders . . .*, ii, f. 22).

[5] Earl Bathurst, *Catalogue of the Bathurst Collection* (1908), 42–54.

[6] On his monument in St. Martin's Church, Stamford, erected by the earl of Exeter, he is described as 'Quem Batava tellus educavit, Gallia aliquandiu fovit . . .'.

Heneage is almost certainly by Wissing; it is close to Lely in his latest period, but shows tendencies towards thin pigment, cold brown tones and a scratchy quality in the impasto which mark Wissing's variations on Lely's themes, to which he remained very faithful. He was, however, a competent painter, though his drawing is often meagre and his colour unpleasantly steely. He was at ease in elaborate full-length compositions such as *Princess Anne* (*c.* 1685) in the Scottish National Portrait Gallery or the *Countess of Lindsey* (*s.* 1685) at Grimsthorpe, and he was exceedingly successful. He painted Charles II (Windsor Castle), James II (*s.* Midgham) and their queens, and James sent him over to Holland in 1685 to paint Princess Mary and her husband (Pl. 51 *a*): 'ils ont envoyé un peintre d'Angleterre pour faire ceux de leurs Altesses pour le Roy. C'est un disciple de Lely nommé Wissingh, mais il n'est pas encore arrivé à la perfection de son maistre'.[1] He was much patronized by the earl of Exeter, and in two delightful portraits (Burghley) of his sons, Lord Burghley and William Cecil, recaptured the playful mood of Lely's early Arcadian portraits. He died at Burghley on 10 September 1687, at the age of thirty-one, and left unfinished a large family hunting piece.[2] The perfunctoriness of much of the work of Wissing's studio may be due to his collaborator Jan van der Vaart, a versatile minor painter born in Haarlem, who is thought to have come to London in 1674. There, like Lely, he failed with small figure-subjects in landscapes, but he assisted Wissing as a drapery and landscape painter. He painted another of the sons of Lord Exeter in the same convention as Wissing. His independent portraits are perhaps softer than Wissing and contain none of the displays of botanical painting which are a characteristic of Wissing's compositions, but his *Countess of Pembroke* (*s.* 1687) at Wilton is virtually indistinguishable from Wissing, to whose portrait of the earl of Pembroke it is a pendant.

John Greenhill is a good example of a young native painter of

---

[1] Constantin to Christiaan Huygens, 24 August 1685 (*Correspondance*, ix (1901), 23). A signed replica of William is at Windsor, with a pendant of Mary II.

[2] This was presumably the piece eulogized by Prior (*Dialogues of the Dead*, ed. A. R. Waller (1907), 31–32) in which 'Wissin Seven-Times one great Perfection Drew'. The portraits of Lord Burghley and his brother were engraved by John Smith.

moderate talents coming under the influence of Lely and evolving a simplified version of Lely's style of the late 1660's and early 1670's. He was born in Salisbury (c. 1644) and his youthful portrait of his uncle, Alderman James Abbot, which is still in the Town Hall there, is an entirely pedestrian piece in the provincial English tradition, innocent of any more sophisticated influence. Soon after his arrival in London he was mixing with the stage and seems to have specialized in portraits in coloured chalks of actors in costume. Two of these survive: *Thomas Betterton as Bajazet* (s. 1663) at Kingston Lacy and *Joseph Harris as Cardinal Wolsey* (s. 1664) at Magdalen College, Oxford,[1] which show no influence of Lely and are uncertain and tentative. They are close in character to the very English portrait (Pl. 51 b: s.) of the second wife of the actor William Cartwright, though the technique now shows a slight influence of Lely.[2]

After his entry into Lely's studio he seems to have been regarded as a particularly promising pupil and later he may have had a few years in an independent practice. Among his patrons, perhaps from motives of local patriotism or because of his disgust at Verelst's intolerable conceit,[3] was the 1st earl of Shaftesbury. Three portraits at St. Giles's House show Greenhill's relation to Lely: a portrait of a certain Mr. Montagu (s.), a bust in a painted carved oval; a full-length (s.) of Shaftesbury in Lord Chancellor's robes; and a smaller portrait of 'false Achitophel' which is probably correctly attributed to Greenhill.[4] All of them are dependent on Lely's style of the earlier 1670's, but the technique is broader, lacks Lely's subtlety and gives no sense of volume. The figures have nothing of Lely's assurance, but there is a freshness and reserve, almost a timidity, in his sitters which reveal Greenhill's essential

---

[1] J. Woodward, *Tudor and Stuart Drawings* (1951), Pls. 51, 53.

[2] The impressive *Self-portrait* at Dulwich can hardly be much later, but seems to show signs of Lely's direct influence in the draperies.

[3] Vertue, i. 32.

[4] The full-length is rep. Collins Baker, ii. 8. The signature and date read *J. Geenhill* [sic]/*November*/*1649*, which is clearly impossible; it appears to have been clumsily superimposed over the original inscription, where the date appears to be 1673, which fits with Shaftesbury's appointment. The other portrait of Shaftesbury is rep. *Country Life*, xciv (1943), 464.

Englishness.[1] His love of raffish company and 'loose and un-guarded Manner of Living' brought him to an early death on 19 May 1676, after a drunken orgy at the Vine tavern.

An untimely fate overtook another young English painter of some promise: Henry Tilson, who entered Lely's studio a short time before Lely's death. He was in Rome with Dahl (Roger North owned two studies by Tilson from the Farnese Gallery)[2] and he also seems to have been in Venice, where he discussed technique with Bombelli. Tilson's signed *Sir William Dolben* (*c.* 1690) at the Guild-hall is a serious, competent portrait close in treatment to Dahl; but his practice is said to have been jeopardized by his generous recommendation of Dahl. Overcome with a sense of his difficul-ties, and suffering from unrequited love, he shot himself through the heart in 1695 at the age of thirty-six.

We are in calmer waters with the well-documented and tedious Mary Beale, daughter of a Suffolk rector who was probably an amateur painter of still-lifes.[3] Her husband, Charles Beale, was Deputy Clerk of the Patents, owned books on the fine arts, and planned to translate lives of some of the great Italian painters, but also carried on a more lucrative trade as an artist's colourman. His lovingly conscientious notes of the painting activities of his 'deare heart' provide an unrivalled picture of life in the artistic circles which radiated from Lely's studio.[4] Mary may have had some in-struction from Walker, but their friend Thomas Flatman definitely speaks of her as 'my Scholar'.[5] The Beales were also close friends

[1] The same qualities and the same dependence on Lely can be seen in the drawn *Self-portrait* in the B.M. (J. Woodward, op. cit., Pl. 49); see also E. K. Waterhouse, 'John Greenhill', *Old Master Drawings*, xi (1937), xliv, 69–70, and R. B. Beckett, 'Notes on Greenhill', *Burl. Mag.* xcii (1950), 294.

[2] B.M., MS. 32504, f. 18v.; for Dahl see below, pp. 198–200.

[3] See below, p. 281, n. 3.

[4] His notes were made in the blank leaves at the end of yearly almanacs. Vertue was lent seven of these, for the years 1661, 1671, 1672, 1674, 1676, 1677 and 1681, and transcribed considerable extracts (iv. 168–71, 172–6, 178; v. 14–15); two of the almanacs survive, one in the N.P.G. and the other in the Bodleian (MS. 8o Rawl. 572). See E. Walsh, 'Mrs. Mary Beale, Paintress', *Connoisseur*, cxxxi (1953), 3–8. She was no doubt more prolific, and is much better known, than other female painters, but was probably no better than Joan Carlile (see below, p. 284) or Sarah Broman (*fl.* 1652).

[5] E. Walsh, 'The Flatman Letters', *Life and Letters*, lxi (1949), 218–22; see above, p. 97.

of Lely, who bought colours from Charles Beale and was a patient and kindly critic of his wife's work. Mary studied and copied portraits by Lely and Van Dyck and borrowed Italian drawings from the royal collection. She was clearly an agreeable woman and as a painter was particularly popular with Anglican divines: Samuel Woodforde, Tillotson, Stillingfleet, Simon Patrick and William Owtram were among her sitters. But in spite of all her opportunities and Lely's polite comments on her progress, Mrs. Beale's work never rises above the quality of a hard-working amateur, with no sense of colour or feeling for texture, very limited knowledge of anatomy and an incurably commonplace understanding of character. For her compositions she depended much on Lely; but it would be hard to find a greater contrast to Lely's *1st Earl of Tankerville* at Audley End (*c.* 1672) than such a derivation of its pattern as the (admittedly damaged) portrait of the Marquess of Halifax in the National Portrait Gallery, which was probably painted in 1677. In her later portraits (and she did not die until 1699) she seems to show some influence of Riley, and her *Robert Fairfax* (*s.* 1685) at Gorhambury is already much influenced by Wissing or the earlier Kneller. Her two sons, Bartholomew and Charles, assisted their mother with her draperies and in 1677 Charles started lessons in miniature painting with Flatman. Two groups of drawings by Charles Beale, in the British Museum and the Pierpont Morgan Library (the latter in an album dated 1679), are an interesting indication of the material absorbed by a young student in this milieu.[1]

[1] There are many drawings of details from existing pictures, particularly from Van Dyck; many studies of Lelyesque types and of actual portraits by Lely; and a group of heads drawn *ad vivum*, perhaps from friends or servants (H. S. Reitlinger, 'The Beale Drawings in the British Museum', *Burl. Mag.* xli (1922), 143–7).

Little is to be gained in a volume on this scale by discussing in any detail the more shadowy figures in Lely's *atelier*. John Baptist Gaspar(s), Caspar(s) or Caspers of Antwerp was probably associated with Lely throughout his career in England, assisted him (and perhaps others after him) with draperies and was an independent portrait painter of moderate skill. Prosper Henry Lankrink painted landscapes for Lely and owned a good collection (*Burl. Mag.* lxxxvi–vii (1945), 29–35). Thomas Hawker's full-length of the 1st Duke of Grafton at Euston (Collins Baker, i. 180) is in a flashy Lelyesque style. More obscure are Davenport and Matthew Dixon, of whose wooden imitations of the later Lely a good example was at Ecton in the portrait of James Sotheby

The three most important portrait painters who stand apart from Lely's environment were his fellow Dutchman Gerard Soest, the Flemish Jacob Huysmans and the Scottish Michael Wright. All three might have been dangerous rivals, but Huysmans, though he was immediately successful on his arrival, found his Catholicism a grave liability; and Wright, who was also probably a Catholic, seems, like Soest, to have lacked the temperament and ambition necessary to sustain a fashionable practice.

Huysmans was born and trained in Antwerp; he may have been a pupil of Gilles Backereel and he is recorded in the studio of Frans Wouters in 1649–50. He was among a group of Netherlanders who appeared before the court held by the Painter-Stainers on 30 July 1662 and promised to present a picture to the Company.[1] Soon after his arrival in London Huysmans was painting small Vandyckian religious pieces for the earl of Salisbury and was taken up by Catherine of Braganza. In 1664 Pepys called him 'the great picture drawer' who was 'said to exceed Lilly' and saw in his studio at Westminster portraits of Huysmans's patroness as St. Catherine[2] and as a shepherdess (Pl. 50 a): devoid of life or taste, crowded with accessories, and painted in cold, liverish colour. Huysmans was a thoroughly unattractive painter, though he could achieve a simpler and more sensitive realization of character in, for example, his *Izaak Walton* (s.) in the National Portrait Gallery. Very little is known of his later years and he died in 1696.

The career of Benedetto Gennari, after his arrival in England in 1674, provides a parallel with Huysmans. His more elaborate portraits, with their lavish and carefully described accessories, are close to Huysmans in intention and are, in their own way, almost as

---

(1679); and those who are scarcely above the level of copyists, such as Joseph Bokshoorn or Buckshorn, and W. P. Claret (though the two full-lengths by Claret of William III and Queen Mary (both *s.*) in the County Court Room at Northampton are sound and un-Lelyesque). In the account kept by Lely's executors (B.M., MS. 16174) there are numerous references to Sonnius, Tilson, Lankrink, Gaspar(s), Wissing, and Hawker; their part in the settlement of their master's affairs included finishing portraits left unfinished at his death.

[1] *Booke of Orders . . .*, ii, f. 71.

[2] Several versions of this exist, e.g. at St. James's Palace.

repulsive. His *Catherine of Braganza* (*s.*), painted for the countess of Arlington and now at Goodwood, is a sequel, some fifteen years later, to Huysmans' portrait at Windsor. His habit of painting his sitters in a historical or mythological context is seen in *MiLedi Beti Felton figurata in una Cleopatra*, which survives at Kingston Lacy. In the full-length *Countess of Arlington* (Euston) the head is curiously close to Lely.

The more flamboyant portraits of Huysmans and Gennari, with their tasteless accessories and empty allegories, no doubt reflect clearly one aspect of the taste of the Restoration court. A complete contrast is provided by Gerard Soest, who never, as far as we know, was honoured with a royal sitting or penetrated court circles. When he died in London on 11 February 1681 he was thought by his contemporaries to be nearly eighty years old. He had probably left his native Holland for this country by the time of Charles I's execution and his earliest portraits have a slight Dobsonesque feeling. He was a serious and conscientious painter, more direct and sometimes more intense than Lely, less openly indebted to Van Dyck and more obviously Dutch. The grave sense of character, the soft play of shadow, the blond hair, and the light across a fair eyelash in portraits such as Soest's *Ferdinando Lyttelton* (probably painted in 1651; Hagley), the fine *20th Earl of Oxford* (Dulwich), or a strange *Unknown Man* (Knole), which are probably slightly later, are qualities often seen in Terborch, on a smaller scale[1] and at a later date.

Soest's sense of colour was very personal, with a remarkable variety of greys, orange, metallic blue, or cool scarlet, permeated by a warm brown underpaint. His draperies are unmistakable: sweeping, inflated folds of satin, cut about into almost arbitrary patterns of light and shadow. They are particularly obvious in such portraits as *Lady Margaret Hay* (*s.*: *c.* 1670).[2] It will be seen at a glance that a constitutional inability to flatter his sitters or to evolve

---

[1] The portrait at Knole is reproduced in the catalogue, *Exhibition of Paintings*, Worcester (1951), Pl. v. Terborch's *Guitar Lesson* in the N.G. contains details which seem very reminiscent of Soest.

[2] *17th Century Art in Europe*, R.A., 1938, illustrated souvenir Pl. 97 (at Yester); the hunched nearer arm and hanging splayed hand are very characteristic.

a compromise between his innate realism and a necessary elegance must have rendered Soest unpopular with fashionable female clients. Towards the end of his life he was clearly very eccentric and had 'grown out of humor with the public but particularly with the ladies. which his ruff humour coud never please'; and when Greenhill visited him in his studio in Southampton Buildings he found him engaged on a large picture of a horse.[1] Nevertheless, of congenial sitters Soest could paint most impressive portraits. His austerely Cromwellian *Major Richard Salwey* (s. 1663; still in possession of the family), his archaizing full-length *3rd Lord Baltimore* (s.; c. 1670) at Baltimore[2] or the penetrating portrait of the ageing Sir Richard Rainsford (Pl. 49 b: s. 1678) bring us face to face with the rugged and unperiwigged heads of men of a very different type from the young fops and rake-hells of Wycherley's comedies, who would have been more at home with Verelst, Gascars, or Lely himself. The portrait of Rainsford is a particularly fine study in warm greys, silvers, and cool scarlet. The same sombre and uncompromising gravity can be seen in the small number of portraits painted in England by Pieter Borsseler of Middelburg. He was certainly in England by 14 September 1665, when he signed and dated the *Sir William Dugdale* at Merevale Hall.[3]

Michael Wright was one of the few native painters to spend many years in Italy. At one stage of his career he was working for the King and the duke of York and styled himself 'Pictor Regius', but he was an amateur at heart, had no ambition seriously to rival Lely or build up a studio, and was outstripped by each successive painter of fashion. His career is obscure and even his precise nationality is not known. He was born in London in 1617, the son of James Wright, a tailor and a citizen of London, but in April 1636 he is recorded as an apprentice to George Jamesone, the Scottish

---

[1] Vertue, ii. 72; iv. 29; v. 45.

[2] *17th Century Art in Europe*, illustrated souvenir, Pl. 97; Waterhouse, Pl. 60.

[3] C. H. Collins Baker, 'Pieter Borsseler', *Connoisseur*, lxiv (1922), 5–15; and A. Staring, 'Weinig bekende portrettisten', ii, *Oud-Holland*, lxi (1946), 33–42. He is probably to be identified with 'Petrus Busler' who was charged with recusancy in London in 1673 and 1679; Borsseler was back in Middelburg by 1684 (*London Sessions Records*, ed. Dom. H. Bowler, *Catholic Record Soc.* xxxiv (1934), 157, 213, 221, 238).

portrait painter, in Edinburgh.[1] On certain canvases he describes himself as 'Anglus' and in Rome he was known as the 'pittore inglese'; but Richard Symonds, who met him in Rome, described him as a Scot and Evelyn, in 1662, as 'a Scotsman' who had 'lived long at Rome'.

According to Thomas Hearne,[2] Wright at an early age fell into the clutches of a priest who took the boy, to the grief of his parents, to Scotland and seduced him to the Roman faith; it was perhaps in the company of this priest or at his instigation that Wright went to Rome. He was enrolled in the Accademia di San Luca in 1648 and appears in a list of its members in 1651.[3] From Rome he travelled to Flanders, where he became antiquary to the Archduke Leopold William. He was probably back in England in 1656. After all that he must have seen in Rome at that period and after meeting, in all probability, Poussin, Bernini, and Velazquez, he could only produce such a fundamentally provincial portrait as the *1st Earl of Cardigan* at Deene Park (*s.* 1658). The awkward contrapposto and flat, angular construction reveal weaknesses that Wright never quite overcame. They are still latent after the Restoration in Wright's more grandiose portraits, encumbered with accessories, such as the *1st Duke of Albemarle* (of which a good version, *s.* 1668, is at Longleat) or the *Duchess of Cleveland* (*s.* 1670),[4] which reflects some influence from the 'epidemic malady of our nation, the affectation of the worst of French vanities'. But even his most elaborate pieces show a sincere and kindly sense of character. Wright was 'free and open, and innocently merry' and an unsophisticated frankness is the most marked characteristic of his sitters. Wright's masterpiece, *Colonel John Russell* (Pl. 49 *a*: *s.* 1659), is a touchstone for Wright's personality, individual

[1] *The Register of Apprentices of the City of Edinburgh*, ed. F. J. Grant, *Scottish Record Soc.* (1906), 203; I am very grateful to Mr. Hutchison for sending me this reference and to Professor Waterhouse for placing his notes on Wright at my disposal. Wright seems to have allowed his first name, John, to lapse.

[2] *Reliquiæ Hearnianæ* (ed. Bliss, 1869), ii. 17–20; Hearne's account, which is dated 14 September 1715, is probably substantially accurate.

[3] P. Orlandi, *Abecedario Pittorico* (1753), 329; G. Hoogewerff, *Bescheiden en Italië*, ii (The Hague, 1913), 130; and Waterhouse, 70–71.

[4] *Burl. Mag.* lxxxviii (1946), 227, in the collection of the earl of Lisburne.

in key and one of the most honest English portraits of the century.

For all his learning Wright's sense of composition was very limited, though in his formal *Charles II* (St. James's Palace), in robes and with the regalia, he achieves a convincing and hieratic image of restored monarchy.[1] His technique was entirely unlike Lely's; his paint is thin and his colour normally pale and cold; his drawing and texture is hard and metallic, though the details in costume are freely drawn; and his flesh is dry with a light watery touch in drawing the features, which are curiously open in construction.

Wright was inferior to Lely, but enjoyed, for some years at least, a respectable practice. In 1670 he was commissioned to paint the series of full-lengths of the judges who had been responsible for sorting out the legal problems entailed in rebuilding after the Fire.[2] The status of the leading painters in London can be seen in the decision of the Painter-Stainers' Company on 6 April 1676 to commission a set of royal portraits: Lely was to be asked to paint the King and Huysmans the Queen; Greenhill was to do the duchess of York and Wright the duke.[3] In his studio, next door to the 'Queen's Head' in Great Queen Street, Wright worked in an atmosphere very different from the businesslike activities of Lely's studio nearby, of which he disapproved: 'I have begun . . . diverse ladyes', he wrote to Sir Walter Bagot on 27 July 1676, 'who are all sufficiently satisfied and judge me moderat comparatively to Mr Lilly.'[4]

There is little doubt that Wright had entered the Roman Church and he was certainly popular with Catholic patrons: Bagots, Stonors, Howards, and Arundells are to be found among his sitters and in 1686 he went as chief steward to the earl of Castlemaine on his unfortunate embassy to Innocent XI; he was thus personally associated with James II's schemes to bring England once more

---

[1] Collins Baker, i. 188.

[2] J. L. Howgego, 'The Guildhall Fire Judges', *Guildhall Miscellany*, 2 (February 1953); the names of Huysmans and Hayls were also considered by the Committee.

[3] *Booke of Orders* . . ., ii, f. 198.

[4] W. J. Smith, 'Letters from Michael Wright', *Burl. Mag.* xcv (1953), 233–6.

into the Roman fold.[1] Wright was a good linguist and a scholarly man of antiquarian tastes, but he was obliged to sell his books, coins, and seals; and, just before Lord Castlemaine's departure, he had paid Roger North two pounds for permission to expose his pictures for sale in Lely's old house in Covent Garden.[2]

Very little is known about two painters who must have been active over a long period: John Hayls,[3] or Hales, and Isaac Fuller. Pepys, on a visit to Hayls on 14 February 1666, was so impressed that he determined to have his wife painted by him as St. Catherine, 'he having a very masterly hand'. Two months later the picture was finished and Pepys himself began to sit. He recorded the progress of his portrait with loving and detailed interest and provided an unrivalled account of the experience of sitting for a portrait at this period. The portrait is in the National Portrait Gallery; it is coarsely painted in a completely un-Lelyesque manner, and Pepys was compelled to admit that his friend was much inferior to Lely.

Isaac Fuller was primarily a decorative painter.[4] He was stated by Buckeridge to have studied in France under Perrier, but the extraordinary moon-struck *John Cleveland* (Tate),[5] which was almost certainly painted in Oxford in 1644, is entirely personal. The unusual pattern is repeated in a more restrained mood in the strangely moving *Self-portrait* (Pl. 52 *b: s.* 1670), which has much the same raffish pathos. The draperies in both portraits are a cold black and the flesh is pallid and coarse; the details are struck in with an intemperate bravura.

[1] Wright wrote an account of the mission which was printed in Italian in 1687 and in English, with alterations and additions, in 1688.

[2] B.M., MS. 16174, f. 82*v*. The exact date of Wright's death is not known; he was alive at the end of 1690 and a 'John Right' was buried at Covent Garden on 23 February 1700.

[3] Hayls gave Symonds (B.M. Egerton MS. 1636, f. 15) in London a receipt for grinding vermilion which he had 'learnt from that of Miravelt', but there is no evidence of personal contact with Miereveld or of a visit to Italy. A 'Mr. Hales' appeared before the Court of the Painter-Stainers in connexion with the 'Lacquery Pattent', on 29 June 1669, and a 'Mr. Hals' took the Company's livery on 7 September 1687 (*Booke of Orders* . . ., ii, ff. 106, 311).

[4] See below, pp. 291–2.

[5] Waterhouse, Pl. 52. Fuller was ordered by the Painter-Stainers on 18 September 1657 to 'have the makeing of the peece of the Court of Assistants' (*Booke of Orders* . . ., ii, f. 48).

In the short period between Lely's death and the ascendancy of Kneller a small school of portrait painting in London was founded by John Riley, of whom little is known before Lely's death. Riley's style is quite distinct from Lely's or Kneller's and he and his followers were much less prolific than these two painters. Riley himself was a limited painter, but a sensitive observer of character, and his sincerity and vein of tender melancholy no doubt reflect his courteous, modest nature. We can think of his school as to some extent the heir of the native tradition of Bower and Jackson, leading a life of its own at a lower level than the great foreign rivals, with their unassailable prestige, to whose work, however, it constantly looked for inspiration. And in the history of the English portrait Riley occupies an honoured place in the apostolic succession: Richardson was his pupil and in turn was the master and father-in-law of Thomas Hudson, to whom the young Reynolds was bound apprentice in 1740. Perhaps the artistic ancestry of the greatest English portrait painter should be traced back to Soest and Fuller with whom, according to Graham, Riley studied in his youth.[1]

After Lely's death the Painter-Stainers, on 25 November 1681, asked Riley and Lely's old assistant Gaspars to paint for them a portrait (perhaps not *ad vivum*) of the duchess of York.[2] Riley's extant works were all painted between this period and his prema-ture death in 1691. In his more formal portraits he comes very close to the contemporary fashionable pieces by Wissing or Kneller. His *Sir Charles Cotterell* (Pl. 59 b: s. 1687) has a well-bred, reticent gravity, but on a larger scale Riley's weaknesses are at once apparent. The larger of the two portraits of *Elias Ashmole* (1683) at the Ashmolean, *James Sotheby* (1689; Tate), and *Sir William Coventry* at Longleat are excellent examples of Riley's ability in painting the heads of English gentlemen: with silvery

[1] The writer of the anon. B.M. MS. 22950 which has already been quoted (see above, pp. 77, 174) states categorically (f. 34) that 'Mr. Hale that Stuttered, used to temper colours for Mr Reyley, that learnt . . . first of Mr. Fever'. The William Fever of this manuscript is obscure.

[2] *Booke of Orders* . . ., ii, f. 267; 'Mr John Royly' (a common corruption) was made free of the Company on 15 September 1682, and on 9 September 1691 William Lang-ley, 'Servt. to John Royley', was also made free.

lights and cool brown shadows, and a marked soft greyish tone in the hair. But his manipulation of the rest of the body is very wooden, and the obvious weaknesses of Riley's larger canvases are partly due to dual authorship; Johann Baptist Closterman, a native of Osnabrück, came to London (probably in 1681) after spending about two years in Paris with François de Troy, and entered into partnership with Riley.[1] Riley's *Mrs. Elliot* at Kensington Palace is thus described in Queen Anne's inventory: 'Ryley yᵉ Head Closterman yᵉ Drapery', which sufficiently explains the disparity between the two elements. Riley's full-lengths are rare and unusual and he invests Bridget Holmes (s. 1686; Windsor),[2] the nonagenarian housemaid, with the panoply of the most fashionable portraiture of the day, used more appropriately for his four full-lengths at Belton of Sir John and Sir William Brownlow and their wives. On the accession of William and Mary, Riley was appointed Principal Painter, but he shared the post with Kneller[3] and no portrait by Riley of either of the sovereigns is known.

Closterman lacked Riley's delicacy, but was more capable of assembling an elaborate composition. The group of the children of the 6th duke of Somerset at Syon and the larger group of the duchess of Marlborough and her children (*c.* 1696) at Blenheim (to which the figure of the duke appears to be a later addition) are perhaps the first offspring of Van Dyck's *Pembroke Family*. Closterman's style expanded still further under the influence of his travels. In Madrid in 1698 he painted his remarkable full-length of Alexander Stanhope,[4] who is Wycherley's Don Diego in paint and seems to reflect the influence of Spanish court portraiture of the generation after Velazquez. At some period in his career Closterman was taken up by the 3rd earl of Shaftesbury, who was responsible for his visit to Rome in 1699, when he acquired statues and copied pictures, including landscapes by Salvator Rosa, for his

---

[1] Vertue, i. 44, 61.

[2] Waterhouse, Pl. 80.

[3] A payment of £219. 14s. 6d., for example, was ordered to be made to Riley and Kneller on 7 October 1691 (*Cal. Tr. Bks.*, ix, pt. iii, 1333).

[4] Waterhouse, Pl. 88; at Chevening.

patron.[1] In Rome Closterman painted Maratti and absorbed enough of the Roman manner to paint, among the remarkable portraits by his hand at St. Giles's House, a classicizing portrait of his patron (Pl. 55), which is a convincing image of one whose designs 'run all on *moral* emblems and what relates to Ancient Roman and Greek History, Philosophy, and Virtue'.[2] On the other hand, for his spectacular life-size equestrian *Marlborough* (1705) at Chelsea Hospital he turned to Rubens's *Duke of Buckingham* for inspiration.

Three other painters are of less importance: Thomas Murray, Sir John Medina, and Jonathan Richardson. Murray is an obscure and variable painter. His smaller portraits, such as the *Edmund Halley* and *Richard Waller* (Royal Society) or *William Dampier* (s., National Portrait Gallery), all of which probably date from the 1690's, retain much of Riley's grave feeling for character and something of his sense of colour, but are weaker in technique and construction. His full-length portraits have little more than a certain gawky and provincial charm, for all their attempts to set the figure in an elaborate context;[3] he was not above painting historical portraits for Oxford colleges in the tradition of Strong and Greenbury; and the large fortune which he had amassed at the time of his death in 1734 came, in the words of Vertue, 'rather from usury or improvement of his money . . . than by the great imployments in painting'.[4] John Baptist Medina, the son of a Spanish officer who had settled in Brussels, is stated to have come to England in 1686 and was both more talented and more successful than Murray.[5]

---

[1] R. L. Brett, *The Third Earl of Shaftesbury* (1951), 52–53. See also E. Wind, 'Shaftesbury as a Patron of Art', *Journal of the Warburg Institute*, ii (1938–9), 185–8, and above, p. 13.

[2] Shaftesbury to Sir John Cropley, from Naples, 16 February 1712 (B. Rand, *The Life . . . of Anthony, Earl of Shaftesbury* (1900), 468). The portrait is said to have been painted in 1702.

[3] e.g. two full-lengths formerly at Panshanger (Christie's, 16 October 1953, 99, 100); a full-length at Blair Castle of the 1st duke of Atholl (s. 1705) is still entirely in the Riley tradition, but with the lightening of tone that we find in Closterman and unaffected by Kneller. There is no evidence that as early as 1682 he painted the 2nd duke of Albemarle and his duchess; the relevant portraits at Welbeck seem to have been confused by R. W. Goulding in his *Catalogue of the Pictures . . . at Welbeck Abbey . . .* (1936).   [4] Vertue, iii. 75.

[5] Vertue, i. 48–49; ii. 133.

His earliest portraits are close to Riley and Closterman[1] and his powerful *3rd Earl of Leven*[2] is nearer to those painters than to Kneller. Medina seems to have become a favourite with Scots noblemen and it was apparently Leven who persuaded and assisted him to go to Scotland, where, in the extent and success of his practice (he was knighted in 1706) and in the quality of his portraits, he did much to deserve the title of the Scottish Kneller. He stands in the same relation to Kneller as George Jamesone, earlier in the century, had stood to Mytens and the Anglo-Dutch school and as Aikman stood later in relation to Jervas; Michael Wright, indeed, seems to have been the only painter of Scottish extraction who made a personal contribution to the development of the British portrait in the seventeenth century.[3] Medina's later portraits can probably be conveniently placed within Kneller's orbit, though his handling is looser and his tone redder than Sir Godfrey's.

When Richardson died in 1745 at the age of eighty, Vertue thought of him as 'the last of the Eminent old painters that had been contemporyes in Reputation',[4] but for all his earnestness he never overcame the weaknesses of the school in which he had been trained. At an early age he had deserted the scrivener to whom he was bound apprentice and entered Riley's studio, where he remained until his master's death. His heads in oil and his numerous drawings have the directness of Riley; but he had little sense of colour, his draperies have an unpleasant harsh bravura and in his more ambitious canvases the figure bulks uncomfortably large in

[1] e.g. a double-portrait of Hugh and John Cholmley (*s.* 1693), formerly at Howsham.

[2] In the Scottish N.P.G. *s.* 168(3?); in the same collection Medina's *1st Earl of Melville* (*c.* 1686–8) is signed on the back as painted in Drury Lane. Medina is said to have had a talent for history-pieces and landscape and he designed all but one of the curious illustrations for the first illustrated edition (1688) of *Paradise Lost*.

[3] Two other portrait painters active in Scotland in the second half of our period should be mentioned: L. Schuneman, who was probably in good practice in the Restoration period; and Richard Waitt, whose remarkable series of Highland portraits at Castle Grant (*s.* between 1714 and 1725) have a barbaric eccentricity. For the obscure David, John, and George Scougall see Waterhouse, 83–84.

[4] iii. 125; see also iii. 23, 67, 75. Much information on Richardson is contained in G. W. Snelgrove, *The Work and Theories of Jonathan Richardson*, unpub. Ph.D. thesis, London University (1936). And see above, pp. 13–14.

the canvas. These qualities can be seen in the *Sir John Vanbrugh* (1725) at the College of Arms or the extremely cumbersome *5th Viscount Irwin and his Wife* (c. 1718) at Temple Newsam.[1] In certain portraits, such as the fine *1st Earl Cowper*, formerly at Panshanger,[2] he achieved a quiet and sober simplicity which is worthy of Riley at his best. But the qualities which distinguish the school of Riley were not those required in a large fashionable practice and there was no painter working in England after the death of Lely who could rival the 'bold, pushing forwardness', the organizing power or the tireless brush of Godfrey Kneller.[3]

Considerable ability and the untimely death of all serious rivals assured for Kneller, as they had for Lely, an unchallenged position for nearly forty years as the leading portrait painter in London. He was born (probably in 1649, though possibly in 1646)[4] in Lübeck, where his father, Zacharias Kniller, was surveyor to the city, and he was brought up in easy circumstances. He was apparently intended for a military career, but soon discovered where his natural inclination lay, and, when he was in Holland as a very

---

[1] *Leeds Art Calendar*, 7, no. 23 (1953), 16.

[2] Waterhouse, Pl. 89.

[3] Certain shadowy painters can perhaps be placed somewhere between Riley and Kneller. Friedrich Kerseboom (or Casaubon) was born in Germany, studied in Holland, France, and Italy and later came to England, where he died in 1693; his portrait of Theophilus Leigh at Stoneleigh (s. 1688; Collins Baker, ii. 48) is dry and stiff. His nephew Johann's portrait of Boyle, of which the prototype was produced in or by August 1689, and of which there are good versions in the royal collection and the Royal Society, is no less dry and angular, but the full-length of the Duke of Leeds (lent to the Ministry of Works by the Duke of Leeds) in which he was assisted by his friend Van der Vaart (it is s. 1704 by both painters) is a quiet and attractive portrait nearer to Riley than to Kneller. The grandiloquent portraits by Edmund Lilley of William, Duke of Gloucester (Windsor), and Queen Anne (s. 1703; Blenheim) have a Closterman-like sweep, but no freedom or richness of texture.

The minor members of the Verelst family (see Waterhouse, 102–3, 110) stand likewise between Riley and Kneller; Harman Verelst's portraits (e.g. *John Locke*, s. 1689, in the N.P.G.) have a certain sincerity in the heads for all the poverty of invention elsewhere; John Verelst's portraits (such as the two Brandling portraits at Temple Newsam (s. 1698) or a set of signed female portraits (1697–9) at Norton Conyers) are soft and colourless, but in the same tradition.

[4] Vertue (i. 53) states on good authority that Kneller was sixty-nine in 1718; but on his monument in Westminster Abbey he is said to have been seventy-seven at his death in 1723. See M. Davies, catalogue *British School*, N.G. (1946), 89.

young man, he came into contact with Bol and perhaps also with Rembrandt. A picture at Lübeck of an old scholar (*s.* 1668) or the *Elijah and the Angel* (*s.* 1672) in the Tate Gallery are almost indistinguishable from Bol in type. From Holland he went to Italy; he is said to have met Bernini and Maratti in Rome and to have had some success as a portrait painter in Venice. He arrived in England in 1674 or 1675 with a recommendation to a Hamburg merchant named Banks, in whose house Kneller's work attracted the attention of James Vernon, secretary to the duke of Monmouth. Vernon sat to him in 1677 and the portrait led to a sitting from the duke and eventually from the King himself. Kneller, 'Young full of Fire & Ambition', was well on the way to success.

The portrait of Vernon (National Portrait Gallery) is unambitious in presentation and impersonal in technique, with the accessories loosely painted round the soft and carefully modelled face; in the three-quarter-length *Monmouth* at Bowhill (*s.* 1678)[1] the conventions are Lely's and Wissing's, but the affectation, tiresome contrapposto, and soft, colourless flesh are not far from Mignard. Kneller's early pieces have none of the flamboyance of Lely (though he used many of Lely's patterns) and there are elements of Bol, Mignard, and the portrait painters such as Voet, Maratti, Baciccio, and Bombelli, whose works he must have seen in Italy. By the early 1680's he attained a style of some maturity. He never achieved Lely's richness of texture and his earlier canvases are very thin and tend towards a brown monochrome. But sobriety and restraint may have seemed refreshing to patrons grown tired of Lely; and in his early masterpieces (both *s.* 1685), the *3rd Earl of Leicester* at Penshurst,[2] and the sombre *4th Lord Wharton* (Pl. 54), a deliberate simplicity of setting and tone is combined with an austere spontaneity and understanding to which there is no parallel in Lely.

Kneller painted Charles II more than once and in the next reign produced state portraits of James II and Mary of Modena. The arrogant young face which looks out so confidently from the *Self-portrait* (*s.* 1685) in the National Portrait Gallery is that of a painter so assured of success and of his own abilities that he had not

[1] *Burl. Mag.* xcii (1950), 234. [2] Waterhouse, Pl. 84.

hesitated, the year before, to assault one of the official 'searchers' of the Painter-Stainers' Company who had come to investigate his establishment.[1] His appointment as Principal Painter to the new sovereigns at the Revolution marked a further stage in his ascendancy. An increasing amount of his time was taken up with official routine work. As early as 1684 he had been sent by Charles II to paint Louis XIV,[2] and many distinguished foreign visitors sat to him.[3] He was also faced with the steady demand for versions of the authorized likenesses of the successive sovereigns whom he served. The repetition of royal portraits was not a new problem, but Kneller evolved on a larger scale than Lely or Van Dyck the mechanism associated to this day with the State Portrait. In his full-lengths of William III and Mary II at Windsor,[4] which were said to have prompted his knighthood on 3 March 1692, he created a standard image of the sovereigns. The *William III* owes much to Van Dyck's *Charles I in Robes of State* (s. 1636; Windsor),[5] but the suppleness and romance of the Van Dyck has disappeared. The stiffness of *William III* is marked, compared with portraits of the same purpose in France. In the Restoration and early Revolution periods Lely and Kneller can stand comparison with contemporary fashionable portrait painters in France, Holland, and Italy, and were indeed greatly superior to most of them, but Kneller never approached the splendid baroque and early rococo panoply of Rigaud's portraits of Louis XIV and Louis XV; these were, however, a source of inspiration to Ramsay in his enlivening of the

---

[1] The court ordered on 28 August 1684 that Kneller should be prosecuted for his assault on Mr. Robinson (*Booke of Orders* . . ., ii, f. 289). Kneller was naturalized with his brother on 18 April 1683. Kneller's arrogance and conceit were legendary (see, for example, W. T. Whitley, *Artists and their Friends in England* (1928), i. 19–22).

[2] Versions of the full-length canvas are at Drayton and Heckfield Place; the *ad vivum* drawing, inscribed as drawn at Versailles, is at Windsor (rep. A. P. Oppé, *English Drawings . . . at Windsor Castle* (1950), 70). Vanderbank's engraving dates the mission in 1685.

[3] e.g. the Moroccan Ambassador in 1682 (a life-size equestrian portrait, s. 1684, is at Chatsworth), Potemkin, the Russian Ambassador, in 1682, and Peter the Great (s. 1698) and the Emperor Charles VI, painted for the crown in two full-lengths which are still at Kensington.

[4] They are very dirty, but the portrait of Mary appears to be s. 1692.

[5] Glück, *Van Dyck*, 382.

formula for the use of George III.[1] Nevertheless, Kneller's presentations of William and Mary, Anne and George I, as well as those of George II and Caroline of Anspach, though they are among his dullest works, were repeated in large numbers for gifts to friends or for official purposes.[2]

Kneller was able in every way to bear the strains which a vast practice inevitably imposed on him: in health, in his ability to make a sitting a pleasant experience, in the extreme facility with which he worked, in the complacency with which he regarded his own achievements, and in the efficiency with which he ran his studio. His team of specialized assistants could cover a large area of canvas in a very short time[3] under his supervision; and the portraits which poured from his establishments rarely fall below a sound and workmanlike level. But in his own right as a painter Kneller, 'firm in his drawing & ready at his pencil', deserved his reputation. His full-lengths, for example, show a competence and variety unknown in England since the death of Van Dyck. *James II* (s. 1684; National Portrait Gallery) and *Hugh Hare* (s. 1685)[4] are completely

---

[1] A curious piece in this connexion is the portrait of Wren in the Sheldonian, designed by Verrio and carried out by Kneller and Thornhill (Mrs. Poole, *Catalogue of Portraits* . . ., i (1912), 133–4), which is very close in design to Rigaud's *Samuel Bernard* at Versailles and, with it, anticipates Hogarth's *Captain Coram*.

[2] For example: Kneller was ordered in 1697 to prepare a portrait of William for a present to Louis XIV (N. Luttrell, *Brief Relation* (1857), iv. 309); the earl of Albemarle had the King's permission to have two copies of William's portrait and one of Mary's, for which Kneller was paid in January 1700 at his official rate of £50 for each piece (H.M.C. *Buccleuch MSS.*, ii. ii (1903), 631, 635); a Lord Chamberlain's Warrant was issued on 15 November 1705 for payment of £450 to Kneller for nine whole-lengths of Queen Anne (*Cal. Tr. Bks.*, xx, pt. iii, 546); and in a petition to the earl of Oxford *temp.* Queen Anne he asks for the money due to him on the Lord Chamberlain's Warrant for six whole-lengths of the late king (R. W. Goulding, *Catalogue of the Pictures . . . at Welbeck Abbey* . . . (1936), 455–6).

[3] W. T. Whitley, *Artists and their Friends in England* (1928), i. 4–6. Some of Kneller's assistants are known by name. Jan Pieters III was with him as a pupil and drapery-painter, 1685–c. 1712 (Vertue, iii. 33). John James Baker or Backer, the elder Marcellus Laroon, and Edward Byng were also employed by him (see Waterhouse, 109). The volumes of drawings by Edward and Robert Byng in the B.M. contain a large number of studies of portraits by Kneller, which must have served as an admirable pattern-book and indicate clearly the available repertory of designs.

[4] Lent by the earl of Radnor to the Ministry of Works; Countess of Radnor and W. B. Smith, *Catalogue of the Pictures in the Collection of the Earl of Radnor* (1909), i, 18.

convincing: the one a vigorous likeness as well as a swagger assemblage of the trappings of official portraiture, the other a grave and simple presentation with an attractive harmony of blues and greys against the thin browns of the early period. In another mood, two portraits of the Duchess of Portsmouth at Goodwood (one is s., the other s. 1684)[1] are successful essays in the manner of Lely's *Duchess of Norfolk*; and the *Countess of Arran* (s. 1687) at Althorp is a good example of Kneller's use of the more Frenchified conventions of Wissing and Riley in the reign of James II. He also painted equestrian portraits, which Lely is never known to have tackled: the very grand *1st Duke of Schomberg* (Pl. 83 *b*) at Brocklesby exploits a Flemish equestrian type and there is a definite awareness of Rubens in the pretty little sketch of the victorious Duke of Marlborough on horseback in the National Portrait Gallery.[2] The vitality of such a composition inevitably disappeared when it was worked out on the scale of the vast *William III returning from the Treaty of Ryswick* (s. 1701), which was commissioned for the wall of the First Presence Chamber at Hampton Court on which it still hangs.

In Kneller's later years there is much very perfunctory work and an increasing use of the most tiresome mannerisms, but in his best portraits an underlying soundness of construction is generally apparent. Good examples, in a rather formal context, are the full-lengths of the 2nd Duke of Argyll (s. 1717) at Drumlanrig and the 3rd Earl of Sunderland (s. 1720) at Blenheim.[3] In this phase Kneller is very rococo in spirit, with a light key, and a soft broken texture. By the time of his death, on 27 October 1723, he had reached the heights of worldly success: many of the crowned heads of Europe had sat to him and he was a Knight of the Holy Roman Empire; he had been Principal Painter and a Gentleman of the

[1] The latter is reproduced by Waterhouse, Pl. 83; the other is perhaps slightly earlier.

[2] Kneller went to Flanders *c.* 1697 to paint an equestrian portrait of the elector of Bavaria; he also owned the *modello*, now in the Hermitage, for the central panel of the ceiling of the Banqueting House.

[3] The only painter to imitate successfully this phase of Kneller's style was John Vanderbank, whose dashing handling owes much to Kneller and whose compositions, such as *Lady Yonge* (s. 1737) at Sudbury Hall, are frequently rococo reinterpretations of seventeenth-century patterns.

Privy Chamber in three reigns and in 1715 was given a baronetcy; he lived in great state in his country house at Whitton; he was a D.C.L. of Oxford University and Deputy Lieutenant and Justice of the Peace in the County of Middlesex. He was honoured on his monument in Westminster Abbey with an epitaph by Pope. No one in England had vindicated more fully the dignity of his art. Yet he remains an essentially unsympathetic character, for whom even some of the members of the Whig Kit-Cat Club had scant respect.

The set of portraits in the National Portrait Gallery of the members of this Club is his most instructive achievement, and illustrates the importance to the historian of an *œuvre* which covers so long a span of English history. The portraits, which were painted for the secretary of the club, the publisher Jacob Tonson, bring before us the Whig circle of patronage and the party which was responsible for many of the great achievements of the age of Anne. They are also a microcosm of Kneller's range.[1] Some are thoroughly pompous and stereotyped, but it is remarkable how varied is the interest in the individual heads and how fresh and lively the touch. There is sympathy and distinction in the portrait of Somers, a senatorial *hauteur* in Devonshire, shrewd humour in the portraits of Wharton and Garth and real subtlety in that of Vanbrugh; and the brilliant unfinished head of Lord Shannon, with its light modelling and lovely pure silvers and pinks, is a reminder that great powers as a technician are sometimes concealed in Kneller's portraits by the weight of the conventional accessories. The most remarkable of all, however, is that of Tonson himself (s. 1717), which has an ease, informality, and blunt understanding which anticipate Hogarth. Therein lies Kneller's importance to the historian of British painting. When 'his fancy was warm' he could produce portraits which introduce us to something quite new. For all Lely's great technical gifts (and they were greater than Kneller's) his portraits are invariably set in moulds which had been made earlier and his temperament produced a uniformity of feeling with which his whole *œuvre* is charged. 'It was objected', wrote Dryden in the Preface to his *Poetical Miscellanies* of 1685,

[1] Most of the portraits are signed; dated canvases run between 1702 and 1717. For the Club and its portraits see the special pamphlet issued by the N.P.G. (1945).

'against a late noble Painter, that he drew many graceful Pictures, but few of them were like. And this happen'd to him because he always studied himself, more than those who sat to him'. Kneller, though profoundly indebted to his predecessors, can sometimes, with an understanding beyond Lely's range, take us completely by surprise: with, for example, the deep sympathy of *Mrs. Jennings* (c. 1685) at Althorp or the piercing insight of *Isaac Newton* (s. 1702; National Portrait Gallery). Nor does the average work of his studio prepare us for the *Chinese Convert* (s. 1687; Kensington), with its technical mastery and its echoes of Rome, or for the sheer brilliance of *Matthew Prior* (s. 1700; Trinity College, Cambridge). And he can also, on rare occasions, discard or transcend the conventions of his age. Perhaps his masterpiece, and certainly one of the most eloquent of English portraits, is, appropriately, *John Dryden* (Pl. 56).[1] The canvas is painted with great brilliance, entirely in a grey and silver key; the extreme simplicity of the design, the loose robe, and the easy gesture with which the old man holds his laureate's wreath have an air of Augustan informality which looks forward to the noble simplicity of Reynolds's finest and most sympathetic portraits.

The only painter to maintain at the same period as Kneller a practice of some importance was the Swede Michael Dahl, who was born in Stockholm, probably in 1656, and studied there under Ehrenstrahl. On 30 July 1682 he was given a pass to travel and came to England, as Kneller had done earlier, under the protection of a merchant. In April 1685 he was in Paris on his way to Italy, where he was a close friend of Tilson. They seem to have returned to London in 1689.[2] According to Vertue,[3] 'the Great busines and high carriage of Kneller gave a lustre to the actions or workes of M^r. Dahl . . . a man of great Modesty and few words', and the affable Dahl enjoyed steady patronage. He was patronised by

---

[1] It is sometimes stated to be s. 1697; there is no evidence for this, though it must date from that period. See C. H. Collins Baker, 'The Craftsmanship of Kneller', *Connoisseur*, cxxvii (1951), 29–32, for comments on Kneller's technique.

[2] While in Rome in 1687 he painted Queen Christina; but the portrait of which there are versions at Grimsthorpe and Attingham seems to be by Kneller. Tilson's pass for his journey from Rome to London is dated 29 October 1687; see above, p. 180.   [3] iii. 118.

Prince George of Denmark, painted full-lengths of Queen Anne, and was not tempted in 1698 by the offer of Ehrenstrahl's post as painter to the King of Sweden. At his death at an advanced age on 20 October 1743, he was regarded as the grand old man among portrait painters and his stocky little figure occupies the place of honour in Gawen Hamilton's conversation piece of a *Club of Artists* (1735; National Portrait Gallery). He was, however, slighted by the Hanoverians. Kneller's association with the Kit-Cats indicates that he was a Whig; Dahl was definitely a Tory. When the Tory Sir Justinian Isham wrote to his son on 25 June 1711[1] of his hopes that he would be painted, he made no mention of Kneller: 'you will have leisure to sit for your Picture, wch I wou'd have you do, either at Doll's or Dagars[2] wch you fancy most, and I will pay for it'. Dahl was among the artists, such as Gibbs, Wootton, Thornhill, and Bridgeman, who in 'virtuoso or connoisseur affairs' were in the circle of the Tory 2nd earl of Oxford.[3]

As a painter Dahl was less gifted than his rival. An innate dour honesty fits uneasily with his attempts at fashionable female portraiture. In the series of portraits of peeresses at Petworth, commissioned by the 6th duke of Somerset after a quarrel with Closterman, the dumpy figures have nothing of Kneller's assurance and their tiresome mannerisms are unrelated to the background and accessories.[4] Dahl was more at home with sitters of a different

[1] MS. at Lamport.

[2] This is Charles, son of Jacques D'Agar, a Huguenot refugee who worked as a portrait painter in England and Copenhagen. The son was in London in the 1680's, settled there in 1691, and had a respectable practice (notably as a painter of women), though he had little of the necessary talent. Thomas Gibson, a respectable but very limited portrait painter, is just worthy of mention; his *William Wake* at Christ Church is a colourless Knellerian piece, not without a certain sensitivity of character.

Thomas Hill, a contemporary of Dahl and a friend of Tilson, was in Lord Oxford's circle; there is often a Dahl-like quality in his draperies and his double-portrait of two children of the St. Clere family (*s.* 1699) at Belchamp Hall has something of Dahl's gallicisms with an individual delicacy and understanding (see Waterhouse, 101, and R. W. Goulding, *Catalogue of the Pictures . . . at Welbeck Abbey . . .* (1936), 449–50, for his work for the Strangways family at Melbury).

[3] There are many lively references to this circle in Prior's correspondence, H.M.C. *Bath MSS.*, iii (1908); Oxford was one of Dahl's most generous patrons.

[4] An exception in the Petworth series is the *Countess of Pembroke*, an elegant

temper, *Sir Justinian Isham* (1711) at Lamport or the naval officers
in the National Maritime Museum. The latter have none of the
dash of the best of the portraits by Kneller with which they have
always hung, but as portraits they are completely honest and full
of humanity. Dahl's technique is quite unlike Kneller's: his texture is thinner and more even, the modelling is built up in shorter,
drier strokes and normally has none of Kneller's breadth and ease.
His colour is also quite different and his canvases are suffused by a
soft, greyish powdered tone. His light touch and pastel-like texture often create a completely rococo impression; the delicate
pathos of some of his female sitters, the artificialities and fluttering
draperies of such of his children as the portraits of a boy at Drumlanrig and a girl at Stoneleigh, and the silvery tone of a late full-length
like the *2nd Viscount Weymouth* (s. 1735; Longleat), belong wholly
to the eighteenth century. His masterpiece is the arresting *Self-
portrait* (Pl. 52 a: s. 1691). It is quite personal in colour: cold maroon
and purple-grey against a very plain pale grey background, which
sets off the deeply felt and carefully constructed head. But it is the
Frenchness of the portrait that is most striking; the pose has an air
of Largillierre and passages like the left hand and the bust are
very rococo and could almost have been painted by Mercier.[1]

There is no such dramatic moment in the evolution of the
English portrait in the later Stuart period as the arrival of Van
Dyck at the court of Charles I. As in so much of contemporary
European portraiture the tendency in the closing decades of the
century is towards mannerisms which are at best soundly painted
and at worst infinitely tedious. With the turn of the century, in
Dahl and in Kneller's later phase, the artificiality becomes lighter
and gayer. Only the comparatively small group of masterpieces

standing figure in silver and grey which faintly anticipates the design of Gainsborough's *Mrs. Graham.* Dahl's work at Petworth justifies Walpole's scathing
description (*Anecdotes,* ed. Wornum, ii. 260).

[1] An odd example of Dahl in another vein is the *Holy Family* (s. 1691) in Stockholm;
his largest canvas is the equestrian *Prince George of Denmark* (s. 1704) at Kensington in
which only the figure can be by Dahl. From 1700 Dahl was assisted by his fellow
countryman, Hans Hysing; Hysing's full-length of the 4th duke of Leeds as a boy
in Highland costume (s. 1726; lent by the duke of Leeds to the Ministry of Works)
is still very Dahl-like in handling and mood.

by Kneller stand apart from the degeneration of the Van Dyck tradition, which was at its lowest ebb in the 1720's,[1] and anticipate the fresh approach to that tradition which was to mark the golden age of English painting.

To the uninitiated it will always be a dull period. A survey of this kind can hardly avoid a certain monotony and can only cover the principal developments of the leading painters in London. But the smart London studios could not have been solely responsible for the immense output of portraits between the Restoration and the death of George I. Many painters were at work in the provinces and even some of the bigger men had local connexions. Lely, perhaps just before the Restoration, spent some time 'at gentlemens' houses' near Bury St. Edmunds;[2] Greenhill's connexions with Salisbury probably led to his employment by the Shaftesbury family and by the corporation of his native city; Wissing had a circle of patrons in the neighbourhood of Stamford; and Wright hints in his correspondence at visits to the country in the summer months.[3] With the use of engravings, and perhaps by personal contact, the provincial painters could form their unsophisticated styles. Mr. Comer, for example, was a friend of the Beales who worked in York and in 1683 and 1685 produced for the duke of Newcastle a set of adequate imitations of Lely's fashionable patterns.[4] There were perhaps local painters of greater ability, such as the obscure Stephen Browne, who may have had patrons in the West Country,[5] but much of English painting in the provinces hardly rose above journeyman level. Jeremias van der Eyden, a drapery painter and copyist in Lely's studio, who was later employed in the provinces, especially at Belvoir in the 1670's in

---

[1] It is most revealing that when Vertue saw Walpole's magnificent collection of Van Dycks he noted: 'I cant help thinking that in time to come in pictures of Sʳ. G. Kneller thein [sic] will be found as much truth of Nature, disposition. light & shade. force. as these picture' (i. 110).

[2] He spoke kindly of the 'very good judgment' of the local painter Mr. Blemwell (Roger North, *Lives*, ed. A. Jessopp (1890), ii. 273–4).

[3] W. J. Smith, 'Letters from Michael Wright', *Burl. Mag.* xcv (1953), 236.

[4] R. W. Goulding, *Catalogue of the Pictures . . . at Welbeck Abbey . . .* (1936), 434.

[5] There is a very competent small group at Badminton (s. 1685) of the 1st duke of Beaufort and his family which is close to Netscher (R. Edwards, *Early Conversation Pieces* (1954), 162, Pl. 118).

mending screens as well as in painting pictures,[1] or Jacob de Witt, who produced the grotesque series of kings for Holyroodhouse in 1684, were working in the impersonal craftsman tradition of an earlier age. Even in London and Oxford civic or university patronage gave employment to painters of far humbler status than those with whom this chapter has been mainly concerned. The Merchant Taylors' Company commissioned portraits in 1672–4 from Robert Mallory, Symonds's 'Captayne of the Citty & a doughty painter by the Stocks who hangs out things On the Church Wall'. He was probably their own 'Master' who could be employed (1675) to 'trim up' one of their monuments in St. Botolph's.[2] The portrait painter Willem Sonmans, who worked in Oxford in term-time, was employed to paint a set of the Founders of the Colleges of Oxford which still decorates Duke Humphrey's Library and of which sets of engravings were made available to visitors.[3]

Work of this nature could remain within a purely native tradition; Thomas Sadler's *Bunyan* (*s.* 1684) or John Wollaston's *Thomas Britton* (*s.* 1703), the musician and coal-merchant, in the National Portrait Gallery, are wholly in the spirit of Gilbert Jackson. Painting was still a polite accomplishment for amateur artists: women like Mrs. Pepys, whose lessons from Mr. Browne in 1665–6 caused her husband such pleasure, despite her neglect of housekeeping and a possible over-fondness for her instructor, and Anne Killigrew, the minor poetess to whom Dryden addressed an ode and who painted little portraits and Lelyesque subject-pieces;[4] or, most interesting of all, Hugh Howard, 'son to a worthy gentleman . . . a doctor of physic', whose father agreed to his travelling on the Continent to study painting, but who, despite the know-

[1] H.M.C. *Rutland MSS.* iv (1905), 552; this provides a useful link with the journeyman work done nearly a hundred years earlier by John Matthewe of Nottingham for the same family (see above, p. 80 n.) For local painters at this date see also Waterhouse, 77, Duleep Singh, *Portraits in Norfolk Houses* (1927), and Rev. E. Farrer, *Portraits in Suffolk Houses, West* (1908).

[2] F. M. Fry, *A Historical Catalogue of the Pictures . . . at Merchant Taylors' Hall* (1907), 59–60, 81, 94, 101.

[3] Mrs. Poole, *Catalogue of Portraits . . .*, i. (1912), 1 et seq.

[4] Sir L. Cust and C. H. Collins Baker, *Burl. Mag.* xxviii (1915), 112.

ledge and expertise which he had acquired in matters of *virtù*, gave up painting for a lucrative post in the Paper Office.[1] Except for the specialist (and often even for him) the temptation to linger over the minor painters in the later Stuart period is very slight. The feeblest painters earlier in the century, if only because of an appealing archaism or, at the lowest, because of the decorative value of the costumes of their sitters, are never wholly devoid of interest; but bad English painting in the late seventeenth and early eighteenth centuries, when the fashionable commonplaces and conventional pomposities are taken over from the big London studios without any ability to give them meaning, is beneath contempt.

[1] H.M.C. *Bath MSS.* iii (1908), 110–11; H.M.C. *Egmont MSS., Egmont Diary,* i (1920), 224–5; many of Howard's books were sold at Sotheby's 11–12 December 1950 and were a very instructive example of a traveller's and connoisseur's library.

There are a great many more names which could be quoted, and for some of them see Waterhouse, 109 (9), and Collins Baker, ii. 186–224, to which the following should perhaps be added: John Linton, who was co-opted on a committee of 'acting painters' of the Painter-Stainers' Company in 1680 and may have worked in the City; Mr. Rapson, who was ordered by the same Company to paint the King's picture in 1664; and Savill, who painted Pepys and his wife (1661–2) to their satisfaction, though they found him 'very silly as to matters of skill in shadows'.

IX

NEW TRENDS IN ARCHITECTURE
AND THE APPLIED ARTS

BETWEEN 1675 and 1690 a change of emphasis can be seen in English architecture. The dependence on Italian High Renaissance models (and therefore, to a large extent, on Inigo Jones) steadily weakens. Dutch and French motives recur, but they are gradually absorbed and combined with new baroque features, coming direct from Italy. It is not, however, possible to trace this evolution in a neat progression of buildings, nor to find precise historical reasons for changes of style. It would be convenient if specifically Roman baroque features could be associated with the reign of the Catholic James II, and if there was an overwhelming Dutch tendency after 1688. Nothing so tidy occurs. Strong baroque elements appear in architecture and decoration about 1680. In the latter, they are no doubt due to the arrival of Antonio Verrio, but it is impossible to believe that that rather inept painter would have modified materially Wren's conception of exterior design. Dutch elements, on the other hand, are far more marked in the architecture of Dr. Robert Hooke in 1676 than they are in the palaces built for William III about 1690. The influence of France is recurrent; Versailles, the Invalides, and the east front of the Louvre have all left their mark on English architecture. But it is not possible to isolate a Roman, a French, or a Dutch phase. All three foreign styles are used during the same years and often in the same buildings (and this applies equally to the period after 1690) but the result is an architecture which is neither Italian, French, nor Dutch baroque, but an increasingly interwoven mixture of the three, combined with elements borrowed from none, which are peculiarly English.[1]

In 1675, however, Wren was still thinking mainly in a High

[1] For a general discussion of English baroque art, and its basis in English thought, see G. Webb, 'Baroque Art', *Proc. Brit. Acad.* xxxiii (1947).

Renaissance idiom. This is nowhere more apparent than in the first secular building of his maturity, the Library of Trinity College, Cambridge (Pl. 45 *b*). As with most of his work, the preliminaries are interesting and revealing. After an abortive project for a new Senate House for the University (presumably to rival the Sheldonian Theatre at Oxford), Wren was commissioned by Dr. Barrow, the Master of Trinity, to build a library. Tradition has it that the Master, disgusted at the inertia of the University, was determined to show what a single college could do. The new library was to stand at the river end of Nevile's Court, and the first design[1] shows a square domed building, circular inside,[2] with a portico on the court front and linked by curved railings to the existing sides of the court. It is beyond all doubt based on Palladio's Villa Rotonda. The second, executed, design was for the oblong building which now closes the end of Nevile's Court. The elevation to the court (which is more important and consequently more elaborate than the river front) is divided into two almost equal storeys, both treated with an order. The Library is entered from the end, consequently there was no need for an accent anywhere on the façade, but a slight emphasis on the centre is given by the four statues by Cibber breaking the skyline. Jones, faced with the same problem at the Banqueting House, had slightly advanced his centre bays, changing the rhythm from pilasters to half-columns. Wren, at any rate early in his architectural career (and this must still be regarded as an early work), is less apt to introduce refinements of this kind unless they are demanded by practical considerations. Trinity College Library, with its simple repeated motives, its sharply defined storeys, its apparently orthodox well-proportioned orders with their unbroken entablatures, is in many

[1] In the Library of All Souls, Oxford. See *Wren Soc.* v. 32, and Pls. xviii–xxi. This volume also contains the drawings for the existing Library, and the interesting correspondence between Wren and the Master, which shows his care for practical detail.

[2] Wren appears to have been interested in the idea of a circular library, since he had provided one in the first design for St. Paul's (see above, p. 164). He was never to execute this or indeed any of his designs for circular buildings (e.g. the Mausoleum for Charles I and the Baptistery for St. Paul's), but they probably counted for something in the complex evolution of the design for the Radcliffe Camera at Oxford, in which both Nicholas Hawksmoor (see below, p. 349) and James Gibbs were concerned.

ways the most Italianate of his buildings, the Italianism being, of course, of the sixteenth rather than of the seventeenth century.[1] The design is, however, less orthodox than it appears, for the floor level of the library is not, as might be expected, at the top of the lower order, but has been dropped to the base of the lunettes filling the arches of the loggia. It had to be at this level, since it was originally intended that the Library should be reached from the first floor of the older buildings at the sides of the court. The high interior resulting from Wren's arrangement is admirably suited to its purpose, for the lower parts of the walls are lined with bookcases, and the tall windows above them give an excellent light for readers. On the exterior the loggia is, perforce, very low, but attention is diverted from it by the emphatic lines of the super-imposed orders. The solution is ingenious, for no complete order could have been fitted in below the floor level, and the alternative of a single giant order would have dwarfed the existing build-ings.

In the same year (1676) that Trinity College Library was begun the King opened Bedlam Hospital, Moorfields (Pl. 45 a), designed by Wren's friend and associate, Dr. Robert Hooke.[2] The contrast between the two buildings affords an admirable illustration of the state of English architecture. Hooke's façade of brick with stone dressings (which is admittedly much longer than Wren's and is not joined to older buildings) is divided into five sections—three similar tall pavilions at the centre and ends, joined by long, lower wings. This method of breaking up a façade is French (Le Vau's design for the river front of the court of the Louvre offers one of many parallels) and the emphasis on the high pitched roof broken by dormers, which affords the strongest possible contrast to Wren's

[1] It is conceivable that he knew of Sansovino's Library of St. Mark's, Venice, also a building with two superimposed orders and unbroken entablatures, though it is not illustrated in any of the Italian treatises on architecture.

[2] For documents see M. I. Batten, 'The Architecture of Dr. Robert Hooke', *Walpole Soc.* xxv (1937), 91. Hooke's building was pulled down in the early nineteenth century, but is recorded in the series of painted medallions which still forms part of the decoration of the Court Room of the Foundling Hospital. Hooke's house for Lord Conway at Ragley showed a similar blend of French and Dutch motives, while his design for Montagu House, Bloomsbury (burnt in 1686), was regarded as peculiarly French (see Evelyn, *Diary*, 11 May and 5 November 1679; 10 October 1683).

horizontal balustrade, may also be ultimately French in origin. But the pavilions, both in their proportion and their design, are Dutch. The introduction of an order on the upper floor only can be seen in contemporary Dutch buildings such as the back of the Gravensteen at Leiden (1670) and the use of festoons between the windows (probably carved in stone against the brick background) is a common Dutch form of decoration. Indeed, the whole appearance of this building, with its sober brick façades, is clearly far closer to Holland than to the architecture of Inigo Jones, though on the other hand, its great length compared with its height would at once proclaim it as English.

Meanwhile, Hugh May was moving in a different direction. Two of his works of the 1670's, Cassiobury Park, built for the Earl of Essex, and his alterations to Windsor Castle, were, indeed, to provide the pattern for English baroque decoration. Unfortunately, Cassiobury was pulled down early in the present century, and the work at Windsor hopelessly mutilated by Wyatville in the reign of George IV, so their importance is easily overlooked. In both, May employed artists who had some continental background: Grinling Gibbons who was born in Rotterdam in 1648, and Antonio Verrio, an Italian. May was also a close friend of Sir Peter Lely, and so appears to have been more cosmopolitan in his contacts than Wren. It was perhaps through Lely that May first met Gibbons. Evelyn relates the romantic story of his discovery of the young carver working in a lonely hut in Deptford Marshes, and of his introduction a couple of months later to Wren and the King.[1] But by then Gibbons had been brought to the notice of Lely by Betterton the actor, for whom he was working on the Duke's Playhouse in Dorsett Garden, and it is probable that Evelyn was not, as he suggests, the sole means of the young man's advancement. And it was certainly May rather than Wren who gave him his first important commissions. May had been in Holland;[2] he must have been familiar with Dutch naturalistic painting (especially flower painting) which is so clearly one of the formative elements in Gibbons's style. It is uncertain where Gibbons had learnt his art, but during the 1650's the Quellin family and their

[1] *Diary*, 18 January 1671.   [2] See above, p. 132.

assistants were carrying out marble decoration inside the Town Hall at Amsterdam (now the Royal Palace) which included flowers, fruit, and shells strung together and treated with extreme naturalism. Gibbons's wood carving as well as his sculpture in stone[1] seems to suggest a dependence on this workshop, and he was possibly trained as a boy in it.

The work at Cassiobury probably preceded that at Windsor[2] and was, therefore, the first appearance of the new form of decoration that was to be dominant for the rest of the century. The architectural framework used by Jones and his school for door-cases and fireplaces begins to disappear. It is replaced by a series of simple mouldings, and interest is concentrated on the trails of flowers and fruit which hang loosely above and beside the pictures. At Cassiobury these were still arranged in relatively tight ropes and bunches; very soon they were to appear to be thrown together haphazard, lightly bound with ribbons or trails of primroses, though the apparent casualness is a mask for consummate skill in design. The process reaches its peak in the decoration which Gibbons was to carry out for Wren in the 1690's at Hampton Court and on the choir-stalls of St. Paul's.

The work at Windsor is of far greater importance, and had even greater consequences for English art. Its significance has been largely neglected,[3] although it occupied an unparalleled position in the history of English domestic architecture, and marks the introduction of a number of new elements. It reveals, further, that Charles II was by no means so completely uninterested in the arts as is generally supposed. In the course of about nine years he was to spend at least £190,000 on the new works at Windsor, an enormous sum for a King who was kept short of money by Parliament. He had already begun a palace at Greenwich,[4] though work there seems to have ceased about 1669, and as soon as the

---

[1] See below, p. 245.

[2] The dates for Cassiobury are not fully established, but Evelyn states (*Diary*, 18 April 1680) that Essex brought marble chimney-pieces from Ireland when he was Lord Deputy, a post he relinquished in 1676. The first payment to Gibbons at Windsor is 1677 (W. St. John Hope, *Windsor Castle* (1914), i. 315).

[3] Except by G. Webb, 'Baroque Art', *Proc. Brit. Acad.* xxxiii (1947).

[4] See above, p. 133.

work at Windsor was nearing completion he started to build a further palace at Winchester.

In 1673 Hugh May, who had hoped for the Royal Surveyorship in 1669, was, perhaps in compensation, made Controller of the Works at Windsor Castle, a post he held until his death in February 1684. By about 1680 he had designed two large new buildings to replace older work on the north terrace, and a new east front had been built. In his exterior designs[1] May respected the general character of the medieval building, and with great tact refrained from disturbing it by a classical design. Far more important was the planning and decoration of the interior.[2] Architecturally, the most novel feature of the castle was perhaps the entrance to the new royal apartments. These were approached through a vestibule, the ceiling of which was supported by two rows of Ionic columns, the walls behind them being decorated by niches which contained 'ancient busts'.[3] This led to an inner vestibule, also adorned with casts of antiques (the *Spinario* being one of them) behind which rose the grand staircase. This, a stone staircase in three flights with an ironwork balustrade, stood within a painted hall and was surmounted by a painted dome. It was certainly the first grand painted staircase executed in England, and its impact on the visitor emerging from the relatively low, columned vestibule, must have been tremendous.

The later of the two blocks built by May contained the King's Staircase, the Chapel Royal, and St. George's Hall as well as other apartments. The King's Stair was different in form, set in a narrow, oblong hall (the entrance in the middle of one long side) with a flight rising on each side of the door, and turning back sharply on itself to reach the landing. The walls were painted with scenes from the Trojan Legend and the dome above with the Battle of the

---

[1] See A. P. Oppé, *The Drawings of Paul and Thomas Sandby at Windsor Castle* (1949), Pl. 3. Engravings by Batty Langley, reproduced in W. St. John Hope, *Windsor Castle* (1914), i, Pl. 35 are not entirely correct. Some windows with heavy unmoulded architraves remain though altered in Henry III's tower.

[2] For the decoration, see below, pp. 296–300.

[3] St. John Hope, *Windsor Castle* (1914), i. 336, quoting George Bickham, junr., *Deliciæ Britannicæ; or the Curiosities of Hampton Court and Windsor Castle delineated*, 1742.

Giants. The whole splendid display would have been visible at once from the door. This staircase must have been the one used by official visitors, since the King's Guard Chamber (the normal approach to the royal presence) was at the top, and its form suggests that it was modelled on the new Escalier des Ambassadeurs at Versailles, finished in 1679.

These great domed and painted staircases were a major innovation, combining, as they did, architecture and painting on a grand scale. The Chapel Royal (Pl. 79 *a*) and St. George's Hall were, however, even more revolutionary, for there the three arts of architecture, painting and carving were combined, and so a true baroque fusion was achieved. Inevitably it was a limited, modified form of baroque, since in an Anglican chapel no sculptured figures beyond *amorini* could be used, and so the complete illusionism of Roman baroque churches in which sculptured saints and angels are mingled with the painted panoply of Heaven is lacking. The carved ornament, for which Gibbons was paid £1,016. 0*s.* 5½*d.*,[1] was of extraordinary richness 'XXVIII Seates and Stalls, carved with Fruit, Flowers, Palmes, Laurells, Pelicans, Pigeons. . . . Six Vasses with Thistles Roses and two Boys[2] Laurel and Palmes and other ornaments in the Front and upon the Topp of the Kings Seate with Drapery, Fruit, Flowers, Crootesses,[3] Starrs, Roses and severall other ornaments of carving about the Altar Pews and other places'. One gets the impression of woodwork freed from architectural restraint, taking on a liveliness of its own, reinforcing the richness of the painted architecture above, and standing as an integral part of the decorated interior. Much, naturally, must have been due to the talents of the individual artists, Verrio and Gibbons, but the credit for the conception of the whole must surely be given to Hugh May, though the part played by the King himself may not have been negligible.

By about 1680 it is evident that Wren was gradually moving away from his dependence on Jones and Palladio. His almost daily

---

[1] St. John Hope, op. cit. 321.

[2] This is the usual term in the seventeenth century (and indeed in the eighteenth century also) for *amorini*, whether winged or not.

[3] Presumably cartouches, i.e. ornamental shields.

contact with Hooke over the City churches must have meant an increasing knowledge of the contemporary architectural books and engravings of which Hooke was so eager a collector, and which, as Wren was never again to leave England, were to be his source of information for French buildings executed after 1665 and for the whole of seventeenth-century Italian architecture. The change in his style, and also his growing maturity as an architect, can perhaps most easily be seen in the evolution of St. Paul's (for plan, see Fig. 8). The east end begun in 1675 still shows him looking to Jones for inspiration. The two-storeyed design with pilasters set in front of a lightly rusticated wall surface, and festoons joining the capitals of the order (and not, as one would expect, decorating the frieze) is directly derived from the Banqueting House. The large round-headed windows with lugged architraves are, however, French, and their introduction, which changes the proportion between voids and solids, at once renders Wren's elevation less strictly Palladian than the work of Jones.

In the centre bay of the east end Wren established a two-storey elevation. The Warrant drawings had made it clear that the medieval church pattern of a high central vessel (choir and nave) flanked by lower aisles was to be followed. Only at the extreme east end and on the transept and west fronts, where the high inner space ran right to the outer walls, would there be an exterior two storeys high. Elsewhere the projecting aisles would present a single-storey elevation, with the upper part of choir or nave set back within and above them. This was the disposition which had been accepted by Jones also in his recasing of the nave in the 1630's. But it does not exist in the executed building. The side view, like that from the east end, shows a two-storey wall rising unbroken from the ground (Pl. 41 *b*). This major change in the design, entailing an alteration from the foundations upwards, must have been made very quickly.[1] The wording of the Warrant permitting

---

[1] J. Summerson, *Sir Christopher Wren* (1953), 104, suggests that all the changes between the Warrant and executed designs below dome level were conceived in 1675. He bases this on the attribution of a drawing at All Souls (*Wren Soc.* i. xix; Summerson, *Wren* (1953), Pl. 6: idem, *Architecture in Britain* (1953), Pl. 81 *a*) to the hand of Edward Woodroffe, who died towards the end of that year. If this is so, the final scheme must be almost contemporary with the Warrant. The All Souls elevation must

10 0 10 20 30 40 60 Feet

FIG. 8. *St. Paul's Cathedral: executed plan*

'variations, rather ornamental than essential' may have been included intentionally, to tie the architect to the Latin cross plan (regarded as 'essential'), but to allow him great freedom in interpretation. The King, who was himself a shrewd man and well used to threading his way through a host of difficulties, may have understood something of the position. The alteration in the elevation is, indeed, both ornamental and essential. There can be no doubt that the outer wall, rising to a great height in a single plane (instead of in the two planes of the medieval form) has a cliff-like grandeur. The building appears as a solid mass of great size, providing a fitting base for the dome resting on it. Viewed from the outside, it would seem that a radical change had also been made in the interior disposition of the church. Windows seem to be set in the upper storey of the walls, suggesting that the aisles are now the same height as the choir. This is not the case. The aisles are still one storey high, and the central vessel is set back above them. The upper part of the walls is in fact a screen (the apparent windows are merely niches)[1] masking a deep trough. In this, rising above the aisle roofs, are flying buttresses which support the vaults of choir and nave; and clerestory windows, as in a medieval church, pierce the inner wall between the buttresses. Wren has often been criticized (mainly by nineteenth-century architectural writers who were still consciously or unconsciously influenced by Ruskin) for the use of these screen walls, which were regarded as false and therefore immoral. Such a view overlooks the fact that, misleading though these walls may be, they do indeed perform an important structural function. They act as stiffening and buttressing masses at precisely that point in the angles of the cross at which the weight of the dome is transmitted to the outer walls. Without them, the upper walls of the church itself might well gradually

in any case be earlier than 1681 (the date of the building of the transept fronts) since the upper part of the transepts is not as built. The sequence is puzzling, for it seems to imply a complete alternative to the Warrant, unsupported by documentary reference, and not a gradual evolution from it. For a brilliant analysis of the final design, see Summerson, 139 f.

[1] The small windows which appear beneath the niches are real and light the passage between the aisle vaults and the sloping roofs above them. The niches themselves are copied from Serlio's plate of the interior of the Pantheon.

have been pushed outwards by the weight of the dome. With them, the weight is distributed over a larger area, and at the same time is more completely controlled.[1]

The design of the transept fronts was also modified. The Warrant plan shows small interior vestibules at the ends of the transepts, entered between columns set flush with the wall. The building, however, has semicircular exterior porches each of six Corinthian columns, which are beautiful in themselves, and which echo the movement of the great dome above. Here, surely, Wren is borrowing from Roman baroque, perhaps from Sta Maria della Pace (of which Hooke had bought a print in 1677),[2] or from S. Andrea al Quirinale. In the decoration of the upper part of the transept fronts, too, a new surface treatment appears (Pl. 42). (The accounts show that the carving was done as soon as the stone was set, and not left to be finished later.) The profusion of fruits and flowers which surround the central window is so disposed that the eye is led from one member to another. The movement is gentle and undramatic, the architectural forms are simple, and there is no element of surprise. Nevertheless, the intention is clear; the different units are bound together in a larger whole by their decoration and the architect is thinking in baroque and not in Palladian terms.

Since, in the early 1680's, Wren had reached the transepts, it might have been expected that he would soon fulfil the terms of the Warrant, and furnish the choir so that services could be held. But Wren chose to ignore the Warrant. By 1684 Edward Strong[3] was working on the north side of the nave, and it was not until a year later that a contract was signed for the great cornice inside the choir. The cathedral, indeed, was not being built by parts! Work now proceeded simultaneously in nave, choir, and transepts (Pl. 41 *b*). The organization necessary for controlling so great a work was immense, and can be deduced from the published accounts.

---

[1] Similar screen walls are used in the west bays of the nave of St. Peter's, added by Maderno at the beginning of the seventeenth century, to mask the fact that the side chapels are lower than the nave. It is possible that Wren may have known of their existence.

[2] *Diary*, 10 June 1677.

[3] Younger brother of Thomas Strong, who had died in 1681.

Four chief master masons were employed (they necessarily changed during the long history of the building, though Edward Strong first appears in the accounts in 1679, and was still at work in 1707). Much of the stone had to be brought round by sea from Portland, and so to risk the dangers of capture by hostile Dutch or French fleets, and, further, a special wharf had to be built for unloading it. Wren, or more frequently later his head clerk Nicholas Hawksmoor, who entered his office in 1679, had to visit the quarries to hasten the delivery of stone. Other stone came from elsewhere, for instance from the Oxfordshire quarries owned by the Strongs, who had so long a connexion with the building. A vast number of bricks were needed, and with the brickmakers and bricklayers, as with all the other trades, the architect was directly concerned. There was no general building contractor, as in modern practice, responsible for sub-contracts; separate contracts were still made by the architect, who was naturally responsible for seeing that they were carried out. The day-to-day volume of work on the Surveyor's shoulders must have been enormous, and it must always be remembered that St. Paul's was only one (though admittedly the greatest) of his many undertakings.[1]

Further alterations were made in the plan. The five bays of the Warrant nave were reduced to three (Pl. 43), thus making it equal to the choir, with a larger domed bay echoing the Great Model at the west. This large bay serves as a vestibule on entering the church, and provides a much-needed space for the assembly of processions. Two chapels were introduced on the north and south sides of the nave. These chapels, though their interior effect is very fine, are sometimes criticized because on the exterior they break the length of the nave. This would not have been distasteful to the architect, whose predilection was for a centrally planned church, with the major accent on the great space under the dome.

[1] Wren evidently visited St. Paul's once a week, as he had noted was Colbert's habit at the Louvre. Roger North (*Lives of the Norths*, ed. Jessopp (1890), ii. 238), speaking of the building, writes: 'We usually went there on Saturdays, which were Sir Christopher Wren's days . . .; and we commonly got a snatch of discourse with him'. For Roger North's own work at Middle Temple Gateway, London, and elsewhere, and his criticisms of Wren, see H. M. Colvin, 'Roger North and Sir Christopher Wren', *Archit. Review*, cx (1951), 257.

Any alteration which offered a distraction from the longitudinal accent would have been acceptable, and the change he had already made in the interior bay design was largely for this purpose.

The development of Wren's architecture away from the High Renaissance Italianism of Jones can also be clearly seen in his two important secular buildings of the early 1680's, the Royal Hospital at Chelsea, built mainly between 1683 and 1690 (Pl. 61 b),[1] and the palace at Winchester begun for Charles II in 1683, but never finished.[2] Both buildings were of brick with stone dressings, and both had wings on either side of a deep court open at one end, and closed at the other by a block with a giant portico in the centre and lower colonnades on either side, and a cupola breaking the skyline. In both cases the giant order is repeated in the side wings, at Chelsea in the middle of each façade, at Winchester, more awkwardly, on two pavilions marking a widening of the court. In neither case does Wren yet seem happy with the new scale imposed by the introduction of his giant order. At Chelsea, the cupola on the block behind it is too light[3] and the conjunction of the great and smaller orders is not well contrived. In the central features of the side wings the windows are awkwardly crushed against the giant pilasters. But the large and simple masses of brickwork are impressive. Wren is no longer thinking in terms of surface decoration, as at Trinity College Library, but is gaining his effect by broad contrasts of colour and texture. It may be that here, in his first use of brick and stone for important public buildings, Wren was influenced by Hooke's choice of the same materials for Bedlam Hospital. His massing is, however, very different. He does not break his building into high pavilions and lower connecting wings, but in this severe and simple linking of blocks equal in height, dominated by the clearly stated horizontal of the roof, and accentuated by the use of stone for central features, he achieves something which is at once grander and more purely

---

[1] *Wren Soc.* xix. 61–86, and Pls. xxx–xlvii.

[2] Ibid. vii. 11–69, 231–3 and Pls. i–v; Evelyn, *Diary*, 16 Sept. 1685. Now completely destroyed, though some of the masonry is re-used in the modern barracks in the Castle Yard.

[3] Wren had wished to use one of Jones's octagonal lanterns from the west front of St. Paul's.

English, and which is at the same time more baroque in conception. Chelsea provides a link with France, since it was built in emulation of the royal foundation of Les Invalides,[1] but there is nothing French in its design. Winchester Palace is, however, far more French. The plan is linked with Le Vau's Versailles, and a recently discovered drawing[2] for the rear elevation shows marked French influence. The building is indeed strongly indicative of Charles II's dependence on France late in his reign, for its very position was probably chosen with an eye to the convenient reception of secret envoys.

The political upheavals of the second half of the decade did not greatly affect Wren's career. His chief work for James II consisted of extensive new buildings at Whitehall between the east side of the Privy Garden and the Banqueting House (Pl. 84).[3] Here brick with stone quoining was used for the first time for a royal palace in London, probably for reasons of haste rather than economy, for the whole work cost £35,000. The most expensive part (beyond the great stone staircase, of which no description remains) was the new Popish chapel, which Evelyn at once admired and deplored.

I went to heare the music of the Italians in the New Chapel, now first opened publickly at Whitehall for the Popish service. Nothing can be finer than the magnificent marblework and architecture at the end, where are four statues representing St. John, St. Peter, St. Paul, and the Church, in white marble, the work of Mr. Gibbons, with all the carving and pillars of exquisite art and great cost. The Altar-piece is the Salutation; the volta in fresca, the Assumption of the Blessed Virgin according to their tradition, with our Blessed Saviour, and a world of figures, painted by Verrio.[4]

It is clear that both here and in the staircase, Hugh May's work at Windsor had made its mark on Wren.

[1] Monmouth asked Louvois for plans of Les Invalides in 1677 (*Cal. S.P. Dom.* (1677–8), 476) which were sent in the next year (Archives de la Guerre, Château de Vincennes, *Minutes de Louvois*, 29 Dec. 1677; Ibid., 14 Nov. 1678).

[2] Ex Marquess of Bute collection. Sold Sotheby's, 22 May 1951, lot 17 (2). (Summerson, Pl. 90 A.)

[3] Evelyn, *Diary*, 18 Oct. 1685. See *Wren Soc.* vii, Pl. vii.

[4] *Diary*, 29 Dec. 1686. For the sculpture of the altarpiece, see below, p. 247. A plan of the chapel, which shows it probably had an oval dome, was among the Bute drawings (sold Sotheby's, 22 May 1951, lot 16 (7)). (See above, p. 7, and below, p. 300.)

Country-house building during the last quarter of the century shows, on the one hand, the persistence of the type of design with hipped roof exploited by Pratt at Coleshill and Clarendon House,[1] and on the other, the introduction of a more grandiose and more baroque house, often using a giant order, and topped by a straight balustrade. Belton House, Lincolnshire (Pl. 64 *b*), begun by Sir John Brownlow in 1684, is probably the outstanding example now remaining of the older type. The architect is unknown,[2] but the design is obviously derived from Clarendon House, though the treatment of the central pedimented section and the proportions of windows to wall are both slightly changed. Within, the placing of hall and saloon is the same as at Coleshill, but the staircase (rebuilt in its original position in 1777) is not in the hall itself, but in a separate staircase hall adjacent to it. The plaster ceilings with a fine free treatment of acanthus scrolls and fruit in very high relief are characteristic of the work of their maker, Edward Goudge, and are typical of the change in English plaster-work since the middle of the century. Ceilings are no longer divided into compartments by the broad flat beams decorated with a guilloche pattern introduced by Jones, and the tight wreaths of fruit which appeared at Coleshill have now given way to a looser and more naturalistic treatment. Goudge's work is of the greatest accomplishment, the relief often being so high that it is evident that parts of the decoration were made separately and wired on to the ground.[3] There is much fine carving in the house between large panels planned for the display of family portraits. This is also naturalistic, in the Gibbons manner, though his name does not

---

[1] See above, pp. 46, 139.

[2] The often-repeated suggestion that Wren was the designer cannot be substantiated, and is basically improbable. The accounts published by Lady E. Cust, *Records of the Cust Family*, series 2, pt. i (1909) (The Brownlows of Belton), give no indication of an architect, but show that the contractor was almost certainly the mason-sculptor, William Stanton. Whether he was capable of the design is an open question. Mr. Howard Colvin's (verbal) attribution to Capt. William Winde (see below, p. 219) is attractive. For illustrations see H. A. Tipping, *English Homes*, IV. i. 205 f.

[3] Some of the drawings by John Webb for ceilings in King Charles's Block, Greenwich, dated in the mid 1660's (Burl. Devonshire Coll., R.I.B.A.) show a treatment of acanthus scrolls in very high relief. This must have been a novelty then, but was common by the 1680's.

appear in the accounts. Indeed, in its design, its interior decoration and in much of its furniture Belton is, for all its anonymity, one of the most complete and most typical houses of its time.

Tradition also largely dominates the work of Captain William Winde (c. 1642–1722), born in Holland where his father was a royalist refugee, and first known as an architect when he succeeded Sir Balthazar Gerbier at Hampstead Marshall in 1667, and worked there till about 1680.[1] The wing he added for the same patron, Lord Craven, to Combe Abbey, Warwickshire,[2] between 1680 and 1684 is, like Belton, based on Pratt's design for Clarendon House, though the proportion is weaker. The same dependence on a type created before the middle of the century, though with added Dutch influence in its detail, may be seen in Powis (afterwards Newcastle) House, Lincoln's Inn Fields (1684–9).[3] Winde had many clients,[4] and, like Inigo Jones and John Webb before him, was prepared to advise his patron on the purchase of pictures. He never held any official position, and seems to have been entirely a domestic architect. His most important commission, Buckingham House (on the site of Buckingham Palace), begun in 1705, shows such strong links in both the plan and elevation of the main block with the style of William Talman that it is possible that Winde was executing a Talman design.[5]

William Talman (1650–1719) is a more important and indeed a

[1] Winde was formerly regarded as Dutch, but it is now known that his father was Henry Winde, Gentleman of the Bedchamber to Charles I. William held an army appointment from 1658, and fought at Sedgmoor in 1688. He was also a military architect (see H. Colvin, *Dictionary*, 682).

[2] Now destroyed, but illustrated in H. A. Tipping, *English Homes*, iv. i, 155 f. For drawings for this and Hampstead Marshall see *Architectural Drawings*, Bodleian Picture Book (1952), 7, Pls. 3, 5, 6.

[3] London County Council, *Survey of London*, St. Giles's in the Fields, i. (1912), 110. Rebuilt by Lutyens in 1930.

[4] For reference to various clients, see his correspondence with Lady Bridgeman, for whom he worked at Castle Bromwich Hall, published by G. Beard, *Country Life*, cxi (1952), 1408 f.

[5] The patron, Lord Normanby, later duke of Buckingham, was included by Vanbrugh in a list of those who had 'suffered vexations' from employing Talman (L. Whistler, 'Talman and Vanbrugh', *Country Life*, cxii (1952), 1648). For plates of Buckingham House, see *Vitruvius Britannicus*, i. 43, 44; for a description, H. Clifford Smith, *Buckingham Palace* (1931), 22 ff.

more mysterious figure in late seventeenth century architecture than Captain Winde. He was the son of a Wiltshire gentleman and nothing is known of his early life[1] or training; he may have come to architecture as an amateur, though it seems possible that he knew something of Hugh May's work at Windsor. Moreover, the date of his first building, Thoresby House, Nottinghamshire (destroyed by fire in 1745), is uncertain, though it is more likely to be of the early 1680's than of 1671 as stated by Campbell in *Vitruvius Britannicus*.[2] Unfortunately we have no record of the original appearance of the house, for there was a fire soon after its completion and the attic was added 'at ye refiting'.[3] It was, however, certainly a very large house, probably rather clumsy in detail, with pediments carved by Cibber and interior decoration by Laguerre.[4] Talman's next commission, and his best known, was for the earl (afterwards duke) of Devonshire at Chatsworth, and was presumably obtained because of his success at Thoresby. It has, however, recently been shown[5] that he only worked there from about 1686 to 1696,[6] and that the south and east fronts alone are from his designs. The south front (Pl. 64 a), which was the first to be built, is Talman's most important contribution, for it set the scale of the whole. It is a landmark in English architecture, for this massive design topped by a straight balustrade ushers in a new type of country house, far more baroque than anything before it. Its general disposition of two storeys above a rusticated basement, with giant pilasters emphasizing a break forward at each end, leaves little doubt that, in spite of the difference of proportions, the source is Bernini's design for the east front of the Louvre,

[1] He held a post in the Customs from 1678 (*Cal. Treasury Bks.* v. ii. 1458). For a more detailed discussion of his work, see M. D. Whinney, 'William Talman', *Journ. of Warburg and Courtauld Institutes*, xviii (1955), 123.

[2] i. 90, 91.

[3] Letter from Hawksmoor to Lord Carlisle, 1731, *Walpole Soc.* xix (1931), 126.

[4] For a full discussion of the evidence, see M. D. Whinney, loc. cit. If the plan in *Vitruvius Britannicus* is the original it shows that Talman had, from the beginning of his career, an interest in fine staircase effects.

[5] See F. Thompson, *A History of Chatsworth* (1949), for full details of the building. Further plates in H. A. Tipping, *English Homes*, IV. i. 313 f.

[6] Campbell's date in *Vitruvius Britannicus* is 1681, i.e. before the earl had succeeded to the property. This encourages a lack of confidence in his dating of Thoresby.

which was easily available in the engraving in the *Grand Marot*. Talman can hardly be blamed for the extreme inconsequence of the plan of Chatsworth which is the result of the earl's method (or lack of method) in rebuilding the Elizabethan house in stages without considering where the next stage would lead him. But from the beginning, since the chapel in the south-west corner runs up through the basement and first floors, it must have been clear that the major suite of state rooms must be above on the second floor, and that a grand approach to them would be required. Talman's skill (and that of his contractor, Benjamin Jackson[1]) in erecting this approach in the old staircase tower was considerable. With its fine iron balustrade by Tijou, the staircase is indeed remarkably impressive[2] and with the baroque painting and sculpture of the chapel (Pl. 81), the woodwork of the State Rooms (carved by Samuel Watson) (Pl. 80) and the dignified layout of the west terrace and stairs, suggest that Talman was not entirely lacking in that sense of display which is a prerequisite for a successful baroque architect.[3]

It was probably owing to the influence of Devonshire that he was made Comptroller of the Office of Works in 1689, a position which he held until 1702. His supervision of Hampton Court Palace is chiefly memorable for its revelation of his jealous nature, in his attempts to make trouble for Wren.[4] The King, however, evidently had some confidence in Talman's abilities,[5] for, probably

[1] Chatsworth was, down to 1699, built by contract and not by the earlier seventeenth-century method of personal agreements between patron and craftsmen; F. Thompson, *History of Chatsworth* (1949), 34. The emergence of the contractor was probably the result of the great undertakings of Wren and the Office of Works, which must have implied a fundamental reorganizing of the building trade.

[2] Celia Fiennes, *Journeys* (ed. Morris, 1947), 97–101, gives a lively account of her visit to Chatsworth in 1697, and was especially impressed with the staircase, which she describes as hanging 'on its self'. It must have been still finer when it was linked with the hall below by two curved flights, instead of the single straight flight which exists today.

[3] For the interior decoration of Chatsworth, see below, p. 303, and for the sculpture, p. 244.

[4] See *Wren Soc.* iv. 59, 73, for his criticisms of the Surveyor.

[5] Talman, indeed, may possibly have been concerned in the Whitehall Palace rebuilding schemes of 1698 (see below, p. 323); for the elevation from the Bute Collection (sold Sotheby's, 23 May 1951, lot 16 (1)) now at All Souls shows a clumsiness in

about the turn of the century, he was instructed to prepare designs for a small palace, a kind of Trianon, at Thames Ditton on the Surrey side of the Thames near Hampton Court, to be connected with the great palace by one of the long avenues radiating from the east front (Pl. 60 b).[1] Its intention and its design are linked with France, and indeed it is not the only point where Talman in his maturity seems to have studied French architectural books. The plan of the one-storeyed building, with an oval saloon in the centre, is French, and so is the whole layout of the formal gardens with cut hedges, statues, and vases, and the two lodges flanking a screen wall closing the entrance court.[2] It is indeed indicative of the prestige of Versailles that Louis XIV's great enemy should plan his own 'Trianon' in so palpably French a manner.[3]

The Thames Ditton Trianon, with its gardens and grottoes, is the most attractive of the designs of William Talman, and was presumably made about the zenith of his career. His undoubted claim to the position of the leading architect in England after Wren was, however, already being challenged, and by 1702 he was to find himself superseded in the Comptrollership, as he had already been superseded as architect to Lord Carlisle, by John Vanbrugh.

Talman's two surviving plans for Castle Howard[4] are less

handling detail which is closer to his later drawings than to any work of Wren or Hawksmoor.

[1] Sixteen drawings, apparently prepared for engraving, at the R.I.B.A., give full particulars of the building. Its purpose as a retreat is suggested by the motto over the door: *Vito superba civium limina* (I avoid the proud thresholds of the state). The project dates from after the death of Queen Mary in 1694, since only one state bedroom is included, and may be after 1700, since the Bushey Park Avenue, which was laid out in that year, appears on the small-scale plan which shows the whole area.

[2] Both the plan, except for the oval saloon, and the design of the entrance front with its portico *in antis* are close to the house at S. Sépulchre, designed by Louis or François Le Vau, and engraved in the *Grand Marot*. An oval saloon does, however, appear in French houses, e.g. Vaux-le-Vicomte and Le Raincy, though on a grander scale.

[3] In the early part of 1699 Portland obtained plans of Versailles, the Trianon, and Marly from J. H. Mansart, and in the correspondence about them Matthew Prior refers to 'the design which his Majesty is now forming' (H.M.C. *Bath MSS.*, iii (1908), Prior Papers, 309, 311, 312, 315, 326, 329, 332). This must surely be connected with William's Trianon project.   [4] Both at the R.I.B.A.

original than that finally executed by Vanbrugh, but one has an oval saloon which is very French, and a fine arrangement of staircases. The other reveals that the exterior was to be treated with giant pilasters, and since Talman had already introduced this motive at Chatsworth, it seems clear that his work was the main source for the idea used with so much accomplishment by Vanbrugh and Hawksmoor at Castle Howard and Easton Neston.[1] Indeed his contribution to English baroque architecture is considerable, both in planning and in exterior design, though he never attained that sense of a dramatic whole which is characteristic of his greater rivals. His house at Dyrham in Gloucestershire,[2] built in 1698 for Mr. Blathwayt, William's Secretary at War, has a somewhat clumsy nobility, while his alterations at Drayton House, Northamptonshire,[3] show imagination in the setting of the cupolas, and the design and ornament of the main front have a charm which is lacking in his more ambitious projects. His arrogance led him to quarrels with many of his patrons, but his interest in the collection of architectural drawings, including important examples of those by Inigo Jones, should not be forgotten.[4]

Talman's exploitation of mass reappears in the work of Thomas Archer (1668 or 1669–1743) whose first known undertaking was the north wing of Chatsworth, built by 1707.[5] The most distinguished features of the design were the treatment of the curved centrepiece with a colossal order, and the introduction of small oval windows set in Borrominesque cartouches.[6] The Cascade House, built about the same time, and though not documented surely his, shows both knowledge of Roman garden ornaments and real skill in shaping the form to that of the hill behind it.[7] He

---

[1] See below, pp. 334, 344.

[2] For illustrations see H. A. Tipping, *English Homes*, IV. i. 351.

[3] I am grateful to Col. Stopford Sackville, the present owner, for allowing me to copy the contract, dated 24 Aug. 1702, which has since been printed in *Arch. Journ.* cx (1953), 189.

[4] *Wren Soc.* xvii. 5; *Vertue*, i. 49.

[5] M. Whiffen, *Thomas Archer* (1950) and Colvin, *Dictionary*, 42, 745. Little is known of Archer's training except that he spent four years abroad.

[6] The façade was much altered by Wyatville in the early nineteenth century.

[7] Another successful small baroque garden pavilion is at Wrest Park, Bedfordshire (c. 1712).

appears to have been less happy in larger buildings. Heythrop Hall, Oxfordshire, is an enormous Roman palazzo built for the duke of Shrewsbury;[1] Roehampton House, Surrey (1712),[2] shows a longing for the gigantic, but is clumsy in detail. It is, however, not quite fair to judge Archer's quality as a house designer on these buildings only, since his other certain works in this field, Hale House, Hampshire, which he built for himself in 1715, Hurstbourne Priors in the same county (after 1712) and the additions to Cliveden House, Buckinghamshire, have all been destroyed or so much altered that it is difficult to assess their merit. Even so, his contributions to English domestic architecture, though markedly baroque in character, can never have been of major importance.[3]

In addition to the public and domestic buildings of professional architects, there are many works of the later years of the century which differ widely in style, and are often the creation of mason contractors. Christopher Kempster of Burford, Oxfordshire,[4] and Robert Grumbold[5] at Cambridge, both worked under Wren. Abingdon town hall, built by the former between 1677 and 1682, is influenced by him (Pl. 62 a), and though Grumbold's earliest work at Clare College, Cambridge is old-fashioned, the north range of the court, built in 1682, shows the fruits of his experience as Master Mason at Trinity College Library. Local masons in Northampton, who built the Sessions House (1673–6) and All Saints' Church (1675–80), were also influenced by London work.[6] The old Ashmolean building at Oxford, however, of about 1680 is conservative, and in its superimposed orders echoes the early seventeenth-century gates of Oxford colleges.

---

[1] Remodelled inside after a fire in the nineteenth century, and now a Jesuit College. Shrewsbury had already acquired a design by a Roman amateur architect, Paolo Falconieri, and Archer's house may be a modification of this (see M. Whiffen, *Archer* (1950), 21, 50–52). For Shrewsbury as a patron, see above, p. 9.

[2] *Vitruvius Britannicus*, i. 80, 81. Added to by Sir Edwin Lutyens when it became Queen Mary's Hospital.

[3] For Archer's ecclesiastical architecture, see below, p. 352.

[4] For Wren's recommendation of Kempster as Master Mason for Tom Tower, see *Wren Soc.* v. 18.

[5] G. Webb, 'Robert Grumbold and the Architecture of the Renaissance at Cambridge', *Burl. Mag.* xlvii (1925), 315; ibid. xlviii (1926), 37.

[6] See *Arch. Journ.* cx (1953), 176, 182.

A slightly different aspect of seventeenth-century building is illustrated by the career of Henry Bell of King's Lynn (1653–1717).[1] The son of a well-to-do merchant, nothing is known of his training, though it is certain he was an engraver as well as an architect.[2] The dominant influence is that of Holland rather than of his English contemporaries, and in his best-known and possibly earliest work, the Merchants' Exchange (now the Custom-house) of 1683 (Pl. 62 b), he borrows freely in its pilastered wall treatment, high-pitched roof, tower, and cupola from Pieter Post's Stadhuis at Maastricht.[3] The house for John Turner (Bell's patron for the Custom-house) in the Tuesday Market Place also has Dutch features, especially in the treatment of the double pediment.[4] These buildings and the Market Cross (built 1707–10 and pulled down in 1831) show that Bell, for all his borrowings, was not without accomplishment. They also form an admirable example of the taste of the merchant community for whom they were built.

It is not only in architecture that the battle of varying influences may be seen at work. The period from the Restoration to the death of Queen Anne was also a great age of design in furniture and silver. Most of the household goods of Charles I had been dispersed during the Commonwealth, and with the return of the court in 1660 came a great demand for furniture in the newer and more luxurious styles of France and Holland. Oak, the wood chiefly used in the first half of the century, gave place to walnut, which was more beautiful in colour and could be cut to more elegant shapes and receive a finer polish.[5] It could, moreover, be

[1] G. Webb, 'Henry Bell of King's Lynn', Burl. Mag. xlvii (1925), 24; A. Oswald, Country Life, cx (1951), 194.

[2] He engraved his own design for the Custom-house. He may be identical with the 'one Bell, an ingenious architect' seen by Hooke in London in August 1676 (Hooke, Diary (ed. 1935), 245).

[3] I am indebted to Dr. Arnoldus Noach for calling my attention to the relation, and for the information that though Post's works were not available in book form until 1715, engravings for the Maastricht building without text were published in 1664. In size and general proportions the Custom-house is also linked with Dutch Waags (i.e. Custom-houses).

[4] Possibly derived from an earlier seventeenth-century local source, Raynham Hall, itself dependent on the Low Countries.

[5] The most comprehensive books on furniture are P. Macquoid, Dictionary of English

used as a veneer, generally on oak, and so a rich patterning could be achieved on a flat surface. New types of furniture, tall chests of drawers, bookcases, dressing tables, writing tables, and, rather later, china cabinets came into use and by the end of the century had spread beyond court circles to the homes of the merchant classes. The need for small tables, which were almost unknown before the Civil War, was created by the new habit of drinking coffee, chocolate, and tea.[1] Folding oval oak or walnut dining tables replaced the heavy long oak tables, and by 1700 walnut side-tables with wooden or marble tops were used instead of the cumbersome oak buffets and court cupboards.

There is a marked change of design in chairs throughout the period. Early seventeenth-century chairs were mainly of oak, with panel backs sometimes carved, and heavy baluster legs. Upholstered chairs, with or without arms, were also in use, though only a relatively small number has survived, such as those at Knole Park, or the 'X chair' in the Victoria and Albert Museum which belonged to Bishop Juxon, who attended Charles I on the scaffold. The Restoration court brought a new form of caned chair, already in use in France and Holland. These were carried out in walnut, and in their lavish use of scroll forms for legs, back, and stretchers (the bars joining the legs) reflect the general tendencies of baroque design (Pl. 68 a). Upholstered chairs are heavily fringed and have legs and stretchers richly carved with *amorini*, foliage or even, as in a splendid set at Ham House of about 1675, with gilt dolphins.

A major change, the introduction of the cabriole leg, and an echo of its curve in the design of the back, resulted from Dutch influence after the accession of William III. The tall cane-backed chairs were gradually ousted, and replaced by types with shorter hooped backs,

Furniture, The Age of Oak (1904), The Age of Walnut (1905), and P. Macquoid and R. Edwards, *Dict. of English Furniture* (1954), 3 vols. See also R. Edwards, *English Chairs*, H.M. Stationery Office (1951); V. & A. booklet, *History of English Furniture* (1955); R. Fastnedge, *English Furniture Styles 1500–1830* (1955). Walnut trees, which take at least fifty years to mature, had been extensively planted in the reign of Queen Elizabeth I, and were now ready for use.

[1] Coffee first appeared as a drink in 1645, the first coffee-house being opened in 1652. Both tea and chocolate were introduced about 1658.

and a fiddle-shaped splat which formed the basis of eighteenth-century developments. The stretcher, too, disappears (though it may still be seen in a set of chairs, which otherwise display the new forms, at Hampton Court Palace, covered with petit-point worked by Queen Mary and her ladies), and by the end of Queen Anne's reign a dignified sober form, with rounded seat and back and cabriole legs ending in a club-foot, or a ball and claw, came into general use (Pl. 68 *b*).

Although the beauty of walnut used by itself was much appreciated, it was also sometimes embellished with gilding or with silver mounts, or it was inlaid with woods of other colours. This inlaid or marquetry furniture had been made in the early part of the century, when an inlay of bone or mother-of-pearl on ebony in the Moorish manner had become fashionable after Charles I's Spanish marriage venture; Restoration marquetry, however, makes great use of a veneer of different coloured woods, buff, brown, black, and red, sometimes combined with green-stained bone or with ivory. These are used about 1670 in Italianate designs of acanthus, arabesques, and birds: later, under Dutch influence, more naturalistic flowers and birds appear. By the end of the century these vanish, and patterns are reduced to very fine acanthus scrolls, imitating the designs carried out in tortoiseshell and metal inlay by the French cabinet-maker Boulle, the patterns being brought over by the French Huguenot craftsmen who took refuge in England after the Revocation of the Edict of Nantes in 1685. The renewal of French influence due to their presence may be seen in many arts; in furniture it vies with Dutch fashions in the reign of William III, for Daniel Marot (*c.* 1660–*c.* 1752), one of the most prolific of Huguenot designers, had entered William's service in Holland in 1685, and had designed and decorated palaces and gardens. Marot was in England in 1694,[1] and some of the decoration and furniture as well as the great tulip-vases at Hampton Court show his style. The corner chimney-pieces surmounted by tiers of shelves are close to his engravings,

[1] A. Lane, 'Daniel Marot: Designer of Delft Vases and Gardens at Hampton Court', *Connoisseur*, cxxiii (1949), 19. His drawing for the gardens now in the Boymans Museum, Rotterdam, is dated 1689, though the alterations were not carried out until 1698/9. See also M. Ozinga, *Daniel Marot* (1938), 89.

and a set of gilt furniture in one of the state bedrooms, with many motives derived from the court of Louis XIV, may be from his designs. It is, perhaps, in the great state beds of the day, with elaborate scrolling ornaments on the cornice and pillow heading, that his lavish style can most clearly be seen (Pl. 80). His engraved works, published in Amsterdam in 1712, were widely known in England, and motives from them were frequently used.

Marot, like other designers of his day, was prepared to work in the Chinese taste. Oriental lacquered furniture had been imported into England as early as the reign of Queen Elizabeth I, and had been imitated by English craftsmen early in the seventeenth century.[1] In the second half of the century the art of 'Japanning' became so popular that it was taught in girls' schools,[2] and in 1688 John Stalker and George Parker published *A Treatise of Japanning and Varnishing*, in which they gave oriental designs 'improved in their proportions'. English lacquer, which is less smooth and less brilliant in its use of metallic pigments than oriental work, was produced in large quantities, though unmounted oriental panels (as well as some furniture) were still imported by the East India Company, and made up into screens or cabinets. Sometimes walls were wainscoted with lacquer. Gerrit Jansen, who was Cabinet-Maker to the Royal Household, 'japanned' a closet at Chatsworth, and also provided mirrors (by now a popular form of decoration), desks in marquetry or inlaid with metal in the Boulle manner, tables and cabinets for Queen Mary,[3] whose Water Gallery at Hampton Court had a 'roome all pannell'd with Jappan' and 'another with Looking Glass'.[4] The oriental fashion was also reflected in the copying of Chinese wallpapers, a patent being granted to William Bayley for this in 1691, and in the imitation of Indian designs in printed cottons for curtains and bed hangings which began to replace the silk hangings by 1700.[5] By then the

[1] R. Edwards, 'The "Master" of the Saddlers' Ballot Box', *Burl. Mag.* lxvii (1936), 232
[2] Letter from Edmund Verney to his daughter Molly, 1683 (*Memoirs of the Verney Family* (1899), iv. 221).
[3] R. Edwards and M. Jourdain, *Country Life*, xci (1942), 996.
[4] C. Fiennes, *Journeys* (ed. C. Morris, 1947), 59. The Water Gallery was destroyed in 1700. For drawings by Gibbons for the japanned room see *Wren Soc.* iv, Pls. xliv, xlvi.
[5] For the use of oriental motives in decorative painting, see below, p. 315.

extreme luxury of the court of Charles II, which can perhaps best be sensed in the sets of silver dressing-table furniture, now at Windsor (Pl. 66 *b*) or Knole, had disappeared, but the standard of comfort then introduced remained, as may be gathered by the descriptions given by Celia Fiennes of the houses she visited in the last years of the century.

If the need for new furniture was great at the Restoration, that for plate was even greater. Much had been sacrificed during the Civil War, and though some relatively modest pieces were made during the Commonwealth, the new King and many of his subjects were in urgent need of new plate.[1] These were days when domestic china was unknown, glass still extremely rare, and many household necessities were made of metal. It is clear too from Pepys's Diary that the acquisition of a piece of plate gave its owner a deep satisfaction and feeling of enhanced prestige. Lavish gifts of plate were made by subjects to the Crown,[2] but the King himself was expected to make such gifts for services rendered to him, and to keep sufficient store of plate in the Jewel House to enable special embassies abroad to be adequately equipped as a matter of prestige.[3]

The favourite form of decoration for Restoration plate is an elaborate embossing in the Dutch manner with naturalistic flowers, birds, and fruit.[4] A typical example is the standing cup and cover

[1] A short modern survey is C. Oman, *English Domestic Silver* (1934, 3rd ed. 1949). See also the same author's 'V. & A. Picture Books', *Charles II Domestic Silver* (1949); *Early Stuart Silver* (1950). For ecclesiastical silver see W. W. Watts, *Old English Silver*, (1924), 123 f. There are a number of important monographs, among the most useful being J. B. Carrington and G. R. Hughes, *The Plate of the Worshipful Company of Goldsmiths* (1926).

[2] For instance the wine-fountain now in the Tower of London presented to Charles II for his coronation by the Borough of Plymouth, the silver furniture at Windsor given by the City of London (Pl. 66 *b*) or the Seymour Salt now belonging to the Goldsmiths' Company, seen by Pepys in the Mayor's House at Portsmouth (*Diary*, 27 April 1662) prior to its presentation to Queen Catherine on her arrival in England.

[3] The pieces so used were sometimes kept as balance for arrears of pay. The presence of the Royal Arms does not therefore necessarily mean that a piece was made for the sovereign's personal use.

[4] Christiaen van Vianen, a noted Dutch goldsmith, who with the two Jan Lutmas of Amsterdam had developed a style using embossed fish forms, had worked for Charles I from 1637 to 1644, and was again in England from 1662 to 1666, and was called 'His Majesty's Silversmith'. He made the Coronation wine-fountain in the Tower, but his fish designs were not widely copied.

given by George Carew to the town of Evesham to commemorate the Restoration (Pl. 66 a). As in contemporary architecture, however, French influences are soon combined with Dutch, for the popular motive of putti among acanthus leaves, seen for instance in the Calverley toilet service (1683/4) in the Victoria and Albert Museum, is probably derived from the engravings of Jean Le Pautre. The other most popular technique was engraving, sometimes used for a coat of arms on an otherwise plain piece, but often for oriental designs which recall the fashion for lacquered furniture and for textiles and porcelain brought from the East by the East India Company (Pl. 67 c). The major change in household plate was the dethronement of the salt, with all its feudal implications. By the end of the reign of Charles I salts had diminished to a modest height of some seven inches, and were generally surmounted by scrolled brackets to support a dish of fruit, as may be seen in Dutch still-life paintings. After the Restoration, however, small salts, circular, quatrefoil, or polygonal, came into use.[1] At the same time, pepper-pots, sugar boxes, and sugar casters begin to appear. Ewers and basins were needed until the end of the century; by then forks with two or three prongs were coming into use, and washing at table became unnecessary. Silver drinking vessels, tankards, cups (often two-handled) were generally used, since glass was rare,[2] while standing cups with covers were still part of ceremonial plate.[3] New objects—teapots,[4] tea-kettles and caddies, coffee- and chocolate-pots—were introduced to serve new needs; silver salvers too are noted as new in 1661: 'used in giving beer or other liquid thing to save the Carpit or Cloathes from drops'.[5]

[1] e.g. the Moody Salt (1664/5) in the V. & A. A few fancy salts were still made, e.g. the Castle Salt presented by the City of Exeter for the coronation of Charles II and the eleven salts in the Tower, made for the same occasion, with detachable domed covers surmounted by a figure of St. George.

[2] See below, p. 232.

[3] Good examples, among many, of these are the embossed coronation cup belonging to the City of Oxford, or the elaborate cup with a pierced design in silver gilt laid on silver presented by Pepys to the Clothworkers' Company in 1667.

[4] The earliest (1670/71, V. & A.) has the tall cylindrical shape of a coffee-pot. Later teapots are gourd-shaped, imitating oriental types, and are small, since tea was expensive.

[5] Thomas Blount, Glossographia, 2nd ed. (1661).

There was, naturally, a great revival of church plate after the Restoration, not only for replacement (which was specially necessary at Oxford) but for the furnishing of new churches in or near London. The first pieces to be made, such as the chalice for Whitehall chapel of *c.* 1664 (Pl. 67 *a*),[1] repeated the Gothic shapes of the Laudian revival, but these were soon superseded by newer fashions. The splendid plate given by Sir Robert Gayer[2] to St. James's, Piccadilly in 1684 (Pl. 37) is embossed with cherubs' heads, fruit, and acanthus, and includes flagons, cups and patens, and a great dish nearly two feet in diameter with a relief of the Last Supper in the centre. Such dishes were probably intended for decoration only;[3] slightly smaller alms-dishes were also made and the provision of altar candlesticks is a further marked feature of the Restoration revival. Occasionally secular plate was given or bequeathed for church use.

The Dutch style of naturalistic embossed decoration was modified by the end of the century owing to the activity of French Huguenot refugees.[4] The official policy of expanding English trade and diminishing imports led to tolerant naturalization orders, the protests of the Goldsmith's Company went unheeded, and in the twenty-five years before 1710 some one hundred and twenty French goldsmiths have been traced in London. They brought with them an ornate style, which they handled with great accomplishment, in which the embossed ornament takes the form of fluting or gadrooning, sometimes accompanied by acanthus or masks. The silver wine-bottle in the Victoria and Albert Museum made by Pierre Platel for General Churchill, Marlborough's brother, between 1702 and 1714 (Pl. 67 *b*) or Marlborough's great wine-cistern with a wine-cooler to match[5] made by Pierre Harache in 1700 are splendid and dignified examples of the new manner.

Though many elaborate pieces were made in the reign of Queen

---

[1] *Cat. Exhib. Royal Plate,* V. & A. (1954), 2.

[2] Evelyn, *Diary,* 7 Dec. 1684.

[3] Other fine examples are at St. George's chapel, Windsor; King's College, Cambridge; Trinity College, Oxford, and in the Tower of London.

[4] See Joan Evans, 'Huguenot Goldsmiths in England and Ireland', *Proc. Huguenot Soc.* xiv (1933), 496, for a detailed study.

[5] Now in the possession of Earl Spencer at Althorp, Northants.

Anne, either by Huguenots or by English goldsmiths imitating them, the prevailing tendency was for a simpler style in which beauty of outline was more important than decoration. Teapots, coffee-pots, salts, and casters are frequently octagonal with plain facets, the angles emphasizing the finely proportioned curves of the simple shapes. When decoration appears it is not embossed, but cut out of thin sheets of metal and applied,[1] always with the greatest moderation, preserving the main outlines. The change was partly due to the introduction in 1697 of the 'Britannia standard' for plate when the silver used had to be finer than that for coinage.[2] The difficulty of embossing the new softer material cannot, however, be the only reason for the change, since, as has been said, embossed designs are common in Huguenot silver. The parallel modification of style which was taking place in furniture suggests both a general change of taste and also a wider demand for articles of beauty and comfort outside the wealthiest classes.

A politer society was, indeed, demanding refinements in all that it handled. This demand can be traced in many and various crafts at the close of the seventeenth century. Two must serve as examples of a wider movement. The development of glass-making in England had received a new impetus from an Italian settler, Giacomo Verzelini: from 1618 to 1653 the monopoly for the manufacture was held by Sir Robert Mansell, whose reputation as a great administrator survives, though few of his wares can be identified. In 1662 there came a new advance. Here, as in other spheres, the newly founded Royal Society encouraged experiments, and one of its fellows, Charles Merret, 'the father of modern Glassmaking' and translator of the great Italian textbook of Antonio Neri, *L'Arte Vetraria*, was mainly responsible for the introduction of lead crystal, often inaccurately known as flint glass. The new invention, soft but brilliant, was from 1672 exploited by the Worshipful Company of Glass Sellers under the control of George

---

[1] This is known as 'cut-card work'.

[2] The measure was framed to prevent the large-scale melting down or clipping of coinage for conversion into plate, and had the support of the Goldsmiths' Company, some of whose members, such as Sir Francis Child and Sir Richard Hoare, were also prominent bankers.

Ravenscroft: and for some thirty years the baroque patterns of the Continent, though without the continental use of colour, were interpreted in this peculiarly English medium.

An almost contemporary and parallel development to this is the employment of salt glaze on stoneware for which John Dwight of Fulham took out a patent in 1671.[1] His busts of royal personages, some of them admirably modelled, are a distinctive if minor feature of English Restoration art. In Staffordshire, where there was already a long tradition of slip ware, the practice came into use in the 1690's under a Dutchman, John Philip Elers; he also began making teapots and other small vessels in an unglazed, hard fired red clay, using Chinese models and patterns. At Bristol, Holland provided the models, and some fine blue and white chargers were made, painted with sprouting tulips, biblical scenes, or royal portraits. As in the greater arts, foreign models were everywhere used and assimilated.

[1] For Hooke's interest in his method, see *Diary*, 89, 103.

X

SCULPTURE AFTER 1660

IN the later part of the seventeenth century sculpture in England, though it rarely achieves great distinction of quality, becomes more closely linked with continental art which is dominated by the great figure of Bernini, the creator of the full baroque style with all its insistence on movement and drama. Two of Stone's sons visited his studio,[1] and John Bushnell must certainly have seen his work. Appreciation of the baroque, however, only appeared in England between the two World Wars and it is still too generally assumed that Bernini's mature work—for instance, the *Sta Teresa* in Sta Maria della Vittoria—sums up the entire style. The position is in fact more complicated, and the repercussions of Italy on northern Europe cannot be understood without some reference to other aspects of Roman baroque art. Bernini's own early work, of which the *Neptune and Triton* recently acquired by the Victoria and Albert Museum is a fine example,[2] has in spite of its new dramatic realism a fundamentally classical basis. And Bernini's two chief rivals, the Fleming François Duquesnoy and Alessandro Algardi, remain throughout their careers far more classical both in spirit and handling. Their treatment of the human figure is more generalized and less realistic (except in portraiture where Algardi exploits the antique tradition of the naturalistic bust), their draperies are smoother, and are not broken and tossed in the Berninesque manner to add to the emotional effect. Both produced work of the highest quality[3] and it is not surprising that

[1] Henry the painter and the younger Nicholas. For the latter's diary see *Walpole Soc.* vii (1919), App. 158.

[2] R. Wittkower, *Bernini* (1955), 4, 179 and Pls. 11, 18.

[3] Duquesnoy's most important works in Rome are the *St. Andrew*, which is the pendant to Bernini's *St. Longinus* under the dome of St. Peter's, and the *St. Cecilia* in Sta Maria di Loreto. Algardi was much more prolific. Notable works are the relief of the *Vision of Attila* and the tomb of Pope Leo XI in St. Peter's. Fine busts can be seen in S. Marcello and other Roman churches. A broad parallel in painting to this classical trend in sculpture can be found in the work of Domenichino and Poussin.

northern artists were attracted by their style, which was no doubt
more easily comprehensible and less demanding in technical skill
than that of Bernini. So far as is known, no English sculptor worked
under either, but among Duquesnoy's most important pupils was
a Fleming, Artus Quellin.[1] His headquarters were in Antwerp,
where he set up a large family studio, but his outstanding work
was the decoration of the Town Hall at Amsterdam (now the
Royal Palace) between 1655 and 1665. This great undertaking,
which entailed a vast amount of figure and decorative work, gave
new life to sculpture in Holland. It introduced the classical-baroque
of the Duquesnoy school, though owing partly to the influence of
Rubens in Antwerp and also to the strongly naturalistic trend of
Dutch painting, the work of Quellin's pupils has qualities which
are completely un-Roman. Grinling Gibbons was certainly greatly
influenced by this group, and a member of the Quellin family,
Artus (or Arnold) III, collaborated with him from 1682 to 1686.
Caius Gabriel Cibber too was probably influenced by the Quellin
workshop. The classical-baroque school dominated France[2] also,
and though there is little documentary evidence connecting English and French sculptors, some stylistic links can be found, and the
influence of the garden sculpture at Versailles is clear enough at
the turn of the century.

English sculpture after the Restoration, therefore, adopts a new
semi-baroque manner which varies both according to the sculptor
and the patron. Some conservative country families still preferred
the old-fashioned types of tomb, with recumbent effigies.[3] Most,
however, required something more up to date. The Grand Tour

[1] J. Gabriels, *Artus Quellien de Oude* (Antwerp, 1930). Both the first Artus and his
nephew, who worked mainly in Antwerp, signed themselves Artus, but are also
referred to in contemporary documents as Arnoldus (T. Levin, 'Handschriftliche
Bemerkungen von Erasmus Quellinus', *Zeitschrift für Bildende Kunst*, 23 (1888), 174,
175). The son of Artus I appears as Arnold in the Wardens' Accounts of the Grocers'
Company (1681/2) but as Artus III in Gabriels, op. cit. 268.

[2] For seventeenth-century sculpture in France, see the relevant chapters of A. F.
Blunt, *Art and Architecture in France 1500–1700* (1953).

[3] Among the latest of these are the Shireburn tombs at Mitton, Yorks., made by
the Stanton workshop in 1699. See K. A. Esdaile, 'A Seventeenth century model
of an English Monument', *Burl. Mag.* lv (1929), 195, and Gunnis, *Dictionary*, 367,
368.

was already taking its place as part of a gentleman's education,[1] and it is probable that the more lively poses of continental sculpture caught many a traveller's eye. Indeed, it is relatively rare after 1660 to find tombs with figures shown in death. Instead, they stand or recline (or more rarely kneel) as in life, and the reference to mortality is restricted to the weeping putti, the skull, or the flaming urn. And with the new freedom in figure sculpture there is a new freedom in architectural setting. The rigid lines of tomb chest and straight canopy are broken up. Sometimes there is now no architectural framework, the figures being set against a black marble background.[2] Alternatively, they stand in a niche with a broken pediment above,[3] or between columns joined by a tent-like drapery.[4] Frequently the figure reclines on one elbow on an altar tomb.[5] Bust monuments continue throughout the century, and are often finer than more ambitious works. Some of these may well have been made from life-masks, for Pepys's description[6] of having his taken suggests that there was a fashion for such things. The portrait set in a medallion also makes its appearance,[7] though it is still a framed portrait in low relief, and not yet the cameo-like profile common in the eighteenth century. Interest in contemporary dress persists but there is also an increasing taste for loose semi-classical draperies,[8] which in the work of sculptors known to have studied abroad are a direct imitation of Roman baroque, while in other works there is a suggestion that grave-clothes have been adapted, often unskilfully, in conformity with the new taste.

[1] See J. W. Stoye, *English Travellers Abroad, 1603–1667* (1952).

[2] e.g. Bushnell's monuments to Lord Mordaunt at Fulham and Lady Ashburnham at Ashburnham, Sussex.

[3] e.g. the monument to Dr. Powell in Gloucester Cathedral, by Thomas Green of Camberwell. Many other examples could be quoted.

[4] e.g. Gibbons's monument to Sir Cloudesley Shovell in Westminster Abbey.

[5] This type is almost too common to quote. The Masters tomb by an unknown sculptor in Cirencester church is a typical example.

[6] *Diary*, 10 Feb. 1669.

[7] e.g. the monument to John Finch (d. 1681) and Thomas Baines (d. 1682) signed by Joseph Catterns at Christ's College, Cambridge, where the heads are taken from portraits (K. A. Esdaile, *English Church Monuments* (1946), 88) or the Cotton monument at Conington, Cambridgeshire, signed by Gibbons, 1697.

[8] The same tendency was common among Restoration portrait painters.

Roman armour too is seen far more frequently than in the first half of the century. Materials also change, for alabaster gradually disappears, though some fine alabaster carving continues until *c.* 1700, and painting also goes out. Important tombs are of black and white marble, or entirely of white, while more modest works are of stone.

Tomb sculpture still forms the bulk of the material in which the history of English sculpture is to be found, but there are a few important secular statues, and far more architectural sculpture than in the reign of Charles I. The series of figures for the Royal Exchange after the Great Fire,[1] the tympana of St. Paul's and Hampton Court, and the garden sculpture for the latter, all provided opportunities. The men who carried out such work, Bushnell, Cibber, and Francis Bird (all of whom had travelled), called themselves 'statuaries', were not members of the Masons' Company, and never worked as building contractors. A number of other sculptors, however, Edward Pierce, Joshua Marshall, Abraham Storey, and Thomas Green of Camberwell among them, preserved the older tradition, and the two first at least undertook extensive building contracts for Wren. But in spite of much recent research, it is still difficult to trace a coherent stylistic development in the period.

John Bushnell was certainly trained in the traditional manner.[2] He was born perhaps about 1630, the son of Richard Bushnell, a plumber, and was apprenticed probably in the mid-1640's to Thomas Burman. Burman (1619–1674) had himself been apprenticed to Edward Marshall,[3] and his name is to be found in the Livery of the Masons' Company from 1663 until his death.[4] He does not appear to have been a sculptor of any great ability. His signed and dated monument to John Dutton at Sherborne,

[1] The Royal Exchange was burnt in 1838. Almost all the statues, except the three by Bushnell on the entrance front, then perished, but models for a few have been identified, see below, pp. 247, 251, 254.

[2] The chief source for Bushnell is Vertue (i. 29, 58, 86, 90, 128; ii. 8). See also K. A. Esdaile, 'John Bushnell', *Walpole Soc.* xv (1927), 21; and 'Additional Notes to John Bushnell', ibid. xxi (1933), 105.   [3] See above, p. 112.

[4] D. Knoop and G P. Jones, *London Mason*, 24; W. L. Spiers, 'Note Book . . . of Nicholas Stone', *Walpole Soc.* vii (1919), 27.

Gloucestershire (1661), shows a standing shrouded figure (a late example of this type) in which the frontal pose has been replaced by a slight turning movement, and the shroud is held across the body like a cloak. The modelling, however, is flat and insipid, small meaningless parallel folds being used for the draperies, though the head is rather livelier in quality.[1] But this is much later than Bushnell's apprenticeship, which ended abruptly when Burman tried to make him marry a servant he himself had seduced. Bushnell fled to the Continent, where, according to his sons, he spent two years in France, and then continued his studies in Rome. Nothing is known of his stay there, but the impact of Bernini may be traced in his later work. He then moved to Venice, where he must have acquired some reputation, for he is said to have spent six years working on the important Mocenigo tomb, still in the church of the Mendicanti.[2] This is an elaborate monument with a standing figure framed in baroque architecture flanked with two large reliefs showing the exploits of the patron in fights against the Turks in 1650. The central figure is in contemporary costume and rather stiffly posed, but his cloak is swept round him and deeply undercut, giving a modified baroque movement.

No other continental work by Bushnell is known, nor is the date of his return to England certain, though he is said to have come back via Vienna and Hamburg.[3] The first fruits of this protracted continental tour were a statue of Mark Antony in marble, now lost, and between 1670 and 1672 the figures of the three Stuart kings and a queen which still remain on Temple Bar.[4] At the same

[1] Other works by Burman are the monument to Mr. and Mrs. Beale, Walton, Bucks. (1672) (Vertue, iv. 169) and a figure of the countess of Shrewsbury on the gate of St. John's College, Cambridge (R. Willis and J. W. Clark, *Cambridge*, ii. 320).

[2] Philip Skippon saw him working on it when he visited Venice probably early in 1663/4 ('An account of a Journey made thro' Part of the Low-Countries, Germany, Italy and France' by Philip Skippon in *A Collection of Voyages and Travels* (ed. Churchill, 1752), vi. 519). See also Vertue, ii. 9. The lower part of the monument has figures signed by Le Court.

[3] Vertue states (i. 29) that he worked in Flanders as well as in Italy and Germany, but does not say when or where. His style does not suggest any contact with the Quellin workshop.

[4] Temple Bar, designed by Wren and built by Joshua Marshall, is now at Theobalds Park, Essex. Bushnell also made the wax and stucco effigy for the funeral of George

time Bushnell must have been working on the first of his statues for the Royal Exchange, since the Charles I (Pl. 70 a) and Charles II were in place on the Cornhill front by 1671. He also finished a Sir Thomas Gresham for the same front, all three figures being now in the Old Bailey.[1] In all these figures Bushnell shows both his knowledge of continental baroque and his eagerness to reproduce its dramatic effects (they must have been a striking novelty to his untravelled contemporaries); they also reveal his basic weakness as a designer. His figures stand unconvincingly on their feet, and though their swirling draperies are intended to give colour and movement they are so incoherently arranged that their main effect is one of confusion. His foreign training had given him the technique of deep undercutting, and the use of a turning pose to give life to his figures, but he had been unable to absorb the idea of a drapery pattern which either emphasized or arrested the main movement.

His most successful attempt in this manner is the figure of Viscount Mordaunt (d. 1675) in Fulham Church where the legs are strengthened by the cloak falling behind them, and the sweep of the drapery across the body is clearly and satisfactorily used as a counterweight to the turn of the head. Moreover the whole design of the monument—the virile white figure standing on a black slab against a narrow black background with an elaborately curved top, the gauntlets and the coronet on separate pedestals at the corners—is new and well conceived. In his other even more ambitious monument at Ashburnham, Sussex, Bushnell is less happy. He has aimed at a full baroque composition making an immediate appeal to the emotions, and indeed the epitaph in which Sir William Ashburnham laments the death of his wife, Jane (d. 1679), who 'was a very great lover', is deeply moving. But the sculpture, though it attempts a reflection of his grief, has not the same nobility. Lady Ashburnham reclines, in a somewhat languishing pose, and is crowned with laurel by a flying putto.

Monck, duke of Albemarle, in 1670 (W. St. John Hope, 'On the Funeral Effigies of the Kings and Queens of England', *Archaeologia*, lx (1907), 561).

[1] He was commissioned for six more royal figures for the Exchange, seen unfinished in his studio by Vertue in 1721.

Her husband kneels at her feet, his hands thrown out in a gesture of despair, while above are curtains, drawn back by two putti. Both figures are in classical dress, but the structure of their bodies (particularly that of the lady's right leg) is maladroit. The male head has real pathos, but that of the lady is distinctly insipid. Though the tomb suggests a desire, rare in England, to give dramatic effect in sculpture to a profound sentiment, it needs only a moment's comparison with any contemporary Roman work to prove that Bushnell, in spite of his training, was incapable of the sustained effort necessary for its accomplishment. The weakness in construction is even more pronounced in the monument to the earl of Thomond at Great Billing, Northamptonshire,[1] which suggests that the madness which overtook Bushnell before his death was affecting his sculpture, for the figures are grotesquely deformed. Vertue clearly felt that some of the unfinished work he saw showed evidence of a strange mind. He speaks of a plaster model of an equestrian statue of Charles II 'almost ruin'd . . . great and spirituous, not elegant nor graceful, consisting chiefly of a manner neither easy nor agreeable.'[2] His prestige in the 1670's must have been considerable, for he had orders from a wide range of patrons,[3] but his difficult and unstable character probably prevented him from obtaining major commissions in the last two decades of the century. He died, apparently an insane miser, at his house in Park Lane, in 1701.

Bushnell is the main representative in England of the emotional,

[1] Mrs. Esdaile (*Walpole Soc.*, loc. cit.) suggests that it was Bushnell's first work after his return from Italy, but the epitaph states that the tomb of Henry, 7th earl of Thomond, who died in 1691, was erected by his widow.

[2] Vertue, ii. 8. He also records that he saw a nude statue of the young Alexander, the 'horse of Troy', and a bust of Mr. Talman, and that many works were destroyed by his sons (Vertue, i. 86).

[3] These included the tablet to Abraham Cowley, erected by the second duke of Buckingham in Westminster Abbey (Vertue, ii. 8), a bust of Mrs. Grew in Christchurch, Newgate Street (destroyed), and probably that of Mrs. Pepys in St. Olave's, Hart Street, and the monuments to Elizabeth, Lady Myddelton, which repeats the pose of Lady Ashburnham, and to Sir Thomas and Lady Myddelton at Chirk, Denbighs. Documents at Chirk Castle relating to the last record 'carrying my ladyes picture for Bushnell the stone cutter to draw a pattern to make her monument' (W. M. Myddelton, *Chirk Castle Accounts, 1666–1763* (privately printed, 1931), 119). See also R. Gunnis, *Dictionary*, 72.

Berninesque aspect of baroque sculpture. In the work of his contemporary, Caius Gabriel Cibber, more complex influences are
to be found. Cibber[1] was born in 1630 at Flensborg, and was the
son of a cabinet-maker to the King of Denmark. According to
Vertue[2] he was sent at the king's expense to study in Rome,
though his master there is unknown. His works suggest that he
also went to Tuscany and Holland. He came to England not long
before the Restoration and was employed as foreman by John
Stone,[3] probably remaining as manager of the workshop until
Stone's death in 1667, for no independent works of this time are
known. He must by then have been a sculptor of some reputation,
for in that same year he was recommended unsuccessfully by the
earl of Manchester to the committee in charge of the rebuilding
of the Royal Exchange.

    A major commission resulting from the Great Fire was executed
by Cibber by 1674, when he was paid for carving the relief at the
base of the Monument (Pl. 69 b).[4] This is of interest both icono-
graphically and stylistically. It is a grand allegorical composition,
with Charles II in the heroic role of rebuilder of the City. Clad in
Roman armour, he directs Architecture and Science to succour the
mourning figure of the City of London, seated on the ruins, and
upheld by Time. A female figure points upwards to Peace and
Plenty enthroned on clouds. Behind London are distraught citizens
and burning buildings; behind the King stand Justice and Fortitude,
and buildings rise anew. Beneath his feet is a hag-like figure which
has been interpreted as Envy or Religious Malice, but which may
well be Havoc.[5] This elaborate allegory, which must have been
approved by the King, offers a parallel to contemporary work in
France, in which Louis XIV appears as the source from which
blessings flow; though the strongly pictorial style of the relief is
closer to the work of the school of Bernini. The whole composition

---

    [1] The main facts of Cibber's life are collected in H. Faber, *Caius Gabriel Cibber*
(1926). He was the father of the dramatist Colley Cibber.
    [2] i. 99.
    [3] See above, p. 112. Faber's suggestion (op. cit. 5) that the introduction to Stone
came through the latter's De Keyser relatives in Holland is likely but unproven.
    [4] *Cal. S.P. Dom.* (1674), 433.
    [5] Strype's edition of Stow's *Survey of London* (1720), i. bk. ii, 180.

is, however, relatively static and the action (in spite of the perspective lines of the buildings to left and right) is parallel to the
plane of the relief, and does not exploit movement into depth.
Moreover, some of the figures, notably that of Architecture, are
awkwardly posed to fit the composition. It lacks the fire of
Bushnell's work, but on the other hand it is more coherent and
more consistent in quality than would have been likely had he been
given the commission.

The same smoothness of modelling which characterizes the
Monument relief is apparent in Cibber's finest tomb, the Sackville
monument in Withyham Church, Sussex, of 1677 (Pl. 69 a).[1]
There is, however, far less evidence of Italian influence though the
appeal to sentiment shown in it is, in itself, baroque. Thomas, the
thirteen-year-old son of the 5th earl of Dorset, reclines on an altar
tomb, his hand resting on a skull, while his mourning parents kneel
on either side gazing at him. By this change from the old pattern
of a wall-tomb with an effigy and kneeling figures at the ends, to a
free-standing tomb with the figures at the sides, Cibber forces the
spectator to play a greater part in the mournful scene. The sentiment is dignified and reticent; the figures, though realistic, have a
simple nobility, and the other children in relief round the sarcophagus, especially the daughters holding skulls and waving palms,
have great charm.

By now it is clear that Cibber had a thriving practice. In 1678 he
was employing five assistants, all apparently foreigners.[2] Much of
his work in the next decade shows the development of a classical-
baroque manner in which there is a direct imitation of the Antique
in the type and treatment of the heads, but often a lack of decision
in the poses, as if the sculptor were afraid of suggesting violent
movement. Draperies and limbs are clumsily disposed, the former
being drawn awkwardly across the body, confusing the eye without giving force or vitality to the whole. These characteristics,
which are perhaps most closely paralleled in the work of the Dutch

---

[1] Contract given in C. J. Phillips, *History of the Sackville Family* (1929), i. 420. The
tomb was to be approved by 'Mr. Peter Lilly, his Ma[tys] painter' before it was set up.
See above, p. 177.

[2] D. Knoop and G. P. Jones, *London Mason*, 25.

followers of Artus Quellin,[1] can be seen in the statues of Divinity, Law, Physics, and Mathematics on the parapet of Trinity College Library, Cambridge,[2] erected in 1681, or in the garden figures of the four Seasons, two Senses and a Juno which he began in 1680 for the 9th earl of Rutland, at Belvoir.[3] His reputation must have been increased by two important works in London, the figures of Raving and Melancholy Madness for the gate of Bedlam Hospital (c. 1680)[4] now in the Guildhall Museum, and a fountain set up in the middle of Soho Square.[5] Both suggest links with Italy, for the fountain on which Charles II in armour stood above the four rivers of England, Thames, Humber, Tyne and Severn, must surely have been inspired by Bernini's fountain in the Piazza Navona, Rome.[6] The Madnesses are perhaps the artist's most famous work.[7] They are of a profound and horrifying realism (they must surely have been studied from the life), and are far more powerful and convincing in modelling than anything else he produced. Since they are semi-nude figures, resting on the two halves of a broken pediment, the 'Raving' with knees drawn up and head thrown back, they have sometimes been held to echo Michelangelo's reclining figures on the Medici tombs. It is true that few figures in this position are entirely independent of this

[1] For instance, in the figure of Juno in the garden behind the Rijksmuseum, Amsterdam, attributed to Rombout Verhulst.

[2] See R. Willis and J. W. Clark, *Cambridge* (1886), ii. 542, for payments to Cibber.

[3] Lady V. Manners, 'Garden Sculpture by Caius Cibber', *Country Life*, lxviii (1930), 382.

[4] Thomas Cartwright (see below, p. 258) had apparently first made figures for the gate (Hooke, *Diary*, 183), and there is no mention of Cibber's figures by Hooke, nor does his name occur in the Court Books (M. I. Batten, 'The Architecture of Dr. Robert Hooke', *Walpole Soc.* xxv (1937), 92). Vertue (i. 99), writing in 1713, includes them in a list of Cibber's works given him by Charles Stoakes, a relative of Cibber's master, John Stone, and Pope, in the *Dunciad* (ed. J. Sutherland (1943), 271), referring to Colley Cibber, speaks of the Madnesses as 'by his fam'd father's hand'. This evidence, though not quite contemporary, seems reasonably conclusive.

[5] Faber, op. cit. 48, and K. A. Esdaile, 'Aubrey's Notes on London and Sussex', *Times Lit. Sup.* 5. vii. 1947. An engraving of the fountain appears in Stow's *Survey of London* (1755 ed.), ii. 660.

[6] The figure of the King is in Soho Square; the river gods in the garden of Grimsdyke, Harrow.

[7] They are of Portland stone, but may always have been painted to imitate bronze. Pope, in the *Dunciad*, refers to them as 'Great Cibber's brazen, brainless brothers . . .'

prototype, and, moreover, the vigour with which the muscular forms are emphasized (in sharp contrast to the pathetic vacancy of the expression) suggests that Cibber had studied Michelangelo's work. The macabre realism is, however, very far from his spirit, and is in some ways closer to the fettered slaves by Pietro Tacca round the base of the monument to the Grand Duke Ferdinand I at Leghorn,[1] though these, for all their realism, seem decorative in comparison with Cibber's unforgettable figures.

He did not, however, produce anything more in this vein, though his success in garden sculpture brought him further commissions. In 1686 he was working for the earl of Kingston at Thoresby,[2] and from there both he and William Talman went on to Chatsworth.[3] His work there, which was done between 1688 and 1691, included the fine sphinxes still on the west terrace, much garden sculpture, the figures of Apollo and Pallas Athene now in niches on the staircase, and those of Faith and Justice[4] on the altarpiece in the chapel (Pl. 81). The whole ensemble of the chapel is one of the most baroque works now to be seen in England, but it is characteristic both of the country and of the artist that the statues should be static in pose, and almost without emotional content.

During the last decade of his life (he died in 1700) Cibber was associated with Wren, working for him at both Hampton Court and St. Paul's. At the former, where there are a number of payments between 1691 and 1696,[5] his pediment sculpture on the park front showing Hercules triumphing over Envy (a direct reference to William III's victories in the war against France) is, though less

---

[1] A terra-cotta model for the 'Raving' in Berlin was indeed for many years attributed to Tacca (Faber, op. cit. 45). Leghorn was an important port in the seventeenth century, frequently used by travellers from the north, so Cibber may very well have known the Ferdinand monument.

[2] See above, p. 220. He made pediment sculpture, statues, busts of Caesars, and sphinxes, none of which has survived.

[3] F. Thompson, *History of Chatsworth* (1949), 36, 67, 86, 91, 124, 126, and H. Faber, op. cit. 49 f. Most of Cibber's garden figures (which have suffered from exposure) have been moved, some being set up on the bridge in 1762.

[4] Described by Vertue as 'Divine Grace & Divine Justice' (iv. 165). For the decoration of the chapel, see below, p. 303.

[5] *Wren Soc.* iv. 25, 32, 33. The metal (presumably lead) figures are lost; his urn is now on the East Terrace at Windsor.

pictorial, in much the same manner as his earlier relief on the
Monument.[1] At St. Paul's he carved the eight keystones of the
great arches supporting the dome,[2] the phoenix above the word
Resurgam in the pediment of the south transept (Pl. 42) and, in
1700, the year of his death, he was carving finials on the south
front.[3] Cibber reveals himself throughout his career as a competent
sculptor, and though he rarely ascends beyond that level he seldom,
if ever, falls below it.

Grinling Gibbons (1648–1721), however, has acquired a reputation which he does not entirely deserve. His unrivalled accomplishment as a woodcarver has given him a prestige which ignores his
frequent failure in other materials. This was perceived in the
eighteenth century by Vertue, who gives the clue to the otherwise
puzzling inequality of his output: 'he was a most excellent carver in
wood, he was neither well skilld or practized in Marble or Brass (i.e.
Bronze) for which works he imployd the best artists he coud
procure'.[4] It seems indeed probable that the few distinguished
works of sculpture which came from his studio were mainly
produced by other men.

Evelyn's discovery of Gibbons and his subsequent success as a
decorator have already been discussed.[5] Of his highly pictorial relief
sculpture in wood the undated Stoning of Stephen in the Victoria
and Albert Museum is the only certain example.[6] The small
classicizing figures, often with long necks, and standing unsteadily

---

[1] The four female figures now at Windsor said to be by Cibber (H. Faber, op. cit.
58) are not his (A. Scott-Elliot, 'The Statues by Francavilla in the Royal Collection',
Burl. Mag. xcviii (1956), 77).

[2] This was done early in 1697/8, i.e. after the church had been opened for worship
(*Wren Soc.* xv. 38).

[3] In 1694 he designed the Danish Church in Wellclose Square, East London (Faber,
op. cit. 61 f.). The lead figures of Faith, Hope, and Charity from the outside of the
church, now at Copenhagen, are certainly his work, but of the four wooden figures
from the reredos, now in the Danish Seamen's church, Poplar, two at least have a
crispness which suggests a different hand.

[4] Vertue, iv. 25.   [5] See above, p. 207.

[6] This was still in his studio at the time of his death in 1721 (though Vertue, who
knew Gibbons, says it was made in Deptford, i.e. early in his life) and was bought by
the duke of Chandos for Canons (Vertue, v. 34). A relief of the Crucifixion at Dun-
ham Massey Hall, Cheshire (*Country Life*, lviii (1925), 694), based on Tintoretto's
painting, may possibly be the work described by Evelyn (*Diary*, 18 Jan. 1671).

on their feet, were to reappear in his larger work. His most important works as a figure sculptor are after 1680, though his designs for the group to stand in Wren's proposed Mausoleum of Charles I show that by 1678 he was prepared to work in either marble or bronze.[1]

It is on the group of royal figures, the Charles II at Chelsea Hospital, the James II formerly at Whitehall and now outside the National Gallery, and the Charles II that stood in the centre of the courtyard of the Royal Exchange, together with the work on James II's altarpiece at Whitehall, that Gibbons's claim to distinction chiefly rests. Some caution, however, must be observed concerning them. About 1680 Arnold (or Artus) Quellin III, the son of the great Artus Quellin, joined Gibbons in England. He was then twenty-seven, that is to say an artist of some experience, as indeed is proved by the quality of his tomb in Westminster Abbey of Thomas Thynn, murdered in Pall Mall in 1682 (Pl. 72 a). The reclining and partially draped figure is not of the standard of Quellin's father's work at Amsterdam, or his cousin's work at Antwerp,[2] but it shows a greater knowledge of design than almost any contemporary work in England. The drapery follows and enhances the flowing lines of the body; the relief below tells the story of the murder with economy, and is sensitively cut, and the mourning putto has a vigour of modelling which is worthy of the best traditions of the Quellin studio. One has only to compare this putto with those on Gibbons's Churchill monument, almost opposite the Thynn tomb, or the sweeping variety of Quellin's looped drapery above the tomb with Gibbons's similar motive above Sir Cloudesley Shovell (Pl. 72 b) to see that Quellin's work has a vitality which is lacking in that of the better-known artist.

There can be little doubt that the Charles II 'in the habit of a Roman Emperor, with a Laurel about his Head, and a truncheon

---

[1] *Wren Soc.* v. 52, Pls. xlii, xliii. There are a few earlier commissions, e.g. the monument to Sir Roger Burgoyne for Sutton Church, ordered by Sir Ralph Verney in 1677, the price of which was to be fixed by Lely and Hugh May when the work was finished (*Memoirs of the Verney Family*, ed. M. M. Verney, iv (1899), 235).

[3] e.g. the confessional in the church of St. Paul, or the high altar in St. Jacques.

in his hand'[1] for the Royal Exchange, though commissioned from Gibbons, was executed by Quellin.[2] The description of this marble figure would fit equally well the famous bronzes of Charles II and James II at Chelsea and Trafalgar Square. The latter, with its easy pose and fine finish, is probably the best statue of the period. Gibbons was paid for both by Tobias Rustat, Yeoman of the Robes,[3] but two Flemish workmen[4] certainly cast the James and probably were responsible for its finish; and not only the pose but the proportions of the two figures, both so much more elegant than in Gibbons's other work, suggest the possibility that the models were made by Quellin.[5] Both masters were concerned with James II's altarpiece at Whitehall but their share is not specified.[6] In spite, however, of the fact that Evelyn states that the standing figures were by Gibbons, they seem even in their present weathered condition to present an easy flow of line, a vitality and an emotional content which is closer to what we know of his partner; and the same is true of the angels, which are much better preserved. Gibbons indeed may well have carved only the elaborate decorative work. At least one outstanding tomb, that of Baptist Noel, Viscount Campden at Exton, Rutlandshire, erected in 1686 is

[1] Strype's ed. of Stow's *Survey of London* (1720), i, Bk. ii, 137.

[2] Vertue (iv. 35) notes that in spite of this a patent forbidding the copying of the statue was granted to Gibbons.

[3] Rustat had already commissioned the equestrian statue of Charles II at Windsor, which is signed *Josias Ibach Stadti Blarensis 1679 fudit*. Gibbons had carved the pedestal. It is uncertain whether Ibach designed or only cast the statue. He may be identical with a 'Mr. Ibeck', a coppersmith who worked at Chatsworth (F. Thompson, *History of Chatsworth* (1949), 36, 124, 204).

[4] Laurens of Malines and Dievot of Brussels (Vertue i. 61, recorded within Gibbons's lifetime).

[5] For a fine model by Quellin in the Soane Museum of Charles II in contemporary dress, see K. A. Esdaile, 'Arnold Quellin's Charles II', *Archit. Review*, cii (1947), 174.

[6] See above, p. 217. The altarpiece was dismantled in 1688, and parts were sent to Hampton Court for use in the chapel. They were never set up, but were given by Queen Anne to Westminster Abbey. In the eighteenth century the angels &c. were made into an altar (see engravings, one from Neale's *Westminster Abbey* of 1822, in *Wren Soc.* vii. 236), but the statues, presumably regarded as idolatrous, were seen by Vertue about 1733 in the Jerusalem Chamber (iv. 57). They now stand in the Canons' Garden at Westminster. The rest of the altarpiece was removed from the Abbey in the nineteenth century, and two angels and four reliefs of cherubs found their way to Burnham Church, Somerset.

probably a partnership work.[1] It appears to introduce a new type, with no architectural frame and with two standing figures in classical dress flanking an urn. No precedent has yet been traced in the Low Countries, and it may indeed be an up-to-date transformation of the familiar Jacobean type of two kneeling figures flanking a prayer desk. The male figure is very close in pose to the Charles II at Chelsea; while the reliefs of Campden's many children show little strutting figures which recall the works of Gibbons's friend Lely (whose monument in St. Paul's, Covent Garden, he had made about 1680).

The possibility that Quellin, who died in 1686,[2] was behind the most distinguished work which goes by the name of Gibbons seems supported by the emptiness of Gibbons's later work. The statue of the 'proud' duke of Somerset in Trinity College Library in 1691[3] shows him in Roman armour (Pl. 70 c), and a fair comparison can therefore be made with the royal figures. It seems inconceivable that this stiff, awkwardly posed figure, with the head badly set on the shoulders, can be designed by the same hand. It is more austere, more coldly classical (and in that sense related to the work of the eldest Artus Quellin) and far less baroque. This rather inept classicism is indeed the keynote of much of Gibbons's later work, for instance the monument to Lady Newdigate at Harefield, Middlesex, or that to Mary Beaufoy in Westminster Abbey. It is a relief to turn from these to a smaller and highly successful work, the charming monument to the grandson of Sir Robert Cotton at Conington, Cambridgeshire, executed in 1697. The boy's head is set in a medallion wreathed in flowers and palms, cut with the same exquisite skill that marks Gibbons's woodcarving.[4] That he was not, even in his own day, regarded as an

---

[1] Vertue, iv. 25, where the large fee of £1,000 is quoted. Campden was the brother-in-law of Cibber's patron, the 9th earl of Rutland, who though he ordered his father's tomb at Bottesford, Leicestershire, from Cibber (H.M.C., *Rutland MSS.* ii. 67) appears to have changed his mind and employed Gibbons (ibid. iv. 228) to make a simplified form of the Exton tomb.

[2] For other works by Quellin see Gunnis, *Dictionary*, 313.

[3] R. Willis and J. W. Clark, *Cambridge*, 1886, ii. 546.

[4] Another successful work with a medallion portrait is the Sir Richard Head (*ob.* 1689) in Rochester cathedral, attributed to Gibbons in Collins's *English Baronetage* (1741), iii. 599.

outstanding sculptor in stone, in spite of the considerable number of his monuments, is perhaps proved by the fact that no commissions for figure-sculpture were given to him at either St. Paul's or Hampton Court. He had been made Master Sculptor and Master Carver to the Crown in 1693, and would therefore normally have been employed on the major undertakings of the Office of Works.[1] It is clear, however, that it was for his woodwork rather than for his sculpture that Wren valued his co-operation.[2] In spite of the lack of quality in his work, his position is not without interest for (with Cibber in some phases of his career) he is the main representative of the continental classical-baroque as opposed to the Berninesque tradition. Unfortunately no English work in this manner can be compared favourably with sculpture in France, or with that of the Quellin studio in Holland.

The only one of the Flemish assistants who worked for Gibbons and Quellin and who built up a good practice of his own, was Jan van Nost (or van Ost) of Malines. He was Quellin's foreman at the time of his death, and subsequently married his widow.[3] Nost seems to have specialized in lead rather than in marble garden figures, and there are many traces of his work in this field in the 1690's at, for instance, Castle Bromwich and Chatsworth.[4] He worked in the gardens of Hampton Court, being responsible for the charming groups of boys supporting baskets of fruit on the gate-piers at the north end of the Long Walk, but his largest remaining group of garden statues is at Melbourne, in Derbyshire. These include a Mercury after Giovanni Bologna, figures of Perseus and Andromeda (the latter also in Bologna's manner), four groups of pairs of *amorini* copied from the painted figures in the corners of the ceiling of the Farnese Gallery, and other single

[1] The unexecuted design for the monument to Queen Mary II (*Wren Soc.* v, frontispiece) is probably his.

[2] Vanbrugh, however, rather surprisingly employed him for figure sculpture at Blenheim (D. Green, *Blenheim Palace* (1951), 239, 247, 250, 257, 283, 284). For further works, see Gunnis, *Dictionary*, 167.

[3] Vertue, iv. 35. His name seems to have become anglicized, as he is referred to as 'Mr. Nost' (or sometimes Noste). Whether he continued to collaborate with Gibbons is uncertain.

[4] G. Beard, *Country Life*, cxi (1952), 1408 f.; F. Thompson, *History of Chatsworth* (1949), 56, 92.

amorini, two of which are copied from works by François Duquesnoy.[1] The re-emergence of interest in Giovanni Bologna must surely be due to the prestige of the garden sculpture at Versailles (where sculptors like Girardon had borrowed freely from him) rather than to any direct Italian influence.

Nost also received commissions as a tomb sculptor. His earliest known work is probably the Sir Hugh Windham at Silton, Dorset, of about 1692.[2] Its elaborate decoration of twisted columns and trails of fruit and flowers forms a link with Gibbons's woodwork, but the easily posed main figure is far more interesting than Gibbons's contemporary and not dissimilar figure of Archbishop Lamplugh at York.[3] Nost's only signed monument which is at Sherborne abbey was probably commissioned by a member of the same family, Rachel Windham, second wife of John Digby, 3rd earl of Bristol (d. 1698) (Pl. 73 *a*). Though the architectural setting is more restrained than in the Judge Windham, the sculpture is extremely rich—the earl standing between his two wives, the first carrying a lighted lamp and the second a flaming heart,[4] flanked by two mourning putti with torches turned downwards. The figures are in a very distinctive style, unlike that of any contemporary artist. Great play is made with the draperies of the female figures which are of very thin material, revealing the details of the nude form beneath, contrasted with swirling looped folds round the hips. Indeed, these aristocratic, elongated, and slightly frivolous figures seem to anticipate, in a curiously stiff manner, the develop-

[1] *Country Life*, vi (1899), p. 40; lxiii (1928), 492, 526 f.; L. Weaver, *Burl. Mag.* vii (1905), 385, 390; ix (1906), 104. For his many other garden ornaments, see Gunnis, *Dictionary*, 280 f. The Farnese figures were widely known from engravings: one of the Duquesnoy figures, Cupid shaping his bow, was made for the prince of Orange (Sandrart, *Academie* . . ., ed. A. R. Peltzer (1925), 232) and was subsequently in Berlin; the other, a Cupid with a curling horn, was also in Berlin, but several versions of both figures are known. I am indebted to Professor R. Wittkower for help in the identification of these sources.

[2] Capt. Winde, in a letter of 23 July 1692, states 'Mr. Noste ye carver is gone into ye country to set upe ye monument of Judge Windham' (*Country Life*, cxi (1952), 1408 f.).

[3] J. B. Morrell, *York Monuments*, n.d., 38 and Pl. xxviii. The bill for £100 is in the Bodleian Library.

[4] This, and the arrangement of the inscription, to which her death date of 1708/9 may have been added, suggests that the monument was commissioned in her lifetime.

ment of rococo sculpture. The monuments to Sir Thomas Spencer at Yarnton, Oxfordshire,[1] and to Sir Josiah Child at Wanstead, Essex,[2] are so close in style that they must surely be by the same hand.

The remaining sculptor to gain important commissions before the end of the reign of Queen Anne was Francis Bird (1667–1731). He was largely trained abroad, for at the age of eleven he was sent to Brussels where he worked under 'Cozins a statuary'.[3] He then went on to Rome and studied under Le Gros, a French follower of Bernini, returning to England when he was about twenty, to work first for Gibbons and then for Cibber. A second short journey to Rome was made, probably before 1700.[4] The monument to Dr. Busby, the famous headmaster of Westminster school, in the south transept of the Abbey, by which Bird made his name, seems to have followed this journey.[5] It is an admirably designed monument in which the reclining figure is most happily proportioned to the setting. The unpretentious draped architectural background and the well-composed figure form a striking contrast to Gibbons's awkward and pompous Sir Cloudesley Shovell of 1707 (Pl. 72 *b*),[6] and reveal the value of Bird's foreign training. The monument to Thomas Shadwell set up by his son after 1700 has a bust (Pl. 71 *b*) which is fully baroque in its ample curves, though it is coarse and insensitive in modelling compared with Edward Pierce's Sir

[1] *Country Life*, cx (1951), 2099.

[2] R.C.H.M., *Essex*, Central and South-west (1921), 249, 250. A further documented work of Nost is the tomb, and its elaborate setting, of James, 2nd duke of Queensberry (d. 1709) at Durisdeer, Dumfriesshire. See also K. A. Esdaile, 'A statuette of William III at South Kensington', *Burl. Mag.* lxxvi (1940), 123; idem, 'Two Royal Sisters, Mary II and Anne in Sculpture', loc. cit. lxxxix (1947), 254.

[3] Vertue, iii. 18, 124. 'Cozins' was either Jan Cosyns, a Brussels sculptor who made figures for the tomb of Lamoral III of Thurn and Taxis in the church of the Sablon, or Henry Cosyns (d. in Brussels 1700), who is said (Thieme-Becker, *Künstlerlexikon*) to have lived long in England.

[4] A pass to go to Holland in Oct. 1695 (*Cal. S.P. Dom.* (July–Dec. 1695), 78) may record the start of this journey.

[5] The evidence is confused. Dr. Busby died in 1695. Vertue (iii. 18) dates the monument 1703, and says that it was made from a cast of a death mask (v. 72). Mrs. Esdaile, *Monuments in English Churches* (1937), 42, dates it 1698, but does not give her source.

[6] This was also attributed to Bird by Horace Walpole, *Anecdotes of Painting*, ed. Dalloway, iii. 34, greatly to the detriment of his reputation. Gibbons's receipt for £322 for it is among the Treasury papers (K. A. Esdaile, *English Church Monuments* (1946), 86).

Christopher Wren (frontispiece). Another relatively early work, the monument to Jane Wren, Sir Christopher's daughter who died in 1702, in the crypt of St. Paul's, is a pictorial relief of St. Cecilia (referring to the girl's love of music) and is in the manner of the school of Bernini. Compared with any similar Roman work, it is grossly immature and insensitive in modelling, but it is revealing that now Cibber was dead, Wren should have chosen his assistant Bird for so intimate a work.

They were to be further associated in the final stages of St. Paul's. Bird made the statue of Queen Anne, with attributes of Europe, Asia, Africa, and America on the base, which was erected in front of the cathedral to commemorate its completion in 1711.[1] It can never have been an exciting work, but the subject and the occasion hardly lent itself to originality of treatment. On the building itself he carved the large relief of the Conversion of St. Paul in the pediment of the west front, a series of scenes from the life of the saint round the west door, and the standing figures on the parapet. All are now weathered, some have been replaced, and it is not easy to form a fair estimate of them. The pediment for which Bird was paid £620 in 1706[2] is a spirited attempt to deal with a difficult problem, the groups of horsemen surrounding the falling figure of St. Paul being shown in violent movement, and almost in the round. On either side is a landscape in lower relief, making the dramatic accent on the figures all the stronger, while the explosion of rays of light through clouds is, as is indeed the whole treatment, clear evidence of the sculptor's knowledge of Roman baroque.

Bird's later work is very unequal. The Dr. Robert South (d. 1716) in Westminster Abbey and the Archbishop Sharpe (d. 1714) at York, both monuments with reclining effigies, lack the distinction of Dr. Busby. The John Ernest Grabe (d. 1711), also in the

---

[1] Replaced by a nineteenth-century copy. The original, much weathered, is now in the garden at Holmhurst, near Hastings (R. Gunnis, Dictionary, 54). Other versions probably made in Bird's workshop are in the market-place of Kingston-on-Thames (the surface completely obscured by gilding) and at Minehead, Somerset. The latter was given to the town by Sir Jacob Banks, M.P., and the parish records show a payment to bell-ringers when it was set up in the church in 1715.

[2] Wren Soc. xv. 146. The reliefs round the door were being cut in 1712/13 (ibid. 206) and the statues on the parapet were set up between 1720 and 1723 (ibid. 225, 226).

south transept at Westminster, has much greater originality and
seems to herald the final divorce between architecture and sculpture
which is characteristic of eighteenth-century tombs. Grabe, in
flowing doctor's robes, is seated reading on a variegated marble
sarcophagus, on one side of which is a pile of manuscripts, and on
the other a lamp. There is no architectural background and all
interest is concentrated on the figure, which is treated with a
sympathetic realism. Had all Bird's later works, which fall outside
the scope of this volume, been as fine as this, his position in the
history of English sculpture would be far higher.

The artists so far discussed in this chapter are those who were
termed 'statuaries'. There is, however, far less of a gulf than might
be expected between their work and that of the mason-sculptors.
Indeed, one of the latter, Edward Pierce (or Pearce), is in his busts
at least the equal of any of his grander contemporaries.[1] He was
probably born in the early 1630's, the son of a decorative painter[2]
and became a Freeman of the Painter-Stainers' Company by
patrimony in 1656; though so far as is known he never worked as
a painter, but as a mason, carver, and sculptor, he remained in the
Company until his death in 1695.[3] Nothing, however, is known
of his training as a sculptor, but during the Commonwealth he
appears to have made busts of both Cromwell and Milton.[4] The

[1] See Mrs. Lane Poole, 'Edward Pierce the Sculptor', *Walpole Soc.* xi (1923), 34,
and June Seymour, 'Edward Pearce: Baroque Sculptor of London', *Guildhall Miscellany*, i (1952), 10, where a number of further facts are recorded.

[2] See below, p. 291.

[3] Mrs. Lane Poole and Mrs. Esdaile assumed that he lived until 1698. Miss Seymour
has, however, found evidence that his will was proved on 20 April 1695.

[4] The *Milton* (in clay) at Christ's College, Cambridge, has some appearance of
being made from a life-mask. The signed marble *Cromwell* in the Ashmolean
Museum, Oxford, may have been made during Cromwell's lifetime, but comparison
with the painted portraits suggests that it is an idealized head not made from the life.
A different portrait in bronze at the London Museum is signed and dated 1672 on the
shoulder. The head, cast separately and set in, is certainly based on the life-mask now
at Chequers, traditionally made for Cromwell's family in 1655 (K. Pearson and G. M.
Morant, 'The Portraiture of Oliver Cromwell', *Biometrika*, xxvi (1935), 91, and Pls.
lxii–lxiv; see also E. S. de Beer, 'Notes on the Portraits of Cromwell', *History*, xxiii
(1928) 129). Several copies, probably of later date, exist of this version (e.g. N.P.G.
and R. J. Haentjens Dekker collection, Amsterdam). The bust at King's College,
Cambridge, said by Mrs. Lane Poole to be one of them, is a different version and does
not appear to be a work of the seventeenth century.

Cromwell busts are rather long and almost frontal, suggesting a link with the work of the foreign sculptors in the reign of Charles I. Pierce worked as a mason-carver at Horseheath for Sir Roger Pratt from 1663–5,[1] and from 1671 onwards was almost continuously employed on the rebuilding of London.[2] He was capable of designing as well as carrying out a building,[3] and the woodcarving which he carried out at St. Lawrence Jewry and elsewhere, though lacking the extreme virtuosity of the work of Gibbons, is of high quality.[4] He was also able to work in bronze, for he was paid £50 each for the four dragons at the base of the Monument.[5]

It is perhaps therefore not surprising that he had little time for sculpture. In 1685 he made two of the statues for the Royal Exchange, the Queen Elizabeth I and the Edward III, the former given by the Fishmongers' Company and the second by the Skinners'.[6] A gilded terra-cotta model for the latter survives in the Company's Hall. Though less distinguished in design than Quellin's Charles II, it yet suggests an ability to manage a turning movement of the heavily armoured figure and so to give it a liveliness which was lacking in the armoured figures of Le Sueur. A year or two earlier he had carved the large wooden figure of Sir William Walworth which still stands on the staircase of Fishmongers' Hall.

It is, however, in his remaining busts that Pierce's true ability can

[1] *The Architecture of Sir Roger Pratt*, ed. R. T. Gunther (1928), 130.

[2] He worked as mason and carver at the Guildhall, 1671–3, built and decorated St. Lawrence Jewry, 1671–8, worked at St. Matthew's, Friday Street, 1682–7, St. Clement Danes, 1680–2, St. Andrew's, Holborn, 1684 and held a mason's contract for the south side of St. Paul's from *c.* 1679–1690 (D. Knoop and G. P. Jones, *London Mason*, 25, n. 4).

[3] H. Colvin and A. Oswald, 'The Bishop's Palace at Lichfield', *Country Life*, cxvi (1954), 2312. The palace was designed by Pierce in 1686–7.

[4] The pulpit he made for St. Matthew's, Friday Street, is now in St. Peter's Church, Reporton Street, Fulham. For his staircase at Sudbury Hall, Derby, see M. Jourdain, *Interior Decoration, 1500–1830* (1950), 40; for woodwork at Combe Abbey and Castle Bromwich Hall, G. Beard, *Country Life*, cxi (1952), 1408 f.

[5] Vertue, v. 80, and *Wren Soc.* v. 50.

[6] An eighteenth-century drawing by John Carter in the possession of the Royal Exchange Assurance Co. shows that the statue of Elizabeth I was, rather surprisingly, based on Maximilian Colt's effigy on her tomb in Westminster Abbey. The sculptor may have known that Nicholas Stone's earlier statue of the Queen in classical robes standing on a phoenix (see above, p. 108) had proved unacceptable. Moreover, judging by the Edward III, pains were now being taken to represent the earlier monarchs in the costume of their own time.

best be seen. The first is that of Wren (frontispiece), made in 1673 (perhaps on the occasion of his knighthood) and given by his son to the Ashmolean Museum, Oxford,[1] which shows a vast change, both in style and quality, from his Cromwell and Milton. It is a wide baroque bust, with voluminous drapery covering the shoulders and falling in a great looped fold on the left of the chest. The long curling hair, deeply undercut, adds to the baroque effect. But it is a French rather than an Italian baroque. There is none of the diagonal play of the most dramatic of the Bernini busts, in which the sharp turn of the head is counterbalanced by a swirling mass of drapery or hair.[2] Here, as in the busts of Coysevox, all sense of the theatrical is avoided by the quiet frontality of the head. As a portrait of the greatest man Pierce knew it is extremely sensitive, for it is in no way an official portrait but an intimate, almost tender, presentation of an intellectual who is also a man of broad humanity. It is by far the most revealing of all the portraits of Wren, and probably the best piece of sculpture made by an Englishman in the century. The bust of Thomas Evans, Master of the Painter-Stainers' Company, made in 1688, is also a remarkable work. It is more robust than the Wren and a little coarser in modelling; the head being lifted and slightly turned, so that the vigorous character of the sitter is conveyed more by the design than by psychological understanding.[3] It is lamentable that so fine a sculptor should have had so little time for his art.[4]

Other mason-sculptors carried on practices inherited from an older generation. Joshua Marshall, who had worked with his father

[1] Vertue, iv. 9.

[2] A bust in this manner, presumably made in England, is the *Charles II* signed Honoré Pelle (who is otherwise unknown) and dated 1684 at the V. & A. Another version, dated 1682, is on the balcony in the courtyard at Burghley House.

[3] The bust of Dr. Hamey at the Royal College of Physicians, ordered in Feb. 1675 (Hooke, *Diary* (ed. 1935), 148, 178), wrongly published by Mrs. Esdaile as by Bushnell (*Walpole Soc.* xv (1927), 39 and Pl. xii *b*), seems to have the same vigour, but it is too high to see easily and the surface is disfigured by paint. A drawing for it by Pierce is in the Ashmolean Museum, Oxford.

[4] The urn which he made for Hampton Court (now at Windsor) is less agreeable in form than Cibber's, but the small fauns round the base are beautifully designed and finely cut (*Wren Soc.* iv. 32, 33). No tombs by him can be identified, though there is a drawing in the B.M. for an elaborate monument to the 2nd duke of Buckingham.

in the first half of the century, was to become Master of the Masons' Company in 1670 and 1677,[1] and Master Mason to the Crown in 1676–7. He remained virtually untouched by the new foreign influences; indeed, unless a work is precisely dated it is often hard to say if it were made before or after the Civil War. The large signed tomb of Edward Noel, Viscount Campden at Chipping Campden, Gloucestershire, is a case in point. Campden died in 1642, and his wife, who erected the tomb, in 1664. The two white marble figures stand hand in hand in their shrouds in a black marble sepulchre, the doors of which open to reveal them as in his father's much earlier Curwen monument at Amersham. The over-large heads and somewhat laboured treatment of the drapery show him as a less accomplished sculptor. Other monuments suggest that he had a certain reputation for busts. The signed Whatton monument at St. Martin's, Leicester,[2] has three, set in ovals, the Crispe monument at Birchington, Kent, unsigned but very close to it in style, no less than six. As a carver he had some competence, as may be seen from the urn in the north aisle of Henry VII's chapel, Westminster, made in 1678 to contain the recently discovered bones of Edward V and his brother, murdered in the Tower, or from the base of Le Sueur's equestrian statue of Charles I at Charing Cross.

The Stanton workshop[3] was even more active in the second half of the century. After Thomas Stanton's death in 1674 it was under the control first of his nephew, William (1639–1705),[4] and then of the latter's son, Edward, most of whose work falls within the eighteenth century. William produced a great number of monuments of varied types, ranging from wall-tablets without figures[5]

---

[1] D. Knoop and G. P. Jones, *London Mason*, 35. Marshall was one of the original contractors for St. Paul's, built six of the City churches and Temple Bar, and was Master Mason to Hugh May at Windsor from 1673 till his death in 1678.

[2] For a further list of signed or documented monuments, see R. Gunnis, *Dictionary*, 254.   [3] See above, p. 113.

[4] D. Knoop and G. P. Jones, *London Mason*, 20, 21. He was made free of the Masons' Company in 1663 and was Master in 1688 and 1689. He was associated with Edward Pierce in the building contract for St. Andrew's, Holborn, and also built Belton House, Lincolnshire. See also K. A. Esdaile, 'The Stantons of Holborn', *Arch. Journ.* lxxxv (1928), 157 f.

[5] Typical signed examples are: Richard Newdigate, d. 1677, at Harefield, Middle-

to bust monuments and tombs with standing, kneeling, or reclining figures. His distinguished altar tombs, at Mitton, Yorkshire, have already been mentioned as among the latest examples of the medieval recumbent effigy. The Shireburns for whom they were made were a Catholic family, evidently with a strong sense of continuity.[1] William Stanton was, however, well aware of the new movements in sculpture. His monument to Chancellor Lucy (d. 1697) at Christchurch, Brecon, shows Lucy standing at the foot of the tomb on which his wife reclines with her infant son. He wears a long curled periwig and has his arm thrown across his body in a rhetorical gesture, while the skirts of his coat flutter about his knees. The design of the tomb as a whole is awkward, but the standing figure shows a real attempt at a baroque pose.

Elsewhere, in for instance the Earl Rivers (d. 1694) at Macclesfield, Cheshire,[2] or the Thomas, Lord Coventry at Elmley Castle, Worcestershire (1699), he sets a baroque reclining figure under a canopy (either with curtains looped back, or with Virtues seated on a curved pediment) which seems a direct continuation of the Nicholas Stone tradition. In most of his work the portraiture is vigorous and it is therefore not surprising that he had so large a practice.[3] This same quality reappears in the work of his son, Edward, as may be seen in the signed bust monument of Edward Tyson (d. 1709) now at All Hallows, Twickenham.[4] In the great number of other monuments made by him before about 1715[5]

sex; Charles Holloway, St. Mary the Virgin, Oxford; Judith Chester, d. 1702, Barkway, Herts., though many others could be quoted.

[1] The payment for the tomb of Richard and Isabel Shireburn was made to Edward, who was still his father's apprentice, so probably the design and perhaps the terracotta model in the V. & A. were by William. The latter was paid in 1703 for the tomb of the young Richard Shireburn (given by Mrs. Esdaile to Edward) showing the boy starting back from a skull. No payment has been found for the earliest tomb, with the fine recumbent figure of Richard Shireburn, d. 1690, but it seems fairly safe to assume that it is by William. R. Gunnis, *Dictionary*, 367, 368.

[2] F. H. Crossley, 'Post-Reformation Effigies . . . of Cheshire', *Trans. Hist. Soc. Lancs. and Cheshire*, xci (1939), 24, 77.

[3] For further signed and documented works see R. Gunnis, *Dictionary*, 367, 368. Mrs. Esdaile's article *Arch. Journ.* loc. cit. contains many further attributions.

[4] Formerly in All Hallows, Lombard Street.

[5] He supplied the antiquary John Le Neve with a list of over one hundred and forty (B.M. Harl. MSS. 3605, 16).

many follow types already used by his father, and though his drapery patterns are more lively and varied,[1] his actual cutting is more superficial. The Stanton family workshop is perhaps the best and most typical example of a continuous tradition of sound workmanship, and willingness to cater for both conservative and advanced taste.

Other Masters of the Masons' Company had probably larger practices than their few known works suggest. Jasper Latham in his mutilated tomb of Archbishop Sheldon (1676) in Croydon parish church,[2] Thomas Cartwright[3] in that of Sir John and Lady Lewys at Ledsham, Yorkshire (1677), and Abraham Storey[4] in his monument to Lord Crofts at Little Saxham, Suffolk (c. 1678), all attempt a certain baroque liveliness of pose in their reclining figures. Richard Crutcher,[5] a pupil of Edward Pierce, seems from his one signed monument to Sir Robert Clayton, Lord Mayor of London, at Bletchingley, Surrey (1705), to have been a man of some skill (Pl. 73 b). The two standing figures in contemporary dress are admirable portraits, and stand under a great canopy supported on Corinthian columns, the long inscription commemorating Clayton's record of public service being placed on drapery beneath clustered cherubs' heads. It is as good an example as can be found of the taste of the wealthy merchant community, who by now had absorbed the baroque style introduced by Wren and his associates, and who no doubt found in it a comfortable richness.

Another London sculptor, Thomas Green of Camberwell, who was working in the first twenty years of the eighteenth century, produced some elaborate monuments, the largest being that to the Furnese family at Waldershare, Kent, erected in 1712, a freestanding tomb with four seated mourning figures at the base and

[1] For instance in the Sir William Lytton and the Sir George Strode at Knebworth, Hertfordshire, or the Sir Francis Russell at Strensham, Worcestershire.

[2] Latham was one of the mason-contractors at St. Paul's in the 1680's. For his career as a mason see D. Knoop and G. P. Jones, op. cit. 20, n. 4, and R. Gunnis, *Dictionary*, 234, for his few certain works of sculpture.

[3] For other work, see D. Knoop and G. P. Jones, op. cit. 38; R. Gunnis, *Dictionary*, 87.

[4] D. Knoop and G. P. Jones, op. cit. 21, n. 2; R. Gunnis, *Dictionary*, 374.

[5] R. Gunnis, *Dictionary*, 117.

four putti with emblems above. Other monuments, the Richard Welby at Denton, Lincolnshire (1714), and the Dr. John Powell (1713) at Gloucester cathedral have a figure in contemporary dress standing on an oval pedestal in front of a niche. Green is more successful in these than in the semi-classical figures on the Waldershare tomb, and with Crutcher suggests that London work after the turn of the century was reaching a high standard.[1]

Too little is at present known of sculptors working outside London for any account of their work to be given, but signed or documented monuments by Samuel Carpenter in York,[2] or the Ferrars tomb at Tamworth, Staffordshire, by Samuel Watson, the Chatsworth carver,[3] can be cited as examples of fairly high quality. Prosperous centres like Bristol, Norwich or York, or districts with good local stone, such as Oxfordshire or Northamptonshire, no doubt supported local schools of mason-sculptors, though the landed gentry and even the richer merchants tended to order their tombs from London workshops.

Finally, some mention must be made of the innumerable wall tablets of the seventeenth century, in which the changes of taste are reflected. Few of them are signed, and here, perhaps more easily than in more ambitious work, it is possible to detect local schools, and also to see how slowly a new fashion penetrated to remote districts. Tablets with clumsy architectural detail or figures seated on pediments which seem to travesty the style of Nicholas Stone or the Christmases are found in Herefordshire late in the reign of Charles II. By then, elsewhere, although the architectural tablet with a pediment and shield supported on colonnettes was still being made, new types with the epitaph on a scrolled cartouche, often backed by drapery, and embellished with the heads of winged putti, flowers or palms reflect the new baroque manner (Pl. 71 a). Indeed, it is often in such work, rather than in figure sculpture, that English craftsmen are to be seen at their best.

[1] Green also made some smaller monuments, William and Thomas Chew (1712) at Dunstable, Bedfordshire; Bishop Cumberland (1718) in the ambulatory of Peterborough cathedral; and Peter Seaman (1715) at St. Gregory's, Norwich. The last has a lively but rather coarsely cut bust. See also R. Gunnis, *Dictionary*, 179.

[2] J. B. Morell, *York Monuments*, n.d., 39, and Pl. xxv.

[3] R. Gunnis, *Country Life*, cix (1951), 393. See also above, p. 221.

XI

LANDSCAPE PAINTING AND THE LESSER GENRES

IN a letter to Archdeacon Nicolson of 10 November 1699 John Evelyn wrote disparagingly of 'our English paynters, who, greedy of getting present money for their work, seldom arrive to any farther excellency in the art than face-painting'.[1] Under the Stuarts a native tradition in landscape and genre painting was less formed than in the painting of portraits. A number of landscapes, seascapes, genre scenes, and still-lifes was painted or drawn during that period, but many of them by foreigners who had settled in, or were passing through, this country. Nevertheless many of the great achievements of English artists in other forms of painting than the portrait in the eighteenth century were foreshadowed by the tentative and sporadic efforts of their predecessors in the seventeenth century, and spring largely from the fusion in this earlier period of Dutch and, to a lesser extent, Flemish, French, and Italian influences. Early in the century Norgate could write of landscape painting that it was 'an Art soe new in England, and soe lately come a shore, as all the Language within our fower Seas cannot find it a Name, but a borrowed one, and that from a people that are noe great Lenders but upon good Securitie, the Duch'.[2]

'For to say truth', Norgate continues, 'the Art is theirs, and the best in that kind that ever I saw speake Dutch, viz. Paulo Brill . . . Adam Elshamer . . . Momper, Bruegel, Coningslo.' These painters and their like were well represented in the great Caroline collections and the work of the foreign landscape painters in the service of Charles I was almost wholly within the Italo-Netherlandish tradition which they had formed. The landscapes of Alexander Keirincx have the artificiality, strong contrasts of light and shade, rich foliage, and fine surface of Coninxloo; and Cornelis van Poelenburgh, who collaborated with Keirincx in England, brought

---

[1] Evelyn, *Diary*, iv. 25.　　　　[2] *Miniatura*, ed. M. Hardie (1919), 42.

to this country a more Italianate form of romantic landscape which is particularly associated with Utrecht and in which the figures play a larger part.[1] Adriaen van Stalbempt's little view, in the royal collection, of the park and palace at Greenwich, from the hill on which the observatory now stands, is, on the other hand, a naturalistic and freely painted attempt to record the appearance and atmosphere, as seen through Flemish eyes, of the lower reaches of the Thames.[2]

The King and the duke of Buckingham also owned, among their pictures by Rubens, examples of the most brilliant and advanced landscape painting of the age. Buckingham possessed at least five landscapes by Rubens and Charles's *Landscape with St. George*[3] marks the consummation of the achievements in landscape painting of Rubens and his predecessors. It was a too sophisticated synthesis of the natural and the ideal to have any influence in England. Van Dyck's landscape drawings, done in pen and water-colour and in rare moments of relaxation from the strains of portrait painting, were even more advanced. Those of an identified scene (such as the views of Rye) are Flemish in feeling, but the handful of very mature drawings of English lanes, woods and fields, and the exquisite drawing in the British Museum of a sow-thistle and other plants, were unsurpassed, for the delicacy and understanding with which they record the most intimate qualities in the English countryside, until the age of Gainsborough.[4]

[1] In July 1639 forty-five pounds was paid as part of the rent for 'sev'll houses and gardens' in Orchard Street, Westminster, which had been let to the King 'for the use & dwellings of Cornelius Van Pollenburgh and Alexander Keyrinx two Dutch-Painters' (P.R.O., E 403/2758, f. 53*v*.). The tiny landscape by the English Sir Nathaniel Bacon (see above, pp. 82–83) in the Ashmolean Museum is entirely in the tradition of Brill.

[2] The little figures of Charles I and his family and courtiers were inserted by Belcamp and the canvas is signed by both artists; from the figures it can be dated *c*. 1632 and the Queen's House is seen in an uncompleted state.

[3] See above, p. 5.

[4] The number of landscape drawings by Van Dyck is comparatively slight and very few of the scenes, some of which may have been in Flanders, are identifiable. A convenient group is in the B.M. (A. M. Hind in *Catalogue of Drawings by Dutch and Flemish Artists . . . in the British Museum*, ii (1923), 72–75); one is dated 1634; no. 80 is a good example of his mature Flemish manner and no. 87 is a particularly beautiful instance of his most advanced (and presumably English) water-colours painted with

The destruction of the civilization which had fostered Rubens and Van Dyck prevented their work in this country from laying the foundations of a native school of landscape painting, and the limitations of patronage did not encourage English painters to turn to the English scene for inspiration. Until the Restoration, and to some extent thereafter, the painting or drawing of landscapes in England was sporadic, and such landscape painting as there was showed a predominant interest in topography. The quality of much of the work is very mediocre and the pictures themselves often concern the antiquarian more than the art-historian.

The interest in topography was by no means new and many continental parallels could be quoted. At the end of the sixteenth century Theobalds had contained a series of landscapes of the most important towns in Christendom, which had probably been assembled by Lord Burghley or his elder son; sketches of various English castles and palaces and paintings of the principal cities of the world were seen at Whitehall and Theobalds by the duke of Saxe-Weimar in 1613;[1] and Charles I commissioned, among other views, ten pictures of his Scottish houses from Keirincx. Henry Peacham had already, in the chapter on landscape in his *Gentleman's Exercise*,[2] chosen the best sites for the landscape painter in England: 'Winsor, and the Country thereabouts, the prospect which you take of the City of London upon Highgate, all the Country about Roiston, with many other places'; but the capital itself inspired the best and most interesting topographical pieces in the earlier half of our period. Claude de Jongh's tranquil view of the Thames and London Bridge (Pl. 75 *a*: *s*. 1630) is of doubtful value topographically but is close in handling, and in its attractive pale tone, to Esaias van de Velde or Van Goyen; the barges and lesser craft glide noiselessly in a dead calm at low water. The three views of London and the river in the Evelyn collection,[3] probably

full body-colour. See also A. P. Oppé, 'Sir Anthony Van Dyck in England', *Burl. Mag.* lxxix (1941), 190, and L. Burchard, 'A View of Rye by Anthonie Van Dyck' *Old Master Drawings*, xii (1938), 47–48.

[1] W. B. Rye, *England as seen by Foreigners* (1865), 44–45, 159–67.
[2] See above, p. 82. [3] Now at Stonor Park.

painted (*c.* 1660) for the diarist by the obscure Dutchman, Cornelius Bol,[1] are of less good quality; but there is an attempt to render the lowering skies and fitful sunlight of the English climate. The picture (Pl. 75 *b*) of the shipping in the river below the Tower foreshadows Samuel Scott, and the two views, looking up and down the north bank of the river from Arundel House, directly anticipate Canaletto's pair of canvases (at Windsor) of the Thames from the neighbouring terrace of Somerset House. And there is perhaps a Venetian feeling in the painting (in the royal collection) of the procession of barges on Lord Mayor's Day (? 1683), with its lively rendering of the strong breeze on the crowded waterway and the straggling river-front of Whitehall Palace. Occasionally painters of London were provided with more dramatic material: eye-witness accounts in paint of the Fire of London[2] manage to convey something of the scale and horror of the catastrophe; Abraham Hondius's picture of the frozen Thames in the London Museum (*s.* 1677) gives a lively impression of the unearthly light and strange scene late on a winter's afternoon.[3]

The first professional landscape painter to work in England for a considerable period was the Dutchman Hendrick Danckerts or Danckers who, when he came to England from The Hague in the summer of 1650, was closely associated with Hugh May and Lely.[4] Much of Danckerts's time was taken up with straightforward topography in oil and tempera: his extensive work for the Crown included views of Tangier, Plymouth, Windsor, Greenwich,

[1] Vertue stated (iv. 53) that they were by Bol; one of the canvases is very close to a drawing in the B.M. attributed to Keirincx (Hind, op. cit., ii. 115, Pl. lix). A signed variant of the view of Westminster in the Evelyn set is at Dulwich.

[2] e.g. at Badminton; Vertue states (i. 106; ii. 30; v. 69) that Thomas Wyck, Waggoner, and Jan Griffier painted this subject.

[3] See also the volumes of the *London Topographical Record*, published by the London Topographical Soc., and, for an example of minor work, two drawings attributed to Jacob Esselens *c.* 1660 (H. Reitlinger, 'Two Seventeenth-Century Views of London', *Burl. Mag.* lxviii (1936), 294).

[4] In a letter in the Cottrell-Dormer manuscripts at Rousham, May wrote to Sir Charles Cotterell, who was then in The Hague, that he had obtained a letter 'from my freind Mr Lely to one Danckers (who is comeing over from the Hague speedily to him)' and that he was 'expected here dayly'. The letter was probably written on 30 June 1650, and it is possible that Danckerts returned thereafter to The Hague.

and Hampton Court, a large view of Pendennis (s. 1674; Windsor) and two pictures of Portsmouth from the sea and the land.[1] Pepys, who admired Danckerts greatly, commissioned him on 20 January 1669 to paint four landscapes for the panels in his dining room. He chose 'the four houses of the King' at Whitehall, Hampton Court, Greenwich and Windsor, and when the view of Greenwich was finished he made a special visit to the actual site to compare it with Danckerts's rendering. Before the new pictures were completed Pepys decided to have, instead of Hampton Court, a 'prospect' of Rome. Danckerts described it as 'a capricio of his owne, made up out of 2 or 3 different churches'. In 1653 he had been in Italy and the drawings that he had made on the spot were used in his large decorative classical landscapes. These were particularly popular with his royal patrons: Charles II commissioned at least three and James II seems to have brought a further fifteen into the royal collection. Many of these survive,[2] and show Danckerts to be a painter of little quality. The atmosphere is strangely airless, the tone is pallid and the drawing and handling very pedestrian; but in these big canvases (e.g. Pl. 53 a) the quiet sunset mood, the ruins, overgrown temples and statuary, Arcadian shepherds with their flocks and the great masses of care-

---

[1] These were formerly at Hampton Court; one is stated to be s. 1675. The view of Tangier at Hampton Court (s. 1669) is probably the one which Pepys saw at Whitehall on 2 May 1669; he stated that it was designed by Sir Charles Harbord and it is possible that Danckerts never actually went so far afield. Nevertheless the earl of Sandwich admired it 'as being the truest picture that ever he saw in his life' and presumably commissioned the view of Tangier (s. 1669) which is still at Hinchingbrooke with a landscape of Plymouth.

[2] Of the classical landscapes at Windsor at least two are signed and dated (1674, 1677). In 1675 and 1679 Danckerts was paid a total of £109. 3s. 6d. for 'several prospect pictures and landskips by the King's command' (Cal. Tr. Bks. iv. 769; v. 1278). The components of these landscapes were well defined by Roger North in describing a landscape he had bought, 'of yᵉ River Tyber, with a prospect of yᵉ citty of Rome, wherein yᵉ Dome of sᵗ peters Appears In lontano. It was done by Dankers and is after yᵉ life, Except some Invention upon yᵉ foreground' (B.M. MS. 32504, f. 22v.).

More spontaneous attempts to record the Italian scene are to be found in the hurried drawings by men like Thomas Manby, who apparently visited Italy a number of times, and the sketches by English travellers and amateur draughtsmen such as Evelyn and Symonds.

fully placed foliage, which frame the 'prospects' of actual Italian towns and buildings, sound at least an echo of Claude.

One of Danckerts's pictures for Charles II was *A Landskip of Ruaignes & Water. for ov^r a doore* and his landscapes were often designed to be hung up in such positions. With his successors an element of fantasy grows more and more predominant until these decorative pieces become indistinguishable from scenery-painting.[1] The landscapes by Robert Streeter and Robert Aggas were, no doubt, largely of this type.[2] Occasionally, as in the landscape attributed to Streeter at Dulwich, there is a combination of careful topography in the middle distance with a light and decorative treatment of the foreground; and in the *Boscobel House and White-Ladies* (Hampton Court), which he painted for Charles II, Streeter must have been at pains to record with a certain accuracy the setting for the most hazardous and celebrated moment in his patron's escape after the battle of Worcester. But it is, in his *œuvre*, an isolated piece of topography, done for a special purpose. The climax of the topographer's art in the Stuart period is to be seen in the work of the Bohemian, Wenceslaus Hollar, the Dutchman, Leonard Knyff, and the Fleming, Jan Siberechts.

Hollar is among the most fascinating and indefatigable artists at work in England in the seventeenth century. He records many aspects of English life, and the subject-matter with which he dealt touched upon all the interests of the educated Englishman of the day.[3] 'We may justly pronounce', wrote Evelyn of Hollar's

[1] The principal painters concerned are: the Dutchmen Jan Looten (who was settled in London by July 1662) and Gerard van Edema (a pupil of Allaert van Everdingen) who specialized in wild, tempestuous, mountainous scenes and, in the case of Edema, in wintry landscapes in the manner of Abraham Beerstraten; and Adriaen van Diest, whose work is the lightest and most theatrical of the three.

[2] See below, pp. 293-5.

[3] Hollar was born in Prague in 1607 and left there in 1627; he may have studied etching under Matthäus Merian the elder in Frankfort. He travelled in Germany and was finally taken into Arundel's service when the earl was passing through Cologne on his embassy to Vienna in 1636 (see above, p. 4, n. 3). Although he was under the special protection of Arundel, he was also drawing master to the duke of York (and possibly to the prince of Wales); he was captured at the siege of Basing House in 1645, but left England for Antwerp in the same year. He returned finally in 1652 (A. M. Hind, *Wenceslaus Hollar and his Views of London and Windsor in the Seventeenth Century*

achievement, 'there is not a more useful and instructive Collection to be made'. Hollar's immense output surpassed that of any graphic artist who had worked in England earlier. It included a large number of plates of biblical and hagiographical subjects for such books as *The Christians Zodiake* (1643) or the little *Manual of Prayers and Letanies* (1672). His extensive sets of plates (some of them after designs by such artists as Streeter, Cleyn, and Barlow) for sumptuous editions of classical authors[1] mark an important stage in the development of English book-illustration. The maps which he drew for the publications of John Ogilby and Richard Blome played an important part in the growth of English map-making. His plates of the costumes of the inhabitants of the Old and New Worlds, which are in the tradition of the records of native life made by John White on Raleigh's expedition to Virginia, would have served or aroused the interests of Englishmen in the customs of foreign parts; and his designs, with their engaging fantasy, for such books as *A New and Perfect Boock of Beasts, Flowers, Fruit, &c.* (1663) provided no less exciting material on the flora and fauna of distant lands. Hollar's plates of coins and medals, and of heraldic and historical subjects, would have formed part of every antiquarian's and historian's library. He also produced contemporary portraits, some of them *ad vivum* and others based on existing likenesses, and his little etchings of current events, such as the trial and execution of Strafford (with its remarkable impression of the enormous crowd on Tower Hill), the plans and maps of some of the early campaigns in the Civil War or his survey of Charles II's coronation, are historical documents of great interest. Hollar made a special study of female costume in the charming portraits used to symbolize the *Seasons* (1641, 1643–4) and in the little costume pieces for his *Ornatus Muliebris Anglicanus* (1640) and *Theatrum Mulierum* (1643). Throughout his career he devoted much of his energies to faithful reproductions of the works of other artists

(1922); John Aubrey, *Brief Lives*, ed. A. Clark (1898), i. 407; G. Parthey's *Wenzel Hollar* (1853) and *Nachträge* (1858), F. Sprinzels, *Hollar Handzeichnungen* (1938) and J. Urzidil, *Hollar* (1942)).

[1] e.g. Ogilby's editions of Virgil (1654 et seq.) and Homer (1660, 1665) and Stapleton's *Juvenal* (1660). Ogilby was the greatest publisher of splendidly illustrated volumes at this date (see *D.N.B.*).

which are a valuable source for the art-historian today. It was for work of this nature that Arundel specially wished to secure his services, and Hollar's plates of the pictures, miniatures, drawings, and sculpture in his patron's great collections are sympathetic and honest.

The importance of Hollar's topographical work can hardly be overestimated. Some of his careful surveys of medieval buildings are reproductions of the work of men like Thomas Johnson, Richard Hall, or Mascall, but none are so fine as the plates of St. Paul's (e.g. Pl. 4 a), with a splendid set of views of the interior, which Hollar made for Dugdale's *History of St. Paul's Cathedral* (1658). His maps and plans of towns are equally important, culminating in his elaborate surveys of London before and after the Fire.[1] His skill in designing bird's-eye views is seen at its best in the aerial view of Windsor (Pl. 74 a),[2] which is among the set of plates drawn and etched by Hollar for Ashmole's *Institution, Laws and Ceremonies . . . of the Garter* (1672); it is a remarkable combination of mathematical precision with an indefinable charm and atmosphere, and illustrates clearly the extreme delicacy of his line and the 'simple probity' with which he used the etcher's technique.[3]

Hollar's skill as a topographer was officially recognized and in November 1666 he was sworn in as His Majesty's Scenographer and Designer of Prospects,[4] but was treated with scant generosity by the Crown. His most arduous official task was the survey of England's new possession, the fortress and naval base of Tangier. Hollar had earlier made a large map of Tangier, but not at first hand, and in March 1669 he proposed that he should go there in

[1] Hind, op. cit. 33–50, Pls. xi–xxvii; the most important are the long *London*, published in 1647 on six plates; *The Prospect of London and Westminster, &c.*; the parallel views of London before and after the Fire (1666); and Ogilby's and William Morgan's *Large and Accurate Map, &c.* (1677). The international celebrity of the Great Fire prompted numerous plagiarisms of Hollar's work.

[2] In his diary Ashmole wrote on 25 May 1659 that he took Hollar with him to Windsor to take views of the castle.

[3] In 1656 Richard Symonds spoke with Hollar about his technical methods (B.M., Egerton MS. 1635, ff. 81v.–82). Vertue (*Description* . . . (1759), 133–6) prints *Mr. Wenceslaus Hollar's Ground for Etching in Copper or Brass; with his Directions how to use it.*   [4] *Cal. S.P. Dom.* (1666–7), 256.

person, under the auspices of the Ambassador, Lord Henry Howard, the grandson of his old patron, to 'examine all, and take designs, and give his Majesty much better satisfaction'.[1] The result was a number of preparatory drawings and the set of large official drawings in pen and water-colour (in the British Museum) which give a lively picture of the town and of the life of the garrison there. Some years later he published a smaller series of views 'Exactly delineated by W: Hollar . . . and by him afterwards, to satisfie the curious, etshed in Copper'.

It is, however, his picture of London and the English country-side, whether in the etchings or in the water-colours, with their delicate ink or pencil outlines and their pale washes, that makes Hollar so important an artist in the development of landscape painting and drawing in England. His English landscapes follow the design and method of his earlier views in Germany and the Netherlands,[2] and the Germanic and sixteenth-century elements in his style would have been kept alive in the atmosphere of Arundel's collections. There is an echo in Hollar's spiky line of the precision of the Breughels and Brill, but nothing of their fantasy; only a supreme competence, which never degenerates into lifelessness, and a wholly enchanting sense of narrative. The diminutive, fairy-story quality of the subject is enhanced by the low horizon which Hollar almost invariably used and which provokes comparisons with such Dutch artists as Esaias van de Velde. His English drawings range between small, intimate little pieces such as the *Richmond Palace* in the British Museum; the view of the shipping on the river at the Tower (in the same collection) with its silvery blue and pale green washes; and the signed drawing at Windsor[3] of the curve of the river, with the rowing boats in the foreground drawn with a vigorous swelling line. The etchings provide a fuller picture of the English scene, but always in the same unruffled mood: Covent Garden (Pl. 4 *b*); the coach and riders galloping up to Albury House (Pl. 74 *b*); the view down the river from the roof of Arundel House; Westminster Hall (1647) and its row of waiting

---

[1] *Cal. S.P. Dom.* (1668–9), 256.

[2] e.g. the drawings of Rheineck, Bonn, and Amsterdam (1634) in the B.M.

[3] A. P. Oppé, *English Drawings . . . at Windsor Castle* (1950), Pl. 64.

carriages; or the quiet waters and the little fisherman at the Waterhouse at Islington (1665).[1] Hollar has a special place in the hearts of students of the English seventeenth century, for no other artist evokes with such subtle poetry the very atmosphere of the English scene of three hundred years ago.[2]

The surveys of English towns and buildings, to the development of which Hollar contributed so much, culminate in the Stuart period in the activities of Johannes Kip and Leonard Knyff. Their work, whether done singly or in partnership, is as ambitious as Hollar's but entirely without his quality. Kip's enormous engraved *Veue et Perspective de la Ville de Londre* (1710), for example, is a very elaborate panorama of the capital from St. James's Park, but has nothing of Hollar's delicacy. Knyff's large painted aerial views such as those of Windsor (*s.*), Hampton Court, or Clandon (*s.* 1708)[3] are equally pedestrian in quality, but pleasant in colour and abounding in anecdotal interest in the light they shed on the life that revolved round a great house. Knyff also produced a series of eighty drawings of royal palaces and country houses; these ('le tout dessiné sur les lieux') were engraved by Kip for his *Britannia Illustrata* or *Nouveau Théâtre de la Grande Bretagne* (1707–8). This extensive surveying of the larger English houses gave to families an opportunity to secure as careful a record of their

---

[1] Almost all these are reproduced by Hind, op. cit. Pls. xliii–iv, xlvii–viii, li, lix.

[2] Hollar's influence on such graphic artists as Daniel King, John Dunstall, Charles Woodfield and Richard Gaywood was considerable, but the only artist to recapture something of his spirit was Francis Place, a member of that pleasant circle of virtuosi in York which included Henry Gyles, the glass-painter, and William Lodge, the traveller, connoisseur, and amateur painter (Vertue, i. 74–75, 119–21; ii. 35, 89). Place was essentially an amateur, but he was a close friend of Hollar and profoundly influenced by him in his drawings and etchings. In the drawings of the later part of his career, however, such as those of Scarborough and Knaresborough in the B.M., Place relied much more for his atmosphere on a fuller use of wash than is found in Hollar. See Sir H. M. Hake, 'Some Contemporary Records relating to Francis Place', *Walpole Soc.* x (1922), 39–69; and J. Woodward, *Tudor and Stuart Drawings* (1951), Pls. 54 *b*, 56–57.

[3] They all hang in the appropriate places. Knyff, son of the Dutch landscape painter, Wouter Knyff, was born in Haarlem in 1650 and established in London (where he died in 1722) by 1681. He was also a picture-dealer; see H. Honour, 'Leonard Knyff', *Leeds Art Calendar*, vii, no. 23 (1953), 20–25, and *Burl. Mag.* xcvi (1954), 337–8; and below, pp. 279–80.

properties as of their countenances: in a letter to her daughter, the widowed duchess of Beaufort wrote, 'I have had Mr Kniff heer, who is doing three drafts . . . and one hee do's upon his owne account of Chelsy, Mr White . . . is doing y^r Fathers by that at Chelsy my designe when these are all done is to have some of them bound in books & give them to friends indeed my cheife aime is to show what a noble place my deare Lord has left . . . I have now printed the pedigres.'[1]

Jan Siberechts probably came to this country in 1674,[2] possibly under the protection of the duke of Buckingham. His style had matured in Flanders and he always saw the English countryside through Flemish eyes. The repertory of his scenes of country life was limited; they are often oddly out of scale and have a curious and engaging gaucherie: the stocky, wooden figures and animals are still and silent in an airless landscape against patterned foliage and even the splashing water of which he was so fond is seen in slow motion. Siberechts' colour is cool and pleasant and his handling is dry and broad. In England his subject-matter remained largely unchanged, but the distant scenery, which is used as a background for his troops of country folk with their horses, carts, and flocks, is recognizably English. Among the landscapes at Birdsall, for example, which were painted for Sir Thomas Willoughby, is the *Landscape with a Ford* (Pl. 77 a: s. 1695), in which a team of horses pull a wagon through the stream against a distant view of Wollaton House. Siberechts' more strictly topographical canvases

---

[1] Undated manuscript at Badminton: the duchess died in 1715. For one of Knyff's preliminary unfinished drawings see Pl. 84. Later editions of the *Nouveau Théâtre* were expanded to incorporate additional material. There was a close link between original and engraved topographical work at this date and the very poor quality of much of the painted topography is probably due to the use of engravings. The little views of Windsor by Jan Vorstermans (*c.* 1675), which hang in the castle, are almost alone in their sense of atmosphere and in a sympathetic understanding of the picturesque qualities of a subject which was a great favourite and much plagiarized. Of the other sets of views published at this period the most important are David Loggan's *Oxonia Illustrata* (1675) and his later companion volume for Cambridge. See above, p. 101.

[2] He was born in 1627 in Antwerp and entered the Guild of St. Luke in 1648–9; he was still in Antwerp early in 1672. See T. H. Fokker, *Jan Siberechts* (Brussels and Paris, 1931). No dated canvas is known later than 1698; for his view of Henley in that year see *Country Life*, ciii (1948), 277.

are far more competent than Knyff's bird's-eyes. The huge view of Wollaton (s. 1695; also at Birdsall) is one of the most ambitious and successful topographical pieces of this kind, but his most sensitive and charming views of an English country house are the two views of Longleat which are still in the house; they are signed and dated 1675 (Pl. 77 b) and 1676. In these more aristocratic subjects Siberechts follows closely the form of composition, evolved earlier in France for military and topographical subjects and used repeatedly by painters such as Van der Meulen and the Martins, which is built up of three main elements: a very soft and atmospheric distance, in which the natural features were sometimes slightly falsified for the sake of the composition; a meticulously accurate rendering of the house itself in the middle distance; and more freely painted groups of riders, coaches, dogs and huntsmen in the foreground, which was usually steeply and artificially raised in order to justify the high point from which the house was drawn. Such canvases, formal though they are, foreshadow the more sophisticated views of English houses by Richard Wilson and Canaletto.

Among Siberechts' most advanced landscapes are *Nottingham and the Trent* at Birdsall[1] and the much larger view at Easton Neston of the Thames from Richmond Hill (s. 1677), which is one of the earliest uses of a most popular site in English landscape painting. In these extensive 'prospects' there is a lack of formal design and a sense of sweep and distance which are quite new in English painting on such a scale. Even more spontaneous are Siberechts' water-colour drawings done in the Peak District in 1694 and 1699.[2] They are full of weaknesses, but have a real sense of atmosphere and are literal transcriptions from nature, and from much more romantic and picturesque scenery than Siberechts' predecessors had tackled. They are, with the freer of the drawings of Francis Place, among the most important anticipations of the English genius in water-colour in the eighteenth century.

[1] Waterhouse, Pl. 73.
[2] A view of Chatsworth (1694) is in the Rijksmuseum (Fokker, Pl. 43). Three drawings of Derbyshire were sold, Christie's, 21 April 1950 (101–2); one was dated 22 August 1694 and another 1699. On 6 May 1699 Siberechts was paid £10 'in part for Painting a Landskip of Chatsworth' for the Duke of Devonshire, who also commissioned Knyff to make a pictorial record of his new house and gardens.

The development of landscape and the lesser genres is linked paradoxically with the evolution of baroque wall-painting in this country: in the part played by pictures of subjects other than portraits in the design of an interior. In the uppermost register of the wainscot panelling, painted with elaborate Jacobean motives, in the Kederminster Library in St. Mary's Church at Langley[1] is a little series of landscapes; they are very coarse, but some of the views, especially one of Windsor, are identifiable. And in the Bower at Castle Ashby[2] seventeen little landscapes, twelve of which are related to the signs of the zodiac and the seasons, play a more prominent part in the decoration of a slightly later room. At Langley and Castle Ashby the landscapes are painted on the panels, but later in the century canvases were inset into the panelling, overdoors and fireplaces, as elements in the design of a room. Landscapes had been used for this purpose earlier in the century in France; in the Hôtel Lambert, for example, landscapes by the elder Patel, Swanevelt and Asselyn had been set into the walls of the Cabinet de l'Amour. The classic examples of this practice in England are in the rooms at Ham House that were redecorated in the 1670's[3] by the duke and duchess of Lauderdale, who employed a team of Dutch and English painters at the time when it was a deliberate policy of the English government to encourage Dutch immigrants. The work at Ham emphasizes the impersonal nature of much of the work to which reputable artists could still be put and the utilitarian purposes for which their work was often required; and it embodies that intertwining of Dutch and English trends which was of such fundamental importance for the future of English painting. It is the clearest example of a method which continued into the eighteenth century: in the age of Vanbrugh painters like Van Diest and Marco Ricci painted overdoors in such houses as Beningbrough and Castle Howard; and the duke of Montagu's team of French artists at Montagu House included Jacques Rousseau, whose landscapes for his patron (some of which

[1] H. A. Tipping, *English Homes*, III. i (1929), li–iv.

[2] Ibid. III. ii (1927), 170.

[3] For this see the *Guide* to Ham by R. Edwards and P. Ward-Jackson (2nd ed. 1951). A very important set of overdoors is at Drayton.

survive at Boughton), and over the doors in Queen Anne's Presence Chamber and Eating Room at Hampton Court, are exactly identical in type with those which he painted for the Gallery at the Hôtel Lambert. The much larger inset landscapes by later painters like Zucchi and Zuccarelli at Saltram, Harewood and Osterley are in the same tradition; and in May 1755 the duke of Bedford paid Gainsborough twenty-one pounds for *A Landscape for a Chimney piece*.[1]

Danckerts, as we should expect, was employed at Ham, but the Lauderdales' favourite landscapist seems to have been Dirck van den Bergen, who painted for them landscapes with shepherds and flocks in a style very close to his master, Adriaen van de Velde. There are also, over the door and fireplace in the Duchess' Private Closet, two macabre pieces by William Gouw Ferguson with the same unearthly light that is used by Jan Griffier in his pictures of figures in a welter of ruins and archaeological fragments. But the greatest painter in the Lauderdales' team was Willem van de Velde the younger: of four canvases by him, inset over the doors in the Duchess' Bedchamber, all are signed and dated 1673 and two are signed as painted in London. The visits to England of Dutch marine painters such as Hendrick Cornelisz. Vroom and Adam Willaerts, and the seapieces by Porcellis and the Vrooms in Charles I's collection, did not foster the growth of a native school of sea-painting; but the arrival of the Van de Veldes from Holland, late in 1672 or early in 1673, brought to this country the two most distinguished naval painters of the age.[2] Charles II and the duke of York took them at once under their protection and derived intense pleasure from their work. In January 1674 Charles expressed to the Lords of the Admiralty his wish that one hundred pounds should be paid annually to each artist: to the father for

---

[1] G. Scott Thomson, 'Two Landscapes by Gainsborough', *Burl. Mag.* xcii (1950), 201–2.

[2] W. Voorbeytel Cannenburg, 'The Van de Veldes', *Mariner's Mirror*, 36, no. 3 (1950), 185–204, and H. P. Baard, *Willem van de Velde de oude . . . de jonge* (Amsterdam, n.d.); H. de Groot's *Catalogue Raisonné . . .* vii (1923) deals with Willem II; *Country Life*, cxiii (1953), 96–97. I am particularly grateful to Mr. Michael Robinson for allowing me to read in manuscript (1954) his introduction to the catalogue of Van de Velde drawings at Greenwich which contains much invaluable new material.

'taking and making draughts of sea-fights' and to the son for putting them into colours for the King's particular use.[1] Father and son were both very highly specialized in the official portraiture of ships and in drawn or painted records of naval engagements. They painted for the Crown, and for some of the leading naval commanders, actions at sea as seen from the English side and pictures of English vessels of all kinds; for these there exist an immense number of preparatory drawings, often done under fire in a galliot. The borderline between the work of the two men is not quite so clear as their warrant implies. They were both employed, for example, on the series of twelve sea-fights, commissioned by the duke of York and still in the royal collection; the dated canvases run between 1675 and 1683. The one canvas which is definitely by the elder painter (s. 1683) is thinner, drier, and much less atmospheric than the work of his son; but some of the son's pieces in this series are packed with incident and are map-like bird's-eye views of battles, which are official records rather than works of art. In quality, however, they are richer and bolder than the work of the older man. In two canvases in the duke of York's set in which fewer ships are engaged (e.g. Pl. 76 a: s. 1677), the younger Van de Velde shows his skill in treating the details of naval architecture, without losing his sense of the bulk of the vessels or the bellying sails, and creates a vivid impression of broken sunlight, a puff of cannon-fire across a quiet sea and billowing clouds of smoke. On a larger scale these qualities give life to such splendid pieces as *The Y at Amsterdam* (s. 1686; Rijksmuseum) with Tromp's flagship, the *Gouden Leeuw*,[2] and the companion piece, *The Battle of the Texel* (s. 1687) in the National Maritime Museum.

To the end of his life the younger Van de Velde made a special study of cloud effects: William Gilpin knew a Thames waterman who had often taken Van de Velde 'out in his boat, both up and down the river, to study the appearances of the sky . . . in all kinds of weather, fair, and foul; and Mr. Vanderveldt took with

---

[1] *Cal. S.P. Dom.* (1673–5), 101; *Cal. Tr. Bks.* iv. 486, 597; the official warrant for payment was dated 20 February 1674, and the salaries were established by Privy Seal, 20 October 1674.

[2] H. P. Baard, op. cit. 55–58.

him large sheets of blue paper, which he would mark all over with black, and white. These expeditions Vanderveldt called . . . *going a skoying*.[1] In the remarkable *Shipwreck* (s. 1696) at Loseley Park a picturesque quality in the treatment of the fury of the elements looks forward to the work of Vernet; and the styles of Scott and Peter Monamy, and ultimately of all the English marine artists of the eighteenth century, were formed entirely on that of the Van de Veldes. They can thus be accurately described as the fathers of English marine painting.

Another of the duke and duchess of Lauderdale's Dutch artists, Jan Wyck, played almost as important a part in the growth of sporting painting in this country. On 17 June 1674 he appeared before the court of the Painter-Stainers and promised to pay his own and his father's 'quarterage'.[2] Jan's signed battle-piece over the fireplace in the Duke's Closet at Ham is perhaps one of his earliest essays in England in a genre in which he specialized and in which he was influenced by Wouwermans. Many of his battle-pieces and equestrian scenes are of an exotic nature, with Turkish or Moorish figures and a histrionic sense of fantasy; but he also painted contemporary battle-scenes and small martial portraits. In a series of battle-pieces at Drumlanrig, probably painted for the duke of Monmouth, is a very interesting picture (s.) of the battle of Bothwell Brig (1679). It has the appearance of an eye-witness account and the panoramic treatment is the equivalent on land of the Van de Veldes' handling of battles at sea. His little military equestrian portraits, such as those of William III (s. 1692) at Blenheim[3] or Major-General Egerton (Pl. 76 b) are lively and vigorous in quality. They established a type which was popular in the

[1] William Gilpin, in his notes on the poem, *On Landscape Painting*, 34 (*Three Essays, &c.*, 1792).

[2] *Booke of Orders*, ii, f. 170.

[3] The best version of a design which was much repeated and copied, often with variations. Wyck's larger equestrian portraits, such as the life-size *6th Duke of Norfolk* (s. 1677) at Drayton, are less successful.

Other battle-painters working in England were Dirk Maes and Stoop; the latter specialized in pictures and engravings of processions, but was probably outclassed by Wyck. Maes was also a weaker painter than Wyck, but was attached to William III's staff in the Irish wars and painted the battle of the Boyne; Vertue's references (v. 50, 52) are probably to the picture at Welbeck.

eighteenth century: John Wootton's *George II* (*s.* 1754) at Hopetoun House,[1] for example, and countless canvases by painters like Morier, derive from Wyck's prototypes. Wootton's bigger military pieces are close to Wyck in composition and quality; and the views at Windsor showing Frederick, prince of Wales, and his family at Park Place near Henley are entirely traditional.

In his hunting scenes Wootton was no less indebted to Wyck and recaptures much of his fresh drawing, attractive fluency, rich colour and light sense of movement. Wootton was the first distinguished English sporting painter and most of his enormous output lies beyond the limits of this volume, but he was at work in the Stuart and very early Georgian periods, before the influence of Wyck and Gaspar Poussin upon his style had become so strong. Walpole saw at Shortgrove in 1762 'many landscapes over Chimnies and doors by Wotton, but done when he was very young'.[2] He was a member of the circle of Tory artists which was grouped round the 2nd earl of Oxford,[3] and an extensive collection of his work is still at Welbeck. Among the pictures which he painted for Lord Conway is a vast canvas (*s.* 1714; Ragley) of horsemen and hounds against a panoramic landscape. Each horse and rider is so carefully drawn that the scene lacks unity, but the free, light sky and spreading landscape are something quite new in English painting on such a scale. Even more ambitious are two large pictures at Welbeck of Lady Henrietta Harley hawking at Wimpole and chasing the hare on Orwell Hill.[4] By this period Wootton had also evolved his standard form of horse-portraiture: a horse austerely seen in profile, held by a groom and stood against a race-course or varied and indeterminate buildings and landscapes. Their primary interest will always be to the student of the turf, as documents in a great age of horse-breeding, but the records which Wootton made in this way of a hunt or a stud were not wholly unprecedented in England. The series at Welbeck of huge pictures

---

[1] *Kings and Queens*, R.A. (1953), illustrated souvenir, 60.

[2] 'Journals of Visits to Country Seats, &c.' ed. Paget Toynbee, *Walpole Soc.* xvi (1928), 33.   [3] See above, p. 199.

[4] W. S. Sparrow, *British Sporting Artists* (1922), 112. Wootton was in the service of the Harleys from at least 1714 and these two large canvases were paid for in November 1716; see R. W. Goulding, *Catalogue of the Pictures . . . at Welbeck . . .* (1936), 492–4.

of horses painted, traditionally by Abraham van Diepenbeeck,[1] for that great horseman, the 1st duke of Newcastle, anticipate (with one or two isolated pieces) Wootton's life-size pictures of horses[2] which he gave up almost entirely for the smaller form. There is no change of scale or intention between them and Stubbs's *Hambletonian* of 1799; Stubbs's very early group of Mr. and Mrs. Wilson with huntsmen and hounds was anticipated to a considerable extent by a group of huntsmen which is signed and dated 1706 by an obscure painter named Byng.[3] Peter Tillemans, who came to England in 1708, was a slighter and more rococo painter than Wootton; his topographical pieces, such as the view of Chelsea Hospital (*s*; at the Hospital), are light and watery, and his small equestrian portrait of the 2nd earl of Ashburnham with two attendants (*s*.)[4] is soft and cool with a curious air of detachment; but it has none of Wootton's skill in assembling such a composition.

The only English painter in the little colony at Ham was Francis Barlow, a less accomplished and successful artist than Jan Wyck or Wootton, but the first Englishman to specialize in paintings of birds, animals, and sporting scenes.[5] Over the doors in the Volary

---

[1] Goulding, op. cit., 438–9. They are a puzzling set; Diepenbeeck is not known to have come to England and his association with Newcastle was during the latter's exile in Antwerp, where Newcastle produced his celebrated *Méthode et Invention Nouvelle de Dresser les Chevaux* (1658) with plates by Diepenbeeck. Three of the canvases have topographical backgrounds, and one a figure in costume, which cannot be much later than 1630, and there may have been at least two hands at work. See A. M. Hind, *Catalogue of Drawings by Dutch and Flemish Artists . . . in the British Museum* (1923), 100–1, 105, Pl. li; and A. S. Turberville, *A History of Welbeck Abbey* (1938), i. 136–40.

[2] For example at Clandon (obscurely *s*.; *c*. 1715); *Lady Oxford's Dun Mare with Thomas the Groom* (1715) at Welbeck; or the portrait of *Scarr* with his groom (*s*. October 1714) at Chatsworth.

[3] The Stubbs (*c*. 1752–4) was exhibited in the Leger Galleries, 1 October–15 November 1952 (9); the Byng was formerly with Messrs. Leggatt.

[4] Ashburnham sale, Sotheby's, 15 July 1953 (115; reproduced in catalogue).

[5] Barlow is stated to have been born in Lincolnshire; he died in London in 1704. In 1650 he was made free of the Painter-Stainers' Company (see above, p. 77) and his earliest extant work is a drawing of *David slaying the Lion* (*s*. 1648) in the B.M. He may have been apprenticed at first to Sheppard, but was in independent practice as a painter of animals, birds, and fishes by 1652–3, when Symonds visited 'Barlow living neare ye Drum in Drury Lane . . . for a quadro of ffishes he made he had 8ˡⁱ he uses to make fowle & birds & colour them from the life. . . . He paynts the ayre first then the cheife thing of his quadro afterward . . .' (B.M. Egerton MS. 1636, f. 95).

are two appropriate pieces by Barlow: a group of birds (s. 1673?) and the delightful *Owl mobbed by Small Birds*;[1] the background and accessories are purely decorative and conceived as places on which to perch the birds that are the fruit of much loving first-hand observation. The same hiatus can be seen in three vast canvases 'of fowle and huntings' which Barlow painted for the hall of Denzil Onslow's house at Pyrford. The scheme anticipates the large canvases of hunting scenes which Wootton was to paint in the reign of George II for the halls at Althorp, Badminton and Longleat. Onslow's pictures survive at Clandon.[2] In the *Landscape with Birds and Fishes* (s. 1667) the setting is thinly painted and completely subordinated to the successful catch on the bank and to the groups of interested birds. There is humour and sympathy in details like the enormous pike in the foreground and the group of three jackdaws in a tree above. The *Decoy* is a more balanced composition, and is again packed with ornithological detail; but in the *Farm Yard*, opposite the pig in his ramshackle sty, is a peacock beneath a wall and the base of a column which are normally to be found in the more elaborate forms of fashionable portrait painting. Denzil Onslow's series was probably completed by the attractive *Southern-Mouthed Hounds* (also at Clandon);[3] the dogs and a hare are welded with that sense of design which Barlow so often reveals into a frieze-like pattern. As a painter Barlow had little quality; his paint is dry and often harsh and his colour normally cool and sober; and the movements of his birds and animals are frozen into immobility by the unmistakable brown outlines with which he rounded off his forms.

This outline is no less characteristic of his drawings. Barlow was a prolific draughtsman of considerable charm and was influenced by Hollar.[4] Many of his studies, normally in sepia ink and wash,

[1] Waterhouse, Pl. 74.

[2] W. S. Sparrow, *British Sporting Artists* (1922), 23, 26, 39.

[3] Ibid. 36.

[4] J. Woodward, *Tudor and Stuart Drawings* (1951), Pls. 26–32; and see W. S. Sparrow, 'Our Earliest Sporting Artist', *Connoisseur*, xcviii (1936), 36–40. Among Barlow's drawings formerly in the Reitlinger collection was one of a rider fallen from his horse (Sotheby's, 27 Jan. 1954 (129), rep. in catalogue); it is hard to resist the temptation to think of this as a skit on the pomposities of Newcastle's horsemanship.

of animals and birds were used in his canvases, and others were designed as engravings and illustrations.[1] Some of them (e.g. Pl. 78 a) have a lively anecdotal interest and great charm, and the drawings for Aesop's *Fables* (1666 et seq.), of which there are a large number in the British Museum, must have been, with their delightful decorative *animalia*, a congenial task. In Barlow's drawings of sporting subjects,[2] such as the *Hare Hunting* (Pl. 78 b), we catch, for all the mannered line, odd proportion and the artificiality with which the backgrounds are sometimes constructed, a breath of the air of the countryside and its pursuits in the seventeenth century and something of the atmosphere of the *Compleat Angler*.

Between two of Barlow's pictures at Clandon hangs a life-size portrait of an old labourer on the Onslow estate. It is possible that it is by Barlow; but it is, in any case, very exceptional as a sympathetic portrait, wholly without satire, of an English farmworker of the seventeenth century. The most vivid picture of the parishioners of an English village is provided by the Fleming Gillis van Tilborch in the fascinating *Tichborne Dole* (s. 1670)[3] at Tichborne Park. In front of the Tudor mansion is grouped a crowd of expectant villagers, as Sir Henry Tichborne, surrounded by his family and servants, advances to distribute his hereditary charity; the heads are painted with great care and the carefully contrasted types and costumes constitute a social document of intense interest.

Abraham Hondius and Leonard Knyff were more competent as animal painters than Barlow. Hondius, a native of Rotterdam, was in London by January 1674.[4] He specialized in savage scenes, which derive from Snyders, with birds pursued by dogs or boars, or bears, wolves, hounds and bulls locked in violent combat; they are bright in colour and very freely painted and, although they per-

---

[1] For example, *Multæ et Diversæ Avium Species* (1658) and *Variæ Quadrupedum Species*, many of which were etched by Hollar.

[2] These were used for such books as the volume of etchings (by Hollar), *Severall Wayes of Hunting, Hawking, and Fishing, according to the English Manner* (1671), and Richard Blome's *Gentleman's Recreation* (1686).

[3] The signature and date are partly illegible; there seems no other evidence for a visit to England by Tilborch.

[4] Of the many references to Hondius in Hooke's diary the earliest is dated 29 January 1674.

haps reflect the English love for such shows in real life, there is a strong element of fantasy in them and nothing of Barlow's obvious love for his material. Leonard Knyff was a less prolific painter of animals and birds than Barlow and his topographical work can have allowed him few opportunities for this genre. In his large picture at Temple Newsam of the 3rd Lord Irwin with a gun, dog, and dead game (for which Knyff was paid thirty-five pounds in 1700) there is again a contrast between the main items in the composition and a purely decorative backcloth. Knyff's feeling for animals and plants marks the two smaller canvases which he painted for Lord Irwin: *Fell-Hounds with a Hare* (s. 1699) and *A Greyhound and a Hare* (s.).[1] The compositions are curiously static, but the animals are drawn with a greater fluency than Barlow; there is a suggestion of Jan Fyt in the freedom and assurance with which the hare is drawn in the latter picture.

Among Barlow's canvases at Clandon are portraits of an ostrich and a cassowary (of which there are versions at Longleat) and his drawings include studies of an elephant with a rhinoceros.[2] The desire to have records of zoological and anthropological rarities was strong among English patrons. In 1710 John Verelst painted for Kensington Palace full-lengths of the four Iroquois 'kings' who had come to visit Queen Anne, and Barlow's more exotic subjects and the canvases done by the Hungarian Jakob Bogdani are documents of some value for the state of zoological and ornithological knowledge and interest at the time. Bogdani was lavishly patronized by Queen Anne and she bought, after the death of Admiral George Churchill in 1710, the series of large canvases (e.g. Pl. 53 *b*) which faithfully describe the inhabitants of the Admiral's magnificent aviary in Windsor Park. These are in the same tradition as Hondecoeter's picture in the Mauritshuis of the animals in William III's menagerie at Het Loo, and are much more artificial than Barlow; like many of Bogdani's flower-pieces they were intended for use as overdoors.[3] These are very close to those of his

[1] The former is at Temple Newsam, the latter in the possession of the earl of Halifax.

[2] J. Woodward, op. cit., Pl. 31; the rhino is based on Dürer.

[3] In Queen Anne's inventory six out of her fourteen Bogdanis were in use as overdoors and some are still in place. The writer of the treatise B.M. Add. MS. 22950

contemporary, Jean Baptiste Monnoyer, who was one of the French artists brought over by the 1st duke of Montagu for the decoration of Montagu House,[1] and ultimately settled in this country, where he died in 1699. Monnoyer had worked as a flower-painter under Le Brun and he was immensely prolific in the output of large or small canvases of an essentially decorative nature: great sheaves of flowers in carved pots, standing on a ledge in an architectural setting with a baroque sweep of drapery.

In France and England flower-painting had also become a polite accomplishment for female amateur painters. In Lely's double-portrait of the two Capel sisters,[2] Elizabeth, countess of Carnarvon, proudly holds one of her little studies of flowers, of which an example (s. 1662) survives at Windsor. Many years later her sister, then the duchess of Beaufort, commissioned the florilegium in water-colours by Daniel Frankcom and Everard Kickius of 'naturall Plants growing at Badminton and Chelsea'. With Alexander Marshal's set of flower-drawings at Windsor (one is dated 1659) they are perhaps the most important sets of botanical drawings of this kind to be executed in England in the seventeenth century.[3]

The invasion of Dutch painters in the second half of the Stuart period, and the ready employment they found with such patrons

(see above, p. 188, n. 1) records a conversation with Bogdani in October 1691 in which the painter told him of his methods and difficulties: 'says he paint in the Spring flowers & in the Somer flowers & Fruits when they are out Lobsters and oyster pieces, In the Winter pieces of Fowell & plate'.

[1] See above, pp. 272–3. Montagu and the Crown almost monopolized Monnoyer's services.   [2] R. B. Beckett, *Lely* (1951), Pl. 36.

[3] These are in two volumes at Badminton; Kyckius' volume is dated 1703–5; see W. Blunt, *The Art of Botanical Illustration* (1950), 129–30. The only other painters of flowers and still-lifes of any merit are: Simon Verelst (see above, p. 175), who seems to have been working as late as 1700; William Gouw Ferguson, who specialized in groups of hanging dead game entirely in the manner of Weenix (e.g. two, one s., the other s. 1684, in the N.G. of Scotland); the two Cradocks or Craddocks, John (a Bachelor of Divinity who presented to the Painter-Stainers on 7 July 1648 one of his paintings of fruit) and Marmaduke or Luke, of whom Vertue thought highly (i. 79–80); the Fleming, Pieter Angillis, who specialized in subject-pieces with piles of still-life in a favourite Flemish convention; and Pieter Roestraten of Haarlem whose elaborate assemblages of vessels, shells, jewellery, and plate (e.g. at Hampton Court and Chatsworth, s. 1678) may have influenced the very obscure painter Arnold (*fl.* 1682–4) and inspired to some extent the curious 'miscellanies' of Evert Collier.

as the Lauderdales, stimulated the admiration in England of those qualities that are perennially admired in all but the greatest Dutch painting: Pepys's delight in a *trompe l'œil*, in the manner of Evert Collier, of objects on a deal board ('not board, but only the picture of a board') and in the deceptive realism of the drops of dew on the leaves of a flower-piece by Verelst ('it is worth going twenty miles to see it')[1] has been shared by collectors and dealers ever since. His pleasure in pictures of involved and imaginary architectural perspective ('strange things to think how they do delude one's eye') is an echo of the popularity at the court of Charles I of the younger Steenwyck's highly elaborate pieces in this manner[2] and is reflected in the more advanced perspectives of Samuel van Hoogstraten, a pupil of Rembrandt who was in this country in the 1660's.[3] This taste is akin to the popularity of the small, highly polished and artificial candle-light scenes by Godfried Schalcken, a pupil of Dou and Hoogstraten. Schalcken, who seems to have come to England in 1692, probably owed much to the encouragement of William III, and in a portrait of the King (*c.* 1692) of which there are versions at Attingham and in the Rijksmuseum, used his favourite trick in a life-size formal portrait.[4] Finally the picturesque harbours, Italian street scenes, or alchemists in their laboratory, in which Thomas, the father of Jan, Wyck specialized, brought to this country an attractive, but much weakened, development of the style of Bamboccio;[5] the pictures of seaports at Ham and the *Alchemist*, painted as an overmantel in the closet next to the Duchess' Bedchamber, are good examples of the elder Wyck's pleasant, fluent style.

According to the strict canon laid down by the French Academy, with which some English collectors and such classical theorists as

---

[1] *Diary*, 15 March 1668 and 11 April 1669.　　　　[2] See above, p. 69, n. 2.

[3] Waterhouse, 77–78. Two of these perspectives contained figures of Sir John Finch (see above, p. 9) and his sister (?) (ex-Burley-on-the-Hill and the Mauritshuis respectively; Sir L. Cust and A. Malloch, 'Portraits by . . . S. van Hoogstraeten', *Burl. Mag.* xxix (1916), 292–7).

[4] Schalcken was still in England in October 1695; see A. M. Crinò, 'Note di Documentazione su due Autoritratti della Collezione degli Uffizi', *Rivista d'Arte*, xxviii (1953), 191–7.

[5] For his relation to Bamboccio and Cerquozzi, see G. Briganti, 'Pieter van Laer e Michelangelo Cerquozzi', *Proporzioni*, iii (1950), 185–98.

Shaftesbury were in sympathy, these lesser genres were anathema, but there is no doubt that they were steadily gaining in popularity among collectors of less lofty minds. The astute publisher Pierce Tempest wrote to Francis Place on 9 January 1686: 'the ladys have solely left painting *Mezzotintos* yet they doe sell a little especially fancy's Heads & bawdy soe I am provideing 3 or four new ones Against the Terme 2 Queens a new Confession 2 Fancys after *Laroone* . . . a *Presbyterian Meeting* of the same Mar. [Master], . . . rather bigger than the *Quakers* it may sell.'[1] The *Quakers* was almost certainly by the Dutch Egbert van Heemskerck, who spent a number of years in England, where, according to Buckeridge, his imitations of Brouwer, Ostade and Steen, his 'Study of Sots Paradice', were popular with 'waggish Collectors, and the lower Rank of *Virtuosi*'. His prolific pieces of boors and their amusements, such as the set at Birdsall which was probably painted for Sir Thomas Willoughby, are faithful to their prototypes, though they are dull in colour and have nothing of their energy; but his pictures of Quaker meetings,[2] in which the satire seems tinged with sympathy, and his masterpiece, the *Oxford Election* (s. 1687; Town Hall, Oxford),[3] are much more interesting. As social documents in paint they are of great rarity at this period and the abounding humour and vivid, but kindly, characterization, enhanced by vigorous, spiky brushwork, directly anticipate Hogarth. Almost the only works that can be classed with them are the elder Marcellus Laroon's studies of figures from the London streets: the set of water-colours in the British Museum of the characters in Italian comedy, in which *Mezzetino* comes curiously close to Watteau, and the designs for the two sets of *Cryes of the City of London*, which were published by Pierce Tempest and which forestall Wheatley in everything but sentiment. At the other end of the social scale are Pieter Angillis' crude little scene of the Installation of a Knight of the Garter by Queen Anne (s.; National Portrait Gallery) or Tillemans' view of the House of Lords at the same date (s.; Kensington Palace). A small number of timid

[1] Sir H. M. Hake, 'Some Contemporary Records . . .', *Walpole Soc.* x (1922), 65.
[2] F. Saxl, 'The Quakers' Meeting', *Journ. of the Warburg and Courtauld Institutes*, vi (1943), 214–16.   [3] Waterhouse, Pl. 94.

little conversation pieces in landscape settings by Joan Carlile[1] are the most important early examples of a genre which was to be fully evolved by Phillips, the Devis family, Hogarth and Zoffany.

Very few of the artists who have been discussed in this chapter would bulk very large in a history of European painting. England produced no Van Goyen, Jacob Ruysdael or Claude to recapture in a native idiom the beauties of the English countryside. The influences of continental landscape painting came fitfully across the North Sea and the Channel to become absorbed into a substantial part of the raw material on which the English achievement in landscapes in oil and water-colour in the next century was to be based. In our period the landscape painter could not count on the continuous employment which the portrait painter could expect and much of his time was taken up with the anonymous work of painting backgrounds for his more successful contemporaries. The backgrounds in portraits of the Stuart period provide a microcosm of the range of the landscape painters. There are topographical backgrounds chosen for their aptness to the sitter; Netherlandish landscapes and seascapes in the manner of Vinckboons and the Vrooms behind Mytens's patrons, and battle-pieces on land and sea, many of which must have been by Jan Wyck and the Van de Veldes, for Kneller and Dahl; and the essays in landscape by the portrait painters themselves: the beautiful fluent plants and rocks around Van Dyck's sitters; the stormy Venetian skies of Dobson; and the backgrounds in Lely's earlier phase which come so close to Both or Berchem. But despite this subordination of the lesser genres to the portrait, and the palpable lack of technical skill which so many of them display, the landscape painters, the topographers, and the sporting artists give us constant precious glimpses of the country background, and of the fields, farmhouses, and cottages as well as the great houses and estates, against which was spent so much of the life of the men and women who went up to London to sit to Van Dyck, Lely or Kneller.

---

[1] M. Toynbee and Sir G. Isham, 'Joan Carlile (1606?–1679)—An Identification', *Burl. Mag.* xcvi (1954), 275–7; nos. 1, 2, and 8 (all *c.* 1650) in the authors' list are the basis upon which an *œuvre* could perhaps be built; I do not think nos. 5, 6, or 7 are by Mrs. Carlile.

XII

DECORATIVE PAINTING

T HE full baroque style was pre-eminently suited for the service of absolute monarchs or to proclaim the doctrines of the post-Tridentine Church. In Italy, France, and Flanders it epitomized and glorified those theories of absolute monarchy, Divine Right and Catholic supremacy, which precipitated the constitutional upheavals in England in the seventeenth century. It could never have become firmly established in its fullest form as an artistic style in England, but its influence in England was felt in no form more strongly than in the growth of an ambitious, if rather sporadic, school of decorative painting. This school, indeed, surpassed in scope anything that was seen before or after in this country and was at times, in style and sometimes in intention, more than a mere reflection of baroque painting in the Catholic countries of Europe. On the other hand, much of the lesser work of the decorative painters of the time was of a very humble nature and throughout the period there was a close connexion between the painted decoration for houses and the more ephemeral tasks of the scene painter. But the growth of English baroque decorative painting perhaps reveals more clearly than the contemporary development of the portrait the extent and limitations of continental influence on painting in this country.[1]

The thriving school of medieval mural painters in England had been effectively destroyed by the Reformation and the impact of the renaissance on this country in the Tudor period had not been sufficiently powerful to create a definite English renaissance style of decorative painting. Even in the royal palaces it seems that wall painting at the end of the sixteenth century consisted mainly of uninspired repetitive patterns, often made up of motives which can be traced back to classical times. At the accession of Charles I

[1] Mr. Edward Croft-Murray has most kindly placed all his material on the Stuart period at my disposal and has assisted me at every point in this chapter.

this was still the most readily available form of decoration and was used in the most illustrious settings. The work was carried out in the workshops of the Sergeant-Painters, who were also responsible for repairing and decorating the royal coaches, ships and barges, and scarcely rises above the level of house-painting. The payments to John De Critz the elder[1] give a vivid picture of the Sergeant-Painters' tasks and of the painted background for the life of the early Stuart court: between 1606 and 1636, for example, he was paid for such items as heraldic work at Theobalds; for 'twice priming stoppinge & painting lead coulor in oile the Cornish Doores and postes at the Lo: Hayes lodginge', and for sixty-four yards of 'Antique woorke wth white and black' in the privy lodgings, at Whitehall; and, in a passage at Denmark House, for eighty-four panels of 'Crotesque worke and an escuchion in the middest wth shells in them guilded and sett out wth other Coulors the edges of the Battens likewise guilded', and for painting the ceiling of the Queen's Closet with grotesque work.[2] The only example that survives of such work done for the Crown is in the Queen's House, where in the Queen's Bedroom[3] the coving between the cornice and the carved framework of the painted area on the flat of the ceiling (which is also partially decorated in the same manner) is painted, probably by De Critz or under his guidance, in tempera with a rather cramped pattern of complex grotesque motives, which incorporate the Queen's arms, against a green-grey or coffee-coloured background. The handling is fresh and the drawing competent; the colours must originally have been very gay and were set off by gilding. Extensive areas of such painting must have been very bright indeed.

Occasionally the monotony of this form of decoration is relieved by more ambitious elements and by slight essays in history-painting. In the Queen's Bedroom there are four little monochrome scenes on the ceiling which are painted to imitate sculptured

---

[1] See above, p. 83; for the Sergeant-Painters see E. Auerbach, *Tudor Artists* (1954); and E. Mercer, 'The Decoration of the Royal Palaces, 1553–1625', *Arch. Journ.* cx (1953), 150–63.

[2] P.R.O. Declared Accounts, A.O.I. 2419/39, 2422/48, 2425/57.

[3] G. H. Chettle, L.C.C., *Survey of London* (14th monograph, n.d.), 74–75, Pls. 78–83.

reliefs, and the payments to De Critz sometimes indicate work of a more varied kind: his decoration of the King's Withdrawing Chamber at Whitehall in 1620–21[1] included the four elements, the fruits of the four winds, the seasons and the four parts of the earth in compartments, set into the normal grotesque work, and in 1629–30 he painted a chimney-piece in Mr. Carey's bedchamber at Whitehall with 'the Storye of Aeneas, carrying Anchises out of Troye, wth the Scroules on each side . . . paynted to expresse them as they were carved'.[2] The treatment of such themes and the relation between the narrative and the purely decorative elements were probably close to Cleyn's designs for Mortlake tapestries or to the more elaborate forms of Jacobean sculptured decoration. The Jacobean and Caroline form of grotesque decoration survived the Interregnum and was taken up again in the eighteenth century by William Kent; but it could never have satisfied a patron of such highly developed and cosmopolitan tastes as Charles I.

Charles's efforts to set England within the orbit of the leading continental artistic movements were very successful in the field of decorative painting. Simon Vouet, who had come to England as a very young man and was later to work for the widowed Henrietta Maria at Colombes, painted for the Queen's Chapel at Oatlands a ceiling[3] representing the blessings of Faith and Love under the union of the lilies and roses in the courtly baroque style which was so popular at the French court; and Orazio Gentileschi[4] painted a ceiling at York House for Buckingham and nine canvases, representing the Muses and the Fine and Liberal Arts, for the ceiling of the Hall in the Queen's House.[5] Far more important was the commission, probably finally given to Rubens on his visit to this country in 1629,[6] to execute the large canvases for the ceiling of the Banqueting House, in the decoration of which Rubens seems to

---

[1] P.R.O., A.O.I. 2423/51.　　　　　　　　[2] Ibid. 2426/60.
[3] Engraved by Dorigny, 1639.　　　　　　[4] See above, p. 5.
[5] The canvases survive in a mutilated condition at Marlborough House; J. Hess, 'Die Gemälde des Orazio Gentileschi', English Miscellany, 3 (Rome, 1952), 159–87, and 'Precisazioni', English Miscellany, 4 (Rome, 1953), 247–56; and A. M. Crinò, 'Due Lettere Autografe di Orazio . . . Gentileschi . . .', Rivista d'Arte, xxix (1954), 203–6.
[6] See above, p. 5.

have been interested since 1621. Some of the sketches for this cycle (e.g. Pl. 23 *a*) may have been done while he was in this country. They show a sense of sweeping, dynamic movement, a creative vitality and nervous energy and a sheer beauty of colour and touch which are unsurpassed in even his *œuvre*. The finished canvases, for which he was paid three thousand pounds, did not arrive in London until late in 1635. The Whitehall ceiling is the richest remembrance of all Charles I's contacts with contemporary foreign artists. The layout was clearly based on Veronese's ceiling in the church of S. Sebastiano in Venice; the full splendour of Rubens's late technique and his wealth of allegory were called into the service of the Stuarts as they were for the Jesuit Fathers of Antwerp, the Hapsburgs, Bourbons and Medici. The great central panel of the apotheosis of James I is flanked by two scenes of the union of the crowns of England and Scotland (where the reminiscences of Veronese and Correggio are particularly strong) and the prosperity of King James's rule, a theme emphasized in the oval canvases in the four corners, which are linked along the two main walls by friezes of putti with animals and fruit. A superb tribute to the infallibility and blessings of kingly government is appropriately paid, in clear and simple iconography, to the arch-champion of the Divine Right of Kings. In October 1639 negotiations were opened with Jordaens, through Sir Balthazar Gerbier, for a series of canvases for the Queen's Cabinet in the Queen's House: nine for the ceiling and thirteen for the walls. At one stage Gerbier thought that the King might prefer Rubens to carry out the work if it could be done for approximately the same price as Jordaens: 'they are both Dutchmen & not to seeke to represent robustrous boistrous druncken headed imaginary Gods, and of the two most certaine Sir Peter Reubens is the gentilest in his representations; his Landskipps more rare, and all other circumstances more proper'.[1] But soon after came the news of Rubens's death. Jordaens's first canvas was ready for dispatch in May 1640; it was well received by the Queen and by the end of the year Jordaens had 'wrought on' several of the canvases. They have disappeared and nothing is known of the subject-matter of this ambitious series, which to some

---

[1] W. N. Sainsbury, *Original Unpublished Papers* . . . (1859), 211–34.

extent anticipated Jordaens's share in the decoration of the Huis-
ten-Bosch for Amalia van Solms. The political upheavals in
England prevented the completion of the scheme, but 'Eight
peeces in one.roome. p^r. Jordaicon' were among the pictures
appraised at Greenwich by the Commonwealth commissioners
after the King's execution and sold for two hundred pounds.

The empty panels in the ceilings of the Hall and the Queen's
Cabinet, and the rich moulded framework which surrounds them,
remain as silent witnesses to the importance of the Queen's House
in the history of decorative painting in England. If its decoration
had survived intact it would have shown, like other aspects of the
King's patronage, the superiority of the imported foreign artists
over the native craftsmen who did little more than provide an
impersonal decorative setting for the work of their rivals. The
organization of the work at Greenwich was one of the episodes
which must have been particularly galling to the Painter-Stainers'
Company.

Although many of the undertakings, commissioned by Charles I,
which showed the greatest advance on the decoration fashionable
in his youth have been destroyed, certain schemes show the effects
of his patronage grafted rather clumsily on to the earlier tradition.
The most important of these, at Ham House and Wilton, were
carried out, significantly, by members of the court circle. In 1637
William Murray, who was later prominent in the negotiations
with Jordaens, began alterations to the interior of Ham. The work
was carried out by Francis Cleyn. In the North Drawing Room
(Pl. 6 b) at Ham are four inset panels, feebly painted in tempera, of
naked children disporting themselves; the one over the fireplace
contains a motive taken direct from Van Dyck's *Five Children of
Charles I* (1637) at Windsor. In the little Miniature Room, or Green
Closet, Cleyn's decoration is more elaborate. The spandrels that
encircle the central panel of the ceiling are painted with a light
form of grotesque pattern; but in the long panels on the cove
between the cornice and the ceiling the landscapes only are Cleyn's
invention: the playing putti are derived either from a set of panels
by Polidoro which were acquired by Charles I from Frizell in
January 1638, or from a series of copies of Polidoro's panels which

are at Ham and which may have been made by Cleyn. Cleyn, though in the most cumbrous manner, was enlivening the old-fashioned forms with material from a more modern and sophisticated source.[1]

The rebuilding of Wilton[2] by the earl of Pembroke involved mural painting on a much more extensive scale than at Ham. No other house of that period shows so clearly the forms of painted decoration which were available to patrons and architects or so impressive an attempt to give painting its place beside sculpture and architecture in the embellishment of an interior. But even in the Double Cube Room (Pl. 8) the painted is far inferior to the carved decoration; and, though very ambitious and not unattractive in tone, it is exceedingly coarse in quality. It is, however, essential to the harmony of the room and serves as a background for the sumptuous treatment of the walls and for the celebrated inset series of family portraits by Van Dyck and his studio. The painted areas are clearly defined. As at Greenwich the coving is filled with a frieze of putti who support swags of fruit and flowers between large painted urns and cartouches of very eccentric shape, with the arms, mottoes, and monograms of the earls of Pembroke. This coving was probably executed by Edward Pierce;[3] it agrees closely with some of his etched designs for friezes and marks a logical development from the ceiling in the Queen's Bedroom at Greenwich, but the pattern is treated on a much larger scale and is

---

[1] See above, pp. 85 and 125–8; H. A. Tipping, *English Homes*, IV. i (1929), 119, 122–3; and R. Edwards and P. Ward-Jackson, *Ham House, A Guide* (2nd ed. 1951), 39–45. Cleyn's work in the Queen's Cabinet at Somerset House is graphically described by Norgate (*Miniatura*, ed. M. Hardie (1919), 64) and seems to have been more ambitious than anything by him that survives.

[2] See above, pp. 39–41.

[3] The attributions for the painted work at Wilton are based on John Aubrey, *Natural History of Wiltshire*, ed. J. Britton (1847), 85, and on Evelyn's visit to Wilton, 20 July 1654, which was probably soon after the completion of the painting. Pierce probably had a considerable practice as a decorative painter, but much of his work has vanished. He was made free of the Painter-Stainers on 26 July 1630, with Francis Wethered; both men had been apprenticed to Rowland Buckett who had done much decorative work (which survives) at Hatfield for the 1st earl of Salisbury. Pierce was closely associated with the Painter-Stainers, was at work in their Hall in 1630 and was chosen to be one of the Company's Wardens in 1647 (*Booke of Orders . . .*, i. ff. 55, 59, 215). For his son, the sculptor, see above, pp. 253–5.

now co-ordinated into a realistic grouping. There is an attempted illusionism in the painted ledge and sculpture (which are partly conceived as an extension of, and link between, the actual sculpture in the ceiling and the cornice and serve as a playground for Pierce's putti) and in the red curtain which hangs down behind. Above Pierce's coving are three large inset canvases by Emanuel De Critz of scenes from the legend of Perseus. In general disposition there is perhaps some recollection of the ceiling of the Banqueting House. Rubens's influence may have been responsible for the foreshortenings, as well as for the elaborate curved architectural background in the central scene, but De Critz's attempts at steep perspective are ludicrous. In the Single Cube Room the panels in the dado are painted, probably by De Critz, with little scenes from Sir Philip Sidney's *Arcadia*, which are fresh and painterly and rather Venetian in quality. Finally, in the 'Hunting Room' the actual panelling is painted by Pierce with two tiers of sporting scenes. They are ultimately based on Tempesta, but Pierce took certain liberties with his sources and in one panel appropriately introduced the 4th earl of Pembroke, who 'pretended to no other qualifications than to understand horses and dogs very well'. The painting in the earl's splendid suite of new rooms thus ranges between an elaborate scheme in the Double Cube Room, which shows English painters fumbling for something more advanced than the work of their predecessors, and little panels of the most modest kind, in the Elizabethan and Jacobean tradition, where the scope of the painted decoration was dependent on the form of the panelling.[1] But the work at Wilton is unworthy of the architecture and carving with which it was conceived and, compared with the work of contemporary painters in Italy, France, and Holland, lamentably provincial.

Isaac Fuller and Robert Streeter or Streater, whose work marks the next stage in the development of English wall-painting, had travelled abroad and were able to make slightly more ambitious attempts at a fully baroque style. All Fuller's decorative work has disappeared. His *Last Judgment* at the east end of the chapel at All

---

[1] C. Latham, *In English Homes* (3rd ed., 1909), 86, 87, 90; A. Stratton, *The English Interior* (1920), Pls. xlii, xliv.

Souls College was seen by Evelyn on 25 October 1664 and was described by him as 'the largest piece of fresco painting (or rather an imitation of it, for it is in oil of Turpentine) in England, not ill design'd by the hand of one Fuller; yet I feare it will not hold long'. It was one of the earliest large-scale pieces of religious painting in England since the Reformation. It was probably a clumsy pastiche of Michelangelo's *Last Judgment,* and Evelyn said prudishly of it, 'it seems too full of nakeds for a chapell'.[1] Fuller also painted, in the more congenial atmosphere of the Mitre Tavern in Fenchurch Street, an entire room with mythological scenes.[2]

Robert Streeter is a more tangible and more sober figure: 'a very civil little man, and lame'. He can probably be identified with 'Robert Streter, A forrin Panter' who undertook (2 April 1641) to support the Painter-Stainers against their opponents.[3] He was made an Assistant to the Company in 1663 and was chosen with Lely and others in 1677 to assist the 'Mr. Strangers' in discussions with representatives of the Company. Apart from easel pieces he painted in All Souls; at Sir Robert Clayton's house in Old Jewry, where Evelyn on 26 September 1672 described the 'historie of the Gyants War' in the dining-room as 'incomparably don by Mr. Streeter, but the figures . . . too neere the eye'; and in St. Michael's, Cornhill, where he painted figures of Moses and Aaron. In March 1663 he was appointed Sergeant-Painter in place of Sir Robert Howard.

Streeter's most important surviving work is his painted ceiling of the Triumph of Truth and the Arts for the Sheldonian Theatre. On 1 February 1669 Pepys was taken by Danckerts to see Streeter and he found him with Wren and other virtuosi looking at the work which was then in progress. It was the most ambitious baroque composition that had been attempted by an Englishman. Putti roll back a bronze-coloured curtain over golden cords (in imitation of the awning which was rolled back over Roman theatres) to disclose a circular sweep of figures in the sky, looking

---

[1] Fuller painted a similar 'fresco' at Magdalen, which can be seen in a water-colour (1811) in the chapel, and in the frontispiece to Addison's *Resurrection* (1718).

[2] Vertue, i. 101–2. For Fuller's work as a portrait painter see above, p. 187.

[3] *Booke of Orders . . .,* i, f. 156.

up at the vision of Truth. The execution is reasonably competent, but the ceiling is cold in colour, there is no real ability to convey unified movement and although the steep perspective of the circle of figures seated on the clouds is not unsuccessfully realized the foreshortenings in the figures that tumble from the heights are largely misunderstood.[1]

Fuller and Streeter remain shadowy figures. Much of their achievement has been destroyed and much of their time was taken up with painting scenery for the London stage. The link between painted decoration as the setting for everyday life (though admittedly life of a grand and rather histrionic nature) and painted backgrounds for the stage is very close, and the theatre provided artists throughout Europe with a magnificent means of appealing to the senses by that concerted effort of all the arts which is the essence of baroque. In England in the earlier part of the century court masques, those splendid and transitory manifestations of Jacobean and Caroline court culture, had come to rely more and more for their success on the lavishness of the costumes, the splendour of the ever-changing sets and the ingenuity of the mechanism. Until the eve of the Civil War they had provided Inigo Jones with incomparable opportunities for the display of his fertile, eclectic, and ingenious imagination,[2] and had given continuous employment to an army of scenery painters. The accounts of the events, settings and transformations of the individual masques read like a literary description of baroque painting of the most advanced kind and the iconography of the decorative work done for the King and Queen by Rubens, Gentileschi, Vouet, and their humbler rivals was perhaps not unrelated to the flood of Inigo's allegories and personifications. In the public theatre in London, however, scenery was hardly in use at the outbreak of the Civil War; and it was the age of the Restoration drama that saw the birth of the modern stage and an increased use of stage machinery and decor.[3] In 1656 Davenant's *Siege of Rhodes* was put on at

[1] For reproductions of Streeter's work see *Burl. Mag.* lxxxiv–lxxxv (1944), 3–12, 81–82, and E. Croft-Murray, *Country Life Annual* (1950), 152.

[2] See above, pp. 16–17.

[3] A. Nicoll, *A History of Restoration Drama 1660–1700* (3rd ed., 1940), 28–60. L. Hotson, *The Commonwealth and Restoration Stage* (1928), 250–3, 348–55.

Rutland House and, 'to recompense the narrowness of the Room', was 'made a Representation by the Art of Prospective in Scenes'; these scenes were, significantly, by John Webb. Within a few years the success or failure of plays came to depend more and more on the extent to which managers could gratify the tastes of their audiences for brilliant, lavish scenery and spectacularly ingenious mechanism: often at the expense, as with the masques, of the purely literary or dramatic qualities of the piece. The scenery was much influenced by continental prototypes. With the continuous demand for new plays and the extremely short runs which even the most successful plays could expect, the demands on the scenery-painters, though their sets were no doubt used for many different plays, must have been heavy. Occasionally the backgrounds they were required to produce give them a place in the development of English landscape painting. Even in the great days of the masque homelier scenes were sometimes required than the constant hells, elysiums, tempests, oceans and caverns: in *Albion's Triumph* by Inigo Jones and Aurelian Townshend one scene was a view of Whitehall Palace and part of the City, and in *Salmacida Spolia* (1640) there had been a 'prospect' of the Thames. At Dorset Gardens in 1685 Dryden's *Albion and Albanius* included a view of the Royal Exchange. The two parts of the stage were partly divided by representations of Le Sueur's statue of Charles I at Charing Cross and a statue of Charles II. Later in the opera views of Dover and of the Thames at Westminster were seen. Most interesting of all was the final transformation which consisted of different 'shots' of Windsor and of the Garter processions and insignia. These scenes were constructed at the time when Verrio was evolving his elaborate glorifications of the Garter and of Charles II's prerogative. The exiled Shaftesbury was cast in very much the same role in the final set piece of *Albion and Albanius* as he played in the ceiling of St. George's Hall.[1] Dryden, Verrio and the scene-painters in Dorset Gardens were thus driving home to

[1] Nicoll, op. cit., 43–48. For further material on scene-painting and stage mechanism see Eleanore Boswell, *The Restoration Court Stage* (1932), 36–30, 148–58, 203, 208–11, 249–52, 255, 258 (particularly for the type of work on which Streeter was engaged in the theatre at Whitehall), and R. Southern, *Changeable Scenery* (1952).

their audiences, in the most baroque manner, the same ultra-royalist propaganda which had been conveyed with more finesse in *Absalom and Achitophel*.

The tastes of the Restoration audiences were essentially those of the court and the King, and it was under Charles II's auspices that a team of baroque artists and craftsmen, more highly organized and more competent than anything that had been seen in England earlier in the century, was created and set to work. The occasion was the King's decision extensively to repair and redecorate Windsor castle, which the Restoration had found 'exceedingly ragged and ruinous'. Charles was perhaps inspired by what he had heard of his cousin's activities at Versailles and was unconsciously obeying Colbert's dictum: 'rien ne marque davantage la grandeur et l'esprit des princes que les bâtiments; et toute la posterité les mesure à l'aune de ces superbes maisons qu'ils ont élevées pendant leur vie';[1] and even such a prudish and insular critic as Celia Fiennes had to confess that 'some of these foolerys are requisite sometymes to create admiration and regard to keep up the state of a kingdom and nation'.[2] It was appropriate that Antonio Verrio and Louis Laguerre, the two leading painters in the decorative field until the early years of the eighteenth century, had passed through the orbit of Le Brun. Verrio retained an essentially Italian lightness and gaiety of tone, though he was a much less competent painter than Laguerre, but the latter's work remained completely French. Verrio left France at a time when comparatively little of the *Grands Appartements* at Versailles, which mark the culmination of the *style Louis XIV* in decorative painting, had been executed; Laguerre saw the completion of these magnificent suites.

In this its most prolific and ambitious phase, mural painting in England never approached in invention or execution the brilliance of the great Italian decorators of the seventeenth century; the inspiration during this phase came from Versailles and English decorative painting stands at one further remove from its source. The style which was evolved in the Hôtel Lambert, at Vaux-le-

---

[1] Quoted in P. de Nolhac, *La Création de Versailles* (1925), 50. For Hugh May's work at Windsor see above, pp. 208–10.

[2] *Journeys*, ed. C. Morris (1947), 280.

Vicomte, and at Versailles was itself a synthesis of earlier Italian decorative styles, primarily those of the Carracci in the Farnese Gallery and of Pietro da Cortona (and Pietro in the Pitti rather than the Palazzo Barberini), and Le Brun's approach to his prototypes was classical and very French. He rarely indulged in the deliberate confusion between the painted and the carved fields which is so marked a feature of Italian interiors, and the composition of his ceilings is lucid and rational. Sometimes Le Brun's painting, and often the work of his assistants, is thoroughly dull and academic, but the magnificent quality of the sculpture that was combined with the work of the painters prevents their ceilings from becoming stereotyped. With the team of highly organized craftsmen, which had grown up under Colbert's intensive patronage on behalf of his master, Le Brun was able to exploit his repertory of motives (which was *au fond* rather limited) over and over again with no risk of repetition because they could be treated with equal ease in gilt, stucco or paint. In England the types and patterns used by Verrio and Laguerre can be traced back almost without exception to Versailles, but there was never the same richness and variety in the use of materials. The absence of a highly organized central authority to control the work of craftsmen in different mediums, and the sporadic nature of English patronage, made it impossible for Verrio, Laguerre, and their like to rely upon the collaboration of craftsmen in setting off their painted surfaces with rich and varied three-dimensional elements. In English baroque painting, elements which could have been treated in France in a number of ways were almost always rendered in paint.

Antonio Verrio was born in Lecce, probably in 1639. In 1661 he was working in Naples and the influence of Luca Giordano is perceptible in his early work. In May 1671 he was enrolled in the Académie Royale in Paris and he probably came to London very soon after, under the auspices of the English ambassador, Ralph Montagu.[1] He probably began painting at Windsor in 1675 and

---

[1] His first work for the English Crown was probably the *Sea Triumph of Charles II* (*s.*) at Hampton Court, a large easel-picture with very strong reminiscences of Luca Giordano. On 5 May 1675 Verrio was given a grant of denization (*Cal. S.P. Dom.* (1675–6), 584).

by August 1678 a great deal of the work was done; the payments
to him, which were exceptionally generous and were reinforced
by the regular payment of an annual pension of two hundred
pounds and by constant special awards and bounties, continued
into the next reign.[1]

Apart from the quality and scope of the work itself, the significance of Verrio's position and activities at Windsor is threefold.
He was the first painter to work in close collaboration with an
English architect in the essentially baroque function of embellishing
and, by the devices of his craft, extending or bursting through the
limits created by Hugh May's walls. As a Catholic he and his
assistants had to be protected by special decree from the dangers
to which they were liable in those momentous years.[2] His religion
and the glamour of his foreign training, if they were dangerous
assets in the country at large, ensured for him very special treatment
from his royal patron. Verrio's position at Windsor in relation to
Streeter was exactly that of Gentileschi, Rubens and Jordaens in
relation to De Critz at Greenwich;[3] and Charles was able, in the
secluded splendours of his new state apartments, to give uncompromising expression to those absolutist principles which his
cousin embodied and with which he was himself so much in
sympathy. The central episode in Verrio's ceiling of St. George's
Hall, carried out at the end of the reign when the tide had at last
turned against the Exclusionists and the earl of Shaftesbury, to
some extent took up the theme of Rubens's Whitehall ceiling and
was an unequivocal statement of that most baroque theme, the
Stuart conception of the royal prerogative. There can have been

[1] W. H. St. John Hope, *Windsor Castle* ... (1913), i. 317, 318, 320, 322, 323, 328,
329–30, 345–6, and *Cal. Tr. Bks.* (many references).

[2] A warrant was issued on 16 November 1678 to prevent 'any molestation or
trouble to several foreigners, being painters and other artists employed in painting and
adorning Windsor Castle ... Popish Recusants'; Verrio's team included his servants,
his wife and two sons, Giovanni Battista and Francesco, Michael Tourarde, Jacob
Coquet, Lanscroon, Bertrand au Mailhey (all of whom are described as painters),
René du Four, Verrio's apprentice, Sernitte his colour-grinder, René Cousin the
gilder and Antonio Montingo, who was Verrio's flower-painter (*Cal. S.P. Dom.*
(1678), 525–6, 549–50).

[3] For the payments to Streeter for work at Windsor, and for the nature of that
work, see St. John Hope, op. cit., i. 315, 316, 319, 320, 321, 323, 329.

few more wholly baroque iconographies in Europe than the glorification of the English Crown with which ceiling after ceiling at Windsor was concerned.

In spite of the destruction by George III and George IV of so much of Charles II's work at Windsor, some of it can be reconstructed in considerable detail.[1] On his walls and ceilings in the castle Verrio introduced the patterns which remained standard until the arrival of the Venetian painters early in the next century. The three ceilings that survive show Verrio's methods of opening Hugh May's rooms to the heavens. His favourite device was to paint, on the shallow coving that rises from the cornice to the flat part of the ceiling, a carved ledge or balcony, which could be decorated in a variety of ways. This balcony was conceived as resting on the walls and the room is thus open to the sky in which Verrio's deities are seen, but never in very steep perspective and without daring effects of illusionism. A possible prototype for this form is the ceiling of the Salle de l'Abondance at Versailles, in which the basis of Houasse's composition is a ledge above the cornice, surmounted by elaborate vessels and draped with brocaded carpets. In the Queen's Audience Chamber at Windsor Catherine of Braganza proceeds in a triumphal car in the clouds to the Temple of Virtue; in her Presence Chamber the Queen presides over a more serious iconography, in which Sedition and Envy are hurled from her presence and actually fall down to the cornice over a complex painted balustrade. The other form of treatment for a ceiling was more specifically French. The central episode is set within an elaborate painted framework; this is supported on a painted architectural structure on the coving which was usually pierced at the corners or along the walls to show the sky. This form was capable of infinite variety. Verrio's use of it on the small ceiling of the Public (or Charles II) Dining Room is skilful, and appropriately festive in colour.

[1] See especially the section on Windsor in George Bickham, *Deliciæ Britannicæ* (1742), and Joseph Pote, *The History and Antiquities of Windsor Castle . . .* (1749); and the illustrations to W. H. Pyne, *The History of the Royal Residences*, 3 vols. (1819). The original water-colours for the latter are preserved in the Royal Library. For an interesting example of an apparent use by Le Brun of a design by Verrio, see E. Croft-Murray, 'A Drawing by Charles Le Brun . . .', *B.M. Quarterly*, xix (1954), 58–59.

The most sumptuous of Verrio's work at Windsor, however, was swept away: the painting of two staircases (of which there are no visual but many printed records) leading up to the royal apartments, St. George's Hall and the Royal Chapel. Verrio received over two thousand pounds for his work in these two apartments, which were probably both unfinished at the death of Charles II. On the north side of St. George's Hall Verrio set his scene in an imaginary extension of the space of the actual room, behind painted columns which form a proscenium and support the feigned structure of the ceiling above. This elaborate construction of an imaginary space, seen through painted columns, can be traced back to Peruzzi's work in the Farnesina,[1] and is more ambitious than any prototype in France. Behind and around the columns in St. George's wound the triumphal procession of the Black Prince; above it a very elaborate framework in the ceiling was pierced to disclose the Triumph of Charles II over Rebellion and Faction (traditionally said to be in the guise of Shaftesbury); little putti were perched on the imitation cornice, holding the blue and white Garter cloaks, or fluttered up into the heavenly spheres. The general impression, with the lavish use of gold, must have been extremely bright. The iconographical emphasis on St. George, the Order of the Garter and its founders anticipated, though in a much less serious vein, the work of Benjamin West.

Perhaps even more spectacular was the transformation by May, Gibbons and Verrio of the Tudor chapel into the Royal Chapel (Pl. 79 a), which occupied the west end of the present St. George's Hall. Verrio's painting was an integral part of the decoration which surpassed anything attempted hitherto in England. The north wall was pierced in the imagination to disclose scenes from the miracles of Christ and in them Verrio inserted himself and May.[2] In this extended space was an elaborate colonnade and an open sky; the eye of the spectator would have been swept up into

[1] Mr. Croft-Murray has also suggested, as a good example of this form of treatment, the decoration (c. 1600) of Giovanni and Cherubino Alberti in the Sala Clementina in the Vatican; the walls of the Salle de Vénus at Versailles were also painted by Rousseau with architectural perspectives, though these do not contain figures and are on a comparatively small scale.

[2] There is a *modello* for the north wall of the Chapel in the royal collection.

the Ascension of Christ in a blaze of glory in the ceiling.[1] The chapel at Windsor was a prelude to the more elaborate one which was built by Wren at Whitehall for James II; here again the 'Volto, in *fresca*' with the Assumption of the Virgin 'and a world of figures painted by Verrio' combined with the sculpture, Gennari's altarpieces and the Catholic ritual to produce the completely cosmopolitan baroque atmosphere of which Evelyn left an unforgettable account.[2] But the source of Verrio's patronage was very precarious; with the destruction of the Catholic chapels in London by the mob on the night of 22 December 1688, the short-lived supremacy of an ultramontane court, on which Catholic painters like Huysmans, Gennari and Verrio largely depended, came to an end.

Verrio had been so excessively favoured by both sovereigns[3] that he could not hope for success at the new court. As early as 1687 he had been working for the 5th earl of Exeter and at the Revolution he found asylum at Burghley with a patron who had refused to take the oaths to William and Mary. Verrio decorated six rooms in the earl's new apartments and began a seventh; the payments to him continue until 10 March 1698[4] and his patron enabled the arrogant Neapolitan to maintain the considerable state to which he had been accustomed and which he was not prepared to forgo.[5] In the last years of the century he returned to the service of the Crown to work in William III's new state apartments at Hampton Court. He received a pension from Anne some two years before his death there on 15 June 1707.[6]

[1] For the subtle interplay of feigned and actual space over the altar see G. Webb, 'Baroque Art', *Proc. Brit. Acad.* xxxiii (1947).

[2] See above, p. 217.

[3] On 30 June 1685 he was appointed by Charles II 'our chief and first painter' in succession to Lely, largely owing to the King's satisfaction with what he had done at Windsor (*Cal. Tr. Bks*, viii. ii. 1188; *Cal. S.P. Dom.* (1684–5), 83).

[4] The documents at Burghley provide an incomparable picture of the daily activities of a grand decorative painter and the small army with which he had settled into his patron's house. With Verrio were his two sons and his assistants, Souville, Ricard (see below, p. 303), Cousin and others. See *Country Life*, cxiv (1953), 2104–7.

[5] Verrio was a troublesome guest, who probably outstayed his welcome, and had to be provided with a coach, horses with expensive furniture, wine of good quality and such nostalgic delicacies as parmesan cheese, bologna sausages, olives and caviar.

[6] The first payment to him for work at Hampton Court seems to have been £100 on account in January 1701. In 1703–4 he was being paid for the Great Staircase and

Verrio's work at Burghley and Hampton Court provides an adequate survey of his achievement. His painted ceilings, rising above richly carved cornices, are an essential part of the decoration of these grand late seventeenth-century interiors. In little rooms, such as the King's Dressing Room at Hampton Court or the Jewel Closet at Burghley, Verrio used his favourite painted balustrade: at Hampton Court surmounted with very elaborate urns filled with flowers, around which putti clamber, and at Burghley skilfully painted as if it was actually catching the light from the window. In the State Bedroom at Burghley there is a fine arrangement of curved pediments in the middle of each wall and broken pediments at the corners, where coupled bronze figures support pale grey reliefs, which, with the putti, swags of flowers, busts in bronze and gold and glimpses of the sky behind, make up one of the best pieces of illusionistic decoration that Verrio and his assistants produced. From the 'Heaven' Room at Burghley and the King's Staircase at Hampton Court we can gain some conception of the former appearance of St. George's Hall. The walls are covered with an elaborate arrangement of columns; they create a setting for the figures and support a painted cornice that occupies the coving and frames the central episode in the sky. This is in each case an assembly of the deities and from it groups of figures pour down over the painted cornice.[1] In the Queen's Drawing Room at Hampton Court (Pl. 79 b) Verrio varied his treatment of the walls by painting the scenes as if they were on tapestries with floreated borders, hanging from the elaborate frieze and flanked by applied pilasters. But the scale and conception of these great rooms cannot conceal Verrio's innate weaknesses as a painter. The painted

Queen's Drawing Room; the latter was finished early in 1705, but Queen Anne in that year 'was pleased to say . . . there was no haste of any more painting' and gave him an annual pension of £200, 'but no more charge of painting' (see the Cal. Tr. Bks. for Verrio's work for William III and Anne). Apart from the state rooms Verrio painted for William the very pretty main room in the Banqueting House at Hampton Court. For the iconography of the King's Staircase see E. Wind, 'Julian the Apostate at Hampton Court', Journ. of the Warburg and Courtauld Institutes, iii (1939–40), 127–37.

[1] Verrio left the great staircase at Burghley unfinished. It was to have been another of his immensely ambitious compositions, close in design to the neighbouring 'Heaven' Room.

architectural elements are always strong and convincing, the purely decorative elements are rich and varied and Verrio's gilders and his painters of flowers and still-life were especially competent; the colour is usually very gay and light. But the figure compositions are often ludicrously weak and the grasp of illusionism is strangely inept. Verrio was not a sufficiently great painter to carry out with complete success the very grand schemes which he had conceived.[1]

Louis Laguerre was a more capable painter and before his arrival in England[2] he had passed through the best academic training in Europe. He was actually born at Versailles (1663), his father was keeper of the royal menagerie and the Grand Monarque himself was his godfather. He was apprenticed to Le Brun. His work in England was, at its best, far superior to the work of Verrio and shows all the technical skill of the supremely efficient school in which he was trained. The decorative elements are always thoroughly well organized on Laguerre's walls, but some of his later work has the monotony inherent in French classical painting at the end of the seventeenth century, when the original inspiration had been stifled by academic precepts and practice.

Laguerre's most important work was done for the dukes of Devonshire and Marlborough. In January 1689 he was already in

---

[1] Verrio also worked at Chatsworth (see below), Lowther Castle, Euston, Cassiobury, and Ashtead. For Christ's Hospital he painted (c. 1684–7) a large group of the presentation by Charles II of the charter of the Hospital's mathematical school (*Wren Soc.* xi, 69, 71–72); it is an ambitiously baroque conception of the later Stuart monarchy. Among painters associated with Verrio were Nicholas Heud, who was working with him at Chatsworth (1690); and Henry Cooke, who carried out the large wall-painting, begun by Verrio, in the hall at Chelsea Hospital of Charles II on horseback surrounded by allegorical figures, was employed by William III on the repairs to Raphael's cartoons and had a respectable practice as a mural painter. George Freeman petitioned the King in 1670 for the place of principal painter and designer of tapestry and worked as a history- and scene-painter. Michael Wright made at least one essay in decorative painting. His ceiling (c. 1665; belonging to the Corporation of Nottingham) for the King's State Bedchamber at Whitehall survives in a mutilated state; it has a scholarly Roman flavour with flying putti, supporting the Royal Oak and a portrait of Charles II, and an angel holding a scroll inscribed TERRAS ASTRÆA REVISIT.

[2] On 5 September 1682 Laguerre was awarded second prize by the Académie Royale for a picture; he was apparently still in Paris in December 1683 (*Procès Verbaux*, ii (1878), 229, 231, 233, 247, 262, 263). He and Ricard may have worked under Verrio at Windsor on their arrival.

the service of the 4th earl of Devonshire (he was raised to the dukedom in 1694) and was paid ten pounds 'in part of my bargaine of Painting made with the Earle of Devonshire at Chatsworth'. The payments to him and Ricard (with whom he came to England) in the Chatsworth building accounts continue until August 1694.[1]

In the Painted Hall at Chatsworth Laguerre probably relied to a considerable extent on his assistants. The painting, which is confined to the level of the gallery, is less good there than elsewhere in the house,[2] but it is competent and on a grand scale. The iconography is devoted to Julius Caesar. On the long wall facing the window the large mural of Caesar approaching the Capitol is (like the enormous ceiling of the Apotheosis of Caesar) virtually a vast easel picture.[3] On either side of it are oval scenes from the life of Caesar, painted to imitate reliefs, supported on seated nude figures, surmounted by putti and flanked by pilasters. On the north end similar pilasters frame the scene of Caesar's murder, and on the south wall the decoration is of the same form. It is treated, however, in relief by the sculptor Samuel Watson and not in feigned relief by Laguerre; the painted surfaces are thus carefully integrated with the decoration of the room.

In the Chapel (Pl. 81), one of the most beautiful interiors in England, the sculpture is more severely independent of the painting, though the little carved putti over the doors in the gallery are echoed in Laguerre's putti in the clouds just above them, and on the end wall are two imitation statues which are conceived as sitting on the altarpiece at right angles to Cibber's Faith and Justice.[4] The painted decoration does not go below the level of the gallery and is to some extent a remodelling, in restrained and academic terms, of Verrio's layout of the Royal Chapel at Windsor. The main wall is occupied, as at Windsor, with Christ healing the sick and the scene takes place among columns, through which are seen buildings and

[1] F. Thompson, *History of Chatsworth* (1949); C. Latham, *In English Homes*, iii (1909), 214–21, and H. A. Tipping, *English Homes*, IV. i (1929), 326–39.
[2] F. Thompson, op. cit., 117–18, and H. A. Tipping, op. cit., 326.
[3] The *modello* was recently on the art market in London as a Le Sueur. The finished mural is signed by Laguerre and dated 1694.   [4] See above, p. 244.

the sky and which support the painted cornice on which rests, in turn, the very elaborate framework of the Ascension in the ceiling. The scene on the main wall is carried round behind the magnificent reredos, into which is set Verrio's *Christ and St. Thomas*.[1] The Ascension on the ceiling is seen through a richly modelled grey and gold painted frame; at each end, coming down over the coving, is a painted relief (repeating the iconography of the walls and altarpiece); and in the corners, conceived as floating on the clouds over the purely decorative elements, are the four Evangelists.[2]

But Laguerre's greatest achievement is the series of ceilings which he executed in four of the Duke's five state rooms. There are no finer ceilings of this kind in England and they play an integral part in the splendours of one of the most magnificent suites of rooms in the country.[3] Few houses in England can rival Chatsworth as an example of the grandeur and beauty against which the life of a great Whig *seigneur* was lived. On each ceiling the main episode is seen through a different framework, which contains the figures completely except in the State Music Room, where they pour down over one corner of it. The figure compositions in the heavens are much more competent than anything produced by Verrio: stronger in drawing, darker and richer in tone, heavier in texture and far more assured in their understanding of perspective. They are wholly French in colour and type and could be paralleled again and again in the work of Le Brun and his team. Laguerre shows his real quality, above all, in the variety of treatment in his covings, with their grasp of illusionism and interplay of bright natural colours against the bronze, grey and gold of the feigned elements. In the State Drawing Room bronze trophies and nudes support the corners, while above the cornice on three walls red curtains are drawn back, behind the framework, to disclose reclining figures in natural colours; and in the State Music Room the corners are deeply recessed to contain figures that sit on the cornice and throw

[1] See above, p. 244. Verrio also painted at Chatsworth the ceiling of the Great Chamber and the Great Stairs; the payments to him run between June 1691 and October 1692. Laguerre painted one room at Burghley. Lord Exeter was married to Devonshire's sister.

[2] This construction can be studied in Laguerre's little *modello* in the V. & A.

[3] Thompson, op. cit., 141, 142, 151, 161; Latham, op. cit., 219–21.

up shadows, as if from the windows, on to the feigned architecture, and in the centre of each wall a very rich painted relief is draped with flowers in natural colours. In the State Bedroom (Pl. 80), which is the finest of them all, huntresses and hounds are grouped most convincingly at the corners and in the middle of each wall a little panel rests on the cornice in a richly gilt frame; this essentially French design is a development of Perrier's coving in the Cabinet des Muses in the Hôtel Lambert.[1]

After the duchess of Marlborough had refused to employ Thornhill in painting the Saloon at Blenheim, the commission was given to Laguerre.[2] For this great room Laguerre turned once again to France for inspiration: the figures representing the four continents who look down into the room and, set low in a vast colonnade, are silhouetted against the sky, are taken from Le Brun's most ambitious creation, the Escalier des Ambassadeurs at Versailles. And the additional area, between the painted cornice and the ceiling, is filled with a simplified treatment of the same space in Le Brun's design.[3] It is a curious paradox that one of the grandest rooms in the duke of Marlborough's palace should be derived from the state staircase of the King whom he had beaten to his knees. In Marlborough House Louis XIV's godson commemorated the duke's victories.[4] In Farquhar's *Beaux' Stratagem* (1707) Mrs. Sullen asks Archer: 'But what think you there of *Alexander's* Battles?' 'We want only a *Le Brun*, Madam', he replies, 'to draw greater Battels, and a greater General of our own —The *Danube*, Madam, wou'd

[1] The same French form of coving can be found in Holland, e.g. in the contemporary Trèves Saloon in the Binnenhof in The Hague.

[2] D. Green, *Blenheim Palace* (1951), gives the date 1719–20 for Laguerre's work in the Saloon; it is signed and includes the artist's self-portrait (ibid. 132); see H. A. Tipping and C. Hussey, *English Homes*, IV, ii (1928), 102–3.

[3] Laguerre and his assistants or rivals could have used the very good official engravings that were made from Le Brun's work for Louis XIV. Decorative painters could also derive much assistance from, for example, the engraved designs for interior decoration of all kinds by Le Paûtre and Marot (e.g. from the latter's *Nouveaux Livre de Lembris . . .*).

[4] Laguerre was at work in Marlborough House in 1713–14 (*Wren Soc.* vii. 228–9). For his murals see *R.C.H.M. West London*, ii (1925), Pls. 211–24, where they are much more visible than they are *in situ*. They can also be studied in the engravings by Du Bosc, Du Guernier, and Vandergucht. The main episodes in the scheme are conceived as pictures set against the wall in imitation painted frames.

make a greater Figure in a Picture than the *Granicus*; and we have our *Ramelies* to match their *Arbela*.' Though they are, in their present condition, among Laguerre's dullest works, the three walls in the saloon devoted to the battle of Blenheim and the large scenes on the staircases devoted to Ramillies and Malplaquet are among the most ambitious and earliest attempts in England to paint episodes from contemporary history in accurate contemporary costume. They are also, with the celebrated series of Flemish tapestries at Blenheim, the most concrete of the schemes for the glorification of Marlborough's victories, in which Kneller's subject pieces[1] and Thornhill's little allegorical sketch at Blenheim play a more embryonic part.

The academic competence and prevailing dullness of Laguerre's later work can be seen on the Grand Stairs at Petworth, which he painted for the 6th duke of Somerset.[2] If the patronage of decorative painters had been guided only by aesthetic considerations, the Venetians who came to England in the reign of Queen Anne would have presented an even more formidable challenge to painters working in the Anglo-French tradition.

---

[1] See above, p. 196.

[2] The staircase at Petworth is a good example of the standard form of painting a staircase in the full English baroque manner; the form was used in particular by Gerrard Lanscroon, who had been in Verrio's train at Windsor, for his staircases at Powis (s. 1705) (the slightly earlier ceiling is a copy, with suitable variations, from Veronese), Burley-on-the-Hill (finished by April 1712), and Drayton (s. 1714/15). Laguerre also worked at Thoresby, Kiveton, Burghley, Sudbury (see p. 314, n. 4), in Kneller's house at Whitton, and in the London houses of the dukes of Buckingham, Devonshire, and Chandos and of Lords Radnor and Dover.

Another French decorative painter, Louis Cheron, came to England (? 1695) under the auspices of the duke of Montagu; but his series of ceilings at Boughton, on the staircase, in the five state rooms and on three other ceilings, owe more to his studies of Raphael and the antique in Rome than to his French training and are perhaps nearer to Verrio than Laguerre. He also worked at Burghley and Chatsworth. The contents of an album of drawings by Cheron, recently acquired by the British Museum and formerly at Knowsley (Vertue, iii. 22, 28), give an illuminating cross-section of a decorative painter's activities: a number of preparatory drawings for ceilings (including those at Boughton); many signed finished drawings of classical and mythological scenes in a hard and classicizing style; a series of studies, presumably made in Rome, of Raphaelesque figures and details from the Farnese ceiling; and a set of large studies from the nude, some of which were probably drawn in one of the academies in London and used in his ceilings.

In 1708 the earl of Manchester brought back with him from Venice, where he had been ambassador since September 1707, two of the city's leading painters, Giovanni Antonio Pellegrini and Marco Ricci. In 1709 Alessandro Scarlatti's opera *Pyrrhus and Demetrius* was presented at the Haymarket with scenery by 'two famous Italian Painters (lately arriv'd from Venice)', who can hardly be other than Manchester's protégés. Pellegrini was set to work at Kimbolton, where Vanbrugh was carrying out extensive alterations for Manchester.[1] From Kimbolton he moved on to Castle Howard, where Vanbrugh was at work for the 3rd earl of Carlisle.[2] Both Manchester and Carlisle were members of the Kit-Cat Club. Pellegrini's success was jeopardized by the return to England of Marco Ricci (c. 1712), from a visit to Venice with his uncle Sebastiano, who had been a formative influence on Pellegrini's style. Pellegrini was again in England in 1718, more than a year after the final departure of the Riccis, and may have remained here until 1721.[3] Apart from the quality of the work of these three Venetians, their arrival in England, their success and their eventual departure (brought on by their own jealousies and by their failure to secure two most important commissions), brought out the recurrent conflict between nationalist feelings in artistic matters and the more cosmopolitan attitude which was stimulated by the Grand Tour. Manchester's interest in the art of the city to which he was accredited is reminiscent of Sir Henry Wotton's activities on behalf of the great Caroline collectors, and his responsibility as a diplomat for a Venetian phase in the history of painting and taste in England looks forward to the days of Consul Smith and Canaletto.

Pellegrini's style, in its European context, is a curious phenomenon. It is in some aspects foreshadowed by the work of Francesco Maffei and Johann Liss in the previous century. Pellegrini and

[1] 'If the Painter y^r L^{d}ship brings over be a good one, he may find work enough; but the New Room at Kimbolton can't be ready for him this Winter'; Vanbrugh to Manchester, 17 August 1708 (*Works*, Nonesuch ed., iv (1928), 26).

[2] The payments to Pellegrini in the archives at Castle Howard run from 6 November 1709 to 25 September 1712, when a total payment of over £852 was finally settled.

[3] Vertue, i. 38–39; there appears to be considerable confusion over the dates of Pellegrini's movements, but Vertue is a reliable source for this period.

Ricci were also the protagonists of the eighteenth-century renaissance in Venetian painting that was based largely on a new appreciation of Veronese and in which Tiepolo was to be the most celebrated figure. Pellegrini's sweeping sense of movement, lightness and wholly rococo range of colour provided architects and patrons with something completely new. There is a sheer quality of paint which few of his predecessors achieved and on his ceilings and walls he dispensed almost entirely with the elaborate feigned architecture within which Verrio and Laguerre had set their scenes. Even in Verrio's gayest conceptions the sun is overcast, but it streams in at Kimbolton and Castle Howard. The painted framework which contains Pellegrini's *Triumph of Caesar* on the main walls of the staircase at Kimbolton[1] is very simple and the subsidiary passages show a new and very personal approach to the older decorative conventions. The *Triumph* itself, which actually continues round between the windows, is a pastiche in Venetian terms of Mantegna's *Triumph* at Hampton Court. It is set against a plain sky. On the ceiling putti hold aloft a portrait of William III. It may not be fanciful to see in Pellegrini's Caesar an echo of William III's unmistakable profile and, as at Chatsworth, we find a form of aristocratic republicanism affecting the iconography chosen by patrons who had played a leading part in the Glorious Revolution.[2]

The little landing at the top of the staircase at Kimbolton is one of the most enchanting pieces of rococo decoration in England. The smaller areas are filled with flowers, female figures in painted niches, trophies and hanging drapery and a monkey and a parrot perched on a bar; in the ceiling putti scatter gold coins and the successive coronets which the Montagus had acquired. On the main wall, up a little staircase, is a completely Venetian episode with musicians and figures leaning out over a stone balcony. Pellegrini's handling is very bold and fluent and his paint extremely thin, with areas of loaded, swirling impasto; and his colour, with its pale

---

[1] H. A. Tipping, *English Homes*, IV, i (1929), 287.

[2] The most elaborate glorification of 1688 in paint was organized by Owen McSwiny, who commissioned in the 1720's a series of allegorical canvases; see Vertue, iv. 149; v. 149–50; *Burl. Mag.* lxix (1936), 245–6; and F. J. B. Watson, ibid. xcv (1953), 362–5.

reds, silvers, blues, cool greens, and pale browns and yellows, is extremely attractive.[1]

His work at Castle Howard, though so much of it was destroyed by fire in 1940, is on a grander scale.[2] The ceiling of the Garden Hall was light and airy and enclosed in a painted framework of a most original form; in the High Saloon (both rooms were destroyed) Pellegrini's ceiling and gilt and stucco surround showed a light rococo fantasy which seems more appropriate to Venice or Vienna than to the North Riding. The main wall on the two staircases that flank the Hall is filled with a large, light and colourful scene; in each case Apollo is the central figure. The handling throughout is free, thin and rather coarse and is applied directly to the stonework with a very slight priming. The areas allotted to painting in the design of the interior are carefully planned and defined. Of the surviving decoration in the Hall the most theatrical and Venetian are the two niches over the arcade on the north side which are each filled with Veronese-like figures who have come straight from the Villa Maser. Before the disastrous fire the apex of this noble interior was Pellegrini's brilliant *Fall of Phaeton* in the dome (Pl. 92 a) where horses, chariot, and rider hurtled from the sky in a blaze of Venetian sunlight.[3]

Sebastiano Ricci was a sounder painter than Pellegrini and his canvases had absorbed more of the sparkle of the Grand Canal, but comparatively little of the work which he did in England has survived. The three big canvases for Lord Burlington are still at Burlington House. His *Resurrection* in the apse of the chapel of Chelsea Hospital, in composition and in relation to the main building, is oddly reminiscent of La Fosse's slightly earlier treatment of the same subject in the chapel at Versailles. It is in a

[1] At Kimbolton Pellegrini also decorated the Chapel and the ceiling of the Boudoir.

[2] C. Latham, *In English Homes*, i (1909), 234–42; H. A. Tipping and C. Hussey, *English Homes*, IV. ii (1928), xxi, 15–26.

[3] According to Vertue, Pellegrini also worked at Cowdray and in the London houses of the duke of Portland and Lords Manchester and Burlington. Easel-pictures by him are not uncommon and a set of mythological figures, painted for the Crown, is still in the royal collection. For the hall of Sir Andrew Fountaine's house at Narford he painted a series of large canvases which survive *in situ*. At Kimbolton and Castle Howard Pellegrini also executed a life-size group of the children of his patrons; both canvases are still in the houses and are wholly Italianate and rococo.

vigorous style with an intensely dramatic sense of swirling movement and flickering contrasts of light and shade; it thus suggests,
perhaps, something of the quality of the chapel which Ricci painted
at Bulstrode for the 1st duke of Portland and for which *modelli*
(e.g. Pl. 82) survive: 'a Noble free invention. great force of lights
& shade. with variety & freedom. in the composition of the parts.'[1]

Vertue truly said of Sebastiano Ricci that he had 'a better &
more masterly Stile than any painter now living or any we have
had for historical subjects in this nation for many years'.[2] The
seductive and superficial brilliance of his technique, which was not
without its effect on native painters in the early eighteenth century,
was wholly different from the more academic quality of his rivals.
Nevertheless the Venetians suffered two major rebuffs in England.
We have seen how a patron's choice of a portrait painter might be
affected by Whig or Tory loyalties; in the decorative field there
are indications of a wider prejudice. When it was proposed, in the
reign of George I, that more rooms at Hampton Court should be
decorated, the duke of Shrewsbury, as Lord Chamberlain and
with the authority with which he conceived that his travels had
invested him, proposed that Ricci should be given the task. But the
earl of Halifax, First Lord of the Treasury and a celebrated
Maecenas, threatened to refuse payment if, by giving a commission
of such importance to a foreigner in preference to Thornhill, so
grievous a blow was given to the prestige and aspiration of native
painters.[3] And on 28 June 1715 the Commissioners of St. Paul's
cathedral, who had been weighing the qualifications of various
artists to paint the dome of the cathedral, gave the appointment
to Thornhill, who was the only English candidate.[4] In carrying off
the most important royal and ecclesiastical commissions Thornhill

---

[1] Vertue, iv. 47–48. A *modello* for the *Resurrection* in Chelsea Hospital is at Dulwich.

[2] i. 39. Another Venetian, Antonio Bellucci or Bellouchi, arrived in England in 1716;
he worked for the duke of Chandos and his paintings for the ceiling of the duke's
chapel at Cannons survive at Witley, Worcs.; see C. H. Collins and M. I. Baker, *The
Life and Circumstances of James Brydges First Duke of Chandos* (1949), and F. J. B. Watson, 'A Venetian Settecento Chapel in the English Countryside', *Arte Veneta* (1954),
295–302.

[3] Vertue, i. 45.

[4] *Wren Soc.* xvi. 108, 109, 116; among the competitors were Cheron and Pellegrini,
who was said to have been Wren's favourite candidate.

brought off, single-handed and at the very end of our period, the final victory over the foreign painters for which his countrymen had fought so long.

James Thornhill's early years and training are still obscure.[1] He was born in Dorset in 1675/6 of a respectable but impoverished family. There is no evidence of personal contact in his early years with Verrio or Laguerre, though he was considerably influenced by the latter; in May 1689 he was bound apprentice to Thomas Highmore (uncle of Joseph Highmore) of the Painter-Stainers and he was made free of the Company in March 1703. In his earliest certain work on a large scale, the painting of the Sabine Room at Chatsworth,[2] he appears as a fully fledged painter working with complete success within the conventions laid down by his predecessors. The entire surface of the room is painted; Thornhill's methods, and the extent to which the figures in the heavens swirl down over his cornice and among his columns, are wholly in the manner of Verrio and Laguerre, but his deeper and very baroque feeling for architecture and sculpture appears in the structure on the chimney-breast and in the colonnade which curves round behind it.[3] His figures are weaker, but they are also slighter and more rococo and painterly, than those of Laguerre. On the ceiling in the Queen's Bedroom at Hampton Court (the commission which he wrested from Sebastiano Ricci and finished by October 1715) the structure under the frame for the central episode is more ambitious than anything attempted by Laguerre, while the scene in the heavens is richer in tone and better composed than Verrio's most mature works.

Thornhill made at least two journeys to the Continent. In the early summer of 1711 he was in Holland and Flanders and six years later he went to France.[4] They must have been welcome

---

[1] The materials for the life and a full catalogue of his work are assembled by W. R. Osmun, unpub. Ph.D. thesis, University of London (1950).

[2] F. Thompson, *History of Chatsworth* (1949), 194; the room was ready in October 1706 for the plasterer who was to prepare it for the painter.

[3] A similar composition was to be seen in Thornhill's painted decoration in the hall at Stoke Edith (destroyed in 1927; C. Latham, *In English Homes*, iii (1909), 252–5).

[4] The two notebooks which he kept on these journeys (formerly in the collection of Mr. Alistair Cobbold) show a professional interest in decoration and also a

holidays in the intervals of work on his two major public commissions: at St. Paul's and in the Painted Hall at Greenwich. Thornhill's work in the dome of the cathedral was finished by October 1717. He made no attempt to open the dome to the heavens with a sweep of figures in steep perspective on the clouds, as some of the other candidates might have done, but set the episodes from the Apostle's life behind, and in the spaces between, an architectural structure which carries up into the lantern the design of the actual architecture. The work is wholly in monochrome, picked out with gold in the decorative parts;[1] and the scenes are reinterpretations of Raphael in terms of the academic, classicizing baroque which Thornhill admired in France.

In working out on a large scale the ideas which first took shape in his *modelli* and drawings the freshness of Thornhill's preliminary conceptions was rarely recaptured. His drawings probably survive in a greater quantity than those of any other native painter of our period.[2] They enable us to follow the growth of a theme in his mind and they possess great charm in their own right. The worked-out drawings for his more elaborate compositions reveal a teeming invention and sometimes provide (e.g. Pl. 93)[3] a clearer indication

considerable interest in architecture and in sculpture. The little sketches that he made of the work of Girardon, for instance, show an attitude towards this kind of source which is taken over into his wall-paintings; he was concerned with what Vanbrugh described as 'the Great expensive part (of architecture) As Collumns, Arches, Bass reliefs &c.' He also bought engravings of the buildings which interested him and pictures on the visit to France; he visited private collections; and was as observant of the works of Poussin and late seventeenth-century French painters as he had been of Rubens and Teniers.

[1] In Dudley Ryder's very interesting account (*Diary*, ed. W. Matthews (1939), 306–8) of a visit (28 August 1716) to the dome while Thornhill was at work, he states that there had been 'a design once proposed to have the whole Dome all in one without the divisions into several stories, but one story of St. Paul would not have been enough and then to have put more together within one arch would have only confounded it'.

[2] A very large number is in the B.M. and other important groups are in the Witt collection, at Greenwich and in Sir Bruce Ingram's possession. In the B.M. is a sketch-book, begun in 1699 and full of material for an understanding of his methods; the histories and allegories are worked out with scholarly thoroughness and the pages bear eloquent witness to his rapidity of touch.

[3] This drawing was among the preparatory studies for the mural at All Souls (destroyed 1870).

of his thoughts than the finished work; and the drawings for less formal themes, especially those in which the landscape is predominant, show an inventiveness and a light and facile touch which sounds an echo of Inigo Jones.[1]

These qualities were submerged on the immense area of painted walls and ceilings in the Painted Hall at Greenwich (Pl. 96), which occupied Thornhill for nearly eighteen years[2] and was the culminating achievement of the baroque decorative school in England. On the huge ceiling of the Lower Hall the central glorification of William and Mary[3] is seen through a great oval frame, supported at the sides by naked slaves among a pile of naval accoutrements and cut into a feigned roof. The latter is open at each end, where Thornhill built up an elaborate arch, conceived in the spirit of Pozzo as an extension of the architecture. The oval frame within a rectangle is perhaps derived from the rich carved framework within which the central canvas of Rubens's Whitehall ceiling is set, and there are other reminiscences at Greenwich of the same source and of Verrio's St. George's Hall. Although Thornhill gave himself such endless opportunities for displaying the *tours de force* of his craft, the scale of the figures throughout is too uniform and the false perspective is no more daring than in the work of Verrio or Laguerre.

The Upper Hall presented Thornhill with a less formidable problem and once again he resorted to the familiar themes in the French tradition, though there is perhaps a Venetian flavour in the figures who look over a balcony into the room. The urns and the deep bronze-gold trophies in the corners of the ceiling and the feigned gold and stucco on the walls are of high quality. In the two scenes on the side walls of the arrival of George I and the landing

[1] Thornhill produced sets for the opera *Arsinoë* at the Theatre Royal in 1705 and for George I's theatre at Hampton Court.

[2] In the summer of 1707 he was already commissioned to paint the Hall itself (perhaps at the instigation of Sir James Bateman); he probably began late in 1708 and had finished it by the summer of 1714. At the end of 1717 he was ordered to paint the Upper Hall, which was probably finished in the summer of 1725; another year was needed in which to finish the Vestibule.

[3] The iconography was fully set out in the *Explanation* which in 1726 the Directors of the Hospital ordered to be printed; Steele's account is reprinted in the current guide to the Palace, Hospital, and College (1952), 9–10.

of William III, Thornhill was faced with the problem that had confronted Laguerre at Marlborough House; but unlike his predecessor he treated these celebrated contemporary events in a classical manner and as vast reliefs[1] in monochrome, of a type which had been constantly used in England and France, though normally on a much smaller scale. On the main wall at the end of the Upper Hall flying figures sweep back the curtains in another grand painted proscenium to reveal the new Hanoverian dynasty, grouped round the seated figure of George I,[2] on a flight of steps at the foot of which Thornhill himself points modestly at the focal point of his great achievement. Behind the columns, curtains and flying putti rises the dome of St. Paul's.

The painting of walls and ceilings on such a scale could naturally only be commissioned (with very few exceptions) by public or ecclesiastical institutions or by the richest or most cosmopolitan members of the aristocracy.[3] Throughout the period (though mainly before 1700) a less expensive form of decoration was used by architects and patrons who wished to embellish a staircase, a ceiling or smaller areas which could be by Verrio, Laguerre, or Thornhill, but would be set within richly carved plaster frames.[4] On a still humbler level the old tradition of painted wainscot panels, like those in the Hunting Room at Wilton, survived throughout the period. A most delightful essay in this tradition

[1] Thornhill's decision to treat these two events in this fashion was not reached without careful thought. For his own musings on the subject (on a drawing in the B.M., L.B. 23) and the place of this episode in the development of history-painting in England see E. Wind, 'The Revolution of History Painting', *Journ. of the Warburg Institute*, ii (1938/9), 121–4, and C. Mitchell, ibid. (1944), vii. 23–27.

At Easton Neston Thornhill's paintings of scenes from the life of Cyrus on the staircase are entirely in monochrome (H. A. Tipping and C. Hussey, *English Homes*, IV. ii (1928), 135).

[2] The royal portraits are harder than his usual style and, in certain cases, seriously out of proportion.

[3] In a very interesting petition, in connexion with the payment for his work at Greenwich, Thornhill cited the payments to other decorative painters by their royal or noble patrons (*Wren Soc.* vi. 77–78).

[4] An example of this is in the Duchess' Bedchamber at Ham; at Sudbury Hall Laguerre painted for George Vernon between 1691 and 1694 (MSS. at Sudbury) sections of the ceilings of the parlour and saloon and of the staircase (C. Latham, *In English Homes*, iii (1909), 142, 145).

was the enchanting set of panels by Robert Robinson in 1696[1] with highly imaginative exotic scenes of native life. Robinson was a scene-painter and the panels, with the strange beasts and the backgrounds in which Wren's City churches are transformed into oriental *capricci*, have the air of fantastic scenery for a pantomime.

Robinson was a member of the Painter-Stainers and Thornhill remained loyal to his old associates. In 1720 he was elected Master of the Company and they must have rejoiced at the honour which he had done to their craft. He was a director of Kneller's academy and became its governor in 1716; and eight years later set up his own academy at his house in Covent Garden. In 1720 he was appointed Sergeant-Painter; in the same year he was knighted and he presented to the King a set of engravings of the work at St. Paul's; he was returned as member of Parliament for Melcombe Regis in 1722 and was elected Fellow of the Royal Society in 1723. His status almost rivalled Kneller's and his success enabled him to buy back the home of his ancestors in Dorset. He had retired for some years before his death on 4 May 1734.[2]

The history of baroque decorative painting in England, and the struggles of native artists to vindicate their rights against the ceaseless threat of the favoured foreigners, reach their climax in Thornhill's appointment in June 1718 as History-Painter in Ordinary to the King and in the recognition that he was not only the greatest native history-painter the country had produced, but the first of whom no court in Europe need be ashamed. But he suffered at the

---

[1] They were painted for a house in Botolph Lane, but when this was destroyed the room was removed to Sir John Cass's School, Aldgate; see E. W. Tristram, *Walpole Soc.* iii (1914), 75–81; and E. Croft-Murray, *Country Life Annual* (1955), 174–9.

[2] In March 1729 he received permission to copy the Raphael cartoons; he completed one set on the original scale and began two sets of smaller copies. There is thus a concentration on the work of Raphael in the last years of his life of which Richardson would have approved.

Of Thornhill's other decorative work the most important is at Blenheim, Charborough and Wimpole, where he painted the chapel for the 2nd earl of Oxford. For his portraits see C. H. Collins Baker, 'Antonio Verrio and Thornhill's early Portraiture', *Connoisseur*, cxxxi (1953), 10–13; he also did a few book-illustrations and designed the rose window in the north transept of Westminster Abbey. For the catalogue of the sale of his collection see *Burl. Mag.* lxxxii (1943), 133–6; the sale included copies by him after Van Dyck and Rembrandt and a large number of Laguerre's sketches.

end of his career a 'mighty mortification' far more cruel and callous than any injury he had inflicted on Pellegrini or Ricci. Both his royal offices entitled him to expect the commission for painting at Kensington Palace, but in March 1722 it was given to William Kent. Kent was a far less distinguished painter than Thornhill and his work for the Crown at Kensington and Hampton Court shows little more than a feeble reworking of the outworn themes of his predecessors and is much less virile than the early attempts of Hogarth (who had, incidentally, eloped with Thornhill's daughter) to reinterpret the baroque tradition in England; but as Vertue said of this episode 'what is Merit when envy joynd with power to oppose it'?[1] The desire for decorative painting on a very large scale was past and in the houses that were now being built the areas allotted to it were shrinking rapidly; but Kent was the protégé of Lord Burlington and therein lies the significance of his victory over Thornhill. The supplanting of a man who was still working in the full Stuart manner by the artist who was so closely linked with the Palladian movement, and the emergence of Lord Burlington as a dispenser of patronage, brings to an end one phase of the Stuart period in the history of the arts in England.

[1] iii. 35.

XIII

THE CULMINATION OF THE BAROQUE STYLE IN ARCHITECTURE

THE reigns of William III (1688–1702) and Queen Anne (1702–14) present the culmination of English baroque architecture. William's dislike of Whitehall and his consequent need for new palaces gave Wren, who was now at the zenith of his career, an opportunity for design on a grand scale which he had hardly enjoyed so far. His activities in this field were, however, to reach their greatest heights in Greenwich Hospital, which was undertaken just before Queen Mary's death in 1694. These were also the years of the completion of the body of St. Paul's cathedral, though the west towers and the dome, which are the crown of Wren's career and the final basis of his claim to greatness, were not built until after 1700.

During this last period of Wren's life, his style shows an increased interest in three-dimensional architecture in contrast to the two-dimensional character of, for instance, Trinity College Library of 1676.[1] He now creates buildings which are interesting from more than one viewpoint, and in which the various parts lead the eye from one to the other. He tends, too, to think in terms of a grand layout, in which various blocks of related buildings are combined in a single whole, with a central dominating feature. And the scale of the individual parts, and even more of the individual details, is as a rule grander, and handled with far greater assurance.

It is not, however, in Wren's work alone that this increased baroque quality may be seen. It appears even more strongly in the work of Sir John Vanbrugh (1664–1726) and Nicholas Hawksmoor (1661–1736). It is echoed in the work of Thomas Archer (1668/9–

---

[1] It is difficult to accept Mr. Summerson's view (see *Architecture in Britain* (1953)) that Wren himself never thought in terms of mass, and that the creation of the baroque style is entirely due to the influence of younger men.

1743),[1] and in the early work of James Gibbs.[2] The interdependence of Wren, Hawksmoor, and Vanbrugh about the turn of the century is one of the most intricate and teasing problems in the history of English architecture, and must be discussed in connexion with the buildings concerned. One broad fact, however, emerges. In the hands of these three men English architecture achieves a new grandeur, which in the work of Vanbrugh and Hawksmoor is specifically heroic in its aim. It is characteristic that in 1707 all three should have signed a preface of recommendation to John James's translation of Pozzo's *Perspectiva*, a work dealing entirely with three-dimensional art. And Wren, in a dictum recorded in *Parentalia*, points out, with his usual common sense, the method whereby the desired results may be achieved:

The architect ought above all things to be well skilled in Perspective: for everything that appears well in the Orthography may not be good in the model, especially where there are many Angles and Projections; and everything that is good in the Model, may not be so when built.[3]

Out of his long experience, Wren was meditating deeply on the problems of his art. He had at last secured a team of craftsmen, capable of carrying out his designs. Many of the names which appear again and again in the accounts of his buildings—Doogood and Grove the plasterers, William Emmett the carver, Edward Pierce carver and mason, Jasper Latham, and the two Strongs, were Englishmen, trained probably by the usual apprentice system. Others, Gibbons, Jean Tijou the Huguenot smith, Cibber, Verrio, and Baptiste, came from abroad. Many Huguenot craftsmen, especially silversmiths and silk weavers, had taken refuge in England after the revocation of the Edict of Nantes in 1685.[4] Wren, writing to Mr. Treasurer Hawes of Christ's Hospital on 24 November 1694,[5] reflects on the differences between English and foreign craftsmanship:

---

[1] See above, p. 223.

[2] Since most of Gibbs's work falls after 1715, it will not be discussed in this volume.

[3] *Parentalia*, 352.   [4] See above, pp. 227, 231.

[5] Wren was a Governor of Christ's Hospital, and was formerly assumed to have designed the Mathematical School and the Writing School. The style of the former (*Wren Soc.* xi, Pl. xlvi) suggests the hand of Dr. Robert Hooke, while the latter is almost certainly by Nicholas Hawksmoor (Summerson, 166 and Pl. 99 a).

It was observed . . . that our English Artists are dull enough at Inventions but when once a foreigne patterne is sett, they imitate soe well that commonly they exceed the originall. I confess the observation is generally true, but this shows that our Natives want not a Genius, but education in that which is the ffoundation of all Mechanick Arts, a practice in designing or drawing, to which everybody in Italy, France and the Low Countries pretends to more or less.[1]

This letter strikes at the basic weakness of English art from the early sixteenth century onwards—the lack of a sound tradition in training. In architecture, great amateurs, Jones, Wren himself, and Vanbrugh, trained themselves during their own practice. In painting, young men were largely dependent on the studios of foreign artists like Lely and Kneller:[2] sculptors of any ambition went abroad. No central school, such as the French Academy (with its daughter institute the French Academy at Rome), existed in England, and the lack of academic standards affected the whole structure of the arts.[3] The apprenticeship system was in itself sound, and a real degree of technical ability was transmitted by it, but it was technical ability only, divorced from any canon of design established at higher levels, and lacking in invention, because it lacked the knowledge and control arising from that training in drawing which Wren advocated. A comparison between the drawings made by Gibbons for decoration at Hampton Court or elsewhere, and those of his imitator, Samuel Watson, for Chatsworth, is clear proof of the soundness of Wren's case.[4] Watson's actual carving is nearly as accomplished as that of Gibbons: his drawings are those of a provincial craftsman who cannot express himself on paper.

At the time Wren wrote his letter to Christ's Hospital he was making heavy demands on the men who worked for him. The

[1] Wren's advice was heeded, and a drawing master, Bernard Lens, who set up an art school in Fleet Street in 1697, was appointed as a visiting master at Christ's Hospital (Stow's *Survey of London*, (ed. Strype, 1720), i. 173, 181).

[2] See above, Chap. VIII.

[3] For the history of academic training, see N. Pevsner, *Academies of Art* (1940).

[4] *Wren Soc.* iv. Pls. xxvii–xlii; F. Thompson, *A History of Chatsworth* (1949), Pls. 51, 59, &c. The lack of invention in the Stanton workshop also supports Wren's statement. (See above, p. 258.)

accession of William and Mary had plunged him into a series of new and great undertakings. St. Paul's was still only a shell, with much of its decoration and all its fittings still to be provided, and in the nineties many of the City churches were to be 'beautified'. The fittings in Trinity College Library, the work of Gibbons and Cornelius Austin,[1] were carried out in the same decade, and there was much routine business such as the devising of a pre-fabricated house for William to take on his Irish campaign, or the setting up of crush-barriers at the time of the Queen's funeral in 1695.[2]

The first of the new commissions for the Crown were Hampton Court and Kensington Palaces. William found Whitehall too damp (he suffered from asthma), and though the Queen completed the new drawing-room and river terrace begun for Mary of Modena, which can be seen in the view of the palace drawn about 1694 (Pl. 84), her energies were quickly diverted to planning healthier palaces. She joined her husband in England in February 1689; by April work was begun at Hampton Court and by July at Kensington. The latter was not an entirely new building, but a series of additions to Nottingham House, built about 1610, bought by William from Daniel Finch, second Earl of Nottingham, and renamed Kensington House. Wren's loosely grouped blocks are simple and well proportioned in themselves but the whole inevitably lacks dignity and coherence.[3]

The problem at Hampton Court Palace[4] was a larger one, also involving older buildings, and its final solution may well have been a great disappointment to the architect. An early plan, which must date from the first months of 1689, proves that at first he conceived a palace on the grandest scale. The whole of the Tudor building

[1] R. Willis and J. W. Clark, *Cambridge* (1886), ii. 544–546; M. D. Whinney, *Grinling Gibbons in Cambridge* (1948).

[2] N. Luttrell, *A Brief Historical Relation of State Affairs* (ed. 1857), ii. 12 and iii. 420.

[3] The interior of Kensington Palace has since been much altered. The original nucleus of Nottingham House was rebuilt and entirely redecorated between 1718 and 1721, and the Palace was mutilated in the late eighteenth and early nineteenth century by being cut up into suites.

[4] For accounts, documents and drawings for Hampton Court, see *Wren Soc.* iv. For an historical account of the palace and its associations, see E. Law, *History of Hampton Court* (1885–91, 3 vols.).

was to be taken down, except for Henry VIII's Great Hall, which was to serve as an axial point in the new design. The grand approach to the palace was to be by the chestnut avenue (as yet unplanted) in Bushey Park to a great court flanked by re-entrant wings converging on the Great Hall. The visitor would pass under the Hall, and find himself with the Grand Front of the new palace on his left. Behind the Grand Front the palace was arranged round a square court nearly four times the size of the present Fountain Court. Several sketches for elevations for this scheme exist, that for the Grand Front being of special interest since it shows a treatment with a giant order rising from the ground, surmounted by an attic and a wide low dome (Pl. 60 a). This is far more baroque in its large scale and its dramatic emphasis than anything yet designed in England.[1] Indeed, the whole conception of a grand layout culminating in an emphatic main front, though a continuation of Wren's experiments at Chelsea Hospital and Winchester Palace, is a great advance upon them. Had the scheme been carried out, Hampton Court would have taken its place as one of the great baroque palaces of Europe.

Presumably, however, the project was considered too expensive and it was quickly abandoned for the present more modest building. A new court (Fountain Court) was added on the park side of the Tudor palace, with the King's Apartments looking on to the garden at the south and the Queen's on the main park front (Pl. 65 a).[2] A simple bay design of four windows of varying shapes set above each other is repeated on both fronts, a combination of brick and stone being used throughout the building. Wren handles this with great skill, using his stone to emphasize his verticals and

[1] Possibly based on Rainaldi's or F. Mansart's designs for the east front of the Louvre, though the closest of all precedents is provided by the west front of St. Peter's, Rome. The plan of the Great Court, which appeared among the Bute drawings (sold Sotheby's 23 May 1951, lot 16–5), wrongly catalogued as for Whitehall, has close links, especially in the arrangement of staircases, with Bernini's plan for the Louvre. An alternative scheme for the Grand Front borrows motives from Le Vau's entrance court at Versailles. Probably both architect and patron had the latter in mind.

[2] No provision was now made for the administrative rooms (i.e. the Council Chamber, &c.) which were to be on the Grand Front in the earlier design, for it was probably realized that the administrative centre could not follow the King but must remain near Parliament.

horizontals—and it is on the balance between verticals and horizontals that the whole design is based—and to give colour and texture to the building. The proportion of the area of brick and stone is sensitively adjusted on the two main fronts, giving scale to the whole, though in Fountain Court, where the bay design of the east front is repeated, the windows are closer together and over-crowded. The simple block-like character of the building is emphasized by the straight sky-line.[1] The quality of the craftsman-ship throughout is extremely high: the brick, which is almost orange in colour, is set with very fine joints and has an amazing smoothness of texture: the carving of the stone ornaments, particularly the keystones and festoons on the south front, and the capitals and frieze of the central feature on the east, is of the utmost virtuosity (Pl. 65 b).

At the time of the Queen's death in December 1694 the fabric of the 'King's side' (i.e. the south front) was finished, though all the windows were not in, and the 'Queen's side' (the park front) was not entirely roofed. Work was broken off and not taken up again until 1699, when the destruction by fire of Whitehall in 1698 and the more stable conditions after the Peace of Ryswick probably turned William's attention again to Hampton Court. Most of the interior woodwork dates from between 1699 and 1702, though the Queen's Apartments were finished by Queen Anne. The two great suites of rooms with their finely proportioned panelling and superb door-cases have cornices and decorations above the fire-places by Gibbons; the ceilings and walls painted by Verrio and Thornhill have already been discussed.[2]

The spectre of a grand palace at Whitehall haunts English architectural history in the seventeenth century. Jones and Webb had both produced great schemes, and Wren had already, probably about 1669, made drawings for a building in which the Banqueting House was to be repeated beyond a great portico.[3] In 1698 he was to plan the finest of all his grand projects, and again it was to come to nothing. The disastrous fire of 4 January destroyed the entire

---

[1] Drawings at the Soane Museum (see *Wren Soc.* iv. Pls. xvii, xviii) show that Wren meant to break the sky-line by statues and vases.

[2] See above, pp. 300, 301, 311.   [3] *Wren Soc.* vii. Pl. xi.

palace except the Banqueting House: before the end of the month Wren had surveyed the ruins; 'his majestie designs to make it a noble palace, which by computation may be finisht in 4 years'.[1] But by March the King directed that only a Council Chamber and 'five lodgings for his own use' should be erected, 'the rest will be omitted till Parliament provides the same'.[2] If Parliament had seen the ambitious layout proposed by Wren (Pl. 85 a) it is not perhaps surprising that it shrank from the undertaking. Two schemes are extant,[3] the larger of which would have entailed a major reconstruction of the whole area from Whitehall to Westminster. The Banqueting House was kept as a single entity, linked by a circular vestibule at either end to long blocks of buildings running down to a terrace on the river front, and back to a formal garden at the end of the Long Water in St. James's Park.[4] From the south wing of the palace a colonnade was to lead to a new Parliament House, placed opposite Westminster Hall. An open piazza lay to the west approached between two small apsed buildings, which recall the similar placing of churches in the Piazza del Popolo in Rome. The whole Westminster area was to be treated as a precinct, with an encircling wall, and a grand entrance to the west of the Abbey. The linking of the various buildings, and the device adopted to mask the awkward relation of the Long Water to the new palace is masterly, and reveals Wren's long experience in planning, and his splendid vision of the possibilities of the site.

The elevations, however, show a curious straining after dramatic effect. A giant portico is applied to the Banqueting House, and domed circular vestibules with giant orders flank it on either side (Pl. 85 b). The river and park fronts have great porticoes of giant columns. It is hard, but not impossible, to believe that this is Wren's architecture. Except for St. Paul's, this must have seemed the

---

[1] Narcissus Luttrell, *A Brief Historical Relation of State Affairs* (ed. 1857), iv. 334.

[2] Ibid. 351.

[3] *Wren Soc.* viii. Pls. i–x. A further elevation, perhaps in Talman's hand, appeared in the Bute Coll. (sold Sotheby's 23 May 1951, lot 16–1) and is now at All Souls. The smaller plan is an enlarged variation of John Webb's last scheme, see above, p. 136.

[4] The Long Water, on Pls. 84 and 85 a, dug immediately after the Restoration by troops for whom neither pay nor occupation could be provided, was 'landscaped' into its present serpentine form by Nash in 1827.

grandest opportunity of his career, and it appears incredible that he should have left the designing of the elevations to his assistant, Nicholas Hawksmoor, or to William Talman. His speed in producing large-scale schemes is proved at Hampton Court and elsewhere and even if the draughtsmanship could be categorically attributed to Hawksmoor (which seems impossible) the ideas are not necessarily his.[1] The grandiose style is puzzling, but Wren may have been spurred by the King on the one hand, and by the leanings of Talman and Hawksmoor towards massive architecture on the other, to attempt a design both more dramatic and more antique than anything built for Louis XIV. Many great artists develop a new personal style in their old age which is freely used by their successors. This is, conceivably, the late style of Wren and there is no reason to suppose that because he was nearly seventy he was incapable of new ideas.

Greenwich Hospital must stand as the most complete example of Wren's civil architecture, but even here he was unable to carry out his original wishes. In 1694 Queen Mary decided to establish a hospital for retired seamen as a complement to the military hospital at Chelsea. The site was granted in October (evidently Greenwich was no more agreeable than Whitehall as a palace) and the first plans must have been made before the Queen's death in December. The two buildings already existing which were materially to affect the new design were King Charles's Block, the single wing of the uncompleted palace begun by John Webb for Charles II, and the Queen's House lying back from the river, on the edge of the Park.[2] Wren's first scheme repeated King Charles's Block on the east side of a wide court open to the river, and added a smaller base block beyond on each side. A second, rather narrower court was projected behind, closed at the south end by a range of buildings containing a hall and chapel with a domed vestibule between them (Pl. 61 a). The view from the Queen's House would have been completely blocked, but the vista from the river would

---

[1] The larger plan (*Wren Soc.* viii. Pl. ii) is certainly in Wren's own hand. The draughtsmanship of the elevations is puzzling, but seems closer to Wren than Hawksmoor. On *Wren Soc.* viii. Pls. iv and v. the figure-sculpture and decoration are added by Gibbons.   [2] See above, pp. 19, 133.

have been terminated by an important feature. The Queen, how-ever, insisted that the view should be preserved; Wren was forced to change his plans, and the project which was accepted by the King in April 1696 and carried out, though with some modifica-tions, left the view open (Fig. 9). The major accent could no longer be at the end of the narrowing courts, for the Queen's House was too low to provide it. Wren therefore moved his hall and chapel forward to the end of the first court and marked them by domes. Behind them the second court is narrower and long, flanked by colonnades whose entablatures provide a strong horizontal, leading the eye gently to the distant low rectangle of Jones's building (Pl. 63). Once more Wren had found a compromise solution to a problem set him—a very skilful one though it could not completely succeed. So great a group of buildings in which the parts are baroque in scale and to which the nature of the site necessitates a single approach, requires a climax—and this was denied to the architect.

Several further alterations were to take place during the long building operations. An engraving[1] shows wards for the pensioners running at right angles to the colonnades, instead of ranged round two back courts (King William's and Queen Mary's Courts) as finally built. No doubt, as at Chelsea, Wren with his practical humanity wished to give the wards the maximum of light and air. The domes, too, in this engraving are insignificant, with neither the height nor the interest of the executed design.

It is difficult to say how far these changes were due to younger men. In 1698 Hawksmoor was made Clerk of the Works at Greenwich, and in 1704 Deputy Surveyor. In 1702 Vanbrugh became Comptroller of the Office of Works, and in the next year his name first appears among those attending the Board Meetings for Greenwich. Thereafter Wren's attendances slackened. He was by now an old man, and his energies must have been mainly given to the completion of St. Paul's. It is possible that the alteration in the domes, which was made by 1702, is partly due to Hawksmoor, though the design of the drums is close to the west towers of St. Paul's. There can be no doubt that the long colonnades of coupled

---

[1] *Wren Soc.* vi. Pl. xlv. This engraving, issued in 1707, shows a design of 1699.

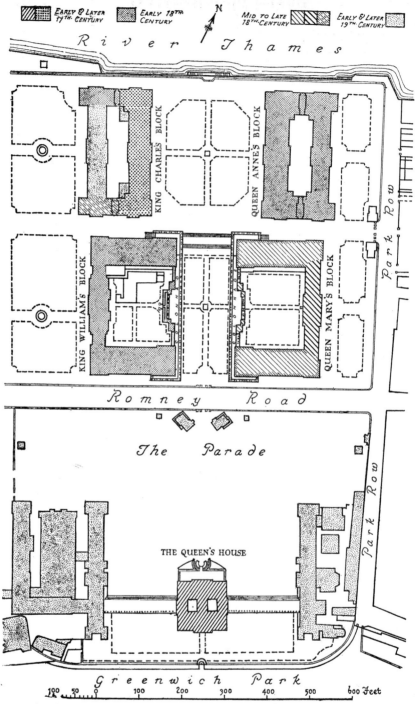

N

River Thames

KING CHARLES BLOCK

QUEEN ANNE'S BLOCK

KING WILLIAM'S BLOCK

QUEEN MARY'S BLOCK

Park Row

Romney Road

The Parade

THE QUEEN'S HOUSE

Park Row

Greenwich Park

100 50 0 100 200 300 400 500 600 Feet

FIG. 9. *Greenwich Hospital, executed plan.*

columns, which are perhaps the most beautiful and most characteristic feature of the Greenwich design, are Wren's invention, for they appear in the 1699 engraving. He had, moreover, already used them on a smaller scale in the fine Ionic colonnade which masks the junction of the old and new work at Hampton Court, and provides the approach to the King's Stair.

It will be convenient to deal here briefly with the further history of Greenwich Hospital. Work was slow, and the cornice on the west colonnade (the first of the two to be built) was not laid till 1714. Hawksmoor had been made Surveyor for Greenwich in 1705, and was living on the job, and the detail here is almost certainly his. The court behind it, King William's Court, which was nearing completion, was however apparently designed by Vanbrugh.[1] The inner front of its west block with its crowded centrepiece is a rather unhappy attempt to change the scale of the design, and so give it an added grandeur. The outer elevation of this same block, with a giant Doric portico, is, however, simpler and more impressive. By now a further change had been made in Wren's scheme when in 1711 King Charles's Block (and subsequently Queen Anne's Block which was being built as its counterpart) was doubled. It was probably about this time[2] that Vanbrugh proposed an ambitious new scheme for the whole inner part of the Hospital. This entailed the taking down of the Queen's House, which was to be rebuilt farther up the hill. It was to be replaced by a fantastic building with a dome and four towers, standing on the short axis of a great oval court, to which Wren's colonnades formed the approach.[3] There can be little doubt that Vanbrugh had studied engravings of Bernini's plan for the piazza of St. Peter's when preparing this scheme, nor that it would have added immeasurably to the grandeur of Greenwich had it been

[1] Summerson, 180, suggests this was designed as early as 1702. For a further discussion of Vanbrugh's and Hawksmoor's share, see ibid., 2nd ed. (1955), 170.

[2] In 1711 Queen Anne gave the Queen's House for the use of the Governor of the Hospital. Between 1697 and 1711 it had been granted to Lord Romney, who had been Ranger of the Park and who had moved the road running through the house.

[3] For the plan, some original drawings (which may be in Hawksmoor's hand) and a reconstruction of the scheme, see *Wren Soc.* vi. Pls. xxxii–xxxiii, xxxvi–xxxix.

carried out. How far his new building with its great masses of stonework and its abrupt movement from part to part would have proved a happy marriage with the suaver architecture of Wren is an open question, but it would at least have been a baroque monument on the grandest scale. Nothing, however, came of the scheme, and the Hospital was continued slowly, the Chapel being begun in 1715, though the dome was not built till 1735, the Great Hall (which had been carried out by Wren) painted by Thornhill between 1707 and 1726,[1] and Queen Mary's Court completed by Ripley after 1729. Greenwich Hospital, as it stands, is Wren's most important and most successful public building, and also one of the major instances of his ability to achieve a compromise solution in hampering conditions. At St. Paul's he was faced with even more difficult problems; and it was in the last years of his life that these were brought to a triumphant conclusion.

In 1687 a change was made in the allocation of the money derived from the tax on sea-coal. Up till then the larger proportion had been given to the City churches, and less to St. Paul's. By now, most of the work on the churches was done, and more money was available for the cathedral. At this date, the foundations for the south-west chapel were being dug, and during the next few years the west front was built. The idea of a giant portico was probably now revived[2] (this would have been in keeping with the general trend of Wren's architecture in the nineties), but the Portland quarries could not provide a sufficient number of large blocks of stone and Wren was forced to fall back on a two-storeyed design. In order to give his small columns greater weight and importance, he used them coupled instead of single, though this may have been for practical reasons also, since, as *Parentalia* states, it made the arrangement of doors easier. In spite, however, of Wren's attempts to give his columns importance both by coupling them, and setting them in front of a deep recess, their scale remains somewhat trivial,

---

[1] See above, p. 313 and Pl. 96.

[2] It had appeared in the Great Model and the Warrant Design (Pl. 40 *a* and *b*) but the drawing of *c.* 1675 (see above, p. 211, and Summerson, Pl. 81 A) shows a two-storeyed portico. For drawings of the giant portico, see *Wren Soc.* ii. Pl. xviii; iii. Pl. xiv; and for discussion of Wren's difficulties and of precedents for the use of coupled columns, *Parentalia*, 287–9.

and the west front of St. Paul's is perhaps the least inspired feature
of the building.

By 1694 the masonry of the choir was at last finished but there
were no fittings, and much decoration remained to be done.
Gibbons, who had been made Master Carver to the Crown in
1693, first worked at St. Paul's in the next year, carving the panels
below the windows on the exterior of the choir. Jasper Latham had
carved the arms of the City with palms and festoons on the east
wall of the north transept in 1686; Gibbons carved the same arms
under one of the south windows of the choir in 1694 or 1695.
Latham's festoons are tightly packed ropes of fruit and flowers,
making a solid mass of decoration. Gibbons's stone carving repeats
his wood technique: flowers and fruit are linked loosely together,
and are so deeply undercut that many of the panels have almost
perished.

It is perhaps not surprising that both the clergy and Parliament
became restive over the long-drawn-out building operations.
Twenty years had gone by since the beginning of the work and
thirty since the Great Fire, and still 'the new choir' was not in
readiness. Gibbons was working on the choir-stalls and organ-case
when in the early months of 1697 Parliament took the drastic step
of suspending half Wren's salary. They coupled this with a charge
of mismanagement of public funds. There was no truth in this,
but it must be admitted that Wren, in his anxiety to get the whole
cathedral built, had deliberately misinterpreted the terms of his
contract.[1] The measure had its effect, for on 2 December 1697 the
choir was opened for the Thanksgiving Service for the Peace of
Ryswick, and the first regular Sunday service was held there three
days later (Pl. 43).[2]

Neither the dome nor the west towers were yet built; indeed
their design was not yet fixed, for the official engravings of 1701–3
show a dome stepped in above the drum, while the western towers

[1] See above, p. 168.

[2] The interior is not now as it was in Wren's day, for until 1872 the organ stood on
a screen across the west end of the choir, closing the central space and also providing
an effective *repoussoir* for the choir vault. Further, the area under the dome was
empty of chairs, and therefore looked even more spacious. See *Wren Soc.* xiv. Pl.
xlviii.

appear as small copies of Bramante's Tempietto. In September 1704, when Queen Anne blazing with jewels, and the duchess of Marlborough in her plain black gown, rode in state to give thanks for the victory of Blenheim, the cathedral was still incomplete. But between that time and the autumn of 1708 both towers and dome were finished. They represent the height of Wren's achievement, the last fruits of long years of thought and experiment. It cannot be doubted that he considered them together, and evolved the broken lines of the towers (Pl. 86) with their contrasting movement of slow curves and jutting angle-columns, their diminishing arched storeys over which the eye is led by the line of urns and buttresses moving towards the summit as a foil to the simple majestic lines of the dome itself. The towers are among the most baroque of Wren's creations;[1] the detail is bolder and heavier than in his earlier work, and is close to the manner of Hawksmoor, but the final drawings are in Wren's own hand.[2]

His final maturity is even more evident in the dome (Pl. 88). Throughout the whole history of the cathedral Wren had been deeply concerned with its support, and had introduced innumerable hidden devices for spreading the load. A long succession of drawings had been made, few of which can be certainly dated, experimenting with ideas borrowed from Bramante, Michelangelo, or Jules Hardouin Mansart at Les Invalides. Now, at last, he was to build his own creation, a masterpiece both of engineering and of design. Other architects had faced the problem of a dome which from the inside would play its part in the space-composition of the interior. Mansart, indeed, had built an inner and an outer dome, the inner open at the top, with light streaming from above. Wren's problem was, however, greater than Mansart's, whose dome is set near the façade of the church. The great length of the nave, and indeed the great size of the church, made it imperative that the dome should rise to a great height, and be surmounted by a tall lantern (Wren had from his very earliest connexion with St. Paul's,

---

[1] They are perhaps influenced by the towers of S. Agnese in Piazza Navona, Rome. Cf. the steeple of St. Vedast (1694) for further Borrominesque influence (see above, p. 161).

[2] Bute collection, sold Sotheby's 23 May 1951, lots 2 and 8.

before the Fire, been determined on a high central feature as a landmark). Michelangelo had placed a great lantern on the dome of St. Peter's, but his dome is of stone, and therefore capable of bearing the weight. Wren's solution of his problems was complex and ingenious. He evolved, probably during the winter of 1704/5, a triple structure (Fig. 10). Within is a low dome which gently closes the great central space, cut by an eye in the centre, through which one looks up to immeasurable heights. Above this, unseen from inside or outside, is a tall masonry cone, which carries the lantern. The outer dome, with its ribs rising to the lantern, is of lead, supported on a timber structure.

Below the dome, the cornice and balustrade of the drum runs in a continuous, unbroken curve, echoing the circle of the dome itself. The columns which surround it stand light against the shadow, carrying the eye up through the attic to the ribs of the dome, and so up to the lantern. Wren has, indeed, combined the continuous peristyle of Bramante with the buttressed drum of Michelangelo, for between every fourth column the black shadows are broken by a niched feature which is in fact a buttress, though it does not break the line of the drum. It is in this harnessing of structural expedient and aesthetic effect in St. Paul's that Wren shows his great quality.

In October 1708 the coppersmith was paid for the ball and the cross on the lantern, but it was not until 1711 that Parliament declared St. Paul's complete, and after a good deal of unpleasantness, the arrears of Wren's salary were paid. He was now almost eighty, and took little more active part in architecture. By mean political jobbery he was deprived of the Surveyorship in 1718. It had been offered to Vanbrugh, who had refused it 'out of tenderness to Sir Christopher Wren' and was finally given to an incompetent nonentity, William Benson. Wren survived till 1723. On the day of his death he paid his annual visit to his great cathedral, and returned to die quietly in his chair. In the south transept of that cathedral is his most abiding epitaph, *Si monumentum requiris, circumspice*. It is not by St. Paul's alone, however, that he must be judged. It is the greatest and most successful of his works, but there, as in almost all his undertakings, he was harassed by

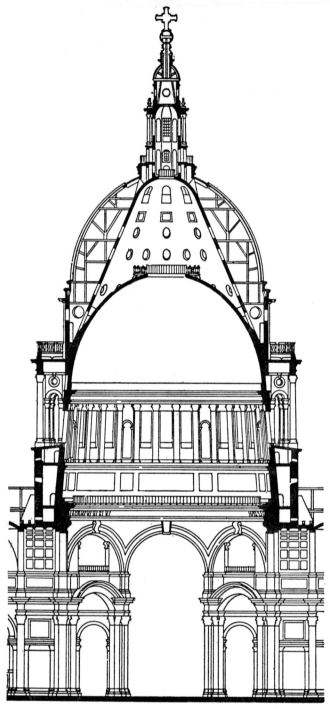

FIG. 10. *St. Paul's Cathedral, section through dome.*

limitations, by opposing interests, by shortage of money or difficulties of material. It was in the very nature of his genius to accept
these limitations and make what he could of them. Sometimes he
succeeds, and sometimes he does not. He is, in fact, one of the
most uneven of great architects. But no other English architect
has matched him in the range and variety of his achievement, and
there are indeed few architects of any country who can show so
great a volume of work. He enjoyed wide patronage, but few, if
any, of his patrons had knowledge of or taste for architecture, and
though he owes much to his opportunities, what he made of them
is his own. Neither the society in which he lived (greatly though it
changed during his fifty years of architectural practice) nor the
scientific temper of his own mind made it possible for him to
create a wholeheartedly baroque architecture. He was not called
upon, like Roman architects, to give visual expression to the ideas
of a militant Church, nor, like the French, to show the glory of
absolute monarchy. Both the English Church and the English
monarchy were, during his lifetime, working out a compromise
solution of their relations to Parliament. Wren's architecture
reflects that compromise. It reflects, too, the abiding English respect
for tradition, and belief in the permanence of the English contribution to civilization. This he expressed in words also:

An architect ought to be jealous of Novelties, in which Fancy blinds
the Judgment; and to think his Judges, as well those that are to live five
centuries after him, as those of his own Time. That which is commendable now for Novelty, will not be a new Invention to Posterity, when
his works are often imitated and when it is unknown which was the
original: but the Glory of that which is good of itself is eternal.[1]

The date of this note is unknown; that it may rightly be applied
to the dome of St. Paul's cannot be questioned.

The reticence and urbanity of Wren's style is a strong contrast to
that of Sir John Vanbrugh, or to the independent work of Nicholas
Hawksmoor.[2] The two men worked for a time as a partnership,

---

[1] *Parentalia*, 351.
[2] The best modern sources for Vanbrugh are: L. Whistler, *The Imagination of
Vanbrugh and his Fellow Artists* (1954); H. A. Tipping and C. Hussey, *English Homes,*

and it is extremely hard to say which had the greater influence on the other. One thing is, however, certain. Hawksmoor, who was born in 1661, went to Wren as a clerk in 1679, and had a long training in architectural practice. By 1700 he had worked at Chelsea, Winchester, Kensington, and St. Paul's, and had perhaps in 1692 designed the library of the Queen's College, Oxford, a building in the full Wren manner. Vanbrugh, on the contrary, had apparently had no training at all. Born in 1664, the child of a marriage between a daughter of Sir Dudley Carleton's nephew and heir and a sugar baker from Ghent, he seems to have retained something of his mother's social status, and early in life to have embarked on a military career. In 1691 he was arrested at Calais as a spy (having probably previously been in Paris) and was imprisoned there and in the Bastille. By 1696 he had begun his association with the stage which was to last twelve years. He wrote eight or nine comedies, the best of which, *The Relapse* and *The Provok'd Wife*, are almost worthy to rank with those of Congreve. His final theatrical venture was connected with the promotion of opera, for which he built the Queen's Theatre, Haymarket,[1] and over which he lost much money.

Suddenly, though apparently without architectural experience, he was asked by the earl of Carlisle to replace Talman at Castle Howard. He was clearly by now on friendly terms with the Whig nobility, for he wrote in 1699 to the earl of Manchester describing a stay at Chatsworth during which he had discussed Carlisle's plans and a model of the house with the duke of Devonshire. The model has disappeared, nor is it possible to say if Vanbrugh alone was responsible for it. The earliest elevations for the house now remain-

---

IV. ii (1928), *The Work of Sir John Vanbrugh and his School*, which has a magnificent series of plates; L. Whistler, *Sir John Vanbrugh* (1938): *Works of Sir John Vanbrugh*, Nonesuch edition, iv (1928), is devoted to his letters, and has a critical introduction to his architecture by Professor Geoffrey Webb. Except for Colvin, *Dictionary*, 272, 747, the literature on Hawksmoor is less adequate. H. Goodhart Rendel, *Nicholas Hawksmoor* (1924), is the best collection of plates of the churches, but the text is biased. Among important recent articles are S. Lang, 'Cambridge and Oxford Reformed', *Archit. Review*, ciii (1948), 157; 'By Hawksmoor out of Gibbs', ibid. cv (1949), 173; and H. Colvin, 'Fifty New Churches', ibid. cvii (1950), 189. For correspondence concerning the Mausoleum at Castle Howard see G. Webb, *Walpole Soc.* xix (1931), iii.

[1] Approximately on the site now occupied by Her Majesty's Theatre.

ing appear to have been drawn by Hawksmoor[1] and suggest a block not too far removed from Talman's Chatsworth or Hawksmoor's own Easton Neston of about 1702.[2] The plan, however, is more accomplished than either, and it seems fair to suppose that in both the first drawings and in the final evolution of the great domed block rising above a series of grouped outbuildings, Hawksmoor's technical experience is used to interpret Vanbrugh's ideas (Pl. 90 *a*).[3] For at Castle Howard and at Blenheim (Pl. 91 *a*), created by the same partnership at almost the same time, a new sense of display and of climax is introduced into English domestic architecture. Wren had experimented with similar ideas, particularly at Greenwich in 1694, but there the functional requirements of hall, chapel, and wards had to some extent controlled the plan. Vanbrugh, though employing similar features—a centre joined to side blocks by quadrants—starts with an idea of magnificence rather than of function. The plan (Pl. 90 *b*), especially that of the main block, however, shows real originality and skill. The core of the house is a great hall, with stairs flanking it on either side, while behind is the Saloon (now the Garden Hall). Opening from the Saloon to right and left are two state suites (antechamber, drawing-room, bedroom, dressing-room, and cabinet or study—in fact an extension of the French *appartement*). Along the inner side of these rooms is a corridor running the whole length of the wings, giving a privacy to the suites which is completely absent at, for instance, Hampton Court.[4] The subsidiary wings on the entrance side, joined to it by quadrant arcades, and containing the chapel and the kitchen, appear, though in not their final form, in the earliest

[1] L. Whistler, 'The Evolution of Castle Howard', *Country Life*, cxiii (1953), 276. Since these drawings apparently remained in the Office of Works, and passed with Wren and Hawksmoor drawings to Wren's family, they may never have been sent to Carlisle. They show no dome and it is just possible that they were connected with the lost model. Both architects were indubitably concerned with the erection of the house, but all contemporary authorities regard it as Vanbrugh's creation.

[2] For Easton Neston see below, p. 344.

[3] Vanbrugh refers in 1706 to the final drawings of the dome then being made by Hawksmoor (L. Whistler, loc. cit.).

[4] Such a corridor appears, however, in some of the unidentified plans by William Talman at the R.I.B.A.

drawings; the great additional courts projected behind them were probably an afterthought.[1]

The elevations are no less interesting than the plan. In both there are certain French elements which suggest that Vanbrugh's knowledge of France had extended beyond Calais and the Bastille, or else that he and Hawksmoor had here studied French architectural books with especial care. The final conception, in the relation of the side blocks to the domed central block with a longer range of buildings on the garden front, is remarkably close to Jean Marot's design for the palace at Mannheim.[2] In plan the relation of hall, saloon, and stairs is not far from that of Le Vau's Vaux-le-Vicomte, while the elevation of the centre block with its round-headed windows and its use of much rather flat decorative sculpture on a channelled wall surface again recalls Le Vau. The giant pilaster treatment could be an echo of Louis XIV's Château de Marly, a building which enjoyed great prestige.[3] The garden front is unorthodox and slightly uncomfortable in its handling of windows with orders of different sizes and was moreover marred when Sir Thomas Robinson, a follower of Lord Burlington, rebuilt the west end in the 1750's.[4] He also spoilt the entrance court and it is only from the engraving in *Vitruvius Britannicus* that the full splendour of Vanbrugh's intention can be judged (Pl. 90 a). Small domes were to act as foils to the central cupola, towers and urns and statues were to be multiplied, and the whole dramatic group was to be approached through a fantastic gateway.

Inside the major innovation was the stone hall, far more monumental in its effect than any earlier English domestic interior (Pls. 89, 92 a). In fact, the same treatment that would be used for a baroque church—giant order and painted dome—is here applied to a room of state. It has a magnificence, a grand theatrical effect,

---

[1] The idea of side courts may follow and not precede those at Blenheim (see L. Whistler, loc. cit.).

[2] Published in the *Grand Marot*. I have to thank Mr. John Shearman for this reference.

[3] Drawings of Marly were available in England (see above, p. 222) and it was also engraved.

[4] A serious fire in 1940 destroyed the upper part of the cupola and much of the interior.

which is gay, in spite of the great scale and clumsy handling of some of the parts.[1] Vanbrugh, moreover, is interested in space-composition in a truly baroque manner, since the side walls of the hall are pierced by arches which open on to the staircases, thus making them spaces subsidiary to the hall itself.[2]

It was probably Carlisle's influence which obtained for Vanbrugh the office of Comptroller of Works in 1702, and in 1705 the commission for Blenheim Palace, to be built for the duke of Marlborough by the grateful nation.[3] On this also Hawksmoor collaborated. In view of the difficulties Vanbrugh had to face, mainly owing to the opposition of the duchess (who would have preferred Wren as an architect)[4] and the criticism which has been levelled at the building, it is important to understand the architect's intentions. These were explained in a letter to Lord Poulet in 1710:[5]

When the Queen declared she would build a house in Woodstock park for the Duke of Marlborough, and that she meant it in Memory of the great services he had done her and the nation, I found it the opinion of all people and of all partys I conversed with, that altho' the building was to be calculated for, and adapted to, a private habitation, yet it ought at the same time, to be considered as both a Royall and a National Monument, and care taken in the design, and the execution, that it might have the qualitys proper to such a monument, vizt. *Beauty, Magnificence and Duration* . . .

Vanbrugh, in fact, was not aiming at a private house (which was what the duchess wanted) but at a building which would express the greatness of England, the glory of military power, and the success of her foreign policy. It was to be heroic and not domestic architecture. Inevitably, his ideas soon outran the original estimate

[1] e.g. the repetition of two circular-headed openings, one above the other at the entrance end of the hall.

[2] For the decoration of Castle Howard, see above, p. 309.

[3] Some new information, drawn from the Marlborough papers, and not included in the admirable account of the house in H. A. Tipping and C. Hussey (op. cit. 63–112), is contained in the official *Guide to Blenheim Palace*, published by the Blenheim Estate Office (1950), and more in D. Green, *Blenheim Palace* (1951).

[4] He appears to have had some hand in the building of Marlborough House for her in 1709–11, though Colen Campbell in *Vitruvius Britannicus*, i. 39, 40, specifically ascribes it to Mr. Christopher Wren, i.e. Wren's son, and must have had grounds for this.   [5] *Works of Sir John Vanbrugh*, Nonesuch ed., iv (1928), 44.

of £100,000, and he found himself between the two fires of the duchess and the Treasury. The house eventually cost about £300,000, of which the nation paid four-fifths and the duke one fifth—but Vanbrugh had disgraced himself with the duchess for ever, and when he went with the Carlisles to see the finished house, he was refused admittance and forced to spend the day in the inn at Woodstock.

The plan is an elaboration of that of Castle Howard; hall, stairs, saloon, and state suites are placed in the same relation to each other, and are flanked by a corridor. To this nucleus are added two long side wings, the east containing the private apartments, and the west the picture gallery, now the library, and the corridors are returned round two small inner courts. This great main block, some 480 feet across, was the original idea for the palace, but to it Vanbrugh added an enormously deep forecourt, with kitchen and stable courts lying on either side.[1]

In the elevations he strove for the maximum grandeur (Pl. 91 a). He does not use the motive of piling up to a high centre, as at Castle Howard, but instead, evokes an effect of sheer mass, in which the height of the main block is repeated in four angle towers. Every part is on a great scale. A huge portico of two columns set within two square piers dominates the entrance front, which is itself treated with a giant order. The junction between the main block and the side wings is masked by quadrants treated with Doric half-columns, which are echoed by the Doric loggias on each side of the court. Windows have heavy flat architraves, and everywhere is a sense of the weight and durability of stone. There is far less surface decoration than at Castle Howard, though the skyline is broken by urns and figures by Gibbons and his school,[2] and the great banded columns which mark the entrance to the side courts are topped by lions savaging the cock of France. Behind these columns are two more great towers, most complex in design, with layer upon layer of stonework cut back to suggest immense thickness of wall, and almost without decoration. In the kitchen court,

---

[1] The stable court on the west was never completed.
[2] There were originally eighteen figures of graces and goddesses above the quadrants; two of these may survive in the niches of the east gate.

carried out under the supervision of Hawksmoor after Vanbrugh's break with the duchess in 1716, the suggestion of military strength is even more forcibly presented. The sides of the court are castellated (though the castellations are given classical mouldings) and the great entrance gate has two bastions on either side which rest on cannon balls.[1] On the south front (which was denuded of its formal garden when Capability Brown 'landscaped' the park in 1764) the architects have attempted to articulate the length by a change of surface texture, moving from rusticated to smooth masonry and then to an engaged and finally to a free-standing order. Here, as elsewhere, the parts are not very happily combined; the elements of surprise or of gradual movement from one unit to the next are not entirely controlled. But in spite of the sneers of the later eighteenth century,[2] Blenheim, with all its faults, fulfils its intention; for it is heroic architecture.

Inside, the house is far more grand though perhaps less attractive than Castle Howard. In the Great Hall Vanbrugh experiments for the first time with an interior effect he was to use again at Seaton Delaval (Pl. 91 b) and Grimsthorpe, achieved by a contrast between heavy and simple forms of unadorned stone, foiled by concentrated areas of fine decoration. Here the decoration is strictly architectural, supplied by the superb capitals and cornice mouldings carved by Gibbons and his assistants. Nowhere in Blenheim does Gibbons use the free, informal decoration usually associated with his name, a clear proof, if proof were needed, that Vanbrugh's remarkable imaginative power controlled the entire undertaking.[3] Much, if not all, of the actual detail was drawn by Hawksmoor; he was closely associated with Vanbrugh from the first, shared his disgrace in 1716, but was reinstated by the duchess after the duke's

[1] This treatment of a gate is perhaps derived from the gates of Paris, the Porte St. Denis or the Porte St. Antoine, though the nearest counterpart is the Porte de Paris at Lille by Simon Vollant. The lions' heads, wreaths, and laurel ropes were added by Sir William Chambers in 1773.

[2] Horace Walpole regarded it as 'execrable within, without, and almost all round'. 'Visits to Country Seats', *Walpole Soc.* xvi (1928), 26. Both Sir Joshua Reynolds (*xiiith Discourse*, 1786) and Robert Adam, *Works*, Introduction to pt. i (1773), 2, Note A, however, admired Vanbrugh, praising his originality of invention, his sense of movement and the poetry of his compositions.

[3] For the painted decoration, see above, p. 305.

death in 1722, and certainly superintended the decoration of the library, a most impressive room in which the severe Doric order is counterbalanced by rich plaster decoration.

In creating his palace which was to be so much more than a private house Vanbrugh had, inevitably, turned his thoughts to those other monuments of military power visible in England, medieval castles, and perhaps also to those great houses of the Elizabethan age like Wollaton which in their form (though not in their detail) are linked with them. He was compelled, as Dryden was, to use classical forms, but like Dryden he had a shrewd suspicion that the English genius best expressed itself when the rules were disregarded.[1] At Blenheim the romantic, castle-like quality is implied rather than directly stated, but during the alterations to Kimbolton which he began for the earl of Manchester in 1707 he wrote:

As to the outside, I thought it absolutely best, to give it something of the castle air, tho' at the same time to make it regular . . . I'm sure this will make a very noble and masculine show; and is of as Warrantable a kind of building as any.

And in a slightly later letter:

I lik'd mighty well what was done, And Coleman[2] own'd he began to discover a gusto in it, that he had no notion of before. I shall be much deceived if people don't see a manly beauty in it when tis up, that they did not conceive could be produced out of such rough materials; but tis certainly the Figure and Proportions that makes the most pleasing Fabrick, and not the delicacy of the ornaments.[3]

This is not the nostalgic romanticism of the eighteenth and nineteenth-century Gothic revivals, but a genuine and penetrating admiration for medieval building. It finds expression again and again in Vanbrugh's architecture: in the Belvedere built for the

---

[1] Cf. Dryden's attempts to defend and explain the character of Shakespeare in his *Essays in Dramatic Criticism.*

[2] Coleman was a local architect, who had previously been asked to provide plans. It is difficult to be certain whether 'gusto' should be read as 'taste', or in the modern sense of enjoyment. It was occasionally used in the latter sense in Vanbrugh's day, e.g. by Pepys and Congreve, but more usually in the former.

[3] *Works of Sir John Vanbrugh*, Nonesuch ed., IV (1928), pp. 14, 15. For illustrations of Kimbolton, see H. A. Tipping and C. Hussey, op. cit. 113–19.

duke of Newcastle in the gardens at Claremont,[1] in the chimneys which imitate castellations and the machicolations of the brew-house at King's Weston;[2] in the fantastic archway to the demesne at Castle Howard,[3] which though it employs classical forms treats them with a medieval ruggedness; and above all in the house which he built for himself at Blackheath, and named 'Vanbrugh Castle'.[4] In the last the plan, as well as the elevation with its round machico-lated towers, is medieval, for it is simply a collection of rooms grouped together haphazard, with no attempt at symmetry.

Though, however, in one way Vanbrugh's approach to medieval architecture is very far removed from that of the later eighteenth century, in another he is the herald of the 'Picturesque' movement. One of the most tremendous rows with the duchess of Marl-borough was over the preservation of the old Manor of Wood-stock, which could be seen from the north front of Blenheim. The duchess, who regarded it as a squalid ruin, wished it removed, but Vanbrugh pressed hard for its retention, suggesting that the en-closure round it should be set with trees 'so that all the building left might appear in two risings amongst them, which would make one of the most agreeable objects that the best of landskip painters can invent'. It is only a short step from here to the idea that a gentleman's park should look like a landscape by Claude Lorrain. At Blenheim Vanbrugh had the gardens laid out in the formal French manner; but at Castle Howard, at the end of his life, he designed the mown way, bordered by statues and sweeping in a great arc up to the temple, a landscape effect on a big scale.

In his later houses, in which Hawksmoor was not concerned, his planning becomes more compact, and there is an increased reliance on stone itself and on types of ornament which emphasize its inherent quality. The surface ornament of Castle Howard completely disappears; instead there is an exploitation of the theme of contrasting surfaces which appeared on the south front of Blen-heim. Eastbury, of which practically nothing now remains, was

[1] For the Belvedere, see ibid. 169.
[2] Ibid. 141–56. For an alternative classical derivation from Perrault's *Vitruvius*, see Summerson, 172.   [3] H. A. Tipping and C. Hussey, op. cit. 51.
[4] Ibid. 187–92; L. Whistler, *The Imagination of Vanbrugh* (1954), 202.

the first building in the new manner;[1] its highest expression is Seaton Delaval (Pls. 91 *b*, 92 *b*). This was built between 1718 and 1728 on the coast of Northumberland which Vanbrugh loved far more than 'the tame sneaking south'.[2] It was gutted in 1822, but the outside was little damaged, and is still among the most impressive buildings in England. It stands at the back of a deep court, along the sides of which run loggias of round headed arches set on heavily rusticated piers. The house, raised on a solid base, is reached by a great flight of steps, on either side of which are four enormous banded columns, set closely together. Beyond them, a smooth wall runs to octagonal angle towers, while on the side fronts are further towers very heavily rusticated, which contained stair-cases, a strongly medieval theme. On the garden front the octagonal towers are repeated, but between them, surprisingly, is a fine Ionic portico, and the windows on this side are more Palladian in char-acter. By now, of course, the new Burlingtonian school was begin-ning to make itself felt. It is a comparatively small house, but for grandeur it is unsurpassed, and it shows Vanbrugh after twenty years of experience, in complete control of his art and able to use classical and medieval motives and to weld them together, and above all able to extract the maximum effect from the durability of his materials. He could not guess that their strength would be tested by fire, and that the house would stand a shell, but not a ruin, buffeted by the winds and infinitely grand in contrast to the villas that are creeping towards it. Its deserted state adds the final touch to its strange colossal quality, and links it fortuitously to the medieval castles Vanbrugh so much admired.

His last work, Grimsthorpe, has not the savage character of Seaton Delaval. It is, moreover, not an entirely new creation but the rebuilding of one range of an Elizabethan house set round a quadrangle.[3] This one wing, however, which forms the entrance

---

[1] Begun about 1718 for George Dodington and destroyed about 1775. A preli-minary design for Eastbury is probably shown in *Vitruvius Britannicus*, ii. 52–55, called 'A New Design for a person of quality, 1716'. For the evolution of the design see L. Whistler, op. cit. 156 f. and Pls. 61–81.

[2] Letter to Brigadier Watkins from York, 26 August 1721 (*Works of Sir John Vanbrugh*, Nonesuch ed., iv (1928), 137).

[3] *Vitruvius Britannicus*, iii. 11–14; H. A. Tipping and C. Hussey, op. cit. 305–22.

front to the house, is very grand. It contains a single great room, with a staircase screened by arcades at either end. The exterior emphasizes the plan, for the centre is treated as a single unit, framed (at the ends of the hall) by the architect's favourite banded columns. The two angle towers, however, reveal the extent of his concessions to the new Palladianism for they show a return to a wall and window treatment not far removed from that of Coleshill (except in the basement) while on their main face the chief feature of the design is a Venetian window.

Vanbrugh is indeed a strange phenomenon. He is an artist of real imaginative power who forces classical forms into romantic expression. The greatest baroque architect, Bernini, was able to create a new romantic architecture which could be understood and followed by his contemporaries because he had an innate understanding of classical architecture, and the disciplined training of an Italian artist. Vanbrugh had neither. He was fighting always against the precepts of the architectural grammars[1] which were too rigid for his exuberant fancy. It is not fair to suggest that he regarded architecture as so much theatrical scenery—his own statements concerning proportion in his letter about Kimbolton are enough to refute that—but in England there were no gigantic Roman ruins to stimulate his sense of display. He turned therefore to the middle ages, and tried to re-create their enduring strength. But in the age in which he lived strength alone was not enough; it must be expressed in the language of the Ancients. Moreover, Vanbrugh was working for that peculiar society, the Whig aristocracy, whose mission to govern England in their own way he fully approved. He created for them a fitting architecture, often strange and uncouth, entirely personal but an enduring monument to his own original mind, and to the greatness of the party which was gathering its strength to dominate England for half a century.

Nicholas Hawksmoor during his long experience in Wren's office had begun to show signs of a personal style, marked by a

---

[1] He certainly owned and used a Palladio, since in 1710 he wrote to ask if he had left it 'in Mr. Strong's shed' at Blenheim. Hawksmoor had a wide knowledge of architectural books. (See G. Webb, 'Letters and Drawings of N. Hawksmoor...', *Walpole Soc.* xix (1931), 111; K. Downes, 'Hawksmoor's Sale Catalogue', *Burl. Mag.* xcv (1953), 332.)

sense of mass and an abrupt movement from part to part, in the early 1690's, when he designed the Writing School at Christ's Hospital.[1] He may have built the Library of the Queen's College, Oxford (1693–6),[2] and was perhaps concerned with the Whitehall schemes of 1698 which, in their feeling for mass though not in their richness of surface, suggest his outlook. Shortly afterwards he began his collaboration with Vanbrugh and it is reasonable to conclude that the latter's exuberant imagination provided the stimulus for the development of Hawksmoor's later, independent style. Most of his work falls after 1715, and so cannot be treated in detail, but some discussion of it is necessary since it is an important phase of English baroque.

The first building by Hawksmoor in the new manner is Easton Neston in Northamptonshire, the exterior of which was apparently finished by 1702.[3] A wooden model[4] shows a two-storey design, with a small projecting centrepiece of superimposed coupled columns. In the house itself, however, the scale has changed, for it is treated like Castle Howard with giant pilasters, the centre on both fronts being marked by giant columns.[5] The general effect is extremely fine, owing mainly to the admirable design and crisp cutting of the architectural details, for there is practically no sculptured ornament. The mouldings and window-cases are lighter and more orthodox than in most of Hawksmoor's later work, and give a considerable air of refinement, which reappears inside in the treatment of the staircase and gallery. In planning, too, the house is very accomplished.

This is Hawksmoor's only independent house; the rest of his work falls into two main groups—London churches and commissions at Oxford.

[1] Summerson, 166 and Pl. 99 A.

[2] R.C.H.M., *City of Oxford* (1939), 110 and Pl. 175.

[3] This date is on the frieze of the garden front and also on rain-water heads. It is impossible to say if the design ante-dates Castle Howard. The interior was not finished in 1731. G. F. Webb, 'Letters . . . of N. Hawksmoor . . .', *Walpole Soc.*, xix (1931), 126. See also H. A. Tipping and C. Hussey, op. cit. 119–40. For Wren's earlier connexion with the site see M. D. Whinney, *Arch. Journ.* cx (1953), 209.

[4] Preserved in the house.

[5] *Vitruvius Britannicus*, i (1715), Pls. 98–100, shows a dramatic build-up to a central lantern, making the resemblance to Castle Howard even more marked.

London had greatly increased in area since the Great Fire of 1666. New suburbs had grown up on the west and north, as well as south of the Thames. At the time of the Fire, the poorer people had 'squatted' beyond the walls at the east, and had stayed there in the district round the East India Dock. These districts had no churches. In 1711, shortly after the Tories came into power, an Act was passed for the erection of fifty new churches;[1] Commissioners, who included Sir Christopher Wren,[2] were appointed, and Hawksmoor and William Dickinson (who was Wren's Deputy Surveyor at Westminster Abbey, and superintended the building of the west towers) were made Surveyors. Dickinson resigned two years later, and was replaced by James Gibbs, who was himself succeeded by John James in 1715. He and Hawksmoor were to act together until the commission ended in 1733. By then sixteen churches had been built.[3]

It is inevitable, and very revealing both historically and stylistically, that comparisons should be drawn between the Commissioners' churches and those of Wren. In his memorandum Wren had advocated economy, recalling that in his own works the exteriors had been kept as plain as possible, except for expenditure on the steeples. He did, however, suggest that for an important site the addition of a portico might be advisable. The Queen and the Tory party were, however, in no mood to listen to such practical advice. These churches were to mark the triumph of the Church party over the Whigs, and were to be worthy of the occasion. A much more lavish policy was therefore adopted. Most of the new churches were to be placed on island sites, whereas Wren's churches are usually set back, with only a small street-frontage, generally used for a tower. All aspects were consequently of importance; the building must be entirely of stone, and usually set on a wide stone base. Attention was indeed concentrated mainly on the exteriors; generally speaking the interior plaster-work and fittings

[1] See Howard Colvin, 'Fifty New Churches', *Archit. Review*, cxvii (1950), 189–95.

[2] It was on this occasion that Wren produced his memorandum on church building (*Wren Soc.* ix. 15). See above, p. 154. For Vanbrugh's more extravagant advice, see L. Whistler, *The Imagination of Vanbrugh* (1954), 250.

[3] Only the churches by Hawksmoor and Archer (who was never a Surveyor) will be discussed in this volume.

are far less sumptuous than in Wren's churches, but it must be remembered that the latter had often been the gift of individual City Companies.

By 1712 Hawksmoor's twelve years' association with Vanbrugh had developed in him a new conception of stone architecture, which he was now to exploit to the full. He seeks always to give a sense of mass and monumentality. His methods, however, are different from those of Vanbrugh. He seldom uses the weapon of sheer size, or of very heavy rustication. Instead he starts from a smooth wall surface, and cuts back in successive layers, thus achieving the effect of immense thickness of masonry. A simple flat band of stonework beneath his windows, massive keystones or unmoulded labels jutting out from the wall surface are all the decoration he permits. His edges are sharp and hard. It is an austere and sombre architecture handled with great accomplishment, and nowhere seen to better advantage than in the side elevation of St. Alphege, Greenwich (Pl. 94 a).[1]

The same motive of cutting back and building out in flat planes is used with great effect in his towers. At Christchurch, Spitalfields, this is combined with a play on round headed and rectangular openings, the whole being topped by a tall, obelisk-like spire. St. Anne, Limehouse (Pl. 87 b), and St. George-in-the-East have octagonal lanterns above the towers, with buttresses set round the pierced core. It is possible that these are a deliberate reminiscence of the medieval lanterns of the Eastern Counties,[2] though it seems on the whole more likely that Hawksmoor is developing, in a highly personal way, the type of lantern used by Wren at, for instance, St. Michael, Paternoster Royal (Pl. 39 b). He flattens Wren's small columns into buttresses and so obtains the sharp edges and black shadows that he loved. St. George, Bloomsbury, has the strangest of all his steeples and reveals most clearly his passion for antiquity, for it is composed of a tall pyramid of steps in imitation of the Mausoleum at Halicarnassus.[3] This church has

[1] Steeple by John James.

[2] e.g. at Boston, Lincolnshire.

[3] It bears a statue of George II, but the lion and unicorn rampant on the steps were removed in the nineteenth century. The Mausoleum had a great fascination for seven-

also a most noble Corinthian portico, the fruit perhaps of the plates of Baalbek which Hawksmoor had drawn for Henry Maundrell's *Journey from Aleppo* (published in 1703) based on the descriptions and on plates in the *Grand Marot*.

In the monumentality of his exteriors, Hawksmoor owes little to the example of Wren: in his planning and his interiors, in spite of the difference in scale, he derives a good deal more. He was clearly far more interested in centrally planned churches than in those with a clear west-to-east axis, but he does not always succeed in integrating his plan, his interior elevation, and his roof treatment as logically as Wren. Indeed, there is sometimes a strange lack of logic, a refusal to follow up and complete an effect which in a less experienced architect might be put down to incompetence, but in Hawksmoor must be deliberate. Wren in his centrally planned churches always set the altar against a straight eastern wall, and so avoided as far as possible a conflicting west-to-east axis; Hawksmoor always placed his altar in an apse. This increased emphasis on the altar may have been pleasing to the High Church party, but it changes materially the interior effect of the building. Not only is the west-east axis strengthened, but the arch leading to the apse becomes a dominant feature in the design. Hawksmoor seldom makes this arch semicircular. Instead he chooses a flat arch (an illogical and unstructural form) which gives a sense of strain and often of conflict with the round-headed window in the apse itself. This love of the flat arch was exploited to the full in St. George-in-the-East (Pl. 95 *b*), perhaps his finest interior, but now, alas, destroyed. The form of the church, with flat ceilings in the corners, and a cross vault supported by barrels in the centre, is the type Wren had used in Sts. Anne and Agnes (Pl. 36 *b*) or St. Martin, Ludgate. The effect, however, is totally different. Wren's supporting columns are slender, set on high bases: Hawksmoor uses an immense Doric order with a massive entablature in which the architrave is weighed down by the frieze. The wide flat arch dominated the line of the vaults, the edges of the barrels being emphasized by a band of heavy coffering. The church had a strange,

teenth-century architects, and Wren among others attempted a reconstruction (see *Parentalia*, 367).

brooding quality which made Vanbrugh's architecture seem gay and enthusiastic in comparison. Something of the same oppressive grandeur appears in St. Mary, Woolnoth.

St. George, Bloomsbury (Pl. 95 a), though it is much less severe, has also an element of disquiet. The oblong plan is reduced to a square by a double screen of columns on the north and south, supporting Hawksmoor's favourite wide flat arch. The central square, higher than the rest, is lit from above by clerestory windows; the rest of the church is dark, and a worshipper entering on the south side behind the columns would have had no clear direction to the altar, set in a small apse to the east.[1] In Christchurch, Spitalfields, the largest and last of Hawksmoor's churches, the long axis is more evident, though some attempt is made to negate it, for screens are set at the west of the nave, and in front of the apse, dividing the church into three sections, a division which is not echoed in the design of the roof. The covering of the aisles with barrel vaults running inwards is borrowed from Wren (e.g. from St. James, Piccadilly) but the motive is changed, the bays are more sharply separated, and by using a flat ceiling instead of a vault to the nave, the architect establishes an abrupt instead of an easy flowing space composition.[2] It is in these four later churches[3] that Hawksmoor really evolves his personal style.

This style is one of the most original creations of English architecture. In it a man of great knowledge and experience turns from the easy, straightforward manner in which he had been trained, and chooses elements of tension and surprise. His aim, and his achievement, is an architecture both more massive and more sombre than that of his master. A greater artist than Hawksmoor, Michelangelo, had chosen the same elements, and had created the Mannerist style, a style which is the perfect expression of the

[1] The altar was moved to its present position on the north in 1871, when the altarpiece, said to have come from Bedford House, was inserted (*Notes and Queries*, ser. 9, vol. v (1900), 332).

[2] There were originally two galleries, above each aisle. These now only remain at the west end. The double gallery must have made the church much darker, and the general effect more crowded and oppressive.

[3] The two earlier churches, St. Alphege, Greenwich, and St. Anne, Limehouse (interior reconstructed), are closer to Wren, but both use the flat arch.

disquiet of his age, when the rational clarity of Bramante and Raphael could no longer reflect the turmoil of men's thoughts. Hawksmoor's position is different. He was working in an age of confidence, not of insecurity. His normal development would have been towards a fuller expression of the baroque trend of the turn of the century. His interest in mass, in space-composition, and in three-dimensional effects[1] suggests that this was a path he could have followed. But the nature of his patronage and the quality of his craftsmen made this impossible. The Anglican Church could not have accepted full baroque architecture, and Hawksmoor (who had no first-hand knowledge of continental baroque) could not temper it to meet English requirements.[2] Hawksmoor was therefore denied the release of a decorative dramatic style; he was forced to rely on the resources of stone alone. These he strained to the uttermost, so that the tension is clearly evident. In his desire to evolve a more emotional style he turns, on occasions, to Gothic. He cannot, however, allow himself the full release that Vanbrugh finds in his castle style, and his sound knowledge of the source books and his deep admiration for Antiquity make it more difficult for him to abandon formulae approved by the High Renaissance. He rises to great heights: his work is both grand and original, but it is an expression rather of his own personality than of his age, for in its sombreness it reflects the bitterness of a mind constantly disappointed of high office.

His work at Oxford is less distinguished than his churches, but he does not always appear to have had a free hand. Above all, he was unable to carry out, either here or at Cambridge, his town planning schemes. Though these are far less accomplished, in their handling of disparate elements, than Wren's 1698 Whitehall project, that for Oxford is of especial interest in its reference to Antiquity, for its 'Great Piazza' was conceived as a Roman forum.[3] In individual colleges too, his antique learning hardly got beyond

[1] e.g. in his steeples.

[2] Gibbs, who was trained in Rome, produced a successful modified form of baroque space-composition in St. Martin's-in-the-Fields.

[3] For this and for its connexion with the Radcliffe Camera, ultimately built by Gibbs, but developed from designs by Hawksmoor, see S. Lang, 'By Hawksmoor out of Gibbs', *Archit. Review*, cv (1949), 173.

the drawing board. At the Queen's College, where he was not tied by medieval buildings, he devised a number of schemes, some of which show the chapel as a peripteral temple, while in another it has an oval form.[1] The executed work falls back on the pattern, used by Wren at Chelsea Hospital, of a hall and chapel joined by a vestibule with a portico and a cupola.[2] This was a novelty for Oxford, but it is less striking (and also probably less expensive) than the abortive schemes. For Worcester College there is a series of most interesting drawings[3] on which the sources of various features are noted: 'the antiquity at Bordeaux' shown in Perrault's *Vitruvius*, 'the Arc de Xaintes' (Saintes) of which there is an engraving in Blondel's *Cours d'Architecture* of 1683 and the 'Tower of Andromachus at Athens' (i.e. the Tower of the Winds) for which Hawksmoor used either Vitruvius's description or the engraving in George Wheler and Dr. Spon's *Journey into Greece*.[4]

At All Souls, which has a complicated building history,[5] Hawksmoor, though at one time advocating a classical design, finally pressed for the retention of the fifteenth-century Front Quadrangle, saying 'whatever is good in its kind should be preserved in respect to antiquity. . . .' and sent with his letter drawings for the new North Quadrangle in which the style of the Gothic chapel should be followed. This is a different approach to non-classical architecture from Vanbrugh's sense of the picturesque quality of the old Manor of Woodstock[6] and even further from the mid-eighteenth-century conception of Gothic as a purely emotional style.[7] Hawksmoor's Gothic centrepiece with the two towers, which are one of the landmarks of Oxford, is a valiant attempt to

[1] I have to thank Mr. Kerry Downes, who is preparing a thesis on Hawksmoor's drawings, for the loan of photographs of these, which are at All Souls.

[2] R.C.H.M., *City of Oxford* (1939), 96–100, Pls. 169, 170, 172, 174.

[3] I was first made aware of these drawings and their sources by the courtesy of Mr. G. D. Boddington, who allowed me to read his unpublished thesis, *The College Work of Nicholas Hawksmoor in Oxford & Cambridge* (School of Architecture, Cambridge, 1947). They have since been discussed by Summerson, 194.

[4] English edition, 1682.

[5] See Summerson, 193; *V.C.H. Oxfordshire*, iii (1954), 190–2.

[6] See above, p. 340.

[7] 'One must have taste to be sensible of the beauties of Grecian Architecture, one wants only passions to feel Gothic' (H. Walpole, *Anecdotes*, ed. Dallaway, i. 119).

build in an alien style (Pl. 94 b). Compared with medieval architecture, the effect is curiously thin and papery, mainly because
Hawksmoor has not realized how much Gothic owes to the
quality and richness of its mouldings. The upper parts of the towers,
however, with their broken silhouettes and their use of buttresses
and pinnacles in the lanterns, are far more successful than the
façades below them, for here Hawksmoor was dealing with
problems he understood. His hall is Gothic outside, and in the
interior he has perhaps adapted a medieval idea of the relation of a
screen to a ribbed vault springing from corbels. But he has expressed the idea in baroque terms. His vaulted ceiling uses his
favourite flat arch (but it is no longer oppressive as in his London
churches) and his management of the play of curves in the pockets
cutting into the vault above the windows, the circle patterns
traced on the crown, and the curved triangles at the ends, is beyond
praise. And the Ionic screen with scrolls and urns above it, acts as a
magnificent *repoussoir* to the lines of the vault.

It is perhaps in his designs for the Universities, and in the great
circular Mausoleum at Castle Howard (and his letters about it)
that Hawksmoor reveals most clearly the truth of his obituary
notice quoted by Vertue:[1]

He was perfectly skilled in the history of Architecture and could give
an exact account of all famous buildings, both antient and modern in
every part of the world, to which his excellent memory, which never
failed him to the very last, greatly contributed. Nor was Architecture
the only Science he was master of, he was bred a scholar, and knew well
the learned as the modern tongues—he was a very skillful mathematician, geographer and geometrician, and in drawing, which he
practized to the last, tho' greatly afflicted with the Chiraga (gout), few
excelled him.

With his master, Wren, he represents in English art, and to the
highest degree, the scientific thought of the Royal Society. He lived
till 1736 to see the world of letters, and to some extent the arts,
changed by the new Platonic aesthetics of Shaftesbury,[2] and by Lord
Burlington's 'Man of Taste', whose approach to Antiquity was
strangely doctrinaire. He may well have felt he had outlived his age.

[1] Vertue, iii. 78.   [2] See above, p. 13.

Two other architects contributed to English baroque church architecture. Henry Aldrich, Dean of Christ Church (1647–1710), who designed All Saints' Church, Oxford,[1] had looked at Wren's churches and at the designs for Blenheim, and the result is a curious collection of ill-adjusted parts. Thomas Archer[2] only just fails to achieve greatness. St. Philip, Birmingham (now the cathedral) (Pl. 87 a), built between 1709 and 1725, has a splendid tower, made up of convex stages, but in the interior, though the components are massive, there is a curious lack of monumentality. His two London churches, St. Paul, Deptford (1712–1730), and St. John, Westminster (1713–1728), are in exterior design worthy of comparison with Hawksmoor. In the former, the play of curves in the portico and steeple is repeated in the interior by circular vestries and staircase towers cutting off the corners of the main rectangle. The baroque conception is not, however, carried through to the end, for the plan cries out for a central dome instead of the almost flat ceiling.[3] The Westminster church, with its fantastic towers and porticoes, is arresting if not entirely successful in its grouping, but again the interior disposition would seem to have been unimpressive.[4] In all his churches Archer borrows details freely from Borromini, from sixteenth-century Roman Mannerists of the school of Michelangelo, and sometimes from Hawksmoor, but he never gives them the personal stamp achieved by his greater contemporary.

English baroque architecture is, as a whole, essentially a compromise style. Indeed, some critics have held that there is no English baroque, but merely an extension of the Italianism of Jones and Webb. The space-composition, the dome and west towers of St. Paul's, the steeples of Wren and still more those of Hawksmoor, the interiors of St. George-in-the-East and St. George, Bloomsbury, and the great houses of Vanbrugh cannot, however, be explained in those terms. They all have a sense of display, which is lacking in early seventeenth-century architecture derived from the

---

[1] R.C.H.M., *City of Oxford* (1939), 125 and Pls. 198, 200.
[2] See above, p. 223.   [3] For the plan, see Summerson, 188.
[4] It was gutted and reconstructed inside in 1744–5, when the interior columns were removed, and burnt again in 1941.

High Renaissance. On the other hand, compared with the baroque of Rome, of Austria, or of France, these buildings, distinguished though they are, lack the final integration and control of every part which gives to the greatest baroque designs a complete unity of expression. The reasons are complex, and for the most part beyond the architects' control. The lack of a classical tradition in England has already been discussed; the causes of this, which are largely to be found in the reign of Henry VIII, lie outside the scope of this volume. Owing to the absence of an assimilated national style, English seventeenth-century architects were at the mercy of fashion, Italian, French, or Dutch, imported in pattern books or by patrons who had visited the Continent, and they had too little time to digest it completely and make it their own. That they achieved so much in the forty years between 1675 and 1715 is remarkable, for in that time they educated not only themselves but their craftsmen (though they relied to some extent on foreigners) and their patrons.

This process, however, was only partial. The three greatest architects of the style, Wren, Hawksmoor, and Vanbrugh, had none of them seen baroque architecture at its most splendid, and even if they had, it is not certain that they would, wholeheartedly, have admired it. For an appeal to the senses is the very essence of the style, and this is alien to the English temperament. Many Englishmen who would have detested the general manifestations of the Puritan spirit would have found themselves at one with it in its suspicion of the pleasures of the eye. Even Sir Thomas More had held that churches should be dark, so that men's thoughts should not be distracted from their devotions, and the stimulus of art as an aid to worship finds no place in *Utopia*. This is an abiding English characteristic acting as a brake on artist and patron alike. Charles II, who was partly a Medici and looked it, was perhaps free from this inhibition, and so at Windsor created one of the major monuments of English baroque. William III, on the other hand, who gave Wren some of his greatest opportunities, was a Dutch Calvinist and so could provide no counterpoise to English reticence. Thus when Vanbrugh at Blenheim was called upon to express national sentiment in terms of architecture he was unable to use the idiom of a Bernini, a Fischer von Erlach, or even of a Jules Hardouin Mansart, in which an architecture fundamentally classical was used in a sensuous form. He was compelled, in order to achieve his heroic architecture, to combine anti-classical with classical forms, and Hawksmoor, as already suggested, found a different though equally anti-classical solution in his church interiors. The final effect differs from the anti-classical architecture of the Italian Mannerists in that it is romantic. Again, however, the romanticism is of a different kind from the continental brand. The quarrel between classics and romantics or between Poussinistes and Rubénistes, which was taking place at this time in France, was basically a quarrel between two different uses of classical art, for on the Continent romantic art, whether it be that of Giorgione, of Rubens, or of Delacroix, includes always a restatement of the classical. In England, romantic art is more complex and less easy to define, for its essence lies in a free play of the imagination, untrammelled by rules. It may include a nostalgia for the ancient world, as in the case of Hawksmoor or of Turner in his paintings of Carthage and Rome, or for the middle ages, like that of Vanbrugh and William Blake. But at every point it creates something new and original, full of shades of half-stated and sometimes half-understood meaning, which it is perilous to interpret in continental terms. Shakespeare's 'cloud-capp'd towers and gorgeous palaces' are akin to Vanbrugh's, and neither the greater nor the lesser artist conforms to rules. It is the measure of Wren's true stature that, starting from the rational basis of science, he is able to add a poetic sensibility to his architecture, and so to create the singing rhythms of the dome of St. Paul's.

BIBLIOGRAPHY

THE following selective bibliography lists the sources, contemporary and modern, which we have found most useful in the preparation of this book. We have limited it to works of importance which generally contain materials and references for more detailed study. Full references to more specialized sources will be found in our text.

For architecture the most important contemporary sources are the drawings of Inigo Jones and John Webb (not fully published, and divided between the Chatsworth and Worcester College, Oxford, collections and the Burlington–Devonshire collection at the Royal Institute of British Architects) and those of Wren and his associates at the Office of Works, which may be studied in the twenty volumes of the *Wren Society*. To these should be added Colen Campbell's *Vitruvius Britannicus* (3 vols., 1715–25), a major source for seventeenth-century houses. Of recent books, John Summerson's *Architecture in Britain 1530–1830* (1953), 2nd ed. (1955) supersedes all earlier general histories, and Howard Colvin's *Dictionary of British Architects 1660–1830* is indispensable for individual architects. The architectural sections in F. Saxl and R. Wittkower, *English Art and the Mediterranean* (1948) can be used with profit for foreign sources, while H. A. Tipping and C. Hussey, *English Homes* (especially III. ii; IV. i and ii) are unrivalled for plates, and contain valuable information.

The series published by the Royal Commission on Historical Monuments and the Victoria County History were thought to be too widely known to need special reference; those volumes of the London County Council's *Survey of London* which are particularly relevant are listed, but the others should not be neglected.

No modern survey of the sculpture of the period exists, but R. Gunnis, *Dictionary of British Sculptors 1660–1830* (1953) contains much information for the years it covers, and Mrs. Esdaile's pioneer work, *English Monumental Sculpture since the Renaissance* (1927) and her pamphlet, *Monuments in English Churches* (1937), can still be used with profit.

The only recent account of painting in England is Professor Ellis Waterhouse's *Painting in Britain 1530–1790* (1953). It replaces the older standard book, C. H. Collins Baker's monumental *Lely and the Stuart Portrait Painters* (1912), though that remains a stimulating work. The Walpole Society published, in the great series of George Vertue's *Notebooks* (1930–47), a major source for the arts in England in the Stuart and early Hanoverian periods. Horace Walpole's *Anecdotes of Painting in England* (1762–71) was largely based on Vertue's material. The only modern accounts of individual painters which are of value are Gustav Glück's *Van Dyck* (Klassiker der

Kunst, 1931), R. B. Beckett's *Lely* (1951) and the catalogue of the exhibition at the Tate Gallery (1951) of the work of William Dobson.

Much material is to be found in periodicals, notably in the *Burlington Magazine, Country Life,* and in the volumes of the *Walpole Society.* The literature published since 1934 is listed in the *Annual Bibliography of British Art* published by the Courtauld Institute. A convenient bibliography of seventeenth-century printed and manuscript material on painting will be found in H. V. S. and M. S. Ogden's *Bibliography (Art Bull.,* N.Y., xxix (1947), 196–201). References will be found in our text to the copious material which only exists in manuscript, but the following are particularly important:

BRITISH MUSEUM

Richard Symonds, Notebooks, Harl. MSS. 942, 943, 991, 1278, Add. 17919, Egerton 1635, 1636.
Account Book &c. of Sir Peter Lely's Executors, MS. 16174.
Roger North's List of his Pictures &c., MS. 32504.
Van der Doort's catalogue of the Chair Room at Whitehall, Add. MS. 10122.
Inventory of James II's pictures (1687), Harl. MS. 1890.
Inventories of William III's pictures, Harl. MSS. 7025, 5150.

BODLEIAN LIBRARY

Richard Symonds's Notebook, Rawl. MS. D. 121.
Van der Doort's Inventories of Charles I's collections, Ashmole MSS. 1513–14.

Manuscripts in the archives at Alnwick, Arbury (now in the County Record Office, Warwick), Boughton, Castle Howard, Hatfield, Lamport, Melbourne Hall and Rousham; in the possession of the Painter-Stainers' Company (especially *The Booke of Orders and Constitutions*), deposited in the Guildhall Library; and in the office of the Surveyor of the Queen's Pictures (inventories of the royal collection Charles I–Anne).

The following are the principal continental architectural treatises which were available to English architects in the Stuart period:

FOREIGN ARCHITECTURAL TREATISES

ALBERTI, L. B. *De re aedificatoria* (Florence, 1550).
DU CERCEAU, J. A. *Les plus excellents bastiments de France . . .* (Paris, 1576–9). Facsimile reprint, Paris, 1868.
FALDA, G. B. *Il nuovo teatro delle fabriche, et edificii . . . di Roma . . .* (Published by G. J. Rossi, Rome, 1665).
FONTANA, C. *Il tempio vaticano e sue origine . . .* (Rome, 1694).
FRÉART, R. *A parallel of the antient architecture with the modern.* John Evelyn translation, 1664.

LE MUET, P. *Manière de bien bastir pour toutes sortes de personnes* (1st ed., Paris 1623. 2nd enlarged ed., Paris, 1647).

LE PAUTRE, A. *Les Œuvres d'Architecture* (Paris, 1652).

MAROT, J. *L'Architecture françoise* (Paris, c. 1670). The 'Grand' Marot. Enlarged edition as vol. 4 of Mariette's *Architecture française.*

MAROT, J. *Recueil des plans, profils et élévations de plusieurs palais, chasteaux, églises, sépultures, grotes et hostels bâtis dans Paris* (Paris, c. 1660–70). The 'Petit' Marot.

PALLADIO, A. *I Quattro Libri dell'Architettura* (Venice, 1570).

ROSSI, DOMENICO DE. *Studio d'architettura civile . . . di Roma . . .* (Rome, 1702).

RUBENS, P. P. *Palazzi di Genova* (Antwerp, 1622).

SANDRART, J. VON. *Insignium Romae Templorum Prospectus.* n.d.

SCAMOZZI, V. *Dell' Idea dell'Architettura Universale* (Venice, 1615).

SERLIO, S. *Tutte l'opere d'architettura et prospetiva* (Venice, 1584). R. Peake's English edition, 1611.

VIGNOLA. *La Regola delli Cinque Ordini d'Architettura* (Venice, 1562).

VINGBOONS, P. *Afbeeldsels der voornamste Gebouwen* (Amsterdam, vol. 1, 1648; vol. 2, 1674).

VITRUVIUS. The most important editions were:

>BARBARO, D. *Dieci libri dell'architettura di M. Vitruvio . . .* (Venice, 1567).
>PERRAULT, CLAUDE. *Les Dix Livres d'architecture . . . traduits . . . en François, avec des notes et des figures . . .* (Paris, 1684).

A great deal of information on the arts is to be found in contemporary historical sources. The diaries, correspondence, and miscellaneous writings of John Evelyn, Samuel Pepys, and the Huygens family are in a class by themselves, but the *Calendars of State Papers* (Domestic and Venetian series), the *Calendar of Treasury Books* and the volumes of the Historical Manuscripts Commission are rich in references to the arts. For exploration in such sources the reader is referred to G. Davies's *Bibliography of British History, Stuart Period* (1934), and the bibliographies in the same author's *Early Stuarts* (1937), G. N. Clark's *Later Stuarts* (1934) and *English Historical Documents 1660–1714* (ed. A. Browning, 1953).

Three standard sources of reference are Thieme-Becker, *Allgemeines Lexikon der bildenden Künstler* (1907–47), the *Dictionary of National Biography*, and the *Complete Peerage* (1910—, incomplete).

Unless otherwise stated the place of publication is London.

CONTEMPORARY SOURCES

AUBREY, J. *Brief Lives* (1669–96), ed. A. Clark, 3 vols. (1898).

BELLORI, G. P. *Le Vite de' Pittori, Scultori et Architetti Moderni* (Rome, 1672).

BUCKERIDGE, B. *An Essay towards an English School*, with English edition (1706 and later) of DE PILES (q.v.).

CAMPBELL, C. *Vitruvius Britannicus*, 3 vols., 1715–25.

CLARENDON, EARL OF. *History of the Rebellion*, ed. W. Macray, 6 vols. (1888).

COLSONI, F. *Le Guide de Londres* (1693, reprinted 1951, *Lond. Topog. Soc.*).

COSIMO III, GRAND DUKE OF TUSCANY. *Travels through England . . . 1669* (1821).

COSIN, J. Correspondence of . . ., i, *Surtees Soc.* lii (1869).

DEFOE, D. *A Tour through England and Wales* (1724–6), ed. G. D. H. Cole, 2 vols. (1928).

Denizations and Naturalizations of Aliens in England and Ireland, ed. W. A. Shaw, *Huguenot Soc.* xviii (1911).

DUGDALE, SIR W. *History of St. Paul's* (1658).

EVELYN, J. *Diary* . . ., ed. W. Bray and H. B. Wheatley, 4 vols. (1906).

—— *Sculptura* (1662), ed. C. F. Bell (1906).

FIENNES, C. *Journeys through England*, ed. C. Morris (1947).

GERBIER, SIR B. *A Brief Discourse concerning the three chief principles of Magnificent Building . . .* (1662). *Counsel and Advise to all Builders* (1663).

GRAHAM, R. *A Short Account of the most Eminent Painters . . .*, with English edition (1695) of DU FRESNOY, C. A., *De Arte Graphica* (Paris, 1667).

HOOKE, DR. R. *Diary*, ed. H. W. Robinson and W. Adams (1935).

HOUBRAKEN, A. *De Groote Schouburgh der Nederlantsche Konstschilders en Schilderessen*, 3 vols. (Amsterdam, 1718–21).

HUYGENS, C. *Œuvres Complètes*, pub. *Soc. Hollandaise des Sciences*, 22 vols. (The Hague, 1888–1950).

HUTCHINSON, L. *Memoirs of Colonel Hutchinson*, ed. C. Firth, 2 vols. (1885).

JONES, I. *Stone-Heng . . . restored* (1655).

KIP, J. *Britannia Illustrata* (1707).

—— *Nouveau Théâtre de la Grande Bretagne* (1715).

LUTTRELL, N. *A Brief Historical Relation of State Affairs 1678–1714*, 6 vols. (ed. 1857).

NORGATE, E. *Miniatura, or the Art of Limning*, ed. M. Hardie (1919).

NORTH, R. *Lives of the Norths*, 3 vols., ed. A. Jessopp (1890).

PEACHAM, H. *The Compleat Gentleman* (1622, enlarged editions 1634 and 1661), ed. G. S. Gordon (1906).

PEPYS, S. *Diary*, ed. H. B. Wheatley, 8 vols. in 3 (1952).

—— *Private Correspondence and Misc. Papers*, ed. J. R. Tanner, 2 vols. (1926).

—— *Letters and the Second Diary*, ed. R. G. Howarth (1932).

PILES, R. DE. *Abrégé de la Vie des Peintres, avec des Réflexions . . .* (Paris, 1699).

PRATT, SIR R. *The Architecture of Sir Roger Pratt*, ed. R. T. Gunther (1928).

RERESBY, SIR J. *Memoirs*, ed. A. Browning (1936).

RICHARDSON, J. *An Essay on the Theory of Painting* (1715).

—— *An Essay on the whole Art of Criticism* (1719).

RICHARDSON, J. *An Argument in behalf of the Science of a Connoisseur* (1719).
—— *An Account of the Statues and Bas-reliefs, Drawings and Pictures in Italy* (1722).
—— *Works* (1725, 1773, 1792).
RUBENS, SIR P. P. *Correspondence . . .,* ed. C. Ruelens and M. Rooses, 6 vols. (Antwerp, 1887–1909).
SANDRART, J. VON. *Academie der Bau-, Bild- und Mahlerey-künste . . .* (1675), ed. with later additions (1679, 1683) A. R. Peltzer (Munich, 1925).
SHAFTESBURY, ANTHONY 3RD EARL OF. *Characteristicks* (2nd ed., 1714).
—— *Life, Unpublished Letters . . .,* ed. B. Rand (1900).
—— *Second Characters or the Language of Forms,* ed. B. Rand (1914).
STONE, N. 'The Note-Books of Nicholas Stone', ed. W. L. Spiers, *Walpole Soc.* vii (1919).
VANBRUGH, SIR J. *Letters* (Nonesuch ed. of *Works,* iv, 1928).
VERTUE, G. *Notebooks,* i, *Walpole Soc.,* xviii (1930); ii, ibid. xx (1932); iii, ibid. xxii (1934); iv, ibid. xxiv (1936); v, ibid. xxvi (1938); Index, ibid. xxix (1947).
WEBB, J. *Vindication of Stone-Heng Restored* (1662).
WOTTON, SIR H. *The Elements of Architecture* (1624).
WREN, CHRISTOPHER and STEPHEN. *Parentalia* (1750).
Wren Society. 20 vols. (1924–43).

LATER WORKS

ADDLESHAW, G. W. O., and ETCHELLS, F. *The Architectural Setting of Anglican Worship* (1948).
ALBION, G. *Charles I and the Court of Rome* (1935).
ALLEN, D. F. 'Abraham van der Doort and the Coinage of Charles I', *Numismatic Chronicle,* 6th ser., i (1941), 54–75.
AUERBACH, E. *Tudor Artists* (1954).

BAKER, C. H. COLLINS. *Lely and the Stuart Portrait Painters,* 2 vols. (1912).
—— *Lely and Kneller* (1922).
—— *Catalogue of the Petworth Collection* (1920).
BAKER, C. H. COLLINS, and CONSTABLE, W. G. *English Painting of the Sixteenth and Seventeenth Centuries* (Florence and Paris, 1930).
BAKER, C. H. COLLINS, and JAMES, M. R. *British Painting* (1933).
BATHURST, EARL. *Catalogue of the Bathurst Collection* (1908).
BATTEN, M. I. 'The Architecture of Dr. Robert Hooke', *Walpole Soc.* xxv (1937), 844.
BECKETT, R. B. *Lely* (1951).

BELL, C. F. 'English Seventeenth Century Portrait Drawings . . .', *Walpole Soc.* v (1917), 1–18, xiv (1926), 43–80.

BELL, C. F., and SIMPSON, P. 'The Masque Designs of Inigo Jones', *Walpole Soc.* xii (1924).

BINYON, L. *Drawings of British Artists . . . in the British Museum*, 4 vols. (1898–1907).

—— *English Water-Colours* (1944).

BIRCH, T. *The Court and Times of Charles I*, 2 vols. (1849).

BLUNT, A. F. *Art and Architecture in France 1500–1700* (1953).

BRETT-JAMES, N. G. *The Growth of Stuart London* (1935).

BRETT, R. L. *The Third Earl of Shaftesbury* (1951).

Burl. Mag. Editorials. 'Sir James Thornhill's Collection', lxxxii–lxxxiii (1943), 133–6.

—— 'Sir Peter Lely's Collection', lxxxiii (1943), 185–91.

—— 'Robert Streater', lxxxiv–lxxxv (1944), 3–12.

—— 'The Serjeant-Painters', lxxxiv–lxxxv (1944), 81–82.

—— 'P. H. Lankrink's Collection', lxxxvi–lxxxvii (1945), 29–35.

CARPENTER, W. HOOKHAM. *Pictorial Notices . . . a Memoir of Sir Anthony Van Dyck . . .* (1844).

CHETTLE, G. H. *The Queen's House, Greenwich*, London County Council Survey of London, 14th monograph, n.d.

—— 'Marlborough House Chapel', *Country Life*, lxxxiv (1938), 450.

CLAPHAM, SIR A. 'The Survival of Gothic in 17th century England', *Arch. Journ.* cvi, Supplement (1952), 4.

COBB, G. *The Old Churches of London* (1942).

COLVIN, H. *Dictionary of British Architects 1660–1830* (1954).

—— 'Fifty New Churches', *Archit. Review*, cvii (1950), 189.

—— 'The South Front of Wilton House', *Arch. Journ.* cxi (1954), 181.

COSNAC, COMTE DE. *Les Richesses du Palais Mazarin* (Paris, 1884).

CUST, SIR L. *Anthony van Dyck* (1900).

—— 'Marcus Gheeraerts', *Walpole Soc.* iii (1914).

—— 'The Triple Portrait of Charles I by Van Dyck, and the Bust by Bernini', *Burl. Mag.* xiv (1909), 337–40.

CUST, SIR L., and HAKE, SIR H. M. 'George Vertue's Notebooks . . .', *Walpole Soc.* iii (1914), 121–39.

DAVIES, R. 'An Inventory of the Duke of Buckingham's Pictures . . . 1635', *Burl. Mag.* x (1907), 376–82.

DOWNES, K. 'Hawksmoor's Sale Catalogue', *Burl. Mag.* xcv (1953), 332.

DULEEP SINGH. *Portraits in Norfolk Houses*, 2 vols. (Norwich, 1927).

EDWARDS, R. *Early Conversation Pieces* (1954). See also under MACQUOID, P.

EDWARDS, R., and WARD-JACKSON, P. *Ham House* (Official Guide, 2nd ed., 1951).

ENGLEFIELD, W. A. D. *The History of the Painter-Stainers Company of London* (1923).

ESDAILE, K. A. *English Monumental Sculpture since the Renaissance* (1927).

—— *Monuments in English Churches* (1937).

—— *English Church Monuments 1510–1840* (1946).

—— 'The Stantons of Holborn', *Arch. Journ.* lxxxv (1928), 149.

—— 'John Bushnell,' *Walpole Soc.* xv (1927), 21, and xxi (1933), 105.

—— 'Two Busts of Charles I and William III', *Burl. Mag.* lxxii (1938), 164–71.

EVANS, J. 'Huguenot Goldsmiths in England and Ireland', *Proc. Huguenot Soc.* xiv (1933).

EXHIBITION CATALOGUES. *National Portraits*, South Kensington (1866–8).

—— *Historical Medals*, B.M. (1924).

—— *British Art*, R.A. (1934); *Commemorative Catalogue* (1935).

—— *Seventeenth Century Art in Europe*, R.A. (1938); and illustrated souvenir.

—— *The Works of British-Born Artists in the Seventeenth Century*, B.F.A.C. (1938).

—— *Nicholas Hilliard and Isaac Oliver*, V. & A. (1947).

—— *The Beginnings of English Topographical and Landscape Drawing*, B.M. (1949).

—— *William and Mary*, V. & A. (1950).

—— *Paintings of the Civil War and Commonwealth*, Worcester (1951).

—— *William Dobson*, Tate Gallery (1951).

—— *Eighteenth Century Venice*, Whitechapel Art Gallery (1951).

—— *English Tapestries*, Birmingham (1951).

—— *Kings and Queens*, R.A. (1953); and illustrated souvenir.

—— *Kings and Queens of England*, Liverpool (1953); and illustrated souvenir.

—— *Flemish Painting*, R.A. (1953).

FABER, H. *Caius Gabriel Cibber* (1926).

FAGAN, L. *A Descriptive Catalogue of the Engraved Works of William Faithorne* (1888).

FARQUHAR, H. 'Portraiture of our Stuart Monarchs on their Coins and Medals', *Brit. Numismatic Journ.* v (1909)–xi (1915).

FARRER, REV. E. *Portraits in Suffolk Houses* (West, 1908).

FINBERG, A. J. 'A Chronological List of Portraits by Cornelius Johnson', *Walpole Soc.* x (1922).

FOKKER, T. H. *Jan Siberechts* (Brussels and Paris, 1931).

GERSON, H. *Ausbreitung und Nachwirkung der holländischen Malerei des 17. Jahrhunderts* (Haarlem, 1942).

GLÜCK, G. *Van Dyck*, Klassiker der Kunst (Stuttgart, 1931).

GOTCH, J. A. *Inigo Jones* (1928).

GOULDING, R. W. 'The Welbeck Abbey Miniatures', *Walpole Soc.* iv (1916).

—— *Catalogue of the Pictures . . . at Welbeck Abbey* (1936).

GRANT, COL. M. H. *Chronological History of the Old English Landscape Painters*, 2 vols. (1926).

GRAY, B. *The English Print* (1937).

GREEN, D. *Blenheim Palace* (1951).

GROSSMANN, F. 'Holbein, Flemish Paintings and Everard Jabach', *Burl. Mag.* xciii (1951), 16–25.

GUNNIS, R. *Dictionary of British Sculptors 1660–1851* (1953).

HAKE, SIR H. M. 'Some Contemporary Records relating to Francis Place', *Walpole Soc.* x (1922), 39–69.

HAKE, SIR H. M., and O'DONOGUE, F. *Catalogue of Engraved British Portraits . . . in the British Museum*, 6 vols. (1908–25).

HALE, J. R. *England and the Italian Renaissance* (1954).

HAUTECŒUR, L. *Histoire de l'Architecture classique en France*, I. ii (1943); II. i and ii (Paris, 1948).

HERVEY, M. F. S. *The Life, Correspondence . . . of Thomas Howard, Earl of Arundel* (1921).

HESS, J. 'Lord Arundel in Rom und sein Auftrag an den Bildhauer Egidio Manetti', *English Misc.* 1 (Rome, 1950), 197–220.

—— 'Die Gemälde des Orazio Gentileschi für das Haus der Königin in Greenwich', *English Misc.* 3 (Rome, 1952), 159–87.

—— 'Precisazioni', *English Misc.* 4 (Rome, 1953), 247–56.

HIND, A. M. *Catalogue of Drawings by Dutch and Flemish Artists . . . in the British Museum*, 4 vols. (1915–31).

—— *Wenceslaus Hollar and his Views of London and Windsor . . .* (1922).

—— *A History of Engraving and Etching* (1923).

—— *Engraving in England in the Sixteenth and Seventeenth Centuries*, i (1952).

—— 'Van Dyck and English Landscape', *Burl. Mag.* li (1927), 292–7.

HOLME, C., and KENNEDY, H. A. *Early English Portrait Miniatures in the Collection of the Duke of Buccleuch* (1917).

HONOUR, H. 'John Talman and William Kent in Italy', *Connoisseur*, cxxxiv (1954), 3–7.

—— 'Leonard Knyff', *Burl. Mag.* xcvi (1954), 337–8.

HOPE, W. ST. JOHN. *Windsor Castle*, 2 vols. (1914).

HOTSON, L. *The Commonwealth and Restoration Stage* (1928).

JOHNSON, B. *Berkeley Square to Bond Street* (1952).

JOURDAIN, M. *The Work of William Kent* (1948).

—— *English Interior Decoration 1500–1830* (1950).

KENT, W. *The Designs of Inigo Jones* (1727).

KEYNES, G. *John Evelyn ... A Bibliography ...* (1937).

KINGSFORD, C. L. *The Early History of Piccadilly* (1925).

KNOOP, D., and JONES, G. P. *The London Mason in the 17th century* (Manchester, 1935).

LANG, S. 'Cambridge and Oxford Reformed', *Archit. Review*, ciii (1948), 157.

—— 'By Hawksmoor out of Gibbs', ibid. cv (1949), 173.

LLOYD, N. *History of English Brickwork* (1934).

LONDON COUNTY COUNCIL. *Survey of London*, xiii (1930), St. Margaret's, Westminster.

—— *Survey of London*, iii (1912), St. Giles in the Fields.

—— *Survey of London*, 14th monograph, The Queen's House, Greenwich.

—— *Survey of London*, 13th monograph (1933), Swakeleys, Middlesex.

—— *Survey of London*, 15th monograph (1944), St. Bride, Fleet Street.

LONG, B. S. *British Miniaturists* (1929).

LUZIO, A. *La Galleria dei Gonzaga venduta all' Inghilterra ...* (Milan, 1913).

MACQUOID, P. *Dictionary of English Furniture*: The Age of Oak (1904); The Age of Walnut (1905).

MACQUOID, P., and EDWARDS, R. *Dictionary of English Furniture* (1924), 3 vols. (revised ed. 1954).

MAHON, D. 'Notes on the Dutch Gift to Charles II', *Burl. Mag.* xci (1949), 303–5, 349–50; xcii (1950), 12–18, 238.

MATHEW, D. *The Age of Charles I* (1951).

MILLAR, O. 'Charles I, Honthorst and Van Dyck', *Burl. Mag.* xcvi (1954), 36–42.

—— 'Notes on British Painting from Archives: iii', *Burl. Mag.* xcvii (1955), 255–6.

NICOLL, A. *The Stuart Masque and the Renaissance Stage* (1937).

—— *A History of Restoration Drama* (3rd ed. 1940).

NISSER, W. *Michael Dahl and the Contemporary Swedish School of Painting in England* (Upsala, 1927).

OGDEN, H. V. S. and M. S. 'Van der Doort's Lists of the Frizell and Nonsuch Palace Pictures ...', *Burl. Mag.* lxxxix (1947), 247–50.

OMAN, C. *English Domestic Silver* (1934, 3rd ed. 1949).

OPPÉ, A. P. *English Drawings ... at Windsor Castle* (1950).

—— 'Sir Anthony Van Dyck in England', *Burl. Mag.* lxxix (1941), 186–90.

OSMUN, W. R. *A Study of the Work of Sir James Thornhill*, unpub. Ph.D. thesis, London Univ. (1950).

OZINGA, M. D. *Daniel Marot* (Amsterdam, 1938).

PARTHEY, G. *Wenzel Hollar* (Berlin, 1853; *Nachträge* 1858).

POOLE, MRS. R. L. *Catalogue of Portraits in . . . Oxford*, 3 vols. (1912–25).

—— 'An outline of the History of the De Critz Family of Painters', *Walpole Soc.* ii (1913).

—— 'Marcus Gheeraerts . . .', *Walpole Soc.* iii (1914).

—— 'Edward Pierce the Sculptor', *Walpole Soc.* xi (1923), 34.

POPE-HENNESSY, J. 'Some Bronze Statuettes by Francesco Fanelli', *Burl. Mag.* xcv (1953), 157-62.

—— *Samson and a Philistine*, V. & A. Monograph 8 (1954).

READE, B. 'William Frizell and the Royal Collection', *Burl. Mag.*, lxxxix (1947), 73–75

RÉAU, L. *Histoire de l'Expansion de l'Art Français*, iii (Paris, 1931).

REDDAWAY, T. F. *The Rebuilding of London* (1940).

REYNOLDS, G. *English Portrait Miniatures* (1952).

—— 'A Miniature Self-Portrait by Thomas Flatman . . .', *Burl. Mag.* lxxxix (1947), 63–67.

ROWE, C. *The Theoretical Drawings of Inigo Jones, their sources and scope*, unpub. Ph.D. thesis, London University (1947).

SAINSBURY, W. N. *Original Unpublished Papers . . .* (1859).

SALERNO, L. 'Seventeenth Century English Literature on Painting', *Journal of the Warburg and Courtauld Institutes*, xiv (1951), 234–58.

SAXL, F., and WITTKOWER, R. *English Art and the Mediterranean* (1948).

SEYMOUR, J. 'Edward Pearce: Baroque Sculptor of London', *Guildhall Miscellany*, i (1952), 10.

SMITH, J. CHALONER. *British Mezzotinto Portraits*, 4 vols. (1878–83).

SMITH, L. P. *The Life and Letters of Sir Henry Wotton*, 2 vols. (1907).

SMITH, W. J. 'Letters from Michael Wright', *Burl. Mag.* xcv (1953), 233–6.

SNELGROVE, G. W. *The Work and Theories of Jonathan Richardson*, unpub. Ph.D. thesis, London University (1936).

SOUTHERN, R. *Changeable Scenery* (1951).

SPARROW, W. S. *British Sporting Artists* (1922).

SPRINZELS, F. *Hollar Handzeichnungen* (1938).

STEEGMAN, J. *The Artist and the Country House* (1949).

STOPES, C. 'Daniel Mytens in England', *Burl. Mag.* xvii (1910), 160-3.

—— 'Gleanings from the Records of the Reigns of James I and Charles I', *Burl. Mag.* xxii (1913), 276–82.

STOYE, J. W. *English Travellers Abroad 1604–67* (1952).

STRATTON, A. *The English Interior* (1920).

SUMMERSON, J. *Architecture in Britain 1530–1830* (1953); 2nd ed. (1955).

—— *Georgian London* (1945).

—— *Sir Christopher Wren* (1953).

SUMNER-SMITH, J. 'The Italian Sources of Inigo Jones's Style', *Burl. Mag.* xciv (1952), 200.

TAYLOR, B. *Animal Painting in England* (1955).
THOMPSON, F. *A History of Chatsworth* (1949).
THOMPSON, W. G. *Tapestry Weaving in England* (1914).
TIPPING, H. A. *English Homes*, III. ii (2nd ed. 1927), Late Tudor and Early Stuart.
—— *English Homes*, IV. i (2nd ed. 1929), Early Stuart.
—— *English Homes*, IV. ii (2nd ed. 1928), Sir John Vanbrugh and his School.
—— *Grinling Gibbons and the Woodwork of his Age* (1914).
TOYNBEE, M. 'Adriaen Hanneman and the English Court in Exile', *Burl. Mag.* xcii (1950), 73–80.

VICTORIA AND ALBERT MUSEUM. *History of English Furniture* (1955).

WALPOLE, H. *Anecdotes of Painting*, ed. J. Dallaway and R. N. Wornum, 3 vols. (1888).
—— 'Journals of Visits to Country Seats &c.', *Walpole Soc.* xvi (1928), 9-80.
WATERHOUSE, E. K. *Painting in Britain 1530-1790* (1953).
—— 'Portraits from Welsh Houses', *Burl. Mag.* xc (1948), 204.
—— 'Paintings from Venice for Seventeenth-Century England', *Italian Studies*, vii (1952), 1–23.
WATSON, F. J. B. 'On the Early History of Collecting in England', *Burl. Mag.* lxxxiv-v (1944), 223-8.
WEBB, G. F. 'Notes on Hubert le Sueur', *Burl. Mag.* lii (1928), 10, 81.
—— 'The Architectural Antecedents of Sir Christopher Wren', *R.I.B.A. Journ.* xi (1933), 573.
—— *Sir Christopher Wren* (1937).
—— 'Baroque Art', *Proc. British Academy*, xxxiii (1947).
—— 'Letters and Drawings of N. Hawksmoor', *Walpole Soc.* xix (1931), III.
—— Introduction to Letters of Vanbrugh: *Works*, Nonesuch ed., iv (1928).
WHIFFEN, M. *Stuart and Georgian Churches outside London* (1947).
—— *Thomas Archer* (1950).
WHINNEY, M. D. 'John Webb's drawings for Whitehall Palace', *Walpole Soc.* xxxi (1943), 45.
—— *St. Paul's Cathedral* (1947).
—— 'William Talman', *Journal of the Warburg and Courtauld Institutes*, xviii (1955), 121.
WHISTLER, L. *Sir John Vanbrugh* (1938).
—— *The Imagination of Vanbrugh and His Fellow-Artists* (1954).
—— 'Talman and Vanbrugh', *Country Life*, cxii (1952), 1648.

WHITLEY, W. T. *Artists and their Friends in England 1700–99*, 2 vols. (1928).

WILLIAMS, I. A. *Early English Watercolours* (1952).

WILLIS, R., and CLARK, J. W. *Architectural History of the University of Cambridge*, 3 vols. (1896).

WIND, E. 'Julian the Apostate at Hampton Court', *Journal of the Warburg and Courtauld Institutes*, iii (1939–40), 127–37.

WITTKOWER, R. 'Inigo Jones, Puritanissimo Fiero', *Burl. Mag.* xc (1948), 50–51.

—— 'Inigo Jones, Architect and Man of Letters', *R.I.B.A. Journ.* lx (1953), 83.

—— 'Bernini Studies, ii: "The Bust of Mr. Baker"', *Burl. Mag.* xcv (1953), 19–22.

—— See also under SAXL, F.

WOODWARD, J. *Tudor and Stuart Drawings* (1951).

INDEX

The dates are provided wherever possible for English artists, or foreign artists who worked in this country, during the years covered by this volume. References to plates are in black type.

Abbot, George, abp. of Canterbury, 115 n. 1.
Abbot, James, 179.
Abingdon, Berks., 224, **62 a.**
Absalom and Achitophel (Dryden), 295.
ACADEMIES, 13–14, 306 n. 2, 315, 319.
— French, 282, 296, 302 n. 2.
Acomb House, York, 79.
Adam, Robert, 147, 339 n. 2.
Addison, Joseph, 14, 292 n. 1.
Ager, —(*fl.* 1641–2), 81.
Aggas, Robert (d. 1679), 265.
Aikman, William (1682–1731), 191.
Aiton, Sir Robert, 121.
Albano, Francesco, 9.
Albemarle, George Monck, 1st duke of, 185, 238 n. 4.
Albemarle, Christopher Monck, 2nd duke of, 140; and duchess, 190 n. 3.
Albemarle, Arnold van Keppel, 1st earl of, 195 n. 2.
Alberti, Cherubino, 299 n. 1.
Alberti, Giovanni, 299 n. 1.
Alberti, Leon Battista, 28, 51.
Albion and Albanius (Dryden), 294–5.
Albion's Triumph (Jones and Townshend), 294.
Albury Park House, Surrey, 87, **74 b.**
Aldrich, Henry (1647–1710), 352.
Algardi, Alessandro, 123, 234–5.
Alington, William, 1st baron, 139.
Alleyn, Edward, 27 n. 2.
Alnwick Castle, Northumberland, 102 n. 4, **26.**
Althorp, Northants., 62, 66, 71 n. 3, 72, 196, 198, 231 n. 5, 278.
Amalia van Solms, w. of Frederick Henry, prince of Orange, 289.
AMATEUR PAINTING, 82, 97, 102–3, 181, 202–3, 269 n. 2, 281.
Amboyna, massacre of, 78.
Amersham, Bucks., 113, **29 a.**
Ampton, Suffolk, 115 n. 1.

Amsterdam, Rijksmuseum, 65 n. 4, 93, 170 n. 2, 274, 282.
— Royal Palace, 208.
Ancrum, Robert Kerr, 1st earl of, 4 n. 3.
Andover, Dorothy, viscountess, 72.
Andrea del Sarto, 4.
Angillis, Pieter (1685–1734), 281 n. 3, 283.
Anguier, François, 122 n. 5.
ANIMAL AND BIRD PAINTING, 276–80.
Anne, q. of England, 98 n. 2, 99 n. 1, 131, 178, 192 n. 3, 195, 199, 225, 227, 232, 247 n. 6, 251 n. 2, 280, 300, 317, 330.
Anne of Denmark, w. of James I, 19, 90 n. 2, 130.
ANTIQUE SCULPTURE, 105, 109–10, 111, 120, 209.
ANTIQUITY, 17, 18, 25, 27, 32, 38, 136, 156, 306 n. 2, 343, 349, 350, 354.
Antwerp, Musée Royal des Beaux-Arts, 5 n. 4.
Arcadia (Sidney), 291.
Archer, Thomas (1668/9–1743), 223–4, 317, 352, **87 a.**
ARCHITECTURAL BOOKS, 18, 34, 44, 51–52, 53, 138, 141, 142, 211, 222, 343, 349.
Argyll, John Campbell, 2nd duke of, 196.
Arlington, Isabella, countess of, 183.
Arnold, — (*fl.* 1682–4), 281 n. 3.
Arran, Anne, countess of, 196.
Arsinoë, 313 n. 1.
ART MARKET, 11, 269 n. 3, 289, 315 n. 2.
Art of Graveing and Etching (Faithorne), 100 n. 2.
Arundel Castle, Sussex, 63, 123, 175, **50 b.**
Arundel, Thomas Howard, earl of, 2, 4, 9, 10, 18, 45 n. 5, 61, 62, 63, 68, 70, 82 n. 2, 102, 105, 122, 123 n. 4, 141, 265 n. 3, 267, 268.
Arundel, Alethia, countess of, 63, 111.
Ashburnham, Jane, 236 n. 2, 239.
Ashburnham, John, 2nd earl of, 277.

I. SIR ANTHONY VAN DYCK: CHARLES I, 1633. H.M. The Queen, Buckingham Palace

2. *a*. INIGO JONES: THE QUEEN'S HOUSE, GREENWICH, 1616–35
b. INIGO JONES: THE BANQUETING HOUSE, WHITEHALL, 1619–22

3. INIGO JONES: THE QUEEN'S CHAPEL, MARLBOROUGH GATE, *c.* 1627

4. *a*. INIGO JONES: ST. PAUL'S CATHEDRAL: WEST FRONT, BEGUN 1633
b. INIGO JONES: COVENT GARDEN PIAZZA, 1630–8

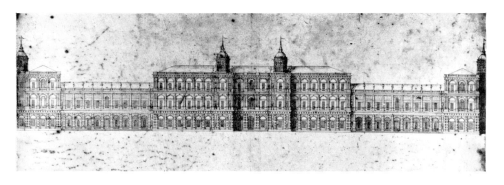

5. *a*. INIGO JONES: DESIGN FOR WHITEHALL PALACE, *c*. 1638. Worcester College, Oxford

   b. INIGO JONES: MASQUE DESIGN: THE ISLE OF DELOS FOR FLORIMENE, 1635

6. *a*. CHEVENING, KENT, *c*. 1630
b. HAM HOUSE, SURREY: THE NORTH DRAWING ROOM, 1637

7. _a_. SWAKELEYS, MIDDLESEX, 1638
_b_. SIR ROGER PRATT: COLESHILL, BERKSHIRE, 1649–62. Burnt 1952

8. INIGO JONES: WILTON HOUSE, WILTSHIRE: THE DOUBLE CUBE ROOM, c. 1649–52

9. SIR ROGER PRATT: COLESHILL, BERKSHIRE: THE HALL, 1649–62

10. *a.* LINCOLN COLLEGE, OXFORD: THE CHAPEL, *c.* 1631

b. ST. JOHN'S COLLEGE, OXFORD: CANTERBURY QUADRANGLE, 1631–6

11. *a.* DURHAM CATHEDRAL: FONT COVER, *c.* 1630
b. FORDE ABBEY, DORSET: STAIRCASE, 1658

12. ATTRIBUTED TO DANIEL MYTENS: ELIZABETH, COUNTESS OF BANBURY
Redlynch House

13. ARTIST UNKNOWN: ANNE, COUNTESS OF STAMFORD
Redlynch House

14. DANIEL MYTENS: ROBERT, 2ND EARL OF WARWICK, 1632
National Maritime Museum

15. SIR ANTHONY VAN DYCK: ROBERT, 2ND EARL OF WARWICK
Metropolitan Museum, New York

16. _a._ CORNELIUS JOHNSON: DOROTHY GODFREY, 1636. George Godfrey-Faussett Coll.
_b._ CORNELIUS JOHNSON: UNKNOWN WOMAN, 1619. Lamport Hall

17. CORNELIUS JOHNSON: THE FAMILY OF ARTHUR, 1ST BARON CAPEL. Earl of Wilton Coll.

18. *a*. SIR ANTHONY VAN DYCK: THOMAS, 1ST EARL OF STRAFFORD. Petworth

b. SIR ANTHONY VAN DYCK: HENRIETTA MARIA. H.M. The Queen, Windsor Castle

19. *a.* SIR NATHANIEL BACON: PORTRAIT OF THE ARTIST. National Portrait Gallery
b. ADRIAEN HANNEMAN: UNKNOWN MAN, 1632? Warwick Castle

20. *a.* ROBERT WALKER: JOHN EVELYN, 1648. The John Evelyn Coll., Christ Church, Oxford

b. ARTIST UNKNOWN: JOHN TRADESCANT II. National Portrait Gallery

21. *a*. GILBERT JACKSON: WILLIAM HICKMAN, 1634. Raveningham Hall

b. EDWARD BOWER: CHARLES I, 1649. H.M. Queen Elizabeth the Queen Mother

22. WILLIAM DOBSON: JOHN, 1ST BARON BYRON. Tabley House

23. *a*. SIR P. P. RUBENS: MINERVA DEFENDING THE THRONE OF JAMES I
Musées-Royaux, Brussels

b. SIR ANTHONY VAN DYCK: CUPID AND PSYCHE. H.M. The Queen

25. WILLIAM DOBSON: PRINCE RUPERT WITH COLS. MURRAY AND RUSSELL. Ombersley Court

26. SIR ANTHONY VAN DYCK: ALGERNON, 10TH EARL OF NORTHUMBERLAND
Alnwick Castle

27. WILLIAM DOBSON: SIR WILLIAM COMPTON (*Identity uncertain*)
Castle Ashby

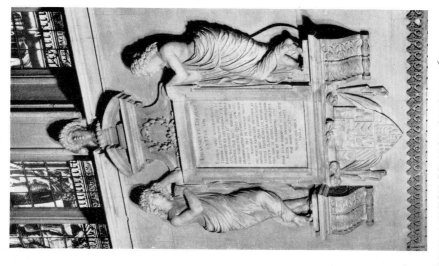

28. *a*. NICHOLAS STONE: MONUMENT TO SIR THOMAS BODLEY: MERTON COLLEGE, OXFORD, 1615

b. NICHOLAS STONE: MONUMENT TO JOHN AND THOMAS LYTTELTON: MAGDALEN COLLEGE, OXFORD, 1634

29. *a.* EDWARD MARSHALL: MONUMENT TO HENRY CURWEN: AMERSHAM CHURCH, BUCKS., 1636
b. THOMAS STANTON: MONUMENT TO DAME JANE BACON: CULFORD CHURCH, SUFFOLK, 1657

30. *a*. HUBERT LE SUEUR: CHARLES I: Stourhead, Wiltshire

b. MORTLAKE TAPESTRY: HERO AND LEANDER: Royal Palace, Stockholm

31. *a*. FRANCESCO FANELLI: CHARLES II AS PRINCE OF WALES: 1640, Welbeck

b. MORTLAKE TAPESTRY: THE MIRACULOUS DRAUGHT OF FISHES: Mobilier National, Paris

32. *a*. SIR CHRISTOPHER WREN: SHELDONIAN THEATRE, OXFORD: SOUTH FRONT, 1664–9
b. JOHN WEBB: KING CHARLES'S BLOCK: GREENWICH, 1663–9

33. *a*. SIR ROGER PRATT: CLARENDON HOUSE, PICCADILLY, 1664–7
b. HUGH MAY: ELTHAM LODGE, KENT, 1664

34. *a*. SIR CHRISTOPHER WREN: ST. BRIDE, FLEET STREET, 1670–84
Gutted 1941
b. SIR CHRISTOPHER WREN: CHRISTCHURCH, NEWGATE STREET, 1677–87
Gutted 1941

35. *a*. SIR CHRISTOPHER WREN: ST. STEPHEN, WALBROOK, 1672–87
b. SIR CHRISTOPHER WREN: ST. MARY-LE-BOW, CHEAPSIDE, 1670–7
Gutted 1941

36. *a.* SIR CHRISTOPHER WREN: ST. MILDRED, BREAD STREET, 1677–83. Gutted 1941
b. SIR CHRISTOPHER WREN: ST. ANNE AND ST. AGNES, GRESHAM STREET, 1677–80

37. GRINLING GIBBONS: REREDOS, ST. JAMES'S, PICCADILLY, 1683

38. *a*. SIR CHRISTOPHER WREN: ST. MARY–LE–BOW, CHEAPSIDE: STEEPLE, 1680
b. SIR CHRISTOPHER WREN: ST. BRIDE, FLEET STREET: STEEPLE, 1701–3

39. *a*. SIR CHRISTOPHER WREN: ST. MARTIN, LUDGATE: STEEPLE, 1677–84
b. SIR CHRISTOPHER WREN: ST. MICHAEL, PATERNOSTER ROYAL: STEEPLE, 1713

40. *a*. SIR CHRISTOPHER WREN: ST. PAUL'S CATHEDRAL: THE GREAT MODEL, 1673
b. SIR CHRISTOPHER WREN: ST. PAUL'S CATHEDRAL: THE WARRANT DESIGN:
SOUTH SIDE, 1675

41. *a*. SIR CHRISTOPHER WREN: ST. PAUL'S CATHEDRAL: THE GREAT
MODEL LOOKING EAST

b. SIR CHRISTOPHER WREN: ST. PAUL'S CATHEDRAL: THE CATHEDRAL
FROM THE SOUTH-EAST

42. SIR CHRISTOPHER WREN: ST. PAUL'S CATHEDRAL: UPPER PART OF SOUTH
TRANSEPT FRONT

43. SIR CHRISTOPHER WREN: ST. PAUL'S CATHEDRAL: LOOKING EAST

44. *a.* EDWARD JARMAN: THE ROYAL EXCHANGE, 1667–71. Burnt 1838
b. SIR CHRISTOPHER WREN: SHELDONIAN THEATRE, OXFORD: INTERIOR,
1664–9. Bodleian Library, Oxford

45. *a*. DR. ROBERT HOOKE: BEDLAM HOSPITAL, LONDON, 1676. Soane Museum
b. SIR CHRISTOPHER WREN: TRINITY COLLEGE, CAMBRIDGE: THE LIBRARY, 1676

46. SIR PETER LELY: THE CHILDREN OF CHARLES I, 1647. Petworth

47. *a*. SIR PETER LELY: LADY JENKINSON. Kingston Lacy

b. SIR PETER LELY: CHARLES, 2ND EARL OF CARNARVON. Lord Porchester Coll.

48. *a*. SIR PETER LELY: SIR THOMAS TEDDEMAN. National Maritime Museum

b. SIR PETER LELY: COUNTESS OF GRAMMONT. H.M. The Queen, Hampton Court

49. *a*. J. M. WRIGHT: COLONEL JOHN RUSSELL, 1659. Ham House
    b. GERARD SOEST: SIR RICHARD RAINSFORD, 1678. Lincoln's Inn

50. *a*. JACOB HUYSMANS: CATHERINE OF BRAGANZA. H.M. The Queen, Windsor Castle
b. SIR PETER LELY: ANNE, DUCHESS OF NORFOLK, 1677? Arundel Castle

51. *a.* WILLIAM WISSING: WILLIAM III. H.M. The Queen, Hampton Court
b. JOHN GREENHILL: MRS. CARTWRIGHT. Dulwich College Picture Gallery

52. *a*. MICHAEL DAHL: PORTRAIT OF THE ARTIST, 1691. National Portrait Gallery

b. ISAAC FULLER: PORTRAIT OF THE ARTIST, 1670. The Bodleian Library, Oxford

53. *a*. HENDRICK DANCKERTS: CLASSICAL LANDSCAPE. H.M. The Queen, Windsor Castle

b. JACOB BOGDANI: A MONKEY WITH ORNAMENTAL BIRDS. H.M. The Queen, Kew Palace

54. SIR GODFREY KNELLER: PHILIP, 4TH BARON WHARTON, 1685
Easton Neston

55. J. B. CLOSTERMAN: ANTHONY, 3RD EARL OF SHAFTESBURY
St. Giles's House

56. SIR GODFREY KNELLER: JOHN DRYDEN. Trinity College, Cambridge

57. *a*. PETER OLIVER: SIR KENELM DIGBY, 1627. Alan Evans Coll.
b. JOHN HOSKINS: UNKNOWN WOMAN. H.M. The Queen, Windsor Castle
c. JOHN HOSKINS: CHARLES I. H.M. The Queen, Windsor Castle
d. JOHN HOSKINS: UNKNOWN MAN, 1659. Fitzwilliam Museum
e. SAMUEL COOPER: UNKNOWN MAN, 1645. H.M. The Queen, Windsor Castle
f. SAMUEL COOPER: REV. MR. STAIRSMORE, 1657. Fitzwilliam Museum

58. *a*. SAMUEL COOPER: CATHERINE OF BRAGANZA. H.M. The Queen, Windsor Castle
b. THOMAS FLATMAN: UNKNOWN MAN. H.M. The Queen, Windsor Castle
c. THOMAS FLATMAN: PORTRAIT OF THE ARTIST, 1673. Victoria and Albert Museum
d. DAVID LOGGAN: MRS. HARRISON, 1681. L. R. Schidlof Coll.

59. *a*. WILLIAM FAITHORNE: SIR ROBERT HENLEY, 1658
b. JOHN RILEY: SIR CHARLES COTTERELL, 1687. Rousham

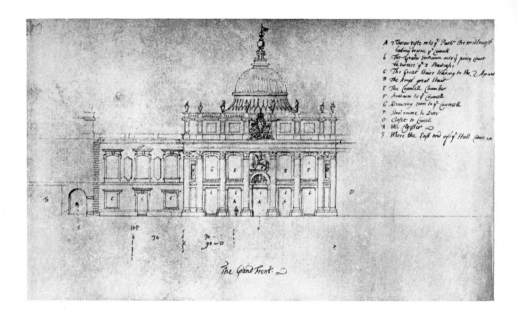

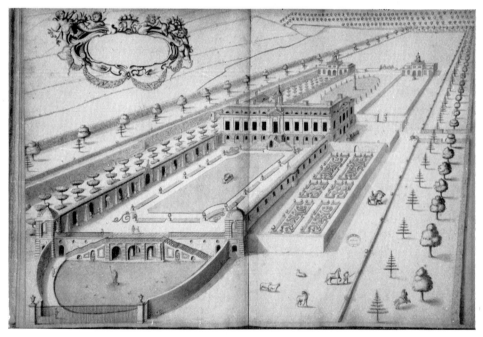

60. *a.* SIR CHRISTOPHER WREN: HAMPTON COURT PALACE: FIRST DESIGN, 1689
Soane Museum
b. WILLIAM TALMAN: THE TRIANON: HAMPTON COURT PALACE, *c.* 1699
Royal Institute of British Architects

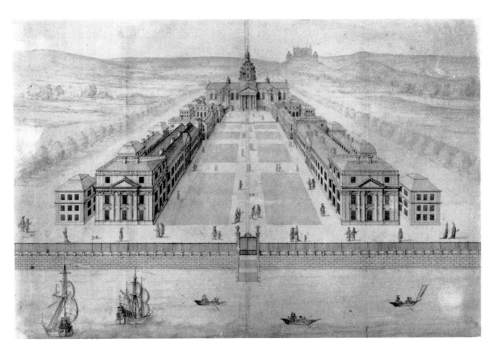

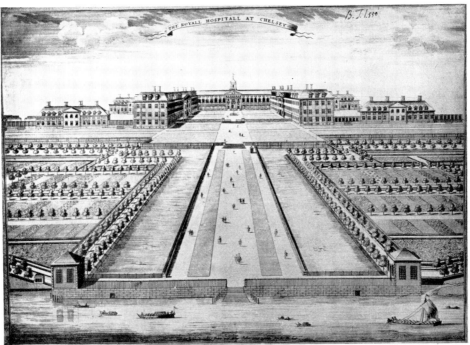

61. *a*. SIR CHRISTOPHER WREN: GREENWICH HOSPITAL: FIRST DESIGN, 1694
Soane Museum
b. SIR CHRISTOPHER WREN: CHELSEA HOSPITAL, 1682–9. Bodleian Library, Oxford

62. *a*. ABINGDON, BERKSHIRE: TOWN HALL, 1677–82

b. HENRY BELL: KING'S LYNN, NORFOLK: THE CUSTOMS HOUSE, 1683

63. SIR CHRISTOPHER WREN: GREENWICH HOSPITAL: BEGUN 1699

64. *a*. WILLIAM TALMAN: CHATSWORTH, DERBYSHIRE: SOUTH FRONT, 1687–8
b. BELTON HOUSE, LINCOLNSHIRE, 1684–9

65. *a*. SIR CHRISTOPHER WREN: HAMPTON COURT PALACE: FROM THE PARK,
1689–*c*. 1702
b. SIR CHRISTOPHER WREN: HAMPTON COURT PALACE: CENTRE OF PARK FRONT,
1689–*c*. 1702

66. *a*. STANDING CUP AND COVER, 1659. Corporation of Evesham
b. SILVER TABLE. Her Majesty the Queen

67. *a.* CHALICE: FROM WHITEHALL CHAPEL, *c.* 1664. Her Majesty the Queen
b. GENERAL CHURCHILL'S WINE BOTTLE. Victoria and Albert Museum
c. TANKARD, 1683. The Worshipful Company of Goldsmiths

68. *a*. CHARLES II CHAIR, *c*. 1670–5. Victoria and Albert Museum
b. QUEEN ANNE CHAIR, *c*. 1715. Victoria and Albert Museum

69. *a*. CAIUS GABRIEL CIBBER: THE SACKVILLE MONUMENT: WITHYHAM,
SUSSEX: DETAIL, 1677
b. CAIUS GABRIEL CIBBER: RELIEF ON THE MONUMENT, LONDON, 1674

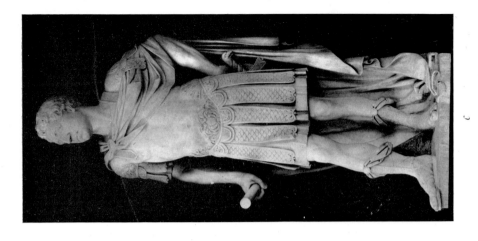

b

a

c

70. *a.* JOHN BUSHNELL: CHARLES I: OLD BAILEY, LONDON, 1671; *b.* HUBERT LE SUEUR: HENRIETTA MARIA: ST. JOHN'S COLLEGE, OXFORD, 1634; *c.* GRINLING GIBBONS: THE DUKE OF SOMERSET: TRINITY COLLEGE, CAMBRIDGE, 1691

71. *a.* ANON.: MONUMENT TO JOHN AND ELIZABETH PEABLES: DEWSBURY, YORKSHIRE, *c.* 1684
b. FRANCIS BIRD: BUST FROM MONUMENT TO THOMAS SHADWELL: WESTMINSTER ABBEY

72. *a*. ARNOLD QUELLIN: MONUMENT TO THOMAS THYNNE: WESTMINSTER ABBEY, 1682

b. GRINLING GIBBONS: MONUMENT TO SIR CLOUDESLEY SHOVELL: WESTMINSTER ABBEY, 1707

73. *a*. JOHN NOST: MONUMENT TO JOHN DIGBY, 3RD EARL OF BRISTOL: SHERBORNE ABBEY, DORSET

c. 1698

b. RICHARD CRUTCHER: MONUMENT TO SIR ROBERT CLAYTON: BLETCHINGLEY, SURREY, 1705

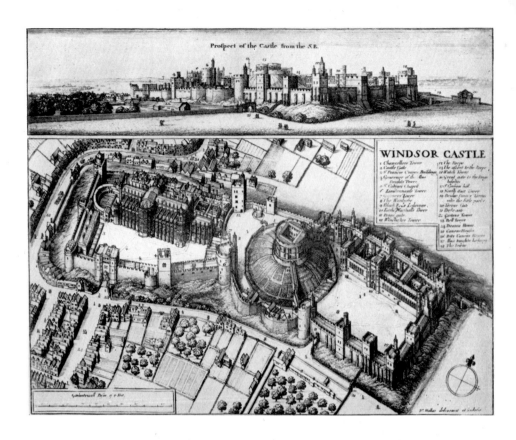

Prospect of the Castle from the S.E.

WINDSOR CASTLE

74. *a*. WENCESLAUS HOLLAR: WINDSOR CASTLE
b. WENCESLAUS HOLLAR: ALBURY

75. *a.* CLAUDE DE JONGH: OLD LONDON BRIDGE, 1630 (DETAIL). Kenwood
b. ATTRIBUTED TO CORNELIUS BOL: VIEW ON THE THAMES
The John Evelyn Coll., Stonor Park

76. *a*. WILLEM VAN DE VELDE II: A SEA FIGHT, 1677. H.M. The Queen,
Buckingham Palace
b. JAN WYCK: MAJOR-GENL. EGERTON. Brig. T. F. J. Collins Coll.

77. *a*. JAN SIBERECHTS: LANDSCAPE WITH A FORD, 1695. Birdsall House
b. JAN SIBERECHTS: A VIEW OF LONGLEAT, 1675. Longleat

78. *a*. FRANCIS BARLOW: PIGS AND DONKEYS. British Museum
b. FRANCIS BARLOW: HUNTING THE HARE. L. G. Duke Coll.

79. *a*. THE ROYAL CHAPEL, WINDSOR. Royal Library, Windsor Castle
b. HAMPTON COURT: THE QUEEN'S DRAWING ROOM

80. CHATSWORTH: THE STATE BEDROOM

81. CHATSWORTH: THE CHAPEL

82. SEBASTIANO RICCI: THE LAST SUPPER. National Gallery of Art, Washington, D.C.

83. *a.* W. MARSHALL AFTER EDWARD BOWER: THOMAS, 3RD BARON FAIRFAX

b. J. SMITH AFTER SIR GODFREY KNELLER: FREDERICK, 1ST DUKE OF SCHOMBERG

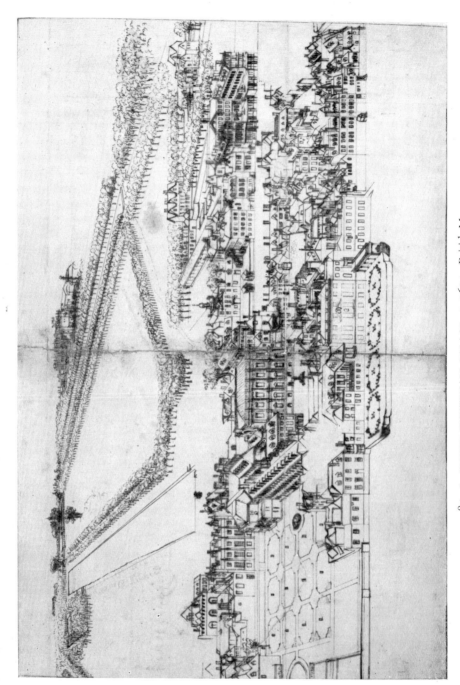

84. L. KNYFF: WHITEHALL PALACE, *c.* 1694. British Museum

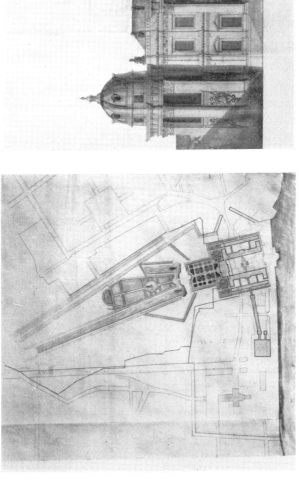

85. *a.* SIR CHRISTOPHER WREN: DESIGN FOR WHITEHALL PALACE: SITE PLAN, 1698. All Souls College, Oxford

b. SIR CHRISTOPHER WREN: DESIGN FOR WHITEHALL PALACE: DETAIL OF CENTRE BLOCK WITH THE BANQUETING HOUSE, 1698
All Souls College, Oxford

86. SIR CHRISTOPHER WREN: WEST TOWERS OF ST. PAUL'S CATHEDRAL, 1705–8

87. *a*. THOMAS ARCHER: ST. PHILIP (NOW THE CATHEDRAL), BIRMINGHAM, 1709–25
b. NICHOLAS HAWKSMOOR: ST. ANNE, LIMEHOUSE, 1714–24

88. SIR CHRISTOPHER WREN: THE DOME OF ST. PAUL'S CATHEDRAL

89. SIR JOHN VANBRUGH: CASTLE HOWARD, YORKSHIRE: THE HALL

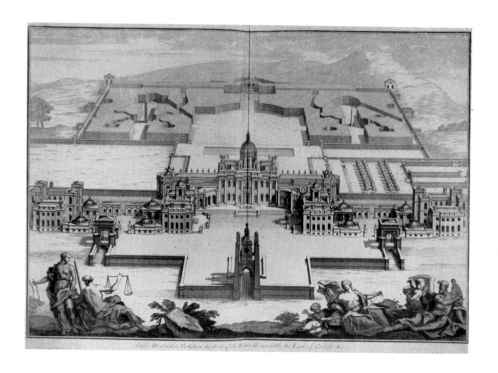

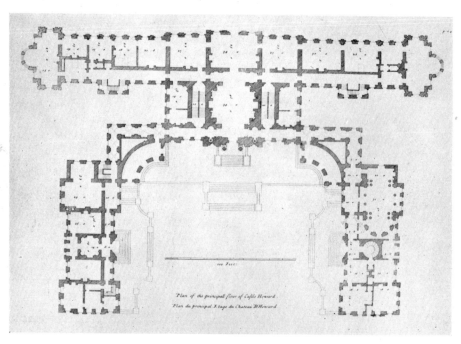

90. *a*. SIR JOHN VANBRUGH: CASTLE HOWARD, YORKSHIRE: PANORAMA
b. SIR JOHN VANBRUGH: CASTLE HOWARD, YORKSHIRE: PLAN

91. *a*. SIR JOHN VANBRUGH: BLENHEIM PALACE, OXFORDSHIRE: THE FORECOURT, 1705–24
b. SIR JOHN VANBRUGH: SEATON DELAVAL, NORTHUMBERLAND, 1718–28

92. *a*. SIR JOHN VANBRUGH AND G. A. PELLEGRINI: CASTLE HOWARD: THE DOME
b. SIR JOHN VANBRUGH: SEATON DELAVAL, NORTHUMBERLAND: THE HALL

93. SIR JAMES THORNHILL: THE RESURRECTION OF ARCHBISHOP CHICHELE
All Souls College, Oxford

94. *a*. NICHOLAS HAWKSMOOR AND JOHN JAMES: ST. ALPHEGE, GREENWICH,
1712–14
b. NICHOLAS HAWKSMOOR: ALL SOULS COLLEGE, OXFORD: THE NORTH
QUADRANGLE

95. *a*. NICHOLAS HAWKSMOOR: ST. GEORGE, BLOOMSBURY, 1716–30
b. NICHOLAS HAWKSMOOR: ST. GEORGE-IN-THE-EAST, 1715–23. Gutted 1941

96. SIR JAMES THORNHILL: THE PAINTED HALL, GREENWICH